The New Labour Rea

The New Labour Reader

Edited by

Andrew Chadwick and Richard Heffernan

polity

First published in 2003 by Polity Press in association with Blackwell Publishing Ltd

Editorial office:
Polity Press
65 Bridge Street
Cambridge CB2 1UR, UK

Marketing and production:
Blackwell Publishing Ltd
108 Cowley Road
Oxford OX4 1JF, UK

Distributed in the USA by
Blackwell Publishing Inc.
350 Main Street
Malden, MA 02148, USA

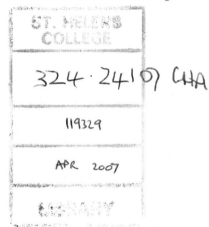
ISBN 0-7456-2943-1
ISBN 0-7456-2944-X (pbk)

A catalogue record for this book is available from the British Library and has been applied for from the Library of Congress.

Typeset in 10 on 12 pt Sabon
by Kolam Information Services Pvt. Ltd, Pondicherry, India
Printed and bound in Great Britain by TJ International, Padstow, Cornwall

For further information on Polity, visit our website: http://www.polity.co.uk

Contents

Acknowledgements

The editors would like to thank all at Polity Press for their assistance in preparing this volume, particularly Sarah Dancy, Rachel Kerr, Louise Knight and David Held. Thanks, too, to Jean van Altena for such splendid copyediting, an essential part of producing any book, and especially valuable in the production of a reader. Through the efforts of Grahame Thompson, currently Head of the Government and Politics Department, the Open University provided some funding to help produce this book. We are very grateful to the institution for providing it and Grahame for arranging it. Most importantly, we would especially like to thank Andrew Gardener for having cheerfully undertaken the onerous task of gathering together a great many materials and for helping us arrange permissions.

Andrew Chadwick
Richard Heffernan

The extracts are drawn from the following sources, and the editors and publishers are grateful for permission to use copyright material. Crown copyright material is reproduced under class licence no. C01W0000283 with the permission of the controller of HMSO and the Queen's Printer for Scotland.

Tony Blair, *The Third Way: New Politics for the New Century*, 1998; reprinted by permission of the Fabian Society, London.

Anthony Giddens, *The Third Way: The Renewal of Social Democracy*, Cambridge: Polity, 1998; reprinted with the permission of the publishers.

Philip Gould, *The Unfinished Revolution*, London: Abacus, 1998; reprinted with the permission of the publishers.

Michael Freeden, 'The Ideology of New Labour', *Political Quarterly*, 70, 1 (1999), pp. 42–51; reprinted with the permission of Blackwell Publishing Ltd.

Richard Heffernan, *New Labour and Thatcherism: Political Change in Britain*, London: Macmillan, 2001; reprinted with the permission of the publishers.

Colin Hay, *The Political Economy of New Labour: Labouring under False Pretences*, Manchester: Manchester University Press, 1999; reprinted with the permission of the publishers.

Michael Kenny and Martin J. Smith, 'Interpreting New Labour: Constraints, Dilemmas and Political Agency', in Steve Ludlam and Martin J. Smith (eds), *New Labour in Government*, London: Macmillan, 2001; reprinted with the permission of the publishers.

David Marquand, 'The Blair Paradox', *Prospect*, May 1998; reprinted with the permission of the publishers.

Stuart Hall, 'The Great Moving Nowhere Show', in *Marxism Today*, 1998.

Anthony Barnett, 'Corporate Populism and Partyless Democracy', *New Left Review*, 11, 3 (2000); reprinted with the permission of the publishers.

Paul Anderson and Nyta Mann, *Safety First: The Making of New Labour*, London: Granta, 1997; reprinted with the permission of the publishers.

The Labour Party, *Labour's Business Manifesto: Equipping Britain for the Future*, London: Labour Party, 1997; reprinted with the permission of the publishers.

Gordon Brown, 'Prudence will be our Watchword': Chancellor's Speech at the Mansion House, 1998, HM Treasury news release 102, 1998, Crown copyright.

Edward Balls, 'Open Macroeconomics in an Open Economy', *Scottish Journal of Political Economy*, 45, 2 (1998); reprinted with the permission of the publishers.

Tony Blair and Gerhard Schröder (1999), *Europe: The Third Way/Die Neue Mitte*, London: The Labour Party; reprinted with the permission of the publishers.

Will Hutton, 'New Keynesianism and New Labour', in Andrew Gamble and Tony Wright (eds), *The New Social Democracy*, Political Quarterly Special Issue, Oxford: Basil Blackwell, 1999; reprinted with the permission of the publishers.

Bill Morris, President's Speech to the TUC Congress, September 2001. Available at <http://www.tuc.org.uk/congress/tuc-3699-f0.cfm>. Last accessed 7 February 2002. Copyright of the author.

Polly Toynbee and David Walker, *Did Things Get Better? An Audit of Labour's Successes and Failures*, Harmondsworth: Penguin, 2001; reprinted with the permission of the publishers.

Gordon Brown, 'Equality – Then and Now', in Dick Leonard (ed.), *Crosland and New Labour*, London: Macmillan, 1999; reprinted with the permission of the publishers.

Julian Le Grand, 'The Third Way Begins with CORA', reprinted with the permission of the *New Statesman*. Copyright © New Statesman Ltd.

Ruth Lister et al., 'Government Must Reconsider its Strategy for More Equal Society', letter to the *Financial Times*, 1 October 1997; reprinted with the permission of the principal author.

Cabinet Office Social Exclusion Unit, *Bringing Britain Together: A National Strategy for Neighbourhood Renewal*, Cm 4045, London: HMSO, 1998. Crown copyright.

Department for Education and Employment, *Excellence in Schools*, London: HMSO, 1997. Crown copyright.

Department of Health, *The New NHS: Modern, Dependable*, London: HMSO, 1997. Crown copyright.

Will Hutton, 'How Big Money is Stitching Up the NHS'; reprinted with the permission of the *Observer.*

Stephen Driver and Luke Martell, *New Labour: Politics after Thatcherism*, Cambridge: Polity, 1998; reprinted with the permission of the publishers.

Nick Ellison, 'From Welfare State to Post-Welfare Society: Labour's Social Policy in Historical and Contemporary Perspective', in Brian Brivati and Tim Bale (eds), *New Labour in Power: Precedents and Prospects*, London: Routledge, 1998; reprinted with the permission of the publishers.

The Cabinet Office, *Modernising Government*, Cm 4310, London: HMSO, 1999. Crown copyright.

Donald Dewar, Foreword to *Scotland's Parliament* (Scottish Devolution White Paper), Cm 3658, London: HMSO, 1997. Crown copyright.

HMSO, The Human Rights Act 1998, London: HMSO, 1998. Crown copyright.

Department of the Environment, Transport and the Regions, *A Mayor and Assembly for London*, White Paper Cm 3897, London: HMSO, 1998. Crown copyright.

The Jenkins Commission, *The Report of the Independent Commission on the Voting System*, Cm 4090-I, II, London: HMSO, 1998. Crown copyright.

Jack Straw, Response to the Jenkins Commission Report, *Hansard*, 318, cols 1032–9, 5 November 1998. Crown copyright.

The Lord Chancellor's Department, *The House of Lords: Completing the Reform*, Cm 5291, London: HMSO, 2001. Crown copyright.

Brendan O'Leary, 'The Nature of the British–Irish Agreement', *New Left Review* 1999, reprinted with the permission of the publishers.

Philip Daniels, 'From Hostility to Constructive Engagement: The Europeanization of the Labour Party', *West European Politics*, 21, 1 (1998), pp. 72–93; reprinted with the permission of Frank Cass publishers.

K. Hughes and E. Smith, 'New Labour – New Europe', *International Affairs*, 74, 1 (London, 1998), pp. 93–103; reprinted with permission.

Tony Blair, Speech at the Launch of the Britain in Europe Campaign, October 1999, Prime Ministerial press release. Crown copyright.

Tony Blair, Speech to the Polish Stock Exchange, Warsaw, October 2000, Prime Ministerial press release. Crown copyright.

Gordon Brown, Speech at the Mansion House, June 2001, HM Treasury press release. Crown copyright.

Gordon Brown, Statement on European Monetary Union to the House of Commons, October 1997, HM Treasury press release. Crown copyright.

Philip Stephens, 'The Blair Government and Europe', *Political Quarterly*, 72, 1 (2001), pp. 67–75; reprinted with the permission of Blackwell Publishing Ltd.

Robin Cook, 'Britain in the World': Speech to The Royal Institute of International Affairs, Chatham House, January 2000, Foreign and Commonwealth Office Press Release. Crown copyright.

Tony Blair, The Doctrine of the International Community, Speech in Chicago, April 1999, Prime Ministerial press release. Crown copyright.

Andrew Rawnsley, *Servants of the People: The Inside Story of New Labour*, Harmondsworth: Penguin, 2001; reprinted with the permission of the publishers.

Michael Foley, *The British Presidency: Tony Blair and the Politics of Public Leadership*, Manchester: Manchester University Press, 2000; reprinted with the permission of the publishers.

Peter Hennessy, *The Prime Minister: The Office and its Holders since 1945*, Harmondsworth: Penguin, 2000; reprinted with the permission of the publishers.

Dennis Kavanagh and Anthony Seldon, *The Powers behind the Prime Minister*, London: Harper Collins, 1999; reprinted with the permission of the publishers.

John Rentoul, *Tony Blair*, London: Little, Brown, 2001; reprinted with the permission of the publishers.

Ivor Gaber, 'Lies, Damn Lies and Political Spin', *British Journalism Review*, 11, 1 (2000), pp. 302–11; reprinted with the permission of the publishers.

Bob Franklin, 'The Hand of History: New Labour, News Management and Governance', in Steve Ludlam and Martin J. Smith (eds), *New Labour in Government*, London: Macmillan, 2001; reprinted with the permission of the publishers.

Nicholas Jones, *Sultans of Spin: The Media and the New Labour Government*, London: Gollancz, 1999; reprinted with the permission of the publishers.

Andrew Chadwick, 'The Electronic Face of Government in the Internet Age', *Information, Communication and Society*, 4, 3 (2001), pp. 46–67; reprinted with the permission of Taylor and Francis.

Philip Cowley, 'The Commons: Mr Blair's Lapdog?', *Parliamentary Affairs*, 54, 1 (2001), pp. 815–27; reprinted with the permission of Oxford University Press.

Publisher's Note

An ellipsis has been used whenever material from the original has been omitted. Where more than one paragraph has been excluded, [...] appears on a line of its own.

Introduction: The New Labour Phenomenon

Andrew Chadwick and Richard Heffernan

The underlying ideological assumptions of the Labour Party were transformed in the 1980s and 1990s, its policies altered to embrace new forms of political discourse, and its organizational structure changed to enhance the role of an assertively reformist leadership. The remaking of Labour under Neil Kinnock, 1983–92, John Smith, 1992–4, and Tony Blair since 1994 has produced a fundamental reordering of the party's doctrine and ethos (Drucker 1979), one that has seen the abandonment of previously cherished policy positions in favour of dramatically different new ones. Labour's current policy stance, and the record of the Blair government since 1997, reflects the fact that the ideological differences between the two principal parties in British politics, Labour and the Conservatives, have narrowed significantly in the past twenty years.

The emergence of New Labour essentially reflects a process of party change, one that was gradual, incremental and caused by a confluence of external political shocks suffered by Labour and the internal responses these shocks engendered. Such shocks, defeat in the general elections of 1979, 1983, 1987 and 1992, the seemingly unstoppable forward march of the Thatcher governments, and the supposed irrelevance of collectivist, statist social democratic politics in the wake of an innovative individualist, anti-statist neo-liberal alternative, all prompted considerable changes in Labour's conception of itself as a political party. For supporters of the Blairite 'project', the reinvention of Labour was necessary to win elections, and to do so by reconnecting with the electorate by becoming politically 'relevant' (a key word in the Blairite lexicon) once again.

In May 1997, having been effectively declared dead in the water in 1983 and again in 1987 and 1992, Labour secured its largest ever parliamentary majority, a thumping 179, the largest since 1945. In June 2001, the Government was re-elected in another landslide, with a majority this time of 166. Throughout the 1997 Parliament, Labour never ceded a commanding opinion poll lead, and as a consequence easily secured, for the first time in its 101-year history, a second term with a more than solid parliamentary majority. These two elections witnessed a dramatic shift in British voting behaviour, so much so that Labour now enjoys the biggest share of support across all social groups excepting class AB ('professional and upper non-manual'), though even here Labour (at 33 per cent) is only seven points behind the Conservatives. Compared with its electoral performance in the 1980s, perhaps most significant is the fact that Labour's support among the C2 'skilled manual' class rocketed to 47 per cent in 2001, while the Conservatives, whose successes in the 1980s and 1990s depended to a great extent on the fabled C2s, slumped to just 29 per cent (Dunleavy 2002: 130). Capturing the 'centre ground' of British politics required that Labour demonstrate that it was dynamic and forward-looking in its approach, while economically and socially cautious in its policies. Appealing to the much-cited 'Mondeo man', named after the dull, solid and value-for-money family saloon car, required that Labour align itself with the zeitgeist of 1990s Britain – conservative (small c) suburban working families, the property price-obsessed, and the 'middle England' of IKEA, TV 'makeover' shows and Britpop.

Declining voter turnouts notwithstanding, New Labour cheerleaders argue that the electoral success of the reformed party is testimony to the political success of the New Labour project. Old Labour stalwarts are not so sure. Critics claim that the political changes brought about under Blair (and Kinnock and Smith) have seen the transformation of the party, not merely its modernization or remaking, and often describe the process as the abandonment of its social democratic traditions (Panitch and Leys 1998; Leys 1996). Roy Hattersley, Old rather than New Labour, deputy leader under Kinnock and a self-confessed democratic socialist of the Labour right, is one typical internal dissident. Arguing that 'the policies which define our philosophy have been rejected by the Prime Minister' (*Observer*, 24 June 2001), he charges New Labour with abandoning a great swathe of the party's key policies, among them progressive taxation, state-funded (and provided) public services, and support for a non-elitist, non-meritocratic education system. As a result, according to Hattersley, Labour now bases 'its whole programme on an alien ideology' (ibid.). According to such commentaries, Labour's political transition is most often described as 'moving to the right'; but what this actually means in the context of British politics since the 1980s has to be made clear. Others suggest that Labour has simply updated the party's programme, applying 'its traditional values in a modern setting'. It is on this distinction – the extent to which Labour has changed and, if it has changed, why – that the debate on the nature and meaning of the New Labour phenomenon centres.

What, then, is New Labour? Why and how has Labour reinvented itself? And to what end? Providing a critical introduction to the New Labour phenomenon is a huge task in itself, but one that might well benefit from a simple and elegant approach derived from one of the architects of the discipline of political science, Harold D. Lasswell. Students, teachers and researchers alike have long been inspired by the parsimony of Lasswell's famous definition of politics as 'who gets what, when, how' (Lasswell 1936: preface). Criticisms of Lasswell's insistence on a behavioural methodology aside, the major strength of this approach is that it 'underlies the working attitude of practicing politicians', embracing a discussion of politics which seeks to understand and explore the exercise of political power through 'the study of influence and the influential' (Lasswell 1936: 1). Assuming that the ultimate goal of all self-respecting political parties in a liberal democracy is capturing government office through the electoral process, a discussion of the politics of New Labour can be usefully (if loosely) structured around Lasswell's questions 'who gets what, when, how?', while adding a very crisp 'why?' to the end of that classic formula.

Who . . . ?

The question 'Who are New Labour?' overlaps with the question 'When was New Labour created?', something dealt with in more detail later. Interpretations of the chronology of the party's transformation have differed. Some writers argue that the process began in 1983 as soon as Kinnock took over from Michael Foot as leader (Westlake 2001; Heffernan 1998; Lent 1997; McSmith 1996). Others focus on the Policy Review process of 1987, which jettisoned many of Labour's 'tax and spend' policies, nationalization and unilateral nuclear disarmament (Kenny and Smith 2001). Still others argue that the real transition did not come until Tony Blair assumed the leadership in 1994, and the changes then made to policy and the internal party machinery, especially the removal of Clause IV in April 1995, which went further than Kinnock or Smith would ever have dared (Gould 1998; Mandelson and Liddle 1996).

The New Labour leaders, foremost among them Tony Blair and Gordon Brown, have been the most decisive actors in prosecuting the remaking of the party, but they did not start from a blank slate. Instead, they were able to capitalize on the efforts of their predecessors. Thus, although Neil Kinnock began the remaking of Labour as far back as 1983, Labour's transformation is seen by many to be the creation of an inner party cadre formed before and after 1994, a collection of like-minded men and women led by Tony Blair and including, most notably, Gordon Brown, Peter Mandelson and Alastair Campbell. At the heart of this cadre has been the Blair–Brown duumvirate, the principal axis on which the New Labour project was formed and upon which the post-1997 Labour government rotates. Today, intra-governmental relations, principally those between Blair and Brown, continue to dominate discussion regarding the government's internal workings. Brown is a putative Prime Minister, the coming man, an obvious alternative to Blair should he falter, and one with a considerable power base within the government and the Parliamentary Labour Party. As the undisputed number two in the government, Brown dominates economic policy, is influential over domestic policy, and has to date a *de facto* veto power over the decision on whether Britain should join the European Single Currency. Once described as 'a French Prime Minister with Blair as a Fifth Republic President' (Hennessy 2000: 513), Brown remains in theory subordinate to Blair (the Prime Minister appoints him and, should he choose, may dismiss or demote him), but in practice is an indispensable figure with whom Blair is obliged to work. As a result, economic policy, and much else in the domestic field, continues to be dominated by the two, so much so that should the Prime Minister and the Chancellor differ on policy choice, this may prove to be an important source of disagreement as Labour's second term progresses.

Most apparent about the 'who' of New Labour is the extent to which the key ideological messages were very much the hand-crafted products of Blair and Brown (and those around them) from the very beginning of Blair's leadership in 1994. Although they were undoubtedly capitalizing on the process of internal change started by Kinnock in the 1980s (continuing, tempered somewhat, by John Smith between 1992 and 1994), it is now clear that Blair and Brown recognized that the strategic direction of the party could be altered only if the leadership tightly controlled the debate. In short, as many of the primary sources reproduced in this book testify, the range of key personnel involved in the re-engineering of Labour's official policies and ideas was, and always has been, strictly limited. In compiling this Reader, for example, we were struck by how few substantive primary ideological statements we could locate which had not been delivered by, or published in the name of, Blair or Brown. Even though background personnel – in particular, figures like Alistair Campbell, Jonathan Powell, David Miliband, Andrew Adonis, Ed Balls, Philip Gould and Geoff Mulgan – have played some role in honing the New Labour message (particularly Campbell and Powell), they have done so by working as agents of the party leadership; the party's *public* presence since 1994 has been very much the product of Tony Blair and Gordon Brown.

Despite this, the fact remains that political parties are always something more than their leaders or their official public declarations. Like Thatcherism and the New Right before it, New Labour has been constructed out of a curious mixture of a small, tightly centralized 'on-message' cadre of 'modernizer' politicians and staff, on the one hand, and a loose network of think-tanks, academics, journalists and opinion pollsters, on the other. Bodies such as the Fabian Society and the Institute for Public Policy Research (IPPR), and even the constitutional reform group Charter 88, although not unqualified in their support for New Labour, have played some part, however small, in popularizing the party's agenda since the early 1990s. Emblematic of the desire to emulate the success of the New Right in the 1970s and 1980s was Blair's and Brown's insistence that individual supporters in the party, the news media and academe (invariably from think-tanks, rather than universities) be co-opted into the policy making process at the very highest levels (particularly in Number 10 and the Treasury).

The scholarly community has not always been supportive, particularly in the area of social policy, which attracted much criticism during the government's first term (Lister et al. 1997). While academics such as Anthony Giddens, Julian Le Grand and Richard Layard, all at the London School of Economics, were also invited to express their opinions to the government (Barnett 2000; Balls 1998; Giddens 1998; Le Grand 1998), public intellectuals have always been considered at best as advisers of the Government, not deciders for it; designated constructive critics or supportive cheerleaders of the New Labour project, rather than active participants in it. For, while claiming that 'politics is first and foremost about ideas' (Blair 1998: 1), Blair also argues that politicians should 'approach issues without ideological preconceptions and . . . search for practical solutions to their problems through honest well-constructed and pragmatic policies' (Blair and Schröder 1999: 15). However, despite efforts to fashion a veneer of intellectual respectability, some more successful than others, the New Labour project reflects first and foremost a policy agenda, a political project, one concerned with propelling Labour into office, building a reliable elect-oral base, and providing a workable set of proposals. It reflects a pragmatic belief that politics can never be anything other than the 'art of the possible'; policy perhaps being 'whatever works' under contemporary economic and social conditions.

If intellectuals have provided some background knowledge to the New Labour project at certain times, they have rarely been assigned to communicate its message. This task has fallen to politicians, trusted officials and *apparatchiks*, spin doctors and a plethora of journalists, especially those in the Murdoch press and, for a brief time, the *Daily Mail*, sedulously courted by Blair prior to the 1997 election. These have played their part in convincing electors, especially swing voters in marginal constituencies, that Labour has changed, and now takes seriously the concerns of suburban 'middle England' – fear of crime, support for upward mobility, self-reliance and consumption (Anderson and Mann 1997: 36–45). The issue of 'spin' reached its apex during Labour's first term, and part of answering the 'who' question must involve discussion of the role played by figures like Peter Mandelson, Alastair Campbell and less successful, but highly representative, individuals like Charlie Whelan, who resigned as Brown's press secretary in January 1999 over his role in the Mandelson loan scandal, when Labour's spinmeister first resigned from the Cabinet.

New Labour took the politics of presentation to new levels of professionalism during the mid-1990s, and this ethos did not desert the party leadership when it took office (Franklin 2000; Gaber 2000; Jones 1999). Peter Mandelson's role is of particular interest here, since his influence may be traced back to the founding of Labour's Shadow Communications Agency in 1986 and the remaking of Labour initiated under Neil Kinnock (McIntyre 2000). The period 1985–90 was one of the defining moments in the transition to the new 'designer politics' (Scammell 1995). Mandelson's close relationship with Blair and his well-documented conflicts with Brown simmered throughout the government's first term. His resignations from the Cabinet, first in 1998 and again in 2001, reflected debates about the politics of spin (and its impacts) that have carried on ever since, revealing much about the ways in which press secretaries and political (rather than 'special') advisers have come to play such crucial roles in the New Labour strategy.

What of the role played by the trade unions in the emergence of New Labour? Historically the main source of party funding by a large margin, trade union donations now account for only around 30 per cent of the party's overall funds. The chief reason for this fall is that ordinary member donations and those from rich 'high-value donors' have increased dramatically (Ludlam 2000: 235). Since the Kinnock and Smith reforms of the 1980s, specifically the shift towards one member one vote, the unions' internal party influence has also diminished. Eager to do all they could to bring about a Labour election victory, the trade unions refused to 'rock the boat', swallowing all disagreements while providing crucial backing to Kinnock's and Blair's reforms, not least in supporting Blair's revision of Clause IV in April 1995. It was not until Labour's second term that the unions began to voice their concerns about the Government's policies, when its insistence following the election victory of 2001 that 'public–private partnerships', mainly under the Private Finance Initiative, be extended across all the public services inflamed leaders of the largest unions, such as Rodney Bickerstaffe of UNISON, John Edmonds of the GMB, and Bill Morris of the TGWU (Morris 2001).

Such instrumental opposition aside, the trade unions have been broadly supportive of the New Labour project, rightly hoping that they would receive more of a hearing from a Labour government than a Conservative one, reluctantly accepting the Labour offer of 'fairness, not favours'. TUC leader John Monks, the architect of the pragmatic 'new unionism', while welcoming the introduction of reforms such as the minimum wage and statutory recognition, has sometimes been mildly critical of employment and industrial policy. Of course, 'new unionism' notwithstanding, essentially a relaunch for the TUC in the face of dwindling membership, the unions have not played anything resembling a centre stage role in the New Labour project, their influence nowhere near what it had been. The divide between the supposed 'political' and 'industrial' wings of the old Labour movement was never as starkly pronounced as it is in this era of New Labour.

What...?

Labour politics have echoed, and occasionally foreshadowed, political and ideological changes. At key moments of its history, the party has found itself in touch with a national mood, able to empathize with, as well as encourage and deepen, a national, progressive zeitgeist. In 1945, as the electoral beneficiary of a national swing in favour of wide-ranging social reform, Labour was deemed the means by which state-sponsored collectivist welfare politics would prevail. Eager to 'win the peace' having 'won the war', the British people propelled Labour into office at an election it did not really expect to win. In 1964–6, albeit to a lesser extent than in 1945, Harold Wilson's dual themes of modernization and technology briefly struck a chord with an electorate critical of a hidebound, class-ridden, old-fashioned Britain and eager to support a forward-looking, innovative and new government. Yet, in the 1980s, Labour found itself seemingly hopelessly old-fashioned, out of touch with the politics of the new Britain supposedly being fashioned by Margaret Thatcher, and in danger of becoming irrelevant and obsolete.

Labour was first called into existence as a party designed to enact programmes of benefit to working-class constituents and the trade union movement. Electoral motivations, as ever, were part of Labour's reform agenda, its pursuit of a more equal society, however defined, being dependent on the ability to win and retain governmental office. Quite obviously, Harold Wilson's famous claim that Labour was 'the natural party of government' was premature. Since first winning an overall majority in the House of Commons in 1945, the party was in government only fleetingly, spending around fifteen of the fifty-two years between 1945 and 1997 in office. The background to the making of New Labour was the fact that the party had been cast out of office in 1979 and routed at the polls in 1979, 1983, 1987 and 1992. Labour pre-Blair was seemingly deemed down and out, no longer a credible electoral force. Back in the 1950s, similar electoral misfortunes had led a number of commentators to suggest that Labour was in terminal decline, the party's failures headlined in book titles such as *Must Labour Lose?* The same claims were made in the 1980s and early 1990s.

Ambitious for office for themselves and their party, electoral realities were imprinted on the minds of Labour's Shadow Cabinet in the 1980s and 1990s, many of whom had never experienced high political office, despite relatively long political careers. In opposition, Labour was merely able to preach politics and pass resolutions or declarations of intent, but only in government could it ever attempt to make a difference and engage with the problems it wanted to solve. In the face of the calamities of the 1980s, New Labour's objective was to become electorally and politically relevant, to again become a party of government, one able to successfully govern in the 'national interest'. In Tony Blair's words, spoken on the morrow of the 1997 victory, the Labour government was 'elected as New Labour and shall govern as New Labour'. In July 1995, having travelled to Perth, Western Australia, to deliver a speech to Rupert Murdoch's News Corporation Leadership Conference, an occasion itself an indication of the journey which Labour had undertaken, Blair had explicitly set out the principal motivation behind the creation of New Labour: 'To become a serious party of government Labour required a quantum leap... [we had to] reconstruct our ideology and organisation... [to begin] the long march back from the dark days of the early 1980s when, frankly, we were unelectable' (Blair 1995). Of course, the reason why a party should reconstruct its 'ideology and organisation' is one question; the means by which it should choose to do so is quite another.

Eric Shaw (1994) suggests that the Labour Party faced a series of interrelated crises both before and after 1983, best described as electoral, ideological and organizational, which in time prompted party change in all three categories. Foremost among these crises, perhaps the issue determining the party's response to the other two, was that Labour had singularly failed to mount a serious electoral challenge to the Conservatives since it narrowly won the October 1974 election. As Andrew Rawnsley writes, 'Tony Blair's rhetoric might be relentlessly futuristic, but he was fixated by the past. This was not surprising. Before 1 May 1997, Labour had not won an election in more than twenty-two years and had not secured a proper parliamentary majority in over three decades' (Rawnsley 2001: p. xiv). Since the defeat of 1992, this record of unmitigated failure in Westminster elections has been rectified. New Labour's electoral strength under Blair has been formidable. Apart from a brief interruption in the midst of the petrol crisis in September 2000, the Labour government has been ahead of the opposition in the polls every month since May 1997. But this amazing opinion poll supremacy goes back all the way to the autumn of 1992, when sterling's ejection from the Exchange Rate Mechanism on 'Black Wednesday' sparked a decline in Conservative support from which the party has yet to recover. In keeping with the performance of his party, Blair's own personal ratings are similarly impressive, and he 'can claim a level of sustained popularity far beyond anything experienced by any other British prime minister in the past 100 years' (*Guardian*, 27 April 2002). The party's electoral domination of British politics since 1997 (no other word suffices) is something indicating, to date at least, that New Labour has spectacularly met the challenge of reinvigorating the party's electoral base.

Drawing upon the two dominant approaches to party competition in political science, we can see that Labour, in common with all major parties, pursues two central goals: office and policies. Parties in parliamentary democracies aspire to win control of the executive branch both for the benefits that accrue and because it grants them the opportunity to introduce their favoured policies (Müller and Strøm 1999; Budge and Laver 1986; Downs 1957). New Labour is no exception. Office- and policy-seeking are intertwined in the 'real world', as Budge and Laver have argued: 'In the first place, the rewards of office may be valued intrinsically, in and for themselves. In the second place, office may be valued only instrumentally for the ability that it gives to influence policy outputs' (Budge and Laver 1986: 490). Managing the relevant tensions and compatibilities between office and policy are part and parcel of any major political party's existence.

In this regard, New Labour has excelled. While its quest for power naturally embraced both office seeking and policy seeking, the hunger for electoral success under Blair's leadership saw the party successfully prioritize the former over the latter. In short, Labour's policy profile was ruthlessly tailored to meet its perceived electoral needs, and the result was the final abandonment of what remained of its social democratic programme of the 1970s and early 1980s. In large part, this was because the Blairites were deeply afraid of becoming Labour's lost generation. In their view, Thatcherism had so reworked the political terrain after 1979 that Labour found itself in danger not merely of missing the electoral bus, but of becoming

completely irrelevant to dealing with the pressing problems of contemporary politics. The Britain of the 1990s was seen to be fundamentally – indeed, irrevocably –
different from the Britain of the 1970s. To take but one example, the great public
enterprises had gone, transferred from the public to the private sector, re-regulated,
and never, it would seem, to be reclaimed by the state. Under the Thatcher and
Major governments, the state, having previously devoted itself to ever increasing the
percentage of the economy in public ownership, rolled itself back, privatizing all
sorts of state industries and public utilities, and selling off telecommunications,
electricity, gas, water and railways, to name only the high-profile examples. This
marketization of the economy forever blurred the distinctions between the public
and the private sectors, deregulation and privatization together encapsulating 'private good, public bad', the watchword of the Thatcher government as applied to the
management of the economy. All this influenced Labour policy modernization,
because a New Labour government had to deal with the world as it found it, not
with the world in a form it would have preferred. Whereas nationalization was the
formal logic of industrial policy in the fifty-odd years before 1979, privatization
became the new logic after 1979 (Feingenbaum, Henig and Hamnett 1999; Wolfe
1996; Saunders and Harris 1994). As a result, nationalization in the form of the
public corporation was deemed to have about the same relevance to contemporary
British politics as would temperance, imperial preference or the Divine Right of
Kings. In industrial and economic policy, this fact above all others came to colour
Labour's policy preference and its political attitudes.

Not merely in the case of privatization, but in other fields too, the Thatcherite
remaking of Britain also saw Labour tailor its policy agenda to what it saw as
contemporary realities. Labour's renewal reflected not merely its own electoral
needs, but the demands which economic and administrative obligations would
place upon it in government. Perhaps the defining feature of New Labour has been
its willingness to accommodate its reform agenda to the political and economic
world within which it finds itself. It is this that has prompted 'Labour's reconcili-
ation with the market economy and with the macro-economic orthodoxy of the
times' (Stephens 2001b: 185), and Labour's belief that markets and competition
ensure that the economy's resources are allocated efficiently. In government, Labour
has eschewed the high levels of taxation and public expenditure prevalent
in continental Europe, claiming it could deliver European levels of public service
at American levels of taxation. Having abandoned old-style collectivism and 'tax
and spend', the Blair government's watchword is prudence and responsibility, its
policy instinct seemingly to prioritize the needs of the private wealth-creating sector
over the public wealth-consuming sector when there is a conflict between the two.
Historically, faced with a choice between managing, focusing, restricting or con-
stricting the market for a social purpose or empowering, freeing and liberalizing the
market in an economic interest, Labour's policy (and its core instinct) was always to
favour the first course of action. It now favours the latter.

As a means to its own particular socialist ends, working with the market economy
in order eventually to supplant it, Old Labour defined its role as managing the
economy by using the state to regulate a market deemed incapable of self-regulation.
It did so at a national level, pursuing stabilization and growth by an active macro-
economic policy and using that growth to fund social reforms. In the post-war
period, this national policy was supplemented by an international regime, the
Bretton Woods system, of managed exchange rates, economic stability and free

trade. The state's role was to provide social income in the form of insurance and related forms of social policy, to empower trade unions and guarantee labour rights, to make substantial public investments, and to vastly extend its direct and indirect control of industry and planned production. By these and other means, Labour would 'domesticate' *laissez-faire* capitalism. Reform-minded Conservatism aside, Labour was the political movement which articulated (and occasionally enacted as policy) social democratic aspirations from the 1940s to the 1970s, pursuing a reformist agenda informed by welfarism. The then twin engines of Labour policy, progressive taxation and increased public expenditure, reflected the state-managed collectivist paradigm of the mid-twentieth century. To this end, Labour ministers set themselves the task of controlling the market through the apparatus of a loosely corporatist state. This is no longer the case, as New Labour clearly testifies. The politics of the Blair government stand as proof positive of the passing of the old social democratic party. Today, with contemporary mainstream politics having moved away from the nostrums of the post-war social democratic era, Labour has acknowledged the demise of this model. Labour now has to govern within a radically different market economy, one based upon a neo-liberal policy paradigm, and these facts necessarily frame and constrain policy.

Labour has 'scorned the demand management on which previous Labour governments relied in favour of macro-economic stability and a social policy rooted in welfare reform and higher spending on education and training. Explicit in all of this was a recognition that the government's ambition of greater social cohesion was contingent on a demonstrable capacity to run the economy competently' (Stephens 2001b: 185). This is not to say that New Labour has not taken some aims of classical social democracy on board, albeit in diluted forms. Whether redistribution of wealth has in fact occurred under the Blair government has acquired totemic significance for New Labour watchers. It is too soon to tell if the answer is affirmative, but preliminary research has shown that although inequality and relative poverty actually increased during Labour's first two years in office, Gordon Brown's budgets have been mildly redistributive, mainly as a result of programmes like the Working Families Tax Credit which benefit those toward the lower end of the income scale by a proportionately larger amount than those at the top (Hills 2001). The Budget of 2002, which substantially increased National Insurance contributions to pay for extra investment in the NHS, was marginally more punitive for high earners, and this led some commentators to claim that the days of redistribution had returned. But raising extra public money to invest in the NHS is not synonymous with redistribution by taxing the wealthy and using the returns to fund higher levels of state benefits. In other words, although they are obviously related, a distinction still needs to be drawn between increasing funding for public services and increasing the amount of money which the less well-off, particularly pensioners, the disabled and the unemployed, receive in the form of direct benefit payments. A helpful explanation of this conundrum is to accept that New Labour believes in redistribution, but only for poverty alleviation, not for the purposes of broader social equality (Goes 2002). The issue then becomes a matter not of absolutes but of degree: redistribution within limits.

Labour's policy agenda clearly reflects the contemporary policy agenda, and because of this it is more obvious today than perhaps at any other time in Labour's history that the two core goals of political parties – office and policy seeking – now seem to happily coincide. Of course, Labour has always been both an office- and a policy-seeking party, wanting to secure office in order to pursue reform. Even the most avowed policy seeker is obliged to recognize the importance of successful office seeking, if not in the short term, then certainly in the long term. The ability to govern is a requirement for any major party that wishes to continue in existence. Labour, New and Old, has always juggled ideological predisposition and practical necessity, and managed the trade-off between principle and pragmatism. The party was inevitably a broad church, its membership embracing both radical and moderate opinion, reaching across the left–right socialist perspective to incorporate those who wished to reform capitalism and those who wished to transcend it. Thanks to the institutional setting of a two-party system copper-fastened by the plurality electoral system, all major British political parties have been such coalitions of interests. With the brief (and unusual) exceptions of the leadership tenures of George Lansbury and Michael Foot, Labour's leadership has long been the reliable redoubt of the centre right of the party (but this is not to say that the left has not enjoyed significant periods of influence). Although informed by its own ideological preconceptions and set of political objectives, Labour has always had to acknowledge the need to both simultaneously work with and seek to change the grain of British politics in whatever contemporary form it has taken. It therefore should not be too surprising that New Labour cuts its policy cloth in the way that it does.

When . . . ?

From when does New Labour date? Did the process begin with the election of Blair as leader in 1994? Is it possible to trace the main features back to 1983, when Kinnock was elected (Westlake 2001; Kinnock 1994)? To complicate matters further, what contributions, if any, were made by John Smith's two-year period as leader? For the most die-hard Labour modernizer, July 1994, the occasion on which Blair became leader, is 'year zero'. Yet the transition from 'Old' to 'New' was, in reality, a slow, incremental process (Heffernan 1998; Lent 1997). Certainly the period from 1983 to 1987 saw the gradual withering of the Bennite left's influence as blame for the 1983 defeat was lain at its door; but in the early years Kinnock was widely perceived to be on what was then known as the 'soft left'. In the 1983 leadership contest, he effectively portrayed himself as a younger, more dynamic version of Michael Foot, someone who would improve Labour's presentation of its existing policies. During the 1983 parliament, however, Kinnock and his supporters within the parliamentary party gradually began to abandon the key tenets of the 1983 manifesto, moving Labour to the right, and doing so in close alliance with key trade union leaders. Symbolic victories, such as a more positive approach to Britain's membership of the European Community, the dilution of nationalization, the acceptance of the Thatcher governments' legislative restrictions on the trade unions, and the expulsion of the Militant Tendency (the means by which the further demonization of the left was secured), it was the Policy Review process of 1987–91 which signalled the extent and breadth of Labour's metamorphosis.

During the early Kinnock years – before the 1987 general election at any rate – the party walked a fine line, seriously diluting many features of the 1983 programme, but still not rejecting the commitment to economic planning and the statist regulation of business. Following the defeat of 1987, and Britain's headlong lunge into the period of high Thatcherism, the Policy Review marked a departure from the post-1983 compromise between Labour Old and New. The Review was the genuine precursor to New Labour, not only in its affirmation of the principles of the market economy and its retreat from nationalization, public spending commitments and unilateral nuclear disarmament, but also in terms of the role it played in allowing the Kinnock leadership to create a 'New Model' party, tightly centralized around the parliamentary leadership and certain members of the Shadow Cabinet, assisted by a compliant National Executive Committee (NEC) (Heffernan 2001b: 79). Two major policy documents were published during the three-year Review, the most important of which was *Meet the Challenge, Make the Change* (1989), and the Annual Conference endorsed both without problems in successive years. While the Policy Review officially ended in 1989, the informal process of revision continued at the level of the leadership right through until the 1992 general election, as two further policy documents, *Looking to the Future* (1990) and *Opportunity Britain* (1991), appeared (Westlake 2001; Taylor 1998). By 1992, Labour had jettisoned many of the commitments of 1983 and 1987, especially those relating to social and economic policy, such as renationalization, and had diluted its commitment to the redistribution of wealth through progressive taxation.

When Labour lost the 1992 election, Kinnock duly fell on his sword and was replaced by John Smith, the old-style alternative leader-in-waiting during most of the 1987 Parliament. To some the role of Smith in the transition to New Labour is perplexing. While he was considered to be an Old Labour 'fixer' by modernizers close to Kinnock, such as Peter Mandelson, Smith also firmly laid the foundations of the economic 'prudence' that was to become Gordon Brown's stock-in-trade. Smith also set in train a significant debate about constitutional reform, or what came to be termed 'democratic renewal', that Blair was obliged to inherit and which subsequently found a place in New Labour's platform for the 1997 general election. At the same time, demonstrating decidedly Old Labour credentials, Smith exhibited a friendlier attitude to the trade unions (McSmith 1994). It should be emphasized, however, that Smith did not reverse any of the changes to Labour's programme and internal structures that had occurred during the Kinnock era. Indeed, at the 1993 conference it was Smith who delivered 'one member one vote' in the selection of Labour parliamentary candidates, removing at a stroke a key plank of trade union involvement in the party, a change Kinnock had long wanted, but was never able to secure.

Looking back, whatever Smith's long-term strategy, and recalling the fact that, on key indices such as economic competence, Labour's opinion poll recovery began under him, the period 1992–4 was but a brief pause in the 'modernization' process. Blair's ascendancy as Smith's successor came just as increased support for Labour in the opinion polls started to show real substance. Under his leadership, Labour ruthlessly set about developing a media-centric strategy, and Blair took the considerable risk of finally ditching Clause IV – a feat never seriously considered by Kinnock or Smith – in April 1995. This symbolic shift demonstrated Blair's determination to pick up where Kinnock had left off, intensifying the modernization dynamic and offering a cast iron pledge on taxation and public spending that was designed to finally purge the demons of the 1980s. In organizational terms, Blair continued the process of centralization, while simultaneously introducing new structures like regional policy forums and a one off party referendum on *The Road to the Manifesto* document in 1996. Above all, Blair succeeded in areas where Kinnock had largely failed, by demonstrating to the electorate that he possessed the qualities of 'strong' and 'dynamic' leadership, personal charisma that appeared to jell with the party's new policies, and a set of relevant, workable and, above all, moderate policy proposals. Instead of the preferred mantra which Blair liked to proclaim, 'education, education, education', New Labour's watchwords were essentially 'reassurance, reassurance, reassurance'. Blair thus became the embodiment of New Labour, much as he strived to assert some symbiotic link between the new Labour Party and a new Britain.

No single point in time can therefore be identified as the 'beginning' of New Labour. There is no year zero. The contemporary party is the product of a cumulative process of change that spanned nearly two decades (Heffernan 2001b, 1998; Hay 1999). Yet one thing is now clear: when Blair announced shortly after the 1997 election that the party was 'elected as New Labour' and would therefore 'govern as New Labour', he was signalling the permanence of the changes to Labour's policy profile and internal organizational discipline. There was to be no going back.

How...?

How did (and does) New Labour pursue its goals? To become electorally successful, the party leadership decided that it had to dramatically alter its programmatic stance; and to alter its programmatic stance, it had to alter its internal structures. In organizational terms, the trajectory mapped out during Labour's transformation was both simple and stark: the parliamentary leadership had to be empowered at the expense of the extra-parliamentary party; Labour's structures had to be altered to grant the leadership *de facto* powers of command. Blair prides himself on leading his party from the front. Of a beleaguered John Major, he once said, 'He follows his party, I lead mine' (Rentoul 2001: 145), perhaps a phrase that best encapsulates Blair's attitude to leadership and party politics.

Of course, changes made to Labour cannot be ascribed solely to Blair's agency. Over time, the building of the 'electoral professional' party (Webb 2000; Panebianco 1988) saw Labour move from its relatively decentralized, federal structure, in which both parliamentary and extra-parliamentary wings coexisted in an occasionally tense, ambiguous relationship, towards a centralized structure. Now the parliamentary leadership, being more autonomous with respect to the extra-parliamentary party, is more fully equipped to point the party's strategic direction. As catch-all, professionalized organizations, political parties are increasingly run from the centre. In the case of Labour, its electoral organizers and campaign professionals are geared to serve the needs of the parliamentary leadership, not local affiliates. As a result, in common with all party elites, the Blair leadership sets out its policy stall as Labour's policy stall, addressing the electorate from a distance, making full use of the news media to frame and disseminate its message, packaging its appeal through carefully chosen imagery, perpetually seeking favourable media coverage. Today's media-driven electoral processes, often blurring personality politics with policy deliberation, further empowers party leaders at the expense of the grass roots. The aim after 1994 was to project the party as the Blair leadership, and the Blair leadership as the party, and this successful strategy has served to further empower the party leadership at the expense of the party at large, in Parliament and in the country.

Once elected, the Labour government quickly sought to translate the principles of centralized, disciplined leadership into a new governing style. Often dismissed by journalists as 'control freakery', New Labour's changes to Whitehall are much more significant than the personal predilections of Blair, because they encompass a programme of Whitehall reform under a 'Modernizing Government' banner (Cabinet Office 1999). Leading 'from the centre' remains a key Blair objective. To this end, strengthening the Downing Street–Cabinet Office nexus in terms of personnel and resources (Hennessy 2000; Burch and Holliday 1999; Kavanagh and Seldon 1999), equipping the Prime Minister and his staff with the means to intervene across Whitehall, and astute use of information and communications technology (Jones 1999; Franklin 2001; Chadwick and May 2003; Chadwick 2001) to publicize Government actions have become central preoccupations. As the Cabinet Office has been gradually brought into the orbit of Downing Street, to serve the Prime Minister rather than the Cabinet collectively, this 'Whitehall Centre' is increasingly organized by and for the Prime Minister, charged with issuing instructions to departments and enabling the Prime Minister to respond to departmental representations. Critics have argued that these reforms have finally 'presidentialized' British government and have continued the ongoing process of building a *de facto* Prime Minister's Department, even if the name itself is deliberately shunned.

Central to Labour's strategy was the very invention of the term 'New Labour'. First used as a slogan at the 1994 party conference, it was an attempt to reconnect with the electorate, and to demonstrate that the election of Blair as leader in succession to John Smith marked a new beginning. In essence, the phrase was deployed to market the party as something different from what it once was, to starkly demonstrate that Labour had changed, had done so fundamentally and irrevocably, and that it would change further. The very term 'New Labour' is therefore a brand, and a key signifier of a reformed political party. The phrase has well and truly stuck. Now used by friend and foe alike, informing both analytical and normative accounts of how the party has been reformed and what the party has been doing in government since 1997, it shows little sign of being past its sell-by date even some eight years after its first appearance.

The phrase 'New Labour' resonates, because it encapsulates change in both ideological and organizational terms. A party defining itself as 'new' is one that wishes to be seen as clean, bright and fresh; no longer sullied by a past best forgotten, and no longer 'old'. More than a marketing device, New Labour was and is a political invention, designed to publicly project the Blair leadership's concept of a modern, vibrant, electorally friendly and, above all, politically viable party. As something pitched to voters at large, as well as to agenda setters, commentators and opinion formers everywhere, New Labour embraced a set of workable and 'realistic' ideas. The re-branding proclaimed the party a safe bet for non-Labour voters, demonstrating that its previous assumptions were well and truly a thing of the past. In their place, Blair-led Labour trumpeted its willingness to pursue market-enhancing, supply-side policies which would bring benefits to 'haves' as well as 'have-nots', appealing to voters who had hitherto provided the core of the Conservative electoral coalition which had propelled Labour into the wilderness after 1979.

This objective involved the construction of a stereotypical Old Labour. Making clear what Labour was not, and what it did not stand for, was the prime objective. The idea that Labour was in thrall to the trade unions, favoured high levels of taxation, would be profligate with taxpayers' money, and 'irresponsible' in its macro-economic policy – all these had to be banished from popular perception. This was the spectre of 'Old' Labour clinically raised to indicate just how fast change was occurring under 'New' Labour. Strangely enough, its target was just as much Jim Callaghan, say, as it was Tony Benn. New Labour now seemingly agreed with Keith Joseph, who had lambasted the party back in 1979 for being wedded to six poisons polluting the UK economy: 'excessive government spending, high direct taxation, egalitarianism, excessive nationalization, a politicized trade union movement associated with Luddism, and an anti-enterprise culture' (Joseph 1975). These were to be drained from the New Labour mind-set, its contemporary solutions to present problems denying any association with the supposedly mad, bad, sad old days.

While several commentators argue that the 'New' is not very different from the 'Old', Blair's desire for it to appear different might well prove to be the leitmotif of his leadership. While aware of the need to genuflect in homage to the party's illustrious past (though with less gusto than his predecessors), Blair has made it clear that he is eager to move Labour forward, a process identified by his adviser, Philip Gould, as 'permanent revolution', an ironic borrowing from that decidedly non-New Labour figure, Leon Trotsky. Gould is a fascinating figure, not least because his critique of Old Labour, based on his analysis of what he terms 'The Land that Labour Forgot' – the hard-working, aspirational suburban consumers in the south of England – encouraged the leadership to painstakingly reconstruct Labour's appeal with the aid of focus groups and poll data (Gould 1998). Gould's personalized narrative of his life as a Labour supporter in the affluent village of Brookwood, just outside Woking, in Surrey, Britain's wealthiest county, where unemployment in January 2002 stood at just 0.9 per cent (Office of National Statistics 2002), is bizarre. At the 1992, 1997 and 2001 general elections, Labour finished third behind the Conservatives and the Liberal Democrats in Woking, and there has never been a Labour MP elected in the constituency (nor, indeed, the county). Since first created in 1950, in common with most of Surrey, Woking has been staunchly Conservative. Perhaps the party can be forgiven for 'forgetting' a place where it has never really been. Still, these facts get in the way of Gould's story and objective, which was not about turning around solid Tory seats based on the support of middle- and upper-middle-class private sector professionals, and was everything to do with convincing non-aligned swing voters of all classes in more marginal constituencies up and down Britain that Labour was not going to interfere with their personal wealth.

Probably more significant in the long term than the media strategy of Philip Gould was New Labour's attempt to frame its policies as the 'Third Way'. According to Blair,

> The Third Way stands for a modernized social democracy, passionate in its commitment to social justice and the goals of the centre-left, but flexible, innovative and forward-looking in the means to achieve them. It is founded on the values that have guided progressive policies for more than a century – democracy, liberty, justice, mutual obligation and internationalism. But it is a Third Way because it moves decisively beyond an Old Left preoccupied by state control, high taxes and producer interests; and a New Right treating public investment, and often the very notions of society and collective endeavour, as evils to be undone. (Blair 1998: 1)

The Third Way suggests that other ways have failed. It chastises traditional socialist ideas, in both their radical and their moderate forms, for being now impractical, and therefore irrelevant, their failings all too apparent, particularly in terms of economic management and in light of transformations wrought in the political landscape by globalization. Neo-liberalism, and the market fundamentalism it engendered, has also proved to be a failed alternative to social democracy. It has been unable to deal with the economic realities of an unequal, unstable, ever-changing world, particularly when markets are neither self-regulating nor able to promote economic development or provide for social justice. In light of the seeming irrelevance of the 'first way', traditional social democracy, and the 'second way', neo-liberalism, to deal with current conditions, the 'Third Way' offers the possibility of discovering new means to manage both economy and society, working with, rather than against, markets, while nurturing and developing civil society. As Anthony Giddens argues, contemporary social conditions, foremost among them globalization, economic and social transformations, particularly the rise of individualism and the erosion of an old-style egalitarian collectivism, all provide the impetus for the renewal of social democracy, something he argues is exemplified by the emergence of New Labour in the UK and by reform-minded projects in other countries headed by centre-left governments (Giddens 2001, 1998).

Unlike Giddens's preferences, a series of normative prescriptions about what the Labour government should do (as opposed to an analysis of what it is actually doing), Blair's version of the Third Way is more slippery and much more pragmatic. The Prime Minister claims to get his inspiration from early twentieth-century new liberals like L. T. Hobhouse and J. A. Hobson. He is not the first Labour politician to acknowledge such debts; progressive liberalism has had affinities with Labourism all the way back to the party's foundation, and has nourished not only its social and economic ideas, but also its discourses of citizenship and constitutionalism (Chadwick 1999). But, posited as a rejection of social democracy and neo-liberalism, Blair's Third Way suffers from a degree of historical amnesia. For it was progressive liberals like Hobhouse, Hobson and, of course, John Maynard Keynes and William Beveridge who played such an important role in defining British social democracy in the first place (Freeden 1999), not least during the 'golden era' of the post-1940 period.

In electoral terms, in the wake of Blair-led Labour's reworking of Britain's electoral landscape, there seems little doubt now that the nature of British politics has shifted. 'Issue voting' has finally come of age, and 'class voting' is being eclipsed, as social and economic trends towards consumerism have at last converged with politics. Gordon Brown's adept management of the economy between 1997 and 2002, narrowly avoiding Britain being pulled into a global downturn, simply consolidated Labour's electoral base. Growth rates remained healthy, inflation stayed low, and wages rose steadily (Toynbee and Walker 2001). Together these facilitated the 'feel good factor' – or at the very least prevented a 'feel bad factor' – which bound Labour's 1997 electorate to the party in 2001. The problems of the manufacturing sector and a potentially damaging North–South divide aside, what we might term the 'cultural economy' – the patterns of consumer behaviour which play such an important role in defining social and therefore political identity in early twenty-first century Britain – have been very kind to New Labour. There is little immediate sign that this will change.

Why...?

Finally, we come to the issue of how commentators have sought to explain New Labour. The debate is rich, complex and still in development, but its main contours can be outlined (Driver and Martell 2002, 1998; Heffernan 2001b; Kenny and Smith 2001; Ludlam and Smith 2001; White 2001; Hay 1999; Shaw 1994). In the broadest terms, certain authors (Kenny and Smith 2001; Giddens 1998) suggest that Labour has merely modernized its traditional policy stance and is still working within the party's historically accepted ideological parameters, while others (Heffernan 2001b; Hay 1999, 1996) argue that Labour has accommodated itself to Thatcherite neo-liberalism and has effectively altered those central principles that had informed its political thought and practice. Ironically, there is considerable overlap between the 'Thatcherism' and the 'non-Thatcherism' schools. Both agree that Labour has changed its policy stance, and has done so dramatically, and acknowledge that, whatever the party's motivation, Blair's policy agenda is demonstrably different from that of, say, Clement Attlee, Hugh Gaitskell or Harold Wilson. Both schools of thought also blend a mixture of contextual factors and the motivations of political leaders, structure and agency, to explain the nature and form of Labour's political change (and of political change in Britain and elsewhere). At the same time, some writers attempt to transcend the divide by arguing that New Labour is the product of 'post-Thatcherite' politics (Driver and Martell 2002, 1998).

Colin Hay argues that five different contexts can be identified in the existing accounts assessing Labour's transformation: party history and traditions, the development of the British state and economy, demographic and other socio-economic trends, the development of European social democracy, and the development of the global political economy (Hay 1999: 12–14). Indeed, when it comes to party change, such contexts are crucial. All political actors are conditioned by historical circumstance and can only express ideas within existing social, political and economic environments (Heffernan 2002, 2001b; Chadwick 2000; Hall 1993, 1989; Steinmo 1993), although they may be able to manipulate such contexts when in office (Dunleavy 1991). Parties often find themselves obliged to adopt policies that work with, rather than against, the grain of societal interests, within and without the state, in line with the demands of the economy, particularly when they are in opposition and prize the attainment of office over all other party goals. Dramatic policy change is the exception, not the rule, and this may be especially true of reformist parties. As Donald Sassoon (1996) rightly suggests, when the needs of capitalism have changed, the strategies of social democracy have inevitably changed too. Thus, the rise of social democracy in the middle of the twentieth century was gradually enacted in light of the perceived failures of the market economy, the collectivist shift in favour of reformist politics encouraged by the growth of mass politics, and the refinement of the holy trinity of state intervention – Keynesian demand management, Beveridgian welfarism and the Morrisonian public corporation – reflected the political, social and economic needs of their time. The insurgence of neo-liberalism in the 1970s unfolded against the background of the economic and political crisis of social democracy and the belief that statism was now part of an economic problem, and no longer a solution (Kavanagh 1997, 1990; Gamble 1994).

Quite obviously, New Labour has not simply imported unthinkingly the high Thatcherism of the 1980s. After all, since 1997, the government has presided over a series of policy changes opposed by the Thatcher- and Major-led Conservatives when they were in office. The thwarted idea of electoral reform notwithstanding (Jenkins Commission 1998; Straw 1998), the constitutional reform agenda, including the introduction of devolution for Scotland (Dewar 1997), Wales and Northern Ireland, the passing of the Human Rights Act (HMSO 1998), elected mayors (DETR 1998), reform of the House of Lords by the abolition of the hereditary principle (Lord Chancellor's Department 2001), provides obvious examples of where the election of the New Labour government has marked a change of direction from Conservative practice. Policies such as the minimum wage, increasing child benefit, and the use of indirect (and direct, at least in the form of increased National Insurance contributions) tax revenues to redistribute resources to the working poor and to fund increased expenditure on public services also mark a departure from the previous Tory agenda.

There are also differences between a Thatcherite and a New Labour view of Europe, though perhaps fewer than is often assumed. Labour's stance on the Euro reflects domestic political and economic considerations almost exclusively. Whereas Thatcher was 'patriotic' and 'anti-European', Labour is simultaneously 'patriotic' and 'pro-European', its Europeanism deriving from the desire that Britain should benefit from membership of a European Union that protects and enhances British interests (Heffernan 2001a; Stephens 2001a; Daniels 1998; Hughes and Smith 1998). Labour is ever conscious of Britain's geo-political traditions, its Atlantic ties, its conception of national sovereignty, and its continuing allegiance to the majoritarian constitutional forms of the Westminster model. Thus, monetary union continues to be the most important European issue facing Labour, its position being that Britain should join the single currency only after overcoming a 'triple veto' of the Cabinet, Parliament and a referendum (Brown 2001, 1997; Stephens 2001a; Blair 2000).

That there are significant differences between Thatcherite Conservatism and New Labour is not in dispute. Yet, in economic policy, social policy and Blair's governing style, there are very important continuities with the Thatcher–Major years. The disjuncture between constitutional radicalism and social and economic conservatism was labelled the 'Blair paradox' early in the first term (Marquand 1998), but promoting business and encouraging entrepreneurship are still the order of the day. In this regard, Peter Mandelson, for many Blair's *eminence grise* and a key architect of New Labour, publicly claimed that New Labour was 'intensely relaxed about people getting filthy rich' (Rawnsley 2001: 213), a phrase without much resonance in Labour's history.

While being himself 'intensely relaxed' about advancing the interests of Britain's entrepreneurial classes (and those of the international community at large), Blair described the 2001 general election as being about '[m]aintaining a strong economy and reforming the public services'. Launching the manifesto on 16 May, he promised: '[W]e make the public investment we need, we target tax cuts on our priorities as affordable, and at all times we never put the stability of the economy at risk' (Blair 2001). For Blair, Labour's 'first term mission was to sort out the economy and begin the process of investment and reform of public services. Our second term mission is to make real and lasting improvements in our public services' (ibid.). Yet, in matters of public sector reform, it is clear that Labour believes the role of the private sector in delivering public services should be increased. The position is both simple and stark: there should be an end to the public–private dichotomy, because '[t]here should be no barriers, no dogma, no vested interests in the way of delivering the best services for people' (ibid.). The government's position, set out in July 2001, is that 'Where it makes sense to use private or voluntary sectors better to deliver public services, we will do so' (ibid.).

In introducing the private sector into the provision of public services, the government is going beyond the introduction of new public management techniques pioneered in the 1980s and 1990s, and much further than the Thatcher and Major governments wanted (or felt able) to go. Labour's willingness to 'think the unthinkable' (in Labour Party terms) regarding, say, part-privatizing the NHS, is an illustration of the road the party has travelled in the past twenty years (Hutton 1998). Thus, having adopted the agenda of Conservative governments, Labour is pursuing a number of public–private partnerships (PPPs) in all forms of public service – in transport (the forced semi-renationalization of Railtrack aside), particularly the London Underground, and in education and the NHS. So far, this has created a great deal of unease among many Labour back-bench MPs and the trade unions. While the government, with the exception of up-and-running PPPs, has so far confined itself to making the general case for private sector involvement, the public sector unions, principally the GMB and UNISON, have reacted strongly to the very idea that private firms should be invited to provide health and education services, disagreeing with ministers that they would be more effective than the public sector. With such opponents threatening to mount a campaign to 'keep public services public', and Labour back-benchers uneasy, and some openly hostile, this issue may come to dominate Labour's second term.

Did demographic change pave the way for New Labour? In common with other European parties of the social democratic left, Labour has had to engage with a changing electoral environment, its previous core vote having dwindled. No longer a party determinedly of and for the organized (and disorganized) working class and those social groups allied with them, Labour slowly, over time, became a 'catch-all' party, broadening its appeal to seek votes from all classes and social interests, becoming 'national' rather than 'sectional'.

This is nothing new. Labour governments have always prioritized national economic interests over the party's preferred sectional interests. MacDonald's 1931 'sacrifice', the Crippsian austerity of 1947–50, and Wilson's defence of sterling before devaluation in 1967 provide but three such historical examples. In 1976, even in the days of Old Labour, Callaghan and Healey's IMF-assisted management of the economy saw a Labour government drastically reduce public expenditure and adopt an unachievable incomes policy culminating in the trade union revolt of 1978–9, the infamous 'winter of discontent'. But whereas in the past a 'national' economic policy was supported by a solid base in the trade union movement, it is reasonably clear that demographic change since the 1970s has shrunk Labour's electoral heartland. Male manual employment in manufacturing industries has continued to decline. Non-unionized jobs have become the norm, and this, together with the growth in the service sector and the relative privileging of skilled manual workers (the C1s and C2s), saw the Conservative Party fashion a new electoral base with which Labour had to engage.

However, with regard to Labour's electoral resurgence, this all points to the context of electoral competition and the Conservatives' strategic failures in the

1990s. While the Conservatives' plight was being undermined after 1992 by poor leadership, economic calamities, pro- and anti-European obsessions, and a general image of 'extremism', 'sleaze' and 'incompetence', Labour became a united *centre party*, no longer of the 'centre-left', able to appeal to electors to its left and right. The Conservatives lost their reputation for sound economic management during Britain's disastrous withdrawal from the Exchange Rate Mechanism in 1992 (Sanders 1996), and, ten years on, they have yet to regain it. Major's period of leadership was characterized by internal divisions reminiscent of Labour's past, and, ever fuelled by the party's suicidal tendencies over Europe, including prioritizing opposition to the single currency during the 2001 election campaign, the mantle was gratefully handed down unaltered to William Hague and to Iain Duncan Smith in turn. Before 1992, opinion poll analysts had persistently argued that the main barriers to a Labour victory were low leadership approval ratings and a poor reputation on economic policy. After 1992, the situation was entirely reversed.

Yet, management of the economy today does not mean what it meant for much of the twentieth century. In today's deregulated, liberalized and globalized market, it is often claimed that it is no longer permissible – or possible – for the state to fully regulate business, the creators of wealth, and the owners of capital. Analyses of globalization have been heavily criticized for their slipperiness, and obviously stretch well beyond explaining party change in one country; but in its central tenets the thesis has been used by New Labour friend and foe alike to account for why such policies as old-style 'tax and spend' will not work. Colin Hay has expressed this new orthodoxy very aptly:

> This posits an increasingly 'borderless world' in which labour and ('footloose' multi-national) capital flow freely – down gradients of unemployment and social protection, and taxation and labour cost, respectively. The result is a much more integrated global economy in which the Darwinian excesses of international competition drive out 'punitive' taxation regimes, 'over-regulated' labour markets, social protection, all but residual welfare regimes and Keynesian economics. This, in turn, serves to establish a pervasive logic of international economics and political convergence – a convergence on neo-liberal terms. At a stroke, it would seem, the liberalisation of capital flows, the deregulation of financial markets and the growth of instantaneous communications technology have eliminated all alternatives to neo-liberalism within the contours of the new global political economy. (Hay 1999: 30)

States therefore find that expanding transnational forces reduce the economic control they can exert over the market; fixed exchange rates, capital controls and Keynesian demand management are therefore deemed not only unnecessary, but also unwise (cf. Friedman 2000; Held and McGrew 2000; Held et al. 1999). If it is argued that globalization is an analytical tool for understanding contemporary political economy, it is also suggested that it is simultaneously a form of ideology used by political elites to strategically justify domestic inaction (Hirst and Thompson 1999; Garrett 1998). Labour's policy realignment met domestic electoral necessities by a shrewd invocation of economic and social forces outside its control. New Labourites could go some way towards silencing critics by pointing to the futility of 'Keynesianism in one country'.

New Labour, in common with most governments in liberal democratic states, has few ideas regarding how to combat the effects of globalization, other than to work with it, rather than against it. New Labour's idea of work has been heavily shaped by the discourses of globalization and 'national competitiveness'. There have been constant references to the need for a globally competitive economy. Skills in the work-force, especially the shift towards a so-called knowledge based service sector, have been central to this strategy. While hints of this may be found in Neil Kinnock's late 1980s concern with supply-side economics, particularly research and development and the acceptance of globalization, the reinterpretation of the labour market as something that must be subject to state intervention only to make workers better equipped for a global economy is a genuinely new element in Labour's thinking. As Margaret Thatcher was reported to have said in the late 1980s, 'you cannot buck the market' (Thatcher 1993). Today New Labour has no intention of doing so, nationally or internationally.

Conclusions

Initially, making clear what Labour was not, what it did not stand for, was the party's prime objective in the search for votes lost in 1983, 1987 and 1992. The idea that Labour was in thrall to the trade unions, favoured high levels of taxation, would be profligate with public monies, and be deliriously, spectacularly irresponsible with the economy, were all to be banished from the public lists. This was the spectre of Old Labour. As a result, more than a carefully crafted marketing device, New Labour was, and remains, a political invention, projecting the Blairite concept of what a modern, electorally friendly and politically relevant party should look like and stand for. Pitched to voters at large, as well as agenda setters, commentators and opinion formers, New Labour above all else embraced a set of workable, realistic ideas, all of which demonstrated that it had a viable programme for government.

In the end, as prior debates about the role and impact of Thatcherism have perhaps demonstrated (Heffernan 2001b; Kavanagh 1997, 1990; Hay 1996; Marsh 1995; Gamble 1994; Hoover and Plant 1989; Marquand 1988; Jenkins 1987), accounting for New Labour will perhaps come down to a more nuanced account, in which generalization becomes qualified with reference to matters of degree and differences across policy sectors. Disentangling the different factors involved and the relationship between ideas and their contexts is an essential preliminary, but there will always be the need to provide an overarching explanation for the New Labour phenomenon. Despite the wealth of literature already in existence, the New Labour debate is only just getting started. Perhaps absent from the current approaches are studies that fully support analytical assertions with detailed empirical material. This is in many respects a product of the novelty of the subject matter, and will hopefully be redressed in due course, especially as the length of Labour's tenure increases. Synthesizing theory with evidence is always a challenge for political scientists, but there is a real need for work making intelligent use of 'thick description' in presenting its case. A natural starting point for such an exercise would be to examine what New Labour has actually done in office since 1997.

The range of responses to New Labour is inevitably explained by its 'complexity' (Smith 2000); yet there is a more fundamental reason for the ambiguity and caginess which we freely admit has hung over our own assessment here. It stems from trying to examine a political party that has, perversely, radically changed its ideology and structure only to accommodate and carry forward a pre-existing agenda, most of which was not of its own making. Analysing Thatcherism was more straightforward. A new, relatively clear, distinctive ideology and policy agenda marked some form of break with post-war collectivism and with many of the economic, social and industrial policies pursued by successive governments, both Labour and Conservative (Heffernan 2002, 2001b; Gamble 1994). Change is often easier to explain than continuity. Huge innovation in Labour's ideology and organization was required, first, to pursue relatively unoriginal policies, and second, to begin to fashion a reform agenda within the neo-liberal policy paradigm bequeathed the Blair government by its Thatcher- and Major-led predecessors. This is the central antinomy of New Labour

The Blairite Third Way agenda argues that statist approaches should be abandoned, but that free-market philosophies be reformed (Blair and Schröder 1999; Blair 1998); as a result, Labour works to reform the *status quo* bequeathed it by successive Conservative governments. New Labour is not Old Thatcherism writ large. While to some degree 'fiscally conservative, [New] Labour is committed to interventionist supply side measures and to incremental redistribution through the tax system' (Smith 2000: 259). That said, it remains the case that fiscal conservatism takes precedence over interventionist measures and incremental redistribution should such objectives conflict. Normative theories of the Third Way aside (Giddens 2001, 1998; Marquand 1998), the Blairite Third Way certainly reflects the remaking of existing ideologies and political theories, but does so as a result of political and policy changes brought about by the eclipse of social democracy amid the rise of neo-liberalism (Heffernan 2002).

In this regard, if in no other, Thatcherism remains a factor in the remaking of Labour. Mainstream politics having moved away from the nostrums of the post-war social democratic era, the Blair government acknowledges the neo-liberal policy paradigm framing and constraining the policy of all governments, and within which it pursues its own distinctive reform agendas. Will the 1997 general election rank as important a turning point in British political history as those of 1906, 1945 and 1979? By themselves, election years may not necessarily change anything other than the administration of the day, and may not change the prevailing policy agenda. Of course, New Labour remains a 'work in progress'. It is probably too soon to tell what will be its impacts in government.

REFERENCES

Anderson, P. and Mann, N. (1997), *Safety First: The Making of New Labour* (London: Granta).

Balls, E. (1998), 'Open Macroeconomics in an Open Economy', *Scottish Journal of Political Economy*, 45 (2).

Barnett, A. (2000), 'Corporate Populism and Partyless Democracy', *New Left Review*, 11 (3), 217–86.

Blair, T. (2001), Speech on the Future of the Public Services, London. Also available at <http://www.number-10.gov.uk/output/page 3194.asp>. Last accessed 21 March 2002.

Blair, T. (2000), Speech to the Polish Stock Exchange, Warsaw. Prime ministerial press release.

Blair, T. (1998), *The Third Way. New Politics for the New Century* (London: Fabian Society).

Blair, T. (1995), Speech to Rupert Murdoch's News Corporation Leadership Conference, Labour Party press release.

Blair, T. and Schröder, G. (1999), *Europe: The Third Way/Die Neue Mitte*. (London: Labour Party).

Brivati, B. and Heffernan, R. (eds), *The Labour Party: A Centenary History* (London: Macmillan).

Brown, G. (2001), Speech at the Mansion House. HM Treasury press release.

Brown, G. (1997), Statement on EMU to the House of Commons, 27 October. HM Treasury press release.

Budge, I. and Laver, M. (1986), 'Office Seeking and Policy Pursuit in Coalition Theory', *Legislative Studies Quarterly*, 11 (4), 485–506.

Burch, M. and Holliday, I. (1999), 'The Prime Minister's and Cabinet Offices: An Executive Office in All But Name', *Parliamentary Affairs*, 52 (1), 32–45.

Cabinet Office (1999), *Modernising Government*, Cm 4310 (London: HMSO).

Chadwick, A. (2001), 'The Electronic Face of Government in the Internet Age', *Information, Communication and Society*, 4 (3), 46–67.

Chadwick, A. (2000), 'Studying Political Ideas: A Public Political Discourse Approach', *Political Studies*, 48 (2), 283–301.

Chadwick, A. (1999), *Augmenting Democracy: Political Movements and Constitutional Reform during the Rise of Labour* (Aldershot: Ashgate).

Chadwick, A. and May, C. (2003), 'Interaction between States and Citizens in the Age of the Internet: "e-government" in the United States, Britain and the European Union', *Governance*, 16 (2), 211–300.

Daniels, P. (1998), 'From Hostility to Constructive Engagement: The Europeanization of the Labour Party', *West European Politics*, 21 (1), 72–93.

Department of the Environment, Transport and the Regions (DETR) (1998), *A Mayor and Assembly for London*, Cm 3897 (London: HMSO).

Dewar, D. (1997), Foreword to *Scotland's Parliament* (Scottish Devolution White Paper), Cm 3658 (London: HMSO).

Downs, A. (1957), *An Economic Theory of Democracy* (New York: Harper and Row).

Driver, S. and Martell, L. (2002), *Blair's Britain* (Cambridge: Polity).

Driver, S. and Martell, L. (1998), *New Labour* (Cambridge: Polity).

Drucker, H. (1979), *Doctrine and Ethos in the Labour Party* (London: Allen & Unwin).

Dunleavy, P. (2002), 'Elections and Party Politics', in P. Dunleavy, A. Gamble, R. Heffernan, I. Holliday and G. Peele (eds), *Developments in British Politics, 6*, rev. edn (London: Macmillan).

Dunleavy, P. (1991), *Democracy, Bureaucracy and Public Choice* (Hemel Hempstead: Harvester Wheatsheaf).

Feingenbaum, H., Henig, J. and Hamnett, C. (1999), *Shrinking the State: The Political Underpinnings of Privatisation* (Cambridge: Cambridge University Press).

Foley, M. (2000), *The British Presidency: Tony Blair and the Politics of Public Leadership* (Manchester: Manchester University Press).

Franklin, B. (2001), 'The Hand of History: New Labour, News Management and Governance', in S. Ludlam and M. J. Smith (eds) *New Labour in Government* (London: Macmillan).

Freeden, M. (1999), 'The Ideology of New Labour', *Political Quarterly*, 70 (1), 42–51.

Friedman, T. (2000), *The Lexus and the Olive Tree* (London: Harper Collins).

Gaber, I. (2000), 'Lies, Damn Lies and Political Spin', *British Journalism Review*, 11 (1), 302–11.

Gamble, A. (1994), *The Free Economy and the Strong State* (London: Macmillan).

Garrett, G. (1998), *Partisan Politics in the Global Economy* (Cambridge: Cambridge University Press).

Giddens, A. (2002), *Where Now for New Labour* (Cambridge: Polity).

Giddens, A. (2001), *The Third Way and its Critics* (Cambridge: Polity).

Giddens, A. (1998), *The Third Way: The Renewal of Social Democracy* (Cambridge: Polity).

Goes, E. (2002), 'New Labour and the Idea of Work: A Public Political Discourse Analysis of the Labour Party 1994–2001' (unpublished Ph.D. thesis, London School of Economics).

Gould, P. (1998), *The Unfinished Revolution* (London: Abacus).

Hall, P. A. (1993), 'Policy Paradigms, Social Learning and the State', *Comparative Politics*, 25 (3), 255–66.

Hall, P. A. (1992), 'The Movement from Keynesianism to Monetarism: Institutional Analysis and British Economic Policy in the 1970s', in S. Steinmo, K. Thelen and F. Longstreth (eds), *Structuring Politics: Historical Institutionalism in Comparative Analysis* (Cambridge: Cambridge University Press).

Hall, P. A. (ed.) (1989), *The Political Power of Economic Ideas: Keynesianism across Nations* (Princeton, NJ: Princeton University Press).

Hay, C. (1999), *The Political Economy of New Labour: Labouring under False Pretences?* (Manchester: Manchester University Press).

Hay, C. (1996), *Restating Social and Political Change* (Buckingham: Open University Press).

Heffernan, R. (2002), 'The "Possible as the Art of Politics": Understanding Consensus Politics', *Political Studies*, 50 (3), 742–60.

Heffernan, R. (2001a), 'Beyond Euro-Scepticism: Exploring the Europeanization of the Labour Party since 1983', *Political Quarterly*, 72 (2), 180–90.

Heffernan, R. (2001b), *New Labour and Thatcherism* (London: Macmillan).

Heffernan, R. (1998), 'Labour's Transformation: A Staged Process with No One Point of Origin', *Politics*, 18 (2), 101–6.

Held, D. and McGrew, A. (2000), *The Global Transformations Reader* (Cambridge: Polity).

Held, D. et al. (1999), *Global Transformations* (Cambridge: Polity).

Hennessy, P. (2000), *The Prime Minister: The Office and its Holders since 1945* (Harmondsworth: Penguin).

Hills, J. (2001), *Taxation for the Enabling State* (London: Centre for Analysis of Social Exclusion, London School of Economics). Also available at <http://sticerd.lse.ac.uk/dps/case/cp/CASEpaper41.pdf>. Last accessed 28 April 2002.

Hirst, P. and Thompson, G. (1999), *Globalization in Question* (Cambridge: Polity).

Hoover, K. and Plant, R. (1989), *Conservative Capitalism in Britain and the United States* (London: Routledge).

HMSO (1998), *Human Rights Act 1998* (London: HMSO).

HM Treasury (2000), *Productivity in the UK: The Evidence and the Government's Approach* (London: HMSO).

Hughes, P. and Smith, D. (1998), 'New Labour, New Europe', *International Affairs*, 74 (1), 93–103.

Hutton, W. (1998), 'How Big Money is Stitching Up the NHS', *Observer*, 13 December.

Jenkins, P. (1987), *Mrs Thatcher's Revolution: The Ending of the Socialist Age* (London: Jonathan Cape).

Jenkins Commission on the Voting System/Home Office (1998), *The Report of the Independent Commission on the Voting System*, Cm 4090-I and 4090-II (London: HMSO).

Jones, N. (1999), *Sultans of Spin: The Media and the New Labour Government* (London: Gollancz).

Joseph, K. (1975), *Reversing the Trend* (London: Barry Rose).

Kavanagh, D. (1997), *The Reordering of British Politics: Politics after Thatcher* (Oxford: Oxford University Press).

Kavanagh, D. (1990), *Thatcherism and British Politics: The End of Consensus* (Oxford: Oxford University Press).

Kavanagh, D. and Seldon, A. (1999), *The Powers behind the Prime Minister* (London: Harper Collins).

Kenny, M. and Smith, M. J. (2000), 'Interpreting New Labour: Constraints, Dilemmas and Political Agency', in S. Ludlam and M. J. Smith (eds), *New Labour in Government* (London: Macmillan).

Kinnock, N. (1994), 'Remaking the Labour Party', *Contemporary Record*, 8 (3), 535–54.

Lasswell, H. D. (1936), *Politics: Who Gets What, When, How* (Glencoe, IL: The Free Press).

Le Grand, J. (1998), 'The Third Way Begins with CORA', *New Statesman*, 6 March.

Lent, A. (1997), 'Labour's Transformation: Searching for the Point of Origin', *Politics*, 17, 10–18.

Leys, C. (1996), 'The Labour Party's Transition from Socialism to Capitalism', in *The Socialist Register 1996* (London: Merlin Press).

Lister, R. et al. (1997), 'Government Must Reconsider its Strategy for More Equal Society', letter to *Financial Times*, 1 October.

Lord Chancellor's Department (2001), *The House of Lords: Completing the Reform*, Cm 5291 (London: HMSO).

Ludlam, S. (2000), 'Norms and Blocks: Trade Unions and the Labour Party since 1964', in B. Brivati and R. Heffernan (eds), *The Labour Party: A Centenary History* (London: Macmillan).

Ludlam, S. and Smith, M. J. (2001), *New Labour in Government* (London: Macmillan).

McIntyre, D. (2000), *Peter Mandelson and the Making of New Labour* (London: Harper Collins).

McSmith, A. (1996), *Faces of Labour: The Inside Story* (London: Verso).

McSmith, A. (1994), *John Smith* (London: Verso).

Mandelson, P. and Liddle, R. (1996), *The Blair Revolution* (London: Faber and Faber).

Marquand, D. (1998), 'The Blair Paradox', *Prospect*, May.

Marquand, D. (1988), *The Unprincipled Society: New Demands and Old Politics* (London: Fontana).

Marsh, D. (1995), 'Explaining "Thatcherite" Policies: Beyond Uni-Dimensional Explanation', *Political Studies*, 43 (4), 595–613.

Morris, B. (2001), President's Speech to the TUC Congress, 10 September. Available at <http://www.tuc.org.uk/congress/tuc-3699-f0.cfm>. Last accessed 7 February 2002.

Müller, W. C. and Strøm, K. (eds) (1999), *Policy, Office or Votes? How Political Parties in Western Europe Make Hard Decisions* (Cambridge: Cambridge University Press).

Nexus (2002), *Nexus Online*, http://www.netnexus.org/. Last accessed 12 April 2002.

Office of National Statistics (2002), *Labour Market Statistics April 2002: South East* (London: HMSO). Available at <http://www.statistics.gov.uk/pdfdir/lmsseast0402.pdf>. Last accessed 24 April 2002.

Panebianco, A. (1988), *Political Parties: Organisation and Power* (Cambridge: Cambridge University Press).

Panitch, L. and Leys, C. (1998), *The End of Parliamentary Socialism?* (London: Verso).

Rawnsley, A. (2001), *Servants of the People: The Inside Story of New Labour* (Harmondsworth: Penguin).

Rentoul, J. (2001), *Tony Blair* (London: Little, Brown).

Sanders, D. (1996), 'Economic Performance, Management Competence and the Outcome of the Next General Election', *Political Studies*, 44 (2), 203–31.

Sassoon, D. (1996), *One Hundred Years of Socialism* (London: Fontana).

Saunders, P. and Harris, C. (1994), *Privatisation and Popular Capitalism* (Buckingham: Open University Press).

Scammell, M. (1995), *Designer Politics: How Elections Are Won* (London: Macmillan).

Seldon, A. (2001), *The Blair Effect* (London: Little, Brown).

Shaw, E. (1994), *The Labour Party since 1979: Crisis and Transformation* (London: Routledge).

Smith, M. J. (2000), 'Conclusion: The Complexity of New Labour', in S. Ludlam and M. J. Smith (eds), *New Labour in Government* (London: Macmillan).

Steinmo, S. (1993), *Taxation and Democracy: Swedish, British and American Approaches to Financing the Modern State* (New Haven: Yale University Press).

Stephens, P. (2001a), 'The Blair Government and Europe', *Political Quarterly*, 72 (1), 67–75.

Stephens, P. (2001b), 'The Treasury under Labour', in A. Seldon (ed.), *The Blair Effect* (London: Little, Brown).

Straw, J. (1998), Home Secretary's Response to the Jenkins Commission Report, *Hansard*, 318, cols 1032–9, 5 November.

Taylor, G. (1998), *Labour's Renewal* (London: Macmillan).

Thatcher, M. (1993), *The Downing Street Years* (London: Harper Collins).

Toynbee, P. and Walker, D. (2001), *Did Things Get Better? An Audit of Labour's Successes and Failures* (Harmondsworth: Penguin).

Webb, P. (2000), *The Modern British Party System* (London: Sage).

Westlake, M. (2001), *Kinnock: The Biography* (London: Little, Brown).

White, S. (2001), *New Labour: The Progressive Future?* (London: Palgrave).

Wolfe, J. (1996), *Power and Privatisation* (London: Macmillan).

Part I

The New Labour Debate

The political and ideological impact of a new government can be assessed in many
different ways. But a good indicator of genuine novelty is the reception it receives in
the academic world. While some may argue that the world of scholarly debate is far
removed from that of *realpolitik*, in fact, modern governments have always craved
intellectual respectability. New Labour is no exception. When Tony Blair was
elected party leader in 1994, he and his Shadow Cabinet sought to learn the lessons
of the Conservatives' success of the 1980s. Although the intellectual aspect of
Thatcherite neo-liberalism had started to turn stale by the early 1990s, the Conservatives had been widely perceived by friend and foe alike as the party of 'big ideas'
like privatization, reducing public expenditure, and 'liberating' business from regulation. All this was underpinned by a healthy cross-over between the world of think-
tanks, the press and some academics who realized that a new political agenda meant
a new research agenda.

New Labour has arguably failed to match the attainments of the Thatcherites in
this regard, but has come close. In part, this is helped by Blair's activist leadership
style. Assisted by seemingly tireless advisers, he takes it upon himself to churn out
article after article, speech after speech, and the odd Fabian Society pamphlet,
attempting to put the New Labour project firmly on the intellectual map. Blair's
notion of the 'Third Way' has been amplified by Anthony Giddens. In trying to steer
a path between the 'first way', neo-liberalism, and the 'second way', 'old-style' social
democracy, Blair and Giddens seek to provide New Labour with a solid intellectual
and ideological foundation. Their efforts are partly aimed at critics who suggest that
Labour has lost its principles (particularly socialist ones), and is nothing more than a
hotchpotch of inherited policies and office-seeking pragmatism. It is not difficult to
see how this perception might have surfaced, especially if we take a glance, as we do
here, at Philip Gould's analysis of the 'Land that Labour Forgot'. Gould's role as
adviser to Blair on electoral and media strategy (the two were almost synonymous
by the mid-1990s) is widely credited with having influenced the drive to secure the
votes of 'middle England', especially swing marginals that Labour needed to win to
gain power. Gould's strange alchemy of autobiography and hard-nosed political
analysis indicates some of the ideas circulating at the very top of the party during

the early Blair period. Still, such pragmatism aside, the riddles of the Third Way are not lost on writers such as Michael Freeden, who provides a perceptive deconstruction of what the phrase might actually mean.

As is well attested, Tony Blair-led Labour in 1997 was a different political animal from Michael Foot-led Labour in 1983. Some commentators describe this as the wholesale abandonment of Labour's social democratic traditions, others suggest it has simply modernized its organization and programme, while others still argue that it is born of a need for Labour to accommodate its policy and practice to a Britain fundamentally altered by eighteen years of radical Conservative governments of the New Right. Whatever the explanation for the transformation of the Labour Party, the emergence of New Labour reflects the recognition of the supposed irrelevance of the old-style collectivist, statist social democratic politics upon which Old Labour was predicated. Some writers suggest that Thatcherism and New Labour have a great many things in common. Richard Heffernan and Colin Hay, in different and complementary ways, provide insights into the continuities of policy and ideology generated as a result of the dynamics of party competition. Heffernan provides a close narrative of the tortuous transition from 'Old' to 'New', a process which, he argues, dates back to the early 1980s, but has no single definable point of origin. Hay has similar aims, focusing on the notion of 'catch-up' to explore the nature of Labour's transition.

Political scientists consider it part of the job description to get away from the hype and journalistic excess, and to try to develop general theories to explain political phenomena. It is no surprise, therefore, to find many writers, among them Michael Kenny and Martin J. Smith, attempting to provide a synthesis of the best competing explanations of the party's transformation and electoral success. Kenny and Smith try to transcend black-and-white and opt for shades of grey by putting the political agency of the Labour leadership in the context of various 'constraints' and 'dilemmas' that any party in a liberal democracy would face. This is a difficult task, as David Marquand's piece on New Labour's 'paradoxes' indicates. One of the foremost social democratic thinkers in British politics, Marquand's support for New Labour's programme of constitutional reform is qualified by his critique of the government's social and economic timidity. Hence the paradox – a constitutional radicalism and a social/ economic conservatism that cannot be reconciled.

Of course, there are any number of voices overtly critical of New Labour and its 'project'. Among them is that of Stuart Hall, who, utilizing his early interpretation of Thatcherism (entitled 'The Great Moving Nowhere Show'), has challenged the vagueness he believes to be the government's major flaw. Hall later broadens his attack to include all progenitors of the Third Way, and offers some penetrating insights into what he believes is New Labour's avoidance of promoting its own distinct values in opposition to those of the right. Along with Hall and others on what used to be known as the 'New Left', Anthony Barnett was a founder of the constitutional reform pressure group Charter 88, and he has turned his attention to what he terms 'corporate populism' to attack Labour's dismissal of the radical implications of 'democratic renewal'.

1

The Third Way: New Politics for the New Century

Tony Blair

I have always believed that politics is first and foremost about ideas. Without a powerful commitment to goals and values, governments are rudderless and ineffective, however large their majorities. Furthermore, ideas need labels if they are to become popular and widely understood. The 'Third Way' is to my mind the best label for the new politics which the progressive centre-left is forging in Britain and beyond.

The Third Way stands for a modernised social democracy, passionate in its commitment to social justice and the goals of the centre-left, but flexible, innovative and forward-looking in the means to achieve them. It is founded on the values which have guided progressive politics for more than a century – democracy, liberty, justice, mutual obligation and internationalism. But it is a *third* way because it moves decisively beyond an Old Left preoccupied by state control, high taxation and producer interests; and a New Right treating public investment, and often the very notions of 'society' and collective endeavour, as evils to be undone.

My vision for the 21st century is of a popular politics reconciling themes which in the past have wrongly been regarded as antagonistic – patriotism *and* internationalism; rights *and* responsibilities; the promotion of enterprise *and* the attack on poverty and discrimination. The Left should be proud of its achievements in the 20th century, not least universal suffrage, a fairer sharing of taxation and growth, and great improvements in working conditions and in welfare, health and educational services. But we still have far to go to build the open, fair and prosperous society to which we aspire.

The Third Way is not an attempt to split the difference between Right and Left. It is about traditional values in a changed world. And it draws vitality from uniting the two great streams of left-of-centre thought – democratic socialism and liberalism – whose divorce this century did so much to weaken progressive politics across the West. Liberals asserted the primacy of individual liberty in the market economy; social democrats promoted social justice with the state as its main agent. There is no necessary conflict between the two, accepting as we now do that state power is one means to achieve our goals, but not the only one and emphatically not an end in itself.

In this respect the Third Way also marks a third way *within* the Left. Debate within the Left has been dominated by two unsatisfactory positions. The fundamentalist Left made nationalisation and state control an end in itself, hardening policy prescription into ideology. Radicalism was judged by the amount of public ownership and spending. In opposition was a moderate Left which too often either accepted this basic direction while arguing for a slower pace of change or ignored the world of ideas. Revisionists periodically tried to change the agenda, but their success was limited. The Third Way is a serious reappraisal of social democracy, reaching deep into the values of the Left to develop radically new approaches.

A decade ago, the Right had a virtual monopoly of power in the democratic West. In America, across Europe, even in Scandinavia, the Right was in power, apparently impregnable. Today, the position is transformed. In most of the European Union the centre-left is in office. While learning lessons about efficiency and choice, particularly in the public sector, we argue as confidently as ever that the Right does not have the answer to the problems of social polarisation, rising crime, failing education and low productivity and growth.

Yet the Left is not returning to the old politics of isolation, nationalisation, bureaucracy and 'tax and spend'. We are acting afresh. Across Europe, social democratic governments are pioneering welfare state reform, tackling social exclusion, engaging business in new partnerships, and establishing a stable economic basis for long-term stability and investment. [...]

Values

My politics are rooted in a belief that we can only realise ourselves as individuals in a thriving civil society, comprising strong families and civic institutions buttressed by intelligent government. For most individuals to succeed, society must be strong. When society is weak, power and rewards go to the few not the many. Values are not absolute, and even the best can conflict. Our mission is to promote and reconcile the four values which are essential to a just society which maximises the freedom and potential of all our people – equal worth, opportunity for all, responsibility and community.

Equal worth

Social justice must be founded on the equal worth of each individual, whatever their background, capability, creed or race. Talent and effort should be encouraged to flourish in all quarters, and governments must act decisively to end discrimination and prejudice. Awareness of discrimination is, rightly, being heightened over time. The attack on racial discrimination now commands general support, as does the value of a multicultural and multiethnic society. A new awareness is growing of the capacity of, for example, disabled and elderly people, as they assert their own rights and dignity. The progressive Left is on their side, recognising that despite two centuries of campaigning for democratic rights, we have a long way to go before people are recognised for their abilities.

Opportunity for all

The new constitution of the Labour Party commits us to seek the widest possible spread of wealth, power and opportunity. I want to highlight opportunity as a key value in the new politics. Its importance has too often been neglected or distorted. For the Right, opportunity is characteristically presented as the freedom of individuals from the state. Yet for most people, opportunities are inseparable from society, in which government action necessarily plays a large part. The Left, by contrast, has in the past too readily downplayed its duty to promote a wide range of opportunities for individuals to advance themselves and their families. At worst, it has stifled opportunity in the name of abstract equality. Gross inequalities continue to be handed down from generation to generation, and the progressive Left must robustly tackle the obstacles to true equality of opportunity. But the promotion of equal opportunities does not imply dull uniformity in welfare provision and public services. Nor does the modern Left take a narrow view of opportunities: the arts and the creative industries should be part of our common culture.

Responsibility

In recent decades, responsibility and duty were the preserve of the Right. They are no longer; and it was a mistake for them ever to become so, for they were powerful forces in the growth of the labour movement in Britain and beyond. For too long, the demand for rights from the state was separated from the duties of citizenship and the imperative for mutual responsibility on the part of individuals and institutions. Unemployment benefits were often paid without strong reciprocal obligations; children went unsupported by absent parents. This issue persists. Our responsibility to protect the environment, for instance, is increasingly pressing. So is the responsibility of parents for their children's education. The rights we enjoy reflect the duties we owe: rights and opportunity without responsibility are engines of selfishness and greed.

Community

Human nature is cooperative as well as competitive, selfless as well as self-interested; and society could not function if it was otherwise. We all depend on collective goods for our independence; and all our lives are enriched – or impoverished – by the communities to which we belong. In deciding where to act on behalf of the national community, whether as regulator or provider, governments must be acutely sensitive not to stifle worthwhile activity by local communities and the voluntary sector. The grievous 20th century error of the fundamentalist Left was the belief that the state could replace civil society and thereby advance freedom. The New Right veers to the other extreme, advocating wholesale dismantling of core state activity in the cause of 'freedom'. The truth is that freedom for the many requires strong government. A key challenge of progressive politics is to use the state as an enabling force, protecting effective communities and voluntary organisations and encouraging their growth to tackle new needs, in partnership as appropriate.

These are the values of the Third Way. Without them, we are adrift. But in giving them practical effect, a large measure of pragmatism is essential. As I say continually, what matters is what works to give effect to our values. Some commentators are disconcerted by this insistence on fixed values and goals but pragmatism about means. There are even claims that it is unprincipled. But I believe that a critical dimension of the Third Way is that policies flow from values, not vice versa. With the right policies, market mechanisms are critical to meeting social objectives, entrepreneurial zeal can promote social justice, and new technology represents an opportunity, not a threat. [...]

The Third Way in a Changing World

Over the last 50 years two major political projects have dominated politics in Britain and many other Western democracies – neo-liberalism and a highly statist brand of social democracy. They have been applied in different ways, according to history, culture and political choice, but the broad intellectual currents are clear. Britain has experienced both in full-blooded form. That is why the term 'Third Way' has particular relevance to Britain, and it is on the basis of British experience since the watershed of the Second World War that I now draw.

The Labour government elected in 1945 was shaped by the legacy of wartime conditions and of pre-war depression and poverty. It proceeded, with a landslide majority and wide public consent, to nationalise industry, manage demand, direct economic activity and expand health and social services on an unprecedented scale. These policies achieved steady and high growth, and a fairer distribution of the benefits of growth. They fitted well with a world of secure jobs, large firms, low unemployment, relatively closed national economies and strong communities underpinned by stable families. Conservative governments of the 1950s made no attempt to dismantle the Attlee settlement, beyond snipping at the edges of the nationalised sector. Yet as the 1970s advanced, post-war social democracy proved steadily less viable. The NHS and much of the welfare state remained – and remain – formidable achievements, at once cost effective and transformative in their impact on the quality of life for the less well-off. But demand management and very high levels of state ownership and direction became increasingly ineffective at promoting growth and containing unemployment in a world of growing competition, external shocks and industrial and technological change. Social democracy proved too inflexible in response. In particular, it was too inefficient and low quality in its provision of public services, notably those such as education, telecommunications and other utilities where it was the near-monopoly supplier.

The Sixties were a decade of personal liberation. But individualism was not taking hold of just the private sphere: it spread rapidly to the realm of political economy. By the early Eighties, neo-liberalism had taken deep root in the form of the Thatcher Government. Some of its reforms were, in retrospect, necessary acts of modernisation, particularly the exposure of much of the state industrial sector to reform and competition. But it went hand-in-hand with a visceral antipathy to the remaining public sector, damaging key national services, notably education and health, even as the ministers preached the language of national competitiveness and individual self-improvement. Meanwhile, deep and bitter divisions within the Left about the appropriate response to these trends led to a decade of infighting within the Labour Party as it sought to reconcile its core values and old policy prescriptions to a changed world.

By the mid-Nineties, the wheel had turned again – not back to a statist social democratic model, but towards a realisation that the dogmatism of the neo-liberal Right had become a serious threat to national cohesion. Too many people were losing out; too many companies were under-performing; too many public services were failing through inattention; and too many communities were endangered by the rise of crime, unemployment and social exclusion. And as the evidence mounted, the Right proved increasingly obtuse in its failure to act – indeed, in its positive desire *not* to act in key areas such as education and social exclusion for fear of the ideological implications. Just as economic and social change were critical to sweeping the Right to power, so they were critical to its undoing. The challenge for the Third Way is to engage fully with the implications of that change.

What are the main features of change? I would highlight the following as particularly important:

- *The growth of increasingly global markets and global culture.* Not only does money cross frontiers within the Western economies faster than ever before, but competition exists on an international scale that has never been known. Products are increasingly made by extended networks threaded across the globe rather than within single organisations. The crises in Asia and Russia are serious, but for the more stable economies of Europe and North America there is no likelihood of a return to policies of isolation.
- *Technological advance and the rise of skills and information as key drivers of employment and new industries,* destroying old patterns of employment and placing an unprecedented premium on the need for high educational standards for the many, not the few.
- *A transformation in the role of women,* questioning forms of social organisation in place for centuries and offering half the population the chance – in the name of equality of opportunity – to fulfil their full potential according to their own choices. Reconciling such changes and opportunities to the strengthening of the family and local communities is among the greatest challenges of contemporary public policy. We need to shape modern institutions of work, and the institutions in which children are brought up, on the basis of enduring values – justice for all, responsibility from all.
- *Radical changes in the nature of politics itself,* with the growth of the European Union and a popular loss of faith with distant, unresponsive and often ineffective political institutions and those who work them. In responding to change governments are having to cope with twin pressures: from localities and regions wanting more control of their own affairs, and from a globalised world in which a growing number of problems depend on international cooperation.

Governments in the course of this century have proved themselves well equipped to cut or raise interest rates, send out benefit cheques, build houses, even fight wars and put men on the moon. Now they need to learn new skills: working in partnership with the private and voluntary sector; sharing responsibility and devolving power; acting flexibly to anticipate problems and to solve them; answering to a much more demanding public; and cooperating internationally not just to fight or avoid wars but to tackle common problems. The replacement of the old certainties of the Cold War by the more insidious threats of organised crime, terrorism, drugs and international environmental degradation, all require flexible forms of international cooperation. What way forward does the Third Way offer in response to these changes and challenges? Not a shopping list of fail-safe policy prescriptions; still less an attempt to reinvent the wheel where existing policies and institutions are broadly successful. Its concern, rather, is to meet four broad policy objectives:

1   A dynamic knowledge-based economy founded on individual empowerment and opportunity, where governments enable, not command, and the power of the market is harnessed to serve the public interest.
2   A strong civil society enshrining rights and responsibilities, where the government is a partner to strong communities.
3   A modern government based on partnership and decentralisation, where democracy is deepened to suit the modern age.
4   And a foreign policy based on international cooperation.

[...]

This is the Third Way – a modernised social democracy for a changing world which will build its prosperity on human and social capital. It is a project built on unshakable values, and a firm commitment to modernisation – to shape the future by embracing change not seeking to defy it. In standing for justice, we assert the historic claim of the centre-left that there is no progress unless every citizen has a real stake in it. Without a fair distribution of the benefits of progress, societies risk falling apart in division, rancour and distrust.

Around the world, governments are seeking to meet the demands of contemporary society. I believe that one of these demands is for a renewal of politics, for a new politics. But the choice of the new politics is not abstract. It is a choice which is already being made, in practice. In Britain, New Labour is the new politics.

The time is now ripe to move beyond defensiveness, beyond compensating for past mistakes and beyond the need to judge policies and politics on the basis of ancient intra-party factionalism. Rather we have the opportunity to shape a new positive agenda, on our own terms, for the future. It will be shaped by the centre-left's values and instincts, applied to a world of rapid change. The challenge is to turn change into progress. We cannot rely on historical inevitability; we have to do it for ourselves.

2

The Third Way: The Renewal of Social Democracy

Anthony Giddens

[...] [C]lassical social democracy and neoliberalism represent two quite distinct political philosophies. I summarize the differences in [...] two boxes [...]. Broad-brush comparisons of this sort carry an obvious danger of caricature. Yet the contrasts signalled here are real and important, and the residues of classical social democracy are everywhere still strong.
[...]

The Doctrines Compared

Neoliberalism might seem to have triumphed across the world. After all, social democracy is in ideological turmoil, and if fifty years ago everyone was a planner, now no one seems to be. It is a considerable reversal, since for at least a century socialists supposed themselves in the vanguard of history.

Yet rather than standing unchallenged, neoliberalism is in trouble, and it is important to see why. The chief reason is that its two halves – market fundamentalism and conservatism – are in tension. Conservatism always meant a cautious, pragmatic approach to social and economic change – an attitude adopted by Burke in the face of the messianic claims of the French Revolution. The continuity of tradition is central to the idea of conservatism. Tradition contains the accumulated wisdom of the past and therefore supplies a guide to the future. Free market philosophy takes quite a different attitude, pinning its hopes for the future on unending economic growth produced by the liberation of market forces.

Devotion to the free market on the one hand, and to the traditional family and nation on the other, is self-contradictory. Individualism and choice are supposed to stop abruptly at the boundaries of the family and national identity, where tradition must stand intact. But nothing is more dissolving of tradition than the 'permanent revolution' of market forces. The dynamism of market societies undermines traditional structures of authority and fractures local communities; neoliberalism creates new risks and uncertainties which it asks citizens simply to ignore. Moreover, it neglects the social basis of markets themselves, which depend upon the very communal forms that market fundamentalism indifferently casts to the winds.

What of old-style social democracy? We can distinguish a cluster of social traits that the Keynesian welfare consensus took for granted – all of which have subsequently disintegrated:

- a social system, and especially a family form – where the husband was the breadwinner and the wife the housewife and mother – which allowed for an unambiguous definition of full employment;
- a homogeneous labour market where men threatened with unemployment were mostly manual workers willing to do any job at a wage that ensured their survival and that of their families;
- the dominance of mass production in basic sectors of the economy, which tended to create stable, if unrewarding, conditions of work for many in the labour force;
- an elitist state, with small groups of public-spirited experts in the state bureaucracy monitoring the fiscal and monetary policies to be followed;
- national economies that were substantially contained within sovereign boundaries, since Keynesianism presumed the predominance of the domestic economy over external trade in goods and services.[1]

The egalitarianism of the old left was noble in intent, but as its rightist critics say has sometimes led to perverse consequences – visible, for example, in the social engineering which has left a legacy of decaying, crime-ridden housing estates. The welfare state, seen by most as the core of social democratic politics, today creates almost as many problems as it resolves.

Classical social democracy *(the old left)*	*Thatcherism, or neoliberalism* *(the new right)*
Pervasive state involvement in social and economic life	Minimal government
State dominates over civil society	Autonomous civil society
Collectivism	Market fundamentalism

Keynesian demand management,
  plus corporatism
	Moral authoritarianism, plus
	  strong economic individualism

Confined role for markets: the mixed
  or social economy
	Labour market clears like any
	  other

Full employment	Acceptance of inequality
Strong egalitarianism	Traditional nationalism

Comprehensive welfare state,
  protecting citizens 'from cradle
  to grave'
	Welfare state as safety net

Linear modernization	Linear modernization
Low ecological consciousness	Low ecological consciousness
Internationalism	Realist theory of international order
Belongs to bipolar world	Belongs to bipolar world

[...]

In terms of this scenario, what are we to make of talk of a third way? The phrase seems to have originated as early as the turn of the century, and was popular among right-wing groups in the 1920s. Mostly, however, it has been used by social demo-crats and socialists. In the early post-war period, social democrats quite explicitly thought of themselves as finding a way distinct from American market capitalism and Soviet communism. At the time of its refounding in 1951 the Socialist Inter-national explicitly spoke of the third way in this fashion. About twenty years later, as employed by the Czech economist Ota Šik and others, it was used to refer to market socialism. Swedish social democrats seem most often to have spoken of the third way, the last version, in the late 1980s, referring to an important programmatic renewal.

The more recent appropriation of 'third way' by Bill Clinton and Tony Blair has met with a lukewarm reception from most Continental social democrats, as well as from old left critics in their respective countries. The critics see the third way in this guise as warmed-over neoliberalism. They look at the US and see a highly dynamic economy, but also a society with the most extreme levels of inequality in the developed world. Clinton promised to 'end welfare as we know it', seeming to echo some of the attitudes of the neoliberal conservatives. On coming to power, his critics say, Blair and New Labour have persisted with the economic policies of Margaret Thatcher.

My aim in what follows is not to assess whether or not such observations are valid, but to consider where the debate about the future of social democracy stands. I shall take it 'third way' refers to a framework of thinking and policy-making that seeks to adapt social democracy to a world which has changed fundamentally over the past two or three decades. It is a third way in the sense that it is an attempt to transcend both old-style social democracy and neoliberalism.

[...]

Third Way Politics

[...] The overall aim of third way politics should be to help citizens pilot their way through the major revolutions of our time: *globalization, transformations in personal life* and our *relationship to nature*. Third way politics should take a positive attitude towards globalization – but, crucially, only as a phenomenon ranging much more widely than the global marketplace. Social democrats need to contest economic and cultural protectionism, the territory of the far right, which sees globalization as a threat to national integrity and traditional values. Economic globalization plainly can have destructive effects upon local self-sufficiency. Yet protectionism is neither sensible nor desirable. Even if it could be made to work, it would create a world of selfish and probably warring economic blocs. Third way politics should not identify globalization with a blanket endorsement of free trade. Free trade can be an engine of economic development, but given the socially and culturally destructive power of markets, its wider consequences need always to be scrutinized.

Third way politics should preserve a core concern with social justice, while accepting that the range of questions which escape the left/right divide is greater than before. Equality and individual freedom may conflict, but egalitarian measures also often increase the range of freedoms open to individuals. Freedom to social democrats should mean autonomy of action, which in turn demands the involve-ment of the wider social community. Having abandoned collectivism, third way politics looks for a new relationship between the individual and the community, a redefinition of rights and obligations.

One might suggest as a prime motto for the new politics, *no rights without responsibilities*. Government has a whole cluster of responsibilities for its citizens and others, including the protection of the vulnerable. Old-style social democracy, however, was inclined to treat rights as unconditional claims. With expanding individualism should come an extension of individual obligations. Unemployment benefits, for example, should carry the obligation to look actively for work, and it is up to governments to ensure that welfare systems do not discourage active search. As an ethical principle, 'no rights without responsibilities' must apply not only to welfare recipients, but to everyone. It is highly important for social democrats to stress this, because otherwise the precept can be held to apply only to the poor or to the needy – as tends to be the case with the political right.

Third way values

Equality
Protection of the vulnerable
Freedom as autonomy
No rights without responsibilities
No authority without democracy
Cosmopolitan pluralism
Philosophic conservatism

A second precept, in today's society, should be *no authority without democracy*. The right has always looked to traditional symbols as the prime means of justifying authority, whether in the nation, government, the family or other institutions.[2] Right-wing thinkers and politicians argue that without tradition, and traditional forms of deference, authority crumbles – people lose the ability to differentiate between right and wrong. Consequently democracy can never be more than partial. Social democrats should oppose this view. In a society where tradition and custom are losing their hold, the only route to the establishing of authority is via democracy. The new individualism doesn't inevitably corrode authority, but demands it be recast on an active or participatory basis.

Other issues with which third way politics is concerned do not belong to the framework of emancipatory politics, or only partially concern such a framework. They include responses to globalization, scientific and technological change, and our relationship to the natural world. The questions to be asked here are not about social justice, but about how we should live after the decline of tradition and custom, how to recreate social solidarity and how to react to ecological problems. In response to these questions, strong emphasis has to be given to cosmopolitan values, and to what might be called philosophic conservatism. In an era of ecological risk, modernization cannot be purely linear and certainly cannot be simply equated with economic growth.

The issue of modernization is a basic one for the new politics. Ecological modernization is one version, but there are others too. Tony Blair's speeches, for example, are peppered with talk of modernization. What should modernization be taken to mean? One thing it means, obviously, is the modernizing of social democracy itself – the breaking away from classical social democratic positions. As an agenda of a wider kind, however, a modernizing strategy can work only if social democrats have a sophisticated understanding of the concept.

Modernization that is ecologically sensitive is not about 'more and more modernity', but is conscious of the problems and limitations of modernizing processes. It is alive to the need to re-establish continuity and develop social cohesion in a world of erratic transformation, where the intrinsically unpredictable energies of scientific and technological innovation play such an important role.

The theme of philosophic conservatism is central. Modernization and conservatism, of course, are normally treated as opposites. However, we must use the tools of modernity to cope with living in a world 'beyond tradition' and 'on the other side of nature', where risk and responsibility have a new mix.

'Conservatism' in this sense has only a loose affinity with the way it has been understood on the political right. It suggests a pragmatic attitude towards coping with change; a nuanced view of science and technology, in recognition of their ambiguous consequences for us; a respect for the past and for history; and in the environmental arena, an adoption of the precautionary principle where feasible. These goals are not only not incompatible with a modernizing agenda; they presuppose it. Science and technology [...] can no longer be left outside the scope of democracy, since they influence our lives in a more direct and far-reaching way than was true for previous generations.

As another example, take the family, which figures in some of the most contentious debates in modern politics. Sustaining continuity in family life, especially protecting the well-being of children, is one of the most important goals of family policy. This can't be achieved, however, through a reactionary stance, an attempt to reinstate the 'traditional family'. [...] [I]t presumes a modernizing agenda of democratization.

NOTES

1   Egon Matzner and Wolfgang Streeck: *Beyond Keynesianism*. Aldershot: Elgar, 1991, pp. 3–4.
2   Julian Le Grand: 'Knights, knaves or pawns', *Journal of Social Policy*, vol. 26, part 2, April 1997.

3

The Land that Labour Forgot

Philip Gould

The People Labour Betrayed

I learned my politics where I grew up, around the small town of Woking in Surrey. Not in great northern cities, the Welsh valleys or crumbling urban estates. Not in places with great political traditions and dramatic folklore. I learned my politics in an unexceptional suburban town where most people were neither privileged nor deprived, but nearly everybody was struggling to get by – which was not pretty, and grew uglier – where people lived in unassuming council estates or in tiny semi-detached houses, where university was out of the question for most and where nearly everyone went to secondary-modern schools. I did not have a deprived upbringing. I had an ordinary upbringing, born and brought up in a twilight suburbia, where post-war council estates nestled alongside small, detached, red-brick Victorian villas.

The party I loved instinctively was to betray the people who lived here, its natural supporters: ordinary people with suburban dreams who worked hard to improve their homes and their lives; to get gradually better cars, washing machines and televisions; to go on holiday in Spain rather than Bournemouth. These people wanted sensible, moderate policies which conformed to their understanding and their daily lives.

Labour became a party enslaved by dogma: it supported unilateral disarmament, immediate withdrawal from the Common Market, nationalisation of the twenty-five largest companies, and marginal taxation rates at 93 per cent. It abandoned the centre ground of British politics and camped out on the margins, forlorn and useless, offering a miasma of extremism, dogmatism, intolerance and wilful elitism which put the hopes and dreams of ordinary people last.

I remember having dinner in 1983 with Michael Foot and his wife, Jill Craigie. They could not understand why the Labour Party had lost the election that June. Labour had offered education, choices and opportunities, but the people had turned on them. They read the *Sun* and abandoned the Labour Party. Yet it was not the people who had betrayed Labour, but Labour who had betrayed the people. The failures and convulsions of the late 1970s and early 1980s were so bitter as to disqualify Labour from power for a generation. Even in the 1997 General Election, an overseas observer of a focus group in Putney said to me, 'What did you do to these people that they fear you so much?'

Labour had failed to understand that the old working class was becoming a new middle class: aspiring, consuming, choosing what was best for themselves and their families. They had outgrown crude collectivism and left it behind in the supermarket car-park. I knew this, because they were my life.

[...]

A New Labour Childhood

In 1954 we moved to Byfleet and then in 1957 to Brookwood, part of the borough of Woking. [...]

At school I learned to respect people's basic impulse to work hard and try to get on. I began to understand the common-sense responses of 'ordinary' people. I developed sympathy for hard-nosed attitudes on crime and defence. David Owen, in his book *Time to Declare*, describes how, as a student working on a building site, he came to respect the tough, uncompromising views on defence of his fellow workers. This sounds condescending, but Owen was right. I developed a strong populist sense at a very early age that the opinions of the majority should be taken seriously.

Whenever I hear people being criticised for their blinkered and reactionary views on crime, or welfare, or aversion to paying taxes, I always ask silently: have you known the dreadful, repetitive tedium of manual work, not just for the long university holidays, but for life; lived in cramped houses, in communities where walking the streets late at night is not a safe option; known the cancerous insecurity of work as clerks or office administrators, not poor, but never safe, and always worrying about the cost of providing for your family?

I sat in the shadow Cabinet room as the self-interest and materialism that was gripping the electorate in the 1980s was described during a polling presentation. I heard the tut-tutting of disdain from the assembled advisers and officials and thought to myself: you all live in big, comfortable houses, have Tuscan holidays and drive large cars. What do you know about the way ordinary people live?

The secondary modern lacked any ambition for its children. I was told that I did not have the ability to take A-levels. I remember talking to my friends in what purported to be the school library and somebody started to talk about university, explaining that it was a place where people like us, who attended a school like ours, never went. I had no idea what university was, but I was determined to go. Eventually I managed it, but almost no one else did, although nearly everybody in the upper streams was quite capable of doing so. The potential that this school, and others like it, killed or maimed was nothing short of educational genocide. That is why I abhor selection at the age of eleven, but also why I abhor the potential that is still being wasted by a comprehensive system that was so badly flawed in design and execution.

The best thing about school was my friends. Most of them were tough kids: Thatcher's children, although they did not know it yet. John Huntly was sensitive and intelligent and wanted to become a vet, which I am pleased to say he did. He was my fishing and country friend. Most nights we would cycle off after school and find some hidden place to fish, hoping to forget the day. He had the misfortune to be the first in our class to be caned for something he did not do.

The rest of my friends were tough-minded and thick-skinned. Roger Gosden, the son of a carpenter; William Mitchell, a plumber's son; John Stuartson, whose father worked in a factory; Barry Richardson, the son of a soldier. These were not privileged boys, not middle-class. They were what would now be called skilled working-class. They should automatically have been Labour supporters, but they were not, because their fathers all wanted to get on. Roger's dad was endlessly improving his house, adding odd bits and pieces to it that did not really work. They would buy and test the latest offerings of the emerging consumer society. They were beginning to take holidays abroad.

And they were tough about their politics. Every political judgement they made was rooted in hard, uncompromising common sense. With Brett Robinson, the son of a civil servant, I canvassed the whole of Woking, or so it felt, for the 1966 General Election. The tiny, grim, forbidding red-brick houses of Goldsworth; the bigger villas further from the centre of the town; the massive over-spill council estate of Sheerwater; the mishmash of suburban housing in Knaphill and Brookwood. Housing that was not pleasing to the eye because each owner, like Roger Gosden's dad, had tried to put their own stamp on it: small porches erected incongruously over front doors; cheap modern windows clashing with Victorian red-brick walls; different shades of paint which owed no allegiance to the house next door; little extras stuck on to make the houses look better, but making them much worse.

Even then their owners were tough on crime, tough on welfare, tough on the Soviet Union. They were fiercely patriotic, as was I. But in the course of their lives they had felt an almost tangible sense of British decline: the great post-war British confidence and achievements were ebbing away. They believed in fair reward for hard work; in responsibility; in standing on your own two feet. They wanted to get on, and they wanted a better life. Given the life they had, this was not surprising. They were early recruits to the new middle class. They might just have voted Labour in 1966, but it was easy to feel the aspirational appeal of the Conservatives. These were the voices, of my friends and their families, which the left stopped listening to. They were to become the new voice of Britain.

By this time I was enthralled by politics and would spend hours arguing with my friends: arguing for Labour, for fairness, for compassion, for society. This was grinding work – my compassionate values clashing uncomfortably with their hard-nosed ambition and unsentimental view of the world.

It was in this tension – between my soft, inner world of decency, fairness and compassion and my hard, outer world of tough-minded working-class aspiration – that my politics began to be formed. Tough and tender; strong but fair. Already I was becoming a New Labour child.

[...]

A New Labour Life

This, then, was my new Labour life.

A life begun in a land of suburban dreams, among ordinary people asking nothing more than to edge slowly forward in their lives.

A life among working people with growing aspirations, gradually emerging as a new middle class, at that time forgotten by the Labour Party, but becoming the most powerful electoral force in British politics.

A life where I learned of the daily struggle of ordinary families – silent heroes making do, getting by.

It was a life that taught me that the children from my rather shabby, second-rate school, and their children after them, had voices which deserved to be heard, and that when Labour stopped listening to them it lost power and began its long slide into betrayal and extremism. I know the suburban sprawl I came from was an ordinary place full of ordinary people. But it was my place, and they were my people. I come from the land that Labour forgot.

4

The Ideology of New Labour

Michael Freeden

[...]

An Ideological Narrative

[...] The age in which we live, far from being post-ideological, is one of ideological experimentation, of the resurrection of past principles combined with new attitudes. On the macro-level, the demotion of politics as an arena of planning, social responsibility and public welfare is its main feature. On the micro-level, current Labourism is, above all, ideologically eclectic; but it is emphatically not ideologically dormant. Indeed, it is brimming with complex ideas, values and practices that draw on all the major British ideological traditions. Paradoxically, the reputedly non-ideological Blair has in the past been keen to attach himself to British ideational movements, though it is frequently liberalism, and not socialism, that has been chosen in this reinvented narrative. Significantly, in a much-publicised lecture delivered in 1995, Blair did not deny the existence or importance of ideology. Rather, he claimed that Labour ideology 'was out of date', having been in the past too narrowly construed around 'one particular strand of socialist thinking, namely, state ownership'. The task he now set his party was 'to reconstruct our ideology around the strength of our values and the way they are expressed. And then to create an organisation to match and reflect the ideology.' One aspect of that 'ideological refoundation' of the party had already been achieved: the revision of Clause Four, with its dogmatically perceived linkage of socialism and nationalisation. Blair went on to associate his political beliefs with David Lloyd George, L. T. Hobhouse, William Beveridge and J. M. Keynes – icons of British liberalism and its pioneering work in clearing the ideological ground for the welfare state – and not only with stalwarts of Labour social democracy such as Aneurin Bevan and Anthony Crosland. Tellingly, he adopted a phrase which had become particularly salient in Labour vocabulary over the previous ten years: 'The aim of socialism is to give greater freedom to the individual.' Similar expressions can be found in Neil Kinnock's 1992 Labour party manifesto as well as in the writings of leading Labour publicists such as Bryan Gould and Roy Hattersley, authors of books that were entitled respectively *Socialism and Freedom* and *Choose Freedom: The Future for Democratic Socialism*. Blair drew attention to the affinity between Labour and 'its progressive liberal cousin'. He was particularly appreciative of a liberalism wedded to 'a credo of social reform and state action to emancipate individuals from the vagaries and oppression of personal circumstance', intent on creating through collective cooperation a quantity of social wealth to be employed for social purposes. That reflected, as it did with the new liberals, a notion of individual interdependence necessary for human flourishing.[1]

[...]

[...] The ideological amalgam of New Labour includes liberal, conservative and (how could it be otherwise!) specifically socialist components as well. In addition, ideational imports from the United States have added a flavour of their own. But New Labour ideology is not identical with any one of the above categories and it deviates from every one of them in crucial areas. Some people, of course, deny that the 'Third Way' is an ideology at all. That is a misconception. Ideologies do not have to be grand narratives; they certainly do not have to be closed, doctrinaire and abstract systems. Ideologies are recurrent, action-oriented patterns of political argument, and it can be empirically demonstrated that New Labour is definitely endowed with those. Moreover, ideologies are not simply superimposed on practices but also embodied in them. What distinguishes New Labour ideology, as indeed any ideology, are the distinctive configurations it forms out of political concepts, the occasional new meanings it assigns to political words in common currency, and the innovative manner in which it blends ideas both external and internal to its traditions. To what extent, then, can Blair's claim that 'our values do not change' be affirmed?

Which Community? Whose Responsibility?

Early in 1998 Julian Le Grand published a spirited endorsement of the 'Third Way'.[2] He detected four components of the distinctive New Labour route between the Scylla of neo-liberalism and the Charybdis of social democracy: community, accountability, responsibility and opportunity. Whichever way one interprets these contested and multi-layered concepts, they come attached to some heavy baggage. Each of these concepts rotates around a full axis of different meanings, but no matter where that rotation is halted, the fourfold combination does not signal a *new* Way, or a *new* ideology. There is little in the principles and values underlying Labour's 'Third Way' that hasn't already been given expression in other places, at other times.

The meaning of community for Le Grand is split between a geographical entity, a locality and a solidaric spirit of cooperation. He also contends that community implies contracts between people and government, and partnerships between individuals and local organisations. But the idea of a social contract is a classical liberal one, suggesting a weak – and possibly commercial – human relationship. Instead, community is also reflected in broader traditions. For new liberals, community had strong organic connotations, according to which social membership was a constituent of individuality, and society as a whole had interests and needs of its own, the fulfilment of which would be crucially conducive both to social and to individual welfare. For many conservatives, community suggests a residue of the one-nation Britain, in which the more fortunate were paternalistically entrusted with the welfare of the less advantaged. For the American sociologist Amitai Etzioni, a recent guest in pro-Labour circles, community entails a form of social control in which neighbourhoods regulate the conduct and morals of their members, demanding support for established norms and less individual assertiveness. To which version does New Labour subscribe? Certainly not to pure forms of the first or the second; but there is more than a hint of the third.

Accountability, a classic component of the liberal rule of law, is interestingly directed towards both local and national communities, though there is far less evidence to endorse its foundational status in Labour discourse. Responsibility, however, has a greater resonance with Etzioni's contrasting of rights with responsibilities. He sees rights as individual claims that are fundamentally confrontational and egoistic, many of them burdensome to society, especially when they threaten the values cherished by a community. At one point Etzioni called for a moratorium on new rights, because in the balance between individual and community he comes down firmly in favour of the individual responsibility to maintain the social fabric, and because he assumes that communities are repositories of a shared moral language and practices. The moral voice of the community (notably couched in the singular) is expressed by what he sees as the transmitters of correct conduct – the family and the schools – with their shared spaces, causes and futures.[3] In the New Labour vision, this is reflected in the insistence of the 1997 manifesto on parents facing up 'to their responsibility for their children's misbehaviour', in a tough attitude to crime and 'anti-social behaviour' and in a strict policy of controlling school standards. In particular, New Labour has adopted Etzioni's preference for guided persuasion over coercion: clean hands in public life, self-discipline, the enhancement of social cooperation. Individual virtue is tantamount to not being a nuisance to others, whether in terms of demanding money, eliciting effort or challenging values. It is particularly exemplified in the opposition to the 'dependency culture', seen as a distorted aspect of the welfare state, rather than the socialist ethic of actively creating networks of interdependent social support. The overriding assumptions are unity in plurality, gentle yet persistent regulation, the existence of a single, beneficent, moral universe transcending the diverse communities of which society is formed – all epitomised in the reassuring paternalism of Britain's new leadership: 'Trust us! We know what is good for you. Have patience! We will give you what you want.' This extraordinary blend of moderate American conservatism, elitist British Fabianism, and populism has resulted in a deficit of the liberal individuality New Labour wishes elsewhere to encourage.

American Attractions

The impact of American public policy is discernible in two other major areas, embodying practices which have contributed to the shaping of New Labour ideology. The first is 'zero tolerance' – a phrase to be found in the 1997 manifesto, and a dramatic linguistic repudiation of the core liberal value of toleration. Recently, surpassing the term's association in the United States with an uncompromising approach towards crime (frequently expressed as 'a third strike and you're out'), the term has been applied in Britain also to underperforming schools. Such schools are quasi-criminalised by implication. In a culture where individual death penalties have been ruled out as unacceptable, schools are potentially subject to an institutional death penalty: in the words of the 1997 manifesto, 'ministers will order a "fresh start" – close the school and start afresh on the same site'.

The second area is 'workfare', which in the United States has been linked to deterrent social policies, aimed at reducing social security bills and implementing a work ethic among the 'underclass'. Notably, New Labour have reformulated this policy as a movement *from* welfare *to* work – a phrase laden with ideological significance. As Blair put it in an interview with the *Guardian* in January 1998, the welfare state was created 'to give the first parts of opportunity to people ... in a society and labour market that doesn't exist any more ... If you were to talk to people and ask them what they think the welfare state should do ... their concept of welfare is the relieving of poverty and the help of people in need.' In the past, the concept of welfare in socialist thought pertained to human flourishing and well-being, to the ethical end of optimising human creativity and eliminating human alienation. It was closely linked to the egalitarian pooling of both human resources and social goods. In current jargon, however, it has been reduced to support services for the marginalised, the handicapped or the unlucky – those who are unable, rather than merely unwilling, to provide adequately for themselves. In many senses this refers to no more than an escape from poverty, a minimal rather than optimal view of human happiness, to which a minority are unequally condemned. That echoes the very social exclusion New Labour has loudly denounced, notably in the establishment of a Social Exclusion Unit. Welfare and work are counterpoised, as if work were not, in mainstream social democratic as well as socialist views, the epitome of human welfare itself.

The Moral Market

All the above is indicative of a new dichotomy: on the one hand stands an unreciprocated catering for basic human needs, rather grudgingly elicited but nevertheless recognised as a humanitarian duty; on the other, a contributory investment of labour in the social and economic fabrics, as an expectation of responsible citizenship, the replacement of the socialist 'right to work' with a puritanical 'duty to work', amid references to human beings as a resource, or as capital. The state still maintains a semblance of the substantive enabling functions that earlier progressive theories accorded it but, as Raymond Plant has pointed out, one of its main roles is the re-skilling of individuals not in order to develop their autonomy and well-being but so as to equip them with employability skills and improve their position in the market. Markets are no longer seen as subservient to governments, but as co-equal with them in a new synergetic relationship.[4] Welfare has emphatically been removed from the core position it had attained in European socialist thought. New Labour aspirations may still be communal and integrative; its political phraseology suggests otherwise.

Is the liberal deficit made good by Le Grand's fourth watchword: opportunity? Does it ensure the predominance of a social liberal ideology to which Blair seemed committed, especially the optimisation of development-enhancing choices as advocated by liberals? This remains unclear. In Le Grand's reading of Labour values, opportunity is provided for a specific activity: for work rather than for the realisation of personal potential. Work is seen not in the socialist terms of human creativity, not even in the social liberal terms of a *quid pro quo* for services granted by the community, with its sense of a common enterprise, but as the far starker assumption of individual responsibility for financial independence, and as an activity subservient to the economic and productivity goals established by market forces. In particular, as Le Grand observes, this version of opportunity dispenses with egalitarian distribution as a linchpin of social justice.

It remains to be seen how New Labour relates to socialism – ironically the most discomforting word in its current vocabulary. The term 'socialism' does not appear in the 1997 manifesto. Instead, it is alluded to via code words such as 'outdated dogma or doctrine' or the 'old left'. When Blair has used it, it appears, carefully unpacked, in the new form of 'social-ism'. In a speech given to the Fabian Society in 1994 Blair recognised the multiple strands of socialism, and stressed the importance of revitalising its ethical tone, 'not a break with its past or its traditions but, on the contrary, a rediscovery of their true meaning' in order to distinguish it from the 'neo-conservatism of the left'. 'Social-ism' identifies what is generally accepted as one of the core concepts of socialism: 'Individuals are socially interdependent human beings ... individuals cannot be divorced from the society to which they belong.' For Blair, this kind of communitarianism signifies the recognition of the duties individuals owe to one another and to society, as well as a view of collective power whose aim is the pursuit of the good and interests of individuals, a formulation familiar to the new liberals a century ago. But it is also linked with a further set of core concepts: social justice, cohesion, the equal worth of each citizen, equality of opportunity. The meaning of socialism has been retained by emphasising cooperation and mutual responsibility, but contained by combining it with a particular vocabulary of fairness towards individuals, greater productivity, consumer choice and, especially, identifying an economic *public* interest in which the market plays a key role. Socialism could thus be diverted away from the old clichés of nationalisation and towards a more complex notion of a society acting in concert to regulate and encourage individual enterprise. This project had of course been set in motion at a far earlier stage of Labour party history, but the crucial linguistic and conceptual turns now effected by New Labour had then been politically inconceivable – not least among them its recent designation by Blair as centre-left.

In Blair's personal ethic, though not in New Labour more generally, there is also a significant Christian strand which underpins his understanding of community as a relationship of mutually respecting and responsible individuals. The sacrament of communion, suggestive of community, is conjoined with an undertone of social sin – 'a purely libertarian ethos' – and punishment for failing one's social duties. That failure is notably one of free will, of willing bad rather than good acts, made all the more culpable in a cohesive society which offers opportunities to individuals as long as they embody what Blair has called 'common norms of conduct' in a 'strong and decent' community. When the substantive value-content of citizenship far outstrips its formal and legal dimensions, the question of ideological pluralism is left dramatically unresolved.

An Ideology Reassembled

The ideological map of New Labour now looks something like this. It is located between the three great Western ideological traditions – liberalism, conservatism and socialism – though it is not equidistant from them all. Liberalism has always concentrated on the pursuit of liberty, on the development of individuality, on human rationality, on open-ended progress, on limiting state power, but also on some notion of the common good. From that ideology New Labour has extracted ideas concerning private choice, the enhancement of human capacities, the further-ance of legitimate individual interests, a respect for individual rights, and a concern with human well-being pursued in part by a welfare state but in the main through the exercise of personal responsibility, underpinned by what Blair identifies as 'talent and ambition ... aspiration and achievement'.

NOTES

1   Tony Blair, *Let Us Face the Future*, London, Fabian Society, 1995, pp. 4, 11–12. For the views of the new liberals see Michael Freeden, *The New Liberalism: An Ideology of Social Reform*, Oxford, Clarendon Press, 1978.
2   Julian Le Grand, 'The Third Way Begins with Cora', *New Statesman*, 6 March 1998.
3   Amitai Etzioni, *The Spirit of Community: Rights, Responsibilities and the Communitarian Agenda*, London, Fontana, 1995, *passim*.
4   Lord Plant, *New Labour – A Third Way?*, London, European Policy Forum, 1998, p. 34; Anthony Giddens, *The Third Way*, Cambridge, Polity, 1998, pp. 99–100.

5

New Labour and Thatcherism

Richard Heffernan

At the 1997 general election, Labour returned from the political wilderness. Its electoral landslide gifting it a Commons majority of 179, the largest in the party's history on 44.4 per cent of votes cast. None the less, with key exceptions involving the constitutional reform, Europe and supply-side modernisation, the agenda of the incoming Labour government reflects policies pursued by the Thatcher and Major governments. Political values preached by Conservative ministers – enterprise, self reliance, anti-statism – find contemporary reflection in the speeches of Labour ministers. The liberalisation of the market economy; the privatisation of national-ised industries, utilities and public sector companies; the divestment of public housing; the introduction of market liberalism to both the public sector and the non-market public sector; the binding of trade unions; the erosion of local govern-ment all collectively represented the wide-ranging redefinition of British political life engineered in the 1980s and 1990s and so serve to structure what Labour in government does.

Indeed, in sharp contrast to its past appeals, Labour's 1997 Manifesto echoed the economic priorities outlined in the 1979 Conservative Manifesto. Then the Tories committed themselves to: controlling inflation as first priority; curbing public ex-penditure; reducing the level of public borrowing; opposition to increases in direct taxation; restoring incentives to business and enterprise; and regulating trade union activities. In endorsing this the Blair government has taken up the economic object-ives of the Thatcher and Major governments organised around four primary areas of policy reform: (1) Ensuring financial stability by promoting sound money and placing the reduction of inflation at the heart of both monetary and fiscal policy; (2) Placing the market at the centre of economic life through deregulation and the rejection of direct state intervention; (3) Privatisation of state-owned industries and utilities so withdrawing the state from direct control over economic activity; (4) Controlling trade union activity by legislation and (together with other measures) so disciplining the labour market.

The long march from the Labour Party led by Michael Foot to that led by Tony Blair is usefully explored in terms of a gradual, staged process altering Labour's programmatic stance and stated political objectives. Labour's transformation was born of a belief that the second, third and fourth successive Conservative victories in 1983, 1987 and 1992 illustrated a deep crisis facing Labour and the left of British politics, which meant that the party had to change and change quickly. Where the 1983 appeal came to be considered as dangerous and extremist, one that supposedly promised 'no compromise with the electorate', that of 1992 and 1997 were considered more suitable to offer Labour an electoral key to access the corridors of Whitehall. The period 1983–97 is one in which explanations of the changing Labour Party are to be found and understood; taken in the round Labour did not so much change or modernise itself as it was changed by the impact of events. In short, where Thatcherism has led, the Labour Party of Kinnock, Smith and Blair followed.

[...]

Labour's transformation reflects a seemingly irreversible shift in the balance of power in favour of right-reformist neo-liberal politics at the expense of left-reformist social democratic politics. Its extent is illustrated by the changes wrought in Labour's ideological outlook and evidenced in policy. This long-drawn-out process of change was characterised by piecemeal and gradual policy qualification followed by revision in the 1983, 1987 and 1992 Parliaments. Labour's policy saw a dramatic alteration in its attitude to the changes brought about by the Thatcher government. Where Martin J. Smith defines this transformation as 'a post-Keynesian revisionism ... for a different era which has learnt the lessons of the 1970's',[1] Eric Shaw more correctly suggests that the period saw 'the abandonment of Keynesian social democracy in favour of pre-Keynesian orthodoxy'.[2] Labour has come to embrace the arm's-length regulated market economy it was once pledged to directly manage and control.

Although cast in the guise of modernisation, the broad economic appeal outlined by 'New' Labour has little historical purchase on 'Old' Labour. Although it retains some affinity with 'Old' Labour, its policy far more closely reflects the preconceptions and prescriptions of the Thatcher and Major governments. In both 1979–83 and (to a far lesser extent) 1983–7, Labour's economic policy was geared toward providing for full employment and better quality public services through government-led reflation, direct management of the economy and an expanded public sector. Between 1983 and 1987, Shadow Chancellor Roy Hattersley demonstrated a marked bias 'in favour of public expenditure rather than personal tax cuts'.[3] A private Shadow Cabinet paper in July 1986 underlined Labour's commitment: 'The social, economic and political advantages of our proposals is that they will finance substantial improvements in health, education, environment and local government programmes as well as reducing unemployment.'[4] Here, as Hattersley later spelled out, Labour's position could be summed up in the phrase: 'Increased public expenditure good; public expenditure cuts bad.'[5]

This economic approach would win a Labour MP few friends at the top of today's party in government: such is the transformation wrought in the party, similar observations now find no echo inside 'New' Labour's high command. Rather than just repudiating 'Bennism', Labour now casts aside policy advocated by the most right-wing members of 'Old' Labour. The personal manifesto issued by Denis Healey in his defence of the deputy leadership against the challenge of Tony Benn in 1981 now makes interesting reading: Healey, a permanent fixture on Labour's right, committed himself four square behind Labour's then 'planned socialist alternative', calling for 'real increases in public expenditure' to 'implement an alternative economic strategy', the centrepiece of which would be 'the restoration of full employment'. In the international sphere, this committed Atlanticist described himself as a 'genuine disarmer' willing to support 'the cancellation of Trident' and the 'reduction of the level of defence expenditure'.[6] These traditional Labour commitments, all firmly within the party mainstream in 1981, were all explicitly cast aside by the Labour Party in the late 1980s and 1990s.

A sharply contrasting new economic discourse dominates Labour politics today, one 'articulated in the language of competition, efficiency, productivity, economic dynamism, profitability, and, above all, that of individual choice and self-fulfilment in the context of a market economy'.[7] Although concerned at the rhetorical level with the promotion of social justice (in common with all serious office-seeking parties in liberal democracies), 'New' Labour is principally concerned with strengthening the power of capital and allowing competition within the market to secure social reforms by virtue of 'trickle down' economics. Blair's designated image for his Labour Party is that it is a party for and of business, one that is 'safe', 'prudent' and 'sensible'; not 'extremist', 'dangerous', 'reckless', or 'profligate'. 'New' Labour today is careful to present itself as a party of an ill-defined centre, no longer a party of the left.[8] In economic terms the party has redefined its task as 'improving' the status quo entrenched by Thatcherism in office since 1979, not reforming the prevailing economic system let alone bring about a 'fundamental and irreversible shift in the balance of wealth and power in favour of working people and their families' promised (but not delivered) in the 1974 manifesto.

For the moment, one additional example may suffice to illustrate the extent of Labour's departure from past practice. In September 1985, a number of Tribune Group MPs argued the need for Labour to 'restate, develop and argue for socialist values in a way that can build popular support and convince the electorate that socialism is relevant to the problems of modern Britain'.[9] In suggesting that 'Economic power must be made publicly accountable through a system of social ownership, planning and industrial democracy, not merely to make the economy more efficient but to restructure it so that power and wealth are used for the public good rather than for a few individuals', this initiative would now be considered deeply unfashionable. Part of the effort of a 'soft' Labour left to distinguish themselves from the 'hard' left, the statement was signed by a number of present-day 'Blairites', among them Gordon Brown (of course better defined as a 'Brownite'), then a junior front bench spokesperson and Labour Chancellor of the Exchequer after 1997.[10]

The name of Tony Blair, although he certainly qualified as a realigning member of the Tribune Group, is notable for its absence. This statement was published in the Conference edition of *Tribune* and carried next to a two-page interview with Neil Kinnock. In addition it also declared a 'determination to disengage immediately from the nuclear arms race' and that 'Britain should retain the option of withdrawal from the EEC'.[11] In addition to Brown, other principal signatories to this declaration who held prominent positions in Tony Blair's new Labour government include: Margaret Beckett, David Blunkett, Robin Cook, Harriet Harman, Clare Short, Chris Smith, Gavin Strang (all members of the 1997 Labour Cabinet), three Ministers of State, Michael Meacher, Derek Fatchett and Mark Fisher. Labour's General Secretary in 1997, Tom Sawyer, and the current Chair of the Parliamentary Party, Clive Soley, were also signatories. Indeed, in 1986, as a rising junior member of the Treasury team, Tony Blair argued that Labour should advocate 'a fairer distribution of taxation to ensure redistribution of wealth away from the wealthiest of our community to the poorest'.[12] It is inconceivable that Blair would advance this case today.

[...]

In detailing Labour's general shift away from its stance of the early 1980s, the years 1983, 1985 and 1987 stand out. The impact of the 1983 reversal set in only slowly as Labour quietly digested the extent of its defeat. It is in the general period embracing the 1983, 1987 and 1992 Parliaments that Labour's transformation can be mapped out. The immediate years following the 1983 election saw the beginning of the end of the 'Bennite' ascendancy. Internal political changes ultimately granted Neil Kinnock and his Shadow Cabinet and National Executive allies the executive authority they required to cautiously strike out to Labour's right. Rather than come to the leadership with a clear programme of reform, Kinnock ran as a candidate of the left in 1983 (albeit of a non-Bennite variety). Presenting himself as a younger and media-friendly version of Michael Foot, the new leader was to move from the 'soft left' to the Labour 'right' following his candidature for the leadership, when he had previously emotionally associated with Foot's policies.

[...] Labour's post-1979 left–right divisions greatly diminished in the face of the precarious electoral position in which the Party saw itself. The rise of a 'soft-left/right' coalition encompassing elements of the Tribune Group with the traditional Labour right inside the Parliamentary Party was decisive. In addition, as Lewis Minkin argues, 'the TUC leadership sought to give full support to the parliamentary leadership...as it became axiomatic that the political running must be left to [this] parliamentary leadership'.[13] Central to these developments was the defeat of the 1984–5 miners' strike and the abortive Labour campaign against ratecapping in 1985 which, for many, served to underline a weakness of the traditional left. The de-polarisation of party disputes was accompanied by a significant recomposition of internal factions following the 1983 defeat. These, in the wake of the apparent unstoppable march of Thatcherism, all made significant contributions to the reassertion of leadership authority over the party.

Labour's gradual shift to the right was neatly symbolised by the expulsion first of Militant and later of other elements of the left in 1985–6 and post-1987 (building on the proscription of the Tendency under Michael Foot in 1982–3[14]). Kinnock's strengthening opposition to the Labour left served also to pave his shift to the right. He appeared to relish taking on the various sacred cows of the left, denouncing what he saw as its timidity and its total lack of realism, setting up Tony Benn and the NUM leader Arthur Scargill as 'enemies within' to be denied office or influence; 'bogeymen' whose isolation would itself prove Labour's newfound moderation and electability. After 1985, the emergence of an 'anti-hard left soft-left', illustrated by the shifting allegiances of Tom Sawyer, David Blunkett and Michael Meacher on the party's NEC, helped the leadership gradually establish a command over the party.[15] Its authority derived from an extended leader's office and the Shadow Cabinet backed up by the then very important NEC (on which Kinnock and later Blair established a reliable and ever increasing majority); a party headquarters (increasingly peopled with Kinnock and later Blair supporters); and the Party Conference where support from leading trade unions was ever more forthcoming after 1987.

[...]

Although always cautious, the Kinnock leadership did not immediately displace the Bennite agenda. Instead it constructed a qualified or 'watered down' version, one which reflected Labour's traditional social democracy and an anti-Thatcherite agenda based upon a moderated version of the 1983 appeal. Thus policy development in the 1983 Parliament was only an incrementalist shift away from the more radical agenda forged earlier. Given the institutional power of trade unions at Conference and the residual powers of the left in both its 'hard' and its 'soft' (travelling to the Kinnockite right) variants, Kinnock was reluctant to go where the party may not follow. As such, while existing 1983 commitments such as opposition to council house sales, immediate withdrawal from the EEC, and statutory planning agreements were quickly excised, in other policy areas the status quo was qualified rather than revised.

In the field of economic policy, while significant changes were made which went beyond repackaging the same policy, Labour continued to believe in the need to tightly regulate the market by state intervention. While the private sector would retain responsibility for capital accumulation, government would use its power to direct economic strategy for politically designated ends; still interventionist, but less interventionist than prior to 1983. Thus, at the 1987 election Labour placed government-led economic regeneration at the heart of its appeal. At the centrepiece of its programme lay a plan for jobs to reduce unemployment by one million in two years through public investment and an industrial strategy to plan the long-term structural development of the economy. While abandoning talk of returning to full employment in the lifetime of a Parliament (preferring instead to concentrate on more moderate aims), Labour promised to establish a neo-corporate National Economic Assessment involving government, business and trade unions in the discussion of economic policy and levels of investment, expenditure and consumption. It pledged itself to an aggressive, comprehensive industrial policy formulated with the direct purpose of facilitating government intervention in the economy and some degree of state co-ordination and control of the market economy. Managing the market was the key to what Neil Kinnock called in 1986 'social control of the market' to plan production and redistribute benefits, to secure economic growth and thereby achieve a number of socialist ends.[16]

At this time Kinnock made it clear that change involved 'a shift in attitudes and presentation, not a change in principles',[17] indicating a continuing association with a watered-down version of the 1983 appeal, one which recognised Labour's failure in office between 1974 and 1979. As Eric Shaw suggests, 'the general pattern of policy change from 1983 to 1987 [was]...a gradual retreat from more ambitious schemes of reform aimed (albeit often loosely) at a recasting of the social order and a return to the revisionist preference for pragmatic and largely consensual reform signalling the abandonment of any sustained challenge to the power and privileges of business.'[18] In the event, Labour's third consecutive election defeat in 1987 combined with the forward march of Thatcherism to encourage the leadership to abandon attempts to moderate the 1983 appeal in favour of its wholesale revision. Where Labour's 1987 pitch was not light-years away from its 1983 appeal (or indeed the broad commitment to economic management that characterised both the 1959 and the 1974 Labour manifestos), the economic approach established after 1983 culminating in the Blair manifesto of 1997 is proof positive of a dramatic shift. Here, the process of policy qualification and dilution which characterised the 1983 Parliament was ultimately replaced by policy revision, a two-stage process encompassing the 1987 and 1992 Parliaments, typified by the outcome of the Policy Review process of 1987–91 and the post-1994 Blairite reformation.

The Policy Review was in many ways the precursor to 'New' Labour, the flagship of the initial 'New Model' party fashioned by the Kinnock leadership. Between 1987 and 1991, it was the mechanism by which Labour's policy stance was altered and the authority of the leadership boosted. Working with the Shadow Cabinet and, when necessary, the 'contact group' of trade union leaders, the Parliamentary leadership became an Inner Core Elite within Labour's highest counsels, its authority such that the opportunities for non-leadership groups to exercise influence over the Labour Party were to be increasingly circumscribed in subsequent years. Couched in the language of earnest review based upon the subscription of ideas and opinions designed to enable Labour to address itself to the needs of the time, the Review process had a simple agenda: it was, in short, not so much a review as a revision of policy, one conducted not merely as an attempt to reapply timeless principles to a modern setting but to respond to perceived changes in the nation's political and economic outlook. Shorn of the intention to radically alter the balance of power within the economy, the 1987 manifesto still placed great emphasis upon the importance of planning the market economy to generate growth and reform its inefficiencies. The Policy Review gradually abandoned this approach in favour of a bolder endorsement (although, when compared with the post-1994 Labour strategy, a somewhat qualified one) of the market mechanism, a process illustrated in the yearly reports submitted to successive Labour Conferences. Over the three full years of the Review, two policy documents were produced by the Review Groups: 'Social Justice and Economic Efficiency' in 1988, and 'Meet the Challenge, Make the Change' in 1989. These were presented to the Shadow Cabinet and agreed by a comfortable majority vote of the NEC. All were endorsed without amendment by the Labour Conference courtesy of a compliant trade union block vote.

In 1990 and 1991 further 'distillations' of the Policy Review entitled 'Looking to the Future' and 'Opportunity Britain', this time heavily influenced by selected members of the Shadow Cabinet, were agreed by the NEC and again endorsed by the autumn Conference. Policy having been successfully reviewed by 1989, the Policy Review machinery ground to a halt although the Review itself continued: policy-making was now almost entirely the preserve of those Shadow Cabinet members whose proposals bore the imprimatur of the Parliamentary leadership. Each policy statement was presented to Conference in a process that had almost as much to do with political communications as it had to do with policy formation. By publicly launching each stage of the Review in a blaze of free publicity the leadership's policy would be presented to the party as an effective *fait accompli* as the chosen corporate image, and the slogan under which the new document was launched provided the theme under which Labour would campaign in the spring and summer and would structure the presentation of the Party Conference in the October.

After 1987, Labour gradually abandoned its commitment to planned action by government in concert with all sides of industry to deal with the problems of the market economy. No longer was it suggested that the market was a good servant but a bad master. The idea that the framework within which economic life proceeds must be substantially determined by government was ruled out. Subject to its responsibility to put in place a responsible fiscal and monetary regime conducive to the workings of a dynamic private sector, it no longer fell to government to determine levels of employment, reform the supply side, or generate sufficient demand. In contrast to previous Labour thinking, the market was said to be both self-regulating and self-correcting, and by itself not wholly responsible for major social and economic divisions. In his introduction to the 1989 Report of the Review, Kinnock stated that the 'economic role of government' should 'help the market system work properly where it can, will and should – and to replace or strengthen it where it can't, won't or shouldn't'.[19] By 1991, he argued that 'the old ideologies – command economy at one extreme, crude free market economies at the other – do not work'.[20]

At the rhetorical level of its policy pronouncements, Labour continued to acknowledge long into the 1980s that the market unaided may not be able to deliver a strong and modern economy. Should the private sector depend upon public sector involvement, the market had to be monitored and regulated in a social interest (if no longer managed in the traditional sense). Thus, early reports of the Policy Review included commitments to some degree of state regulation and control; less than previous but a greater degree than was eventually found in the 1992 and 1997 Labour manifestos. Despite the emphasis placed on interventionist investment in training, research and development and regulatory management, the idea that '[t]he role of the state in economic management was thereafter to be an enabling one, performing tasks which the market was unwilling or unable to accomplish'[21] was a perspective common to policy statements in 1987–91 which was not to be maintained; a 'half-way house' marking the transition away from Labour under Foot and early Kinnock toward that eventually presided over by Tony Blair. For Blair's Labour Party, the role of government is confined to allowing the market economy to work well. At the 1997 election, Blair declared his intention was to 'enhance the dynamism of the market, not undermine it',[22] expressing the belief that 'the post-war Keynesian dream is well and truly buried'.[23]

The political direction in which Labour was travelling is unmistakable after 1989 and the attitude it takes to the reforms pursued by Thatcherism in office is central. In 1989, reporting on the then most recent stage of the Policy Review, Peter Kellner wrote: 'Instead of being a party which found the market guilty until proven innocent, [Labour] was now a party that regarded the market as innocent until proven guilty.'[24] Having granted the market the right of the presumption of innocence in 1989, Labour under Blair after 1994 was to firmly declare it wholly innocent of all (indeed, any) charges brought against it in respect of either economic efficiency or social justice. Early stirrings of Labour's rapprochement with the *realpolitik* of Thatcherism can be evidenced in Kinnock's post-1985 attempts to redefine Labour as a 'party of production', one keen not merely to 'distribute with justice' but also 'produce with efficiency'. This appeal gradually became a common theme in Labour's economic stance after 1986 ('Improved distribution of wealth, however necessary and justifiable, cannot long exceed improved production of wealth'[25]) and grew in strength as the years passed and as Labour increasingly diluted its attachment to redistributive policies.

Influenced by his economics adviser, John Eatwell (later created a peer at Labour's nomination), Kinnock was persuaded after 1987 to emphasise the argument that Labour could make the existing market economy work better than the Conservatives. As the deregulated market place figured larger in Labour's economic plans, it marked a shift away from its traditionalist commitment to state intervention to reform the market mechanism in favour of establishing a framework which would complement the workings of the market. Here, 'reform' of the market is confined to a 'light touch' regulation; the commitment to 'redistribution' over time dramatically overshadowed by the commitment to 'production'.

Despite the relative success of the Policy Review in reorientating Labour away from its election agendas of 1983 and 1987, the party once again crashed to defeat in April 1992. Faced with an electorate willing to 'hold on to the Conservative nurse for fear of something worse' in the midst of recession, John Major's Conservatives played the high-taxation, high-spending anti-Labour card and surprisingly won. Kinnock duly fell on his sword on the morrow of his party's defeat and, following a relatively unprotracted leadership contest, the Shadow Chancellor John Smith was elected in his place, beating Bryan Gould by a margin of 9 to 1 in July 1992. Close Kinnock supporters such as Tony Blair and Peter Mandelson, the party's Director of Communications 1985–90 and MP for Hartlepool since 1992, all 'modernisers' committed to taking Labour to its right, considered Smith's leadership, despite his many abilities, to be suspiciously 'old' Labour. Powerless to prevent his accession, the modernising tendency none the less rejected the notion of 'one more heave', a belief that Labour had only to persevere and wait for a coming election victory; they favoured implementing a more fundamental agenda of party change.

Although Blair and Gordon Brown prospered under Smith's leadership (becoming Shadow Home Secretary and Shadow Chancellor respectively), Mandelson, wholly disliked by Smith, found himself totally frozen out of the party's inner circles. Despite the career advancement of men like Brown and Blair, the two years of Smith's leadership proves in retrospect to have been something of a hiatus for the modernisers. Ever the conservative (small c) politician, Smith was wary of the 'project', the sobriquet applied to modernisation and the 'New' Labour agenda, and unwilling to endorse policy reforms urged upon him by the Blair and Mandelson tendency. He firmly set his face against the idea of revising Clause Four and reportedly 'blew his top' in 1993 when one member of his Shadow Cabinet, Jack Straw, publicly advocated doing so. While prepared to put his leadership on the line in the successful battle to secure the passage of 'One Member One Vote' (OMOV) through the 1993 Labour Conference in the teeth of trade union opposition led by John Edmonds of the GMB, Smith only did so because it was 'unfinished business' left over from the Kinnock regime, a policy he had committed himself to during the 1992 leadership contest.

Many Labour modernisers considered that Smith demonstrated decidedly 'old' Labour credentials in making concessions to trade union opinion on rights at work and the commitment to using the state to return to full employment, but while he may not have significantly advanced the modernisers' agenda nor did he undo any of the Kinnock reforms. In hindsight, Smith's leadership was a period of consolidation, one modernisers privately refer to as an interregnum where their 'project' stalled (if it was in no way reversed). It was only in the wake of Smith's death and the elevation of Tony Blair, moderniser *par excellence*, in his place that the emergent reform project was placed firmly back on track. Where Smith wanted to consolidate the Kinnockite status quo in an attempt to reconstitute the grand old party of, say, Gaitskell or Callaghan, the modernisation agenda was predicated upon the belief that the enterprise culture fashioned by Thatcherism in office structured what Labour should do in opposition and could expect to do in office.

As Leader of the Opposition in 1994–7, Blair was everywhere. The long-established frontrunner to replace Smith once Gordon Brown fell on his sword, he came to office with favourable press coverage, buoyant poll ratings (both for himself and his party) and showed remarkable success in leading his party from the front (symbolised by his success in revising Clause Four in 1995 and winning the endorse-ment of party members for the 'Road to the Manifesto' document in 1996). Blair's leadership was characterised by his commanding his party and seeing it follow (a position he was to skilfully contrast with what he saw as John Major's inability to do likewise in the latter stages of the 1992 Parliament). His time as party leader marked yet a further (but not that dramatic) shift away from Labour's pre-1987 position. Indeed, despite all his efforts, no dramatic shift under Blair since 1994 can be identified (other than a far-reaching tightening of a pre-prepared ratchet); 1994 was not a 'year zero' for the Labour Party because Blair's reforms were built on the firm foundations established before he came to the leadership. Although his tenure of the leadership saw a steady shift in economic and industrial policy it was a shift marked by continuity with the altered political world view of the leadership of the then 'new model' Labour Party fashioned under Kinnock.

As a process, Labour's shift certainly involves an amount of serial disengagement with past practice, but it is not a series of disjointed breaks which suggest that the phenomenon had fundamentally different (as opposed to distinct) characteristics at different times. In identifying distinctive stages in the emergence, rise and consolidation of what is now referred to as the 'Blairite' agenda, a five-stage shift away from the policy stance of 1983 can be evidenced:

1 High-tide: the advance of the left halted, 1981–4
2 Interregnum: Kinnock's quest for control, 1984–5
3 Realignment: the right consolidates its authority, 1985–7
4 Transformation: the Policy Review and after, 1987–94
5 Consolidation: the Blair reformation, post-1994.

Each of these stages had a cumulative effect and all were contributory factors in bringing about Labour's transformation. None can be taken in isolation; all had a collective impact. Here, in the wake of the stalled rise of the Labour left of 1970–84, Labour's modernisation (itself a word that dates back only to the early 1990s; one in vogue only since 1993) is part of a process. It is not in itself an action. To take any key period in isolation at worst obscures and at best only partially maps out the process of change.

Labour's transformation over time reflects a period of transition. As with the chronology of Thatcherism the remaking of Labour has been a 'process' enacted over time, one adjudged in terms of 'stages' with several distinctive points of origin and motivating factors. Hence, there is nothing intrinsically inconsistent in identifying 1983, 1985, post-1987 and 1994 onward as significant 'moments of transition'. They are not by themselves point(s) of origin given that Labour's shift is a staged process. Here, enacted against the backdrop of Thatcherism, a series of key periods (or staging posts) can be identified including the 1983, 1987, 1987 and 1992 General Elections; the shift in the Kinnock leadership in 1983–5; the Policy Review of 1987–91; and the Blair reforms post-1994. Together, these all contributed to the change from the party Labour was in 1980 to that it had become in 1997. With regard to the alteration of the party's politics after 1987, 1988–91 (the Policy Review) and 1994–6 (the Blair 'reformation') are as significant as (but only because they are related to) the 1983, 1987 and 1992 election cycles. Rather than look for one point of origin, a more profitable approach maps out various staging posts in order to fully explore and explain the complex process underpinning Labour's transformation.

NOTES

1 Martin J. Smith, 'A Return to Revisionism', in Martin Smith and Joanna Spear (eds), *The Changing Labour Party*, London: Routledge, 1992, p. 27.
2 Eric Shaw, *The Labour Party Since 1945*, Oxford: Basil Blackwell, 1996, p. 201.
3 Roy Hattersley, *Economic Priorities for a Labour Government*, London: Macmillan, 1987, p. 48.
4 Ibid., p. 6.
5 Ibid., p. 7. [...]
6 Denis Healey, Campaign Statement for the Deputy Leadership of the Labour Party, May 1981. [...]
7 Noel Thompson, *Political Economy and the Labour Party*, London: UCL Press, p. 273.
8 *The Times*, 12 April 1996. [...]
9 *Tribune*, 20 September 1985, 'Democratic Socialism: A Tribune Relaunch Statement'.
10 Ibid.
11 Ibid.
12 *Labour Weekly*, 14 March 1986.
13 Lewis Minkin, *The Contentious Alliance: Trade Unions and the Labour Party*, Edinburgh: Edinburgh University Press, 1991, p. 137.
14 Significant stepping-stones include: The Hayward–Hughes report of 1982; the introduction of the register of constitutional groups in 1982; the proscription of Militant in 1982; the expulsion of five members of the Militant editorial board in February 1983; the NEC investigation of the Liverpool District Labour Party in 1985–6 and the expulsions that followed; and the establishment of the National Constitutional Committee in 1986. Cf. Richard Heffernan and Mike Marqusee, *Defeat from the Jaws of Victory: Inside Kinnock's Labour Party*, London: Verso, 1992; Michael Crick, *The March of Militant*, London: Faber & Faber, 1986; Eric Shaw, *Discipline and Discourse in the Labour Party*, Manchester: Manchester University Press, 1988. Note the significance of Militant ('a pestilential nuisance' according to Michael Foot) as a stick with which to beat the 'mainstream' Labour left.
15 Patrick Seyd, 'Bennism without Benn', *New Socialist*, 27 May 1985; Richard Heffernan and Mike Marqusee, *Defeat from the Jaws of Victory*.
16 Neil Kinnock, *Making Our Way*, Oxford: Basil Blackwell, 1986, p. 192.
17 Neil Kinnock, *The Future of Socialism*, London: Fabian Society, 1985, p. 3.
18 Eric Shaw, *The Labour Party Since 1979: Crisis and Transformation*, London: Routledge, 1993, p. 50.
19 The Labour Party, *Meet the Challenge, Make the Change*, London: The Labour Party, 1989, p. 6.
20 The Labour Party, *Opportunity Britain*, London: The Labour Party, 1991, p. iii.
21 Tudor Jones, *Remaking the Labour Party: From Gaitskell to Blair*, London: Routledge, 1996, p. 126.
22 Tony Blair speech: Labour Party Press Release, 7 April 1997. Labour also published a separate 'Business Manifesto', a 20-page document launched amid much fanfare at an event in the City. Claiming that Labour was now a party both of and for business, Blair went to great lengths during the election campaign to present himself as 'the entrepreneur's champion', winning the endorsement of a number of senior business executives. *The Guardian*, 12 April 1997.
23 *Sunday Telegraph*, 6 April 1997.
24 Quoted in Tudor Jones, *Remaking the Labour Party*, p. 125.
25 Neil Kinnock, *Making Our Way*, p. 97.

6

The Political Economy of New Labour

Colin Hay

[...] My aim [...] is to establish that by the completion of the Policy Review – and, perhaps, some time before that – Labour had ceased effectively to be a social democratic party, committed as it had by then become to a pervasive neo-liberal economic orthodoxy and to a basic acceptance of the legacy of the Thatcher years. In making this argument I suggest, in contrast to much of the existing literature on this period, that the Policy Review itself evidenced a 'Thatcherite revisionism' that reflected in turn the perceived exigencies for Labour of 'the politics of catch-up'. [...]

Though varying somewhat from author to author, the outline of a distinctive 'modernisation' thesis can be traced within the recent literature on the Labour Party [...]. Its central tenets can be summarised in four related hypotheses:

1 that by questioning the assumptions of the Keynesian orthodoxy of the post-war period, Thatcherism has transformed the terms of contemporary political debate in Britain;
2 that in so doing it has in fact facilitated the necessary accommodation of the Labour Party to a qualitatively novel global economic environment characterised by the heightened (if not quite perfect) mobility of goods, labour and, especially, capital;
3 that, as a consequence, Labour's Policy Review and resulting 'renewal' should be seen, somewhat ironically, as the product of the party's years in the electoral wilderness during the 1980s and the requirement to face up to the future that this imposed;
4 that the Review should not therefore be seen as a concession to Thatcherism, but rather as an overdue modernisation which had, for too long, been thwarted by the cloying influence of the trade unions and the inertial impulses of left ex-tremists.

[...]

A central claim of the modernisation thesis is that the Policy Review represented 'an attempt to widen the appeal of the party and to win back some of the working class who voted Conservative in the 1980s' (Smith 1992: 15; Seyd 1993; Sanders 1993). This is undoubtedly the case. However, advocates of, and commentators sympathetic to, Labour's 'modernisation' have tended not to consider the full range of alternative strategies available to the party in reconstituting its appeal to the electorate. In suggesting that the Policy Review was shaped profoundly by the need to win back lost voters, the implicit assumption was made that the only way in which this could be achieved was through a strategy of accommodation to the new-found preferences of the electorate – preferences, it should be noted, which saw the Conservatives re-elected in 1983 and 1987 with sizeable majorities. This psephologically inspired 'politics of catch-up' consigned Labour to a reactive and defensive, preference-accommodating approach – to what Colin Leys terms 'market-research socialism' (1990: 119; see also Shaw 1994: 216–17).

The dangers of such a strategy are threefold. First, in the wake of a crusading government intent on transforming not only the structures of the state but also the 'hearts and minds' of the British electorate, there is a considerable risk of an unwitting accommodation to a Thatcherite agenda internalised within the sensitivities and sensibilities of the electorate. Indeed, by seeking to gauge such preferences as a means of repackaging and representing them as its own, Labour merely served further to establish them as the new 'common sense' in a way that the Conservatives could never have done on their own. It seems plausible to argue [...] that such perceptions of the parameters of political and economic possibility had been circumscribed significantly by the new right's narration of the crisis of the 1970s. They were, moreover, at considerable odds with any attempt to restore an indigenous growth dynamic to the British economy. If this is indeed the case, then it would seem that Labour in fact conspired in reinforcing the very attitudinal changes which would now seem to preclude all but the most orthodox and restrictive of macroeconomic stances.

Second, as Labour would find to its cost in 1992 (and, arguably, had already done so in 1987), preference-accommodation – especially for a traditionally 'programmatic' party (Epstein 1980; Shaw 1994: 60) – was not likely to reap rapid electoral rewards. The risk is that in the initial attempt to poach the core constituencies of one's opponent, the perceived distance between the parties becomes so narrow that, as in 1992, the electorate adopts the view that it is simply 'better to vote for the devil it knows than the devil it doesn't' (see Sanders 1993: 213).

Finally, if the above two propositions are indeed accurate, it is likely that by the time an opposition achieves power by the pursuit of such a preference-accommodating strategy, it will have done so only because the policy implementation of the outgoing government has proved so damaging as to undermine the electorate's faith in its competence. The clear danger is that the incoming party will secure for itself political office at precisely the moment at which the contradictions of the policy paradigm to which it, too, subscribes first become apparent to the electorate. The political fallout arising from any difficulty in establishing economic competence under such conditions may serve to ensure that any period in power is in fact short-lived. Whether this will prove the case for New Labour or not is largely an empirical matter. It is likely to depend on two key factors: (i) the ability of the Conservative Party in opposition to regroup and to define for itself a new political and economic programme; and (ii) Labour's ability to make swift decisions and to establish a hierarchy amongst its current wish list of rather contradictory priorities as, and when, the inevitable recession occurs (on the need to establish a clear sense of priorities see Panitch and Leys 1997: 253; Thompson 1996).

The basis for Labour's renewed appeal to the electorate has not, then, been an attempt to formulate an altogether novel conception of, and response to, the British impasse. Rather, it has sought to appeal to the pre-formulated sensitivities of the electorate, viewed as a fixed constraint to which policy appeals must be oriented. This tendency to 'reify' the attitudinal preferences of the electorate arguably prevented Labour in opposition from learning the lessons of Thatcherism's success, whilst making the party at least somewhat complicit in the latter's dubious achievements. As John Kingdom observes: 'It seemed that socialism could live only by not being socialist; it was not only Thatcherites at the graveside as the earth was shovelled over the coffin of social democracy' (1992: 5–6; see also Crewe 1992; Leys 1990). Thatcherism's success, we should recall, was premised on the ability of the new right to present the moment of the late 1970s as one of crisis. In so doing, it proved itself capable of changing if not the hearts and minds of the electorate then certainly the predominant perceptions of the political context, recruiting subjects to its vision of the 'necessary' response to the crisis of an 'overextended' state 'held to ransom' by the labour movement (Hay 1996a). However incomplete and however far from hegemonic its project remained, its initial success surely lay in this ability to mould perceptions of the nature of the crisis of the 1970s and of the 'painful' remedies required.

There is much that Labour might have learned from this. The similarities between the late 1970s and the early 1990s were considerable. Indeed, both contexts might be seen as providing rare opportunities for the successful pursuit of *preference-shaping* (as opposed to preference-accommodating) strategies. To avail itself of such an opportunity, however, Labour would have had to distance itself from the dominant political and economic orthodoxies of the time, just as the new right did in the 1970s. What applied to Thatcherism then might as easily have been applied to Labour in 1992. Both contexts might be characterised in terms of profound and protracted state failure and economic recession. Moreover, in 1992, as in 1979, the symptoms of such state and economic dislocation were widely perceived and experienced, providing a considerable opportunity for the mobilisation of a populist political and economic project organised around the identification of the nature of the crisis and a vision of an alternative.

Though the more recent 'crisis' might have been defined in a number of different ways, all capable of finding resonance with a variety of personal experiences of state and economic failure, some of the core economic contradictions of the Thatcherite project can be summarised as follows:

1   By pursuing both financial deregulation and a monetarist counter-inflationary strategy, Thatcherite neo-liberalism served to compound conditions discouraging investment in the 'real' economy, thereby exacerbating a persistent structural weakness of the British economy. This has resulted in a situation in which Britain invests more of its available resources overseas than does any of its competitors (Pollin 1995; Watson and Hay 1998).
2   The 'rolling back of the frontiers' of the social democratic state has persistently been pursued for political advantage to the detriment of economic responsibility. This is evidenced in: (i) the short-term asset-stripping of the public sector for the

sake of a 'share- and property-owning democracy' and cosmetic reductions in the public sector borrowing requirement at the expense of long-term improvements in competitiveness and industrial performance; and (ii) the revenue-maximising strategy of transferring public monopolies to the private sector rather than promoting competition by dissolving them. There is little evidence to substantiate Conservative claims that off-loading firms to the private sector has directly improved their performance and competitiveness (Bishop and Kay 1988; Foreman-Peck and Manning 1988; Haq and Temple 1998: 481–8; Parker 1995; Vickers and Yarrow 1995; Yarrow 1986, 1989).

3   The economic strategy of successive Conservative governments during the 1980s and 1990s was directed to securing tax cuts rather than to the channelling of tax incentives and public expenditure towards industrial investment, research and development, training, innovation and (re-)skilling. The result – consumer booms (most notably the 'Lawson boom' of the late 1980s) and import penetration – has undermined the prospects of sustained and sustainable economic growth without a significant expansion in industrial capacity (Michie and Smith 1996).

4   The policy of selective disengagement (if not perhaps outright abstention) from economic intervention resulted in the effective disintegration of both private and public sector training initiatives under the Thatcher governments. This led to a situation in which Britain's training system was, in the judgement of David Ashton *et al.*, 'just about the worst of our international competitors' in an economic context placing an ever greater premium upon reskilling and skill diversification (1989: 137; see also Chapman 1998; Finegold and Soskice 1988). As Bob Jessop and Rob Stones observed, 'at a time when high-grade flexibility depends upon polyvalent skills, the government sponsors flexibility through hire-and-fire industrial relations legislation and adopts a low-cost, low-skill training policy. This has reinforced the low-skill, low-wage, low-productivity character of British industry' (1992: 187). Since the early 1980s, it would appear as though Britain has been forced to compete on the basis of a strategy of 'social dumping in one country' (Hay 1996b: 163–4).

5   The persistent failure of Conservative governments to develop a coherent industrial *strategy* – as distinct from a neo-liberal-engendered neo-Darwinism in which only the fittest have survived – has led to a situation in which, as Jessop observes, 'Britain is fast losing [if it has not already lost] the last vestiges of an independent and coherent manufacturing base which could serve as the basis for an effective national economic strategy' (1992: 37; see also Cowling and Sugden 1990; Glyn 1989; Rowthorn 1989).

6   The systematic stripping of the strategic capacities of the state for intervention on the supply side has compromised its (always meagre) ability to address the persistent pathologies of the British economy and, hence, to promote an investment-led manufacturing renaissance (Ashton *et al.* 1989; Jessop 1992; Jessop *et al.* 1990; Michie and Smith 1996; Watson and Hay 1998).

This list is certainly not exhaustive, but it does begin to illustrate the profound nature of the impasse that is the direct economic legacy of Thatcherism. Its social legacy is no less pronounced and no less inauspicious (see for instance Hills 1996; Oppenheim 1993; Walker and Walker 1987; Webb *et al.* 1996). Once this is considered, it becomes clear that there were – and are – alternatives to the Thatcherite revisionism to which the Labour Party had by 1990 restricted itself. Moreover, the construction of such alternatives was, by that point, a necessary (though not in itself sufficient) condition of Britain's emergence from persistent economic decline and social dislocation.

Conclusion

As I have sought to make clear in the preceding pages, the case for an alternative to Labour's chosen 'politics of catch-up' was in the early 1990s, as it remains today, a compelling one. The deep and palpable dissatisfaction with the policies and personnel of the Major government, which intensified considerably following Britain's ejection from European Exchange Rate Mechanism in September 1992 (Sanders 1996), only demonstrates the potential that existed for Labour in opposition to reap the electoral benefits of preference-shaping. If the crisis of the 1970s was, in the popular fiction of the new right, a crisis of overload and ungovernability, then altogether more plausible was the view that the crisis of the 1990s was, and is, a crisis of *under-load* – of an under-extended, retrenched and debilitated state stripped of the capacity for strategic economic intervention. The adoption, then, of a preference-shaping and, ultimately, a state-shaping strategy might have provided Labour with the basis from which to build a populist political project capable of transcending neo-liberalism and of providing the modernising role that the free play of the market has consistently failed to deliver. [. . .]

What is certain, however, is that such an alternative could not and cannot be constructed out of a nostalgia for a past to which there can be no return. On this much New Labour is surely right. The Keynesian welfare state is gone. The post-war settlement cannot be resurrected. An alternative vision is required. Yet, like all realistic visions, it must be grounded in a tightly focused analysis of the current conjuncture. This presents a considerable challenge to those who would like to present themselves as the 'organic intellectuals' of a resurgent and renewed left. The contradictions of the Thatcherite inheritance are all too apparent. Yet without an alternative vision, we remain ensnared within this 'catastrophic equilibrium' in which the 'old is dying and the new cannot be born' (Gramsci 1971: 176).

References

Ashton, D., Green, F. and Hopkins, M. (1989) 'The Training System of British Capitalism', in F. Green (ed.), *The Restructuring of the UK Economy*. Hemel Hempstead: Harvester Wheatsheaf.

Bishop, M. and Kay, J. (1988) *Does Privatisation Work? Lessons from the UK*. London: London Business School.

Chapman, P. (1998) 'Human Capital Issues', in T. Buxton, P. Chapman, and P. Temple (eds), *Britain's Economic Performance* (2nd edn). London: Routledge.

Cowling, K. and Sugden, R. (eds) (1990) *A New Economic Policy for Britain: Essays on the Development of Industry*. Manchester: Manchester University Press.

Crewe, I. (1992) 'Changing Votes and Unchanging Voters', *Electoral Studies*, 11, 335–45.

Epstein, L. (1980) *Political Parties in Western Democracies*. London: Transaction Publishers.

Finegold, D. and Soskice, D. (1988) 'The Failure of Training in Britain: Analysis and Prescription', *Oxford Review of Economic Policy*, 4 (3), 21–53.

Foreman-Peck, J. and Manning, D. (1988) 'How Well is BT Performing? An International Comparison of Telecommunications Total Factor Productivity', *Fiscal Studies*, 9, 54–67.

Glyn, A. (1989) 'The Macro-anatomy of the Thatcher Years', in F. Green (ed.), *The Restructuring of the UK Economy*. Hemel Hempstead: Harvester Wheatsheaf.

Gramsci, A. (1971) *Selections from Prison Notebooks*. London: Lawrence and Wishart.

Haq, M. and Temple, P. (1998) 'Economic Policy and the Changing International Division of Labour', in T. Buxton, P. Chapman, and P. Temple (eds), *Britain's Economic Performance* (2nd edn). London: Routledge.

Hay, C. (1996a) 'Narrating Crisis: The Discursive Construction of the "Winter of Discontent"', *Sociology*, 30, 253–77.

——(1996b) *Re-stating Social and Political Change*. Buckingham: Open University Press.

Hills, J. (ed.) (1996) *New Inequalities: The Changing Distribution of Income and Wealth in the United Kingdom*. Cambridge: Cambridge University Press.

Jessop, B. (1992) 'From Social Democracy to Thatcherism: Twenty-Five Years of British Politics', in N. Abercrombie and A. Warde (eds), *Social Change in Contemporary Britain*. Cambridge: Polity Press.

——, Bonnett, K. and Bromley, S. (1990) 'Farewell to Thatcherism? Neo-Liberalism and New Times', *New Left Review*, 179, 81–102.

——and Stones, R. (1992) 'Old City and New Times', in L. Budd and S. Whimster (eds), *Global Finance and Urban Living*. London: Routledge.

Kingdom, J. (1992) *No Such Thing as Society? Individualism and Community*. Buckingham: Open University Press.

Leys, C. (1990) 'Still a Question of Hegemony', *New Left Review*, 181, 119–28.

Michie, J. and Smith, J. G. (eds) (1996) *Creating Industrial Capacity: Towards Full Employment*. Oxford: Oxford University Press.

Oppenheim, C. (1993) *Poverty: The Facts*. London: Child Poverty Action Group.

Panitch, L. and Leys, C. (1997) *The End of Parliamentary Socialism: From New Left to New Labour*. London: Verso.

Parker, D. (1995) *Measuring Efficiency Gains from Privatisation*, Occasional Papers in Industrial Strategy No. 36, University of Birmingham.

Pollin, R. (1995) 'Financial Structures and Egalitarian Economic Policy', *New Left Review*, 214, 26–61.

Rowthorn, B. (1989) 'The Thatcher Revolution', in F. Green (ed.), *The Restructuring of the UK Economy*. Hemel Hempstead: Harvester Wheatsheaf.

Sanders, D. (1993) 'Why the Conservative Party Won – Again', in A. King, I. Crewe, D. Denver, K. Newton, P. Norton, D. Sanders and P. Seyd, *Britain at the Polls 1992*. Chatham, NJ: Chatham House.

——(1996) 'Economic Performance, Management Competence and the Outcome of the Next General Election', *Political Studies*, 44, 203–31.

Seyd, P. (1993) 'Labour: The Great Transformation', in A. King, I. Crewe, D. Denver, K. Newton, P. Norton, D. Sanders and P. Seyd, *Britain at the Polls 1992*. Chatham, NJ: Chatham House.

Shaw, E. (1994) *The Labour Party Since 1979: Crisis and Transformation*. London: Routledge.

Smith, M. J. (1992) 'A Return to Revisionism? The Labour Party's Policy Review', in M. J. Smith and J. Spear (eds), *The Changing Labour Party*. London: Routledge.

Thompson, N. (1996) 'Supply Side Socialism: The Political Economy of New Labour', *New Left Review*, 216, 37–54.

Vickers, J. and Yarrow, G. (1995) *Privatisation: An Economic Analysis*. Cambridge, MA: MIT Press.

Walker, A. and Walker, C. (1987) *The Growing Divide: A Social Audit, 1979–87*. London: Child Poverty Action Group.

Watson, M. and Hay, C. (1998) 'In the Dedicated Pursuit of Dedicated Capital: Restoring an Indigenous Investment Ethic to British Capitalism', *New Political Economy*, 3 (3), 407–26.

Webb, S., Kemp, M. and Millar, J. (1996) 'The Changing Face of Low Pay in Britain', *Policy Studies*, 17, 255–71.

Yarrow, G. (1986) 'Privatisation in Theory and Practice', *Economic Policy*, 2, 323–78.

——(1989) 'Privatisation and Economic Performance in Britain', *Carnegie–Rochester Conference Series on Public Policy*, 31, 303–44.

7

Interpreting New Labour: Constraints, Dilemmas and Political Agency

Michael Kenny and Martin J. Smith

Three years into the life of the current Labour administration, observers remain as divided and uncertain about its nature as they were before the election. In this chapter we consider some of the prevalent views of the government's political trajectory, noting particularly the popularity of interpretations which juxtapose Blair's policies with Thatcherite Conservatism and those that regard the government as the culmination of a tradition of 'modernization' of the party according to the changing realities of post-war society. Both of these perspectives have something to offer to our understanding of Labour's current political direction, yet each throws only partial light on it. As an alternative, we propose a general framework for comprehending this complex political phenomenon and offer a rather different account of the ideological and political 'meanings' of so-called 'New Labour'. Though the emphasis in our argument is on treating Labour's development in the 1990s as a complex political problem which requires a multidimensional and disaggregated interpretation, some broader 'generic' conclusions about the political trajectory of the government are also offered. In particular, we hope to show that a better balance needs to be struck between attention to the constraints under which Labour has been operating, a sense of the dilemmas that flow from these pressures and obstacles, and a more nuanced consideration of what sorts of response have been offered to them.
[. . .]

Constraints, Dilemmas and Political Responses

[. . .] The key premise of this framework is that we can detect at least three analytically separable dimensions of the political behaviour of this government. These need to be balanced more completely by Labour's interpreters. The first dimension concerns the *constraints* facing Labour in the British context; we use this term to signal entrenched obstacles and biases arising from certain social and political factors as well as the recurrence of certain challenges over the medium and long terms. Several of these constraints and their significance for understanding Labour's development are outlined indicatively here. Against one recent trend in the analysis of British politics, we believe that there are 'real-world' constraints, structural pressures and causal factors. Yet it is also important to observe that actors' perceptions of what constitutes an obstacle can themselves become a constraint upon what political actors feel able or willing to do. In the study of Labour politics, historians have pointed to the impact of such ideologically generated constraints throughout the party's history. Constraints come in different forms: there are objective ones, the existence and character of which are open to profoundly different interpretation, and also subjectively determined ones that flow from the belief-systems of actors at particular points in time. Both are pertinent in considering the politics of Labour. Our suggestion is that these constraints only enter the realm of everyday politics when they become constructed as 'dilemmas' by political actors.

The second dimension to which we need to attend therefore in understanding contemporary political phenomena is the political *dilemmas* facing the current government (for an extended conceptual discussion of dilemmas see Bevir, 1999). We use this term to signal the emergence of a host of more immediate and often contingent problems and challenges. Many of these stem from the constraints that we can observe, which have been converted into immediate problems and challenges by political actors. Dilemmas assume an immediate and often contingent form. Many dilemmas emerge from the mismatch between actors' perceptions and traditions of belief and the confusing and complex realities that surround them (Bevir, 1999), resulting in a fairly ongoing process of ideological adaptation and adjustment. Interpreted in this way, dilemmas can be regarded as 'constructed' within the webs of belief that actors hold (though again a wider philosophical debate raises the question of whether these exist solely in these perceptual fields). Finally, we separate from both of these dimensions the *responses* that actors adopt to pressures and constraints arising from the social, economic and political contexts in which they operate. These responses take many different forms – from legislative action to internal party debate. They are never predetermined by either the constraints or dilemmas, but they are heavily influenced and their infinity circumscribed by the ways in which 'dilemmas' are actually constructed. Hence the Blair government conceives itself as facing a number of contingent dilemmas – concerning macro-economic policy decisions – arising from the constraints attendant upon its perception of the realities of the global economy. Its responses, in policy and political terms, to these dilemmas are to a large degree shaped by how the constraints and particular dilemmas are perceived. Yet these responses are not foreclosed by the latter: as we shall see, a variety of response-pathways are always available to actors and interpretation needs to be sensitive to these. [...]

Constraints

The economic environment

As some of the 'classic' studies of Labour politics in the twentieth century have rightly observed, the party's policies have often been thwarted through the structural and lobbying power of capital either through capital flight (a key backdrop to the sterling crises Labour experienced in, for instance, the 1960s), direct veto or non-co-operation from business élites. Proposals for greater industrial democracy contained in the Bullock report, for instance, were blocked by a combination of pressure from the CBI and some Cabinet opposition (see Stones, 1990; Coates, 1980; Grant and Marsh, 1977 for consideration of this and other examples). One major constraint facing Labour and other social democratic parties in (capitalist) liberal democracies concerns the influence (or structural power) which can be wielded by entrenched economic interests (see Lindblom, 1977; Poulantzas, 1976; Przeworski, 1985, for a theoretical discussion).

In government, Labour has on occasions abandoned or ignored its own policy commitments; delivery has rarely matched promise. As early as 1968 Labour was attempting to reduce the levels of public expenditure and lessen its commitment to universalism in the provision of welfare benefit levels (see Bale, 1997). Public expenditure cuts have been forced on Labour in order to reassure the markets (see Bale, 1997; Wilson, 1974). In this sense Blair and his Chancellor, Gordon Brown, have internalized a form of argument popular in some academic circles: that there is no option for social democratic political actors except to reassure the principal components of finance capital. This submission to the pressure of capital and the market is a continuous problem for social democratic parties. Consequently, the pressures of a competitive party system have tended to inflect social democratic politics in a generally 'accommodationist' direction with regard to socio-economic arrangements. On certain occasions Labour leaders have translated parts of the social democratic traditions that they have inherited into relatively 'radical' policy-frames, for instance, by developing a 'national plan', calling for the introduction of high marginal rates of taxation, instituting planning agreements with industry, increasing public expenditure in the 1960s, developing proposals for industrial democracy and, at various points, promoting the nationalization of key industries. But the increasingly apparent convergence in policy terms between social democratic parties across central and western Europe (which is rather masked by rhetorical differences over a putative 'third way') suggests that these constraints are both common across different political systems and have been 'framed' in a similar way as a set of powerful dilemmas which appear to necessitate certain programmatic responses (Sassoon, 1997).

Constraints have existed too, since the late 1960s, in the shape of the changing character of the international economic environment, as well as through the perception of these developments by those who have shaped Labour's economic policy-making. For a while now, some of the key decision-makers and opinion-shapers around the government have adhered to a 'strong' version of globalization theory to make sense of economic change, though again one can detect alternative ideas in high places until the early 1990s (Gould, 1998; Giddens, 1998). This constraint is most apparent in two areas. Public expenditure policy is developed around the imperative of not upsetting the global financial markets. Within this perceived structural constraint, Labour's strategy is not to be forced to abandon policy because of the pressure of capital. Blair has chosen to adapt social democratic principle to capitalism in a way that hollows out much of the former. The almost unbridled acceptance of capitalist economic organization combined with a commitment to social justice hints at the influence deriving from US Democrats rather than social democratic thinking here. This particular example illustrates the analytical complexity involved in delineating constraints. Some are undoubtedly external and 'objective' in kind, yet these are extremely hard to separate from the 'baggage' of actors' perceptions of circumstances, the latter representing constraints of a different kind.

The British political system

The party has also been historically constrained by the nature of the political system in which it operates. Though Labour established itself as a presence within the mainstream of political life in the early years of the twentieth century, its value-system and policy priorities have been ambiguously positioned in respect of the prevailing traditions of the British polity. The relationship between Labour and these different ideological and cultural traditions is a complex and nuanced one, being as much about osmosis and adaptation as clear-cut ideological separation. Despite the recent emphasis upon constitutional reform, Labour has not managed to break the embrace of parliamentarianism and the continued potency of key actors' reverence for the Westminster model [...] Indeed it is torn between the degree of control the Westminster system provides for the executive and commitments to considering proportional representation.

Electoral factors

Labour has been constrained by the changing nature of its electoral coalition and particularly the changing social composition and experiences of its 'core' constituency, the working classes. It is impossible to understand Labour's evolution in the 1990s without attending to the impact that repeated electoral failure had on the party. Labour's vote declined overall from 1951 to 1983 (though it rose in the short term in the elections of 1964, 1966 and October 1974), a trend that seemed to require explanation through social as well as political factors. Moreover, the scale of the defeat in 1983 was such that it devastated the party, the leadership and the left opposition. It particularly highlighted the extent of the electorate's disillusionment with the party and undermined the party left's claim that the erosion of support was caused by its drift to the right. Increasing divergence between the policies of Labour and the views of the electorate (Crewe, 1983; Whiteley, 1983) reinforced these electoral problems. The divergence was a reflection of significant social change during the post-war period. The size of the skilled manual workforce has declined whilst there has been a growth in clerical occupations (see Castells, 1996, 307). Moreover, the character of work has changed greatly, with many more people working part-time and substantially more women being employed throughout the economy. In addition, the standard and quality of life have altered, both qualitatively and quantitatively, over the last few decades (Hobsbawm, 1998). In order to win, Labour came to believe that it had to attract a more diverse and volatile electorate whose preferences and concerns were harder to detect and more 'post-material' in kind. And there was evidence to suggest that popular concern had shifted towards issues which come under the heading of 'quality of life' and that the limiting of tax liability had become a major economic priority for the middle classes and skilled working classes.

Dilemmas

Economic competence

Particularly challenging for Labour's leadership after 1994 was the question of establishing a relationship of trust with parts of the electorate beyond its core constituency, and regaining the electorate's confidence in the realm of economic policy. There is considerable evidence that voters did not trust Labour on the economy until the Tory economic debacle of black Wednesday in September 1992 (see Sanders, 1996; Wickham-Jones, 1996; Gould, 1998). As late as 1996 there was still a perception amongst voters that economic improvement would be jeopardized under a Labour government (Gould, 1998a, 276). Fundamental to Labour's strategy under Blair both in opposition and in government, therefore, has been the need to prove that Labour is economically competent and will not repeat the errors that led to the crises of the 1970s. The dilemma that arises from this perception is how to generate the image of competence and make headway in delivering on the goals of social justice. Labour has chosen to 'resolve' this dilemma by reproducing the self-imposed constraints in public expenditure established by the Tories (and indeed by surpassing them in reducing public spending), expressed as a proportion of national income in comparison with the Tories (*The Guardian*, 25 August 1999), reducing the burden of public debt, and maintaining a balanced budget in the medium term. Much of Labour's economic policy has been concerned with retaining the confidence of voters, especially in the imagined community of 'Middle England' and the financial markets. More broadly we might label this the strategy of presenting Labour as the country's 'natural' economic manager. This particular stance is connected in Labour's current rhetoric with the challenges associated with participation in the open and fast-moving international economic environment.

Building an electoral coalition

Despite the overwhelming nature of its victory in 1997, Labour's electoral position has presented a number of dilemmas [...]. A convincing electoral victory requires the votes of its core working-class supporters as well as significant middle-class voting. The coalition that Labour needs to marshal through the ballot box has only been successfully stitched together on three occasions – 1945, 1966 and 1977. A recurrent dilemma for the party's leadership has therefore arisen around the delivery of some of its core values in what it perceives as a hostile electoral environment. The invention of 'New' Labour can thus be seen as a slightly different response to this dilemma, an adjustment to the party's ethos and arguably its very mission in order to secure the Holy Grail of stable electoral support from divergent social constituencies. Not surprisingly, in ideological terms this has encouraged a shifting of the party's political centre-of-gravity, towards the middle of the political and ideological system. Blair is particularly conscious that 'With the possible exception of 1964, Labour has hitherto been unable to recreate the strong consensus of 1945. The truth that we must take seriously is that 1945 was the exception not the rule' (Blair, 1996, 5).

Though different commentators have pointed to the significance of the electoral dimension to Labour's current development, less attention has been focused upon the precise degree and ways in which the parameters of policy have been affected by this 'external' (and now hugely internalized) pressure. Sceptics are right to observe that such factors provide a powerful rationalization for party leaders who want to reorientate the ideological trajectory of the party. But less attention has been devoted to what meaningful alternatives were available to a party operating in a competitive two-party system, facing the kind of challenges that Labour did in the early–mid 1980s. A number of questions need more serious attention here. Would any of the alternative figures displaced, marginalized or replaced by Blair (John Smith, Bryan Gould, Ken Livingstone come to mind) have been able to lead the party to electoral victory without succumbing to the pressures facing the Labour leadership? What degree of space for alternative policy pathways was actually available? Would the more authentically postulated social democracy hinted at as the missed normative alternative by critics (Hay, 1999) really have fared any better in these electoral and political circumstances? These are much harder questions to answer than the rather certain tone of much of the academic writing on Labour in the 1990s implies, and actually requires a greater methodological self-consciousness than has hitherto been displayed. Certainly it is wrong to consider the response to these dilemmas pursued by Labour under Blair as the only one available; this would be to make the error of determinism. But it is equally wrong to posit a pristine political-normative alternative path as the lost or abandoned trajectory which might have magically maintained Labour's true traditions without all the painful compromises and disappointments that the period in office have produced.

The Thatcherite inheritance

A particular dilemma worthy of emphasis concerns the challenge awaiting a party that has to take over the reins of power following more than a decade of government by the opposition party, and the different policy context that the latter has undoubtedly brought into being. This issue is most usefully disaggregated to examine the differential impact of Tory governance in different policy areas, but it is important to consider the most fundamental and generic set of changes which have bequeathed some traps for Labour. The machinery of the British state that Labour has inherited in 1997 looks very different from that which it gave up in 1979. In the first place, through the public sector it could exert indirect control over roughly 20 per cent of the economy at this earlier date. By 1997 the only major industry still in the public sector was the post office. In 1979 there were 505 815 civil servants; and by 1997 there were 431 400, three-quarters of whom work in Next Steps Agencies. In 1979 the state had a range of mechanisms enabling it to intervene within the production process, for instance through the 1972 and 1974 Industry Acts and the creation of the National Enterprise Boards and Sector Working Parties. These mechanisms were reinforced by a range of corporatist institutions such as the National Economic Development Council, the Price Commission and the Manpower Services Commission, all of which were designed to ensure that capital and labour had institutionalized contact with government and the potential to influence policy outcomes. The Thatcher government effectively dismantled this machinery, and even abolished the sponsorship bodies within the DTI (later to be reintroduced) which gave departments contact with key industrial sectors. The DTI itself was emasculated in the Thatcher years; its expenditure was cut dramatically and it shifted from an industrial department to one concerned with trade, the single European market and deregulation.

Consequently, Labour inherited a state that did not have the same capacity for intervention as that which existed in the 1960s and 1970s and that operated according to a very different set of internal 'logics'. To re-establish such a state would have involved tremendous costs, in both resources and political energy. Moreover, the incentives for re-establishing such a state form are low. The collapse of the Labour government in 1979 was linked closely to the failure and collapse of the corporatist, interventionist state model. Certainly a fairly profound adaptation of rhetoric and imagination to the 'realities' of the Thatcherite state is apparent, with the advocacy of public/private partnership, multiple-service deliv[er]ers, and intervention through incentives. It is significant that Labour now adopts the language of 'provider-client' rather than 'state-citizen' relationships (Freeden, 1999, 2). In different respects, there is evidence to suggest that this is not merely a shift of élite opinion. Many within the Labour party now accept that markets should be deployed to deliver a range of goods and services, in both the local and central states. Equally, a distrust of the state is no longer a provenance of the right. Increasingly thinkers on the left are suggesting that social problems need much more complex solutions than the state can provide (see, for example, Hirst, 1997). As Freeden (1999, 1) notes, in Blair's discourse:

> The state is reduced to the status of one actor among many, both internationally and domestically, appearing as pathetically subservient to global economic forces, unwilling to generate policies through its bureaucracies because it no longer believes in the power of politics as a central force for change. Societies have simply become too complex for wielders of political power and authority to manage.

This particular example of the institutional legacy of the Tory governments is important both in its own right and equally as an illustration of the space for political agency that needs to be made in our conceptualization of political challenges (Bevir and Rhodes, 1999); the latter can be handled in different ways, the range of possible responses being in part determined by wider circumstances and pressures. The exercise of agency – the aspects of the political responses of actors that could have been 'otherwise' (Giddens, 1998) – needs to be central to academic understanding of Labour, contrary as that is to the self-understanding of the key political actors involved.

Political Responses: Ideas as Resources

The third dimension highlighted in our interpretative framework is concerned with how responses are generated from the dilemmas facing political actors. Understanding of this process actually requires a context-dependent analysis as well as a consideration of the traditions of thought mobilized by these actors. In particular, we need to consider whether Labour's many responses can be understood as informed by a coherent ideological package or stem from purely pragmatic considerations, as many commentators attest. It is important to consider Labour's development in relation to established political traditions through the notion of 'path dependency'. Current praxis emerges out of the history of the party's thought and practice, as well as in relation to some of the broader traditions of the polity. Indeed these traditions ought to be seen as some of the principal resources enabling the exercise of political agency (Bevir, 1999; MacIntyre, 1981). For all the anti-traditional claims made by Labour's apologists, our suggestion is that 'New Labour' can in fact only be understood through attention to the selective mobilization of some important intellectual and ideological lineages within British politics.

For example, Labour's current approach to economic matters is particularly dependent upon the economic decisions taken with great difficulty by the party élite during the 1970s when the Labour government abandoned the commitment to full employment and other mainstays of its macro-economic thinking. The intellectual shift which generated the proto-monetarist policies adopted then – a neglected precursor to current Labour thinking – are signalled in Prime Minister James Callaghan's famous speech to the 1976 Labour Party conference:

> For too long, perhaps ever since the war, we postponed facing up to fundamental choices and fundamental changes in our society and in our economy. That is what I mean when I say we have been living on borrowed time . . . We used to think that you could spend your way out of a recession and increase employment by cutting taxes and boosting government expenditure. I tell you in all candour that that option no longer exists. (Callaghan, 1987, 425–6)

[. . .]

The latter's ambiguous relationship to social democracy is central. [. . .] According to David Marquand, Labour 'has abandoned the tradition once exemplified by such paladins of social democracy as Willy Brandt, Helmut Schmidt, Ernest Bevin and Hugh Gaitskell. It has also turned its back on Keynes and Beveridge' (Marquand, 1998). But such a judgement is in danger of leading us too far away from what remains one of the sources of current Labour values. Though the state has clearly been shrunk, in ethical terms, support for the moral purposes enshrined in the welfare state remains strong throughout the party, and the state is still confidently envisaged as the agency for intervention to tackle a range of social and economic problems [. . .] State mechanisms and subsidies have been given an important role in transport, employment, economic and social policy. As one government white paper asserts: 'There has been a presumption that the private sector is always best, and insufficient attention has been given to reward in success in the public service and to equipping it with the skills required to develop and deliver strategic policies and services in modern and effective ways' (Cm 4310, 1999, 11). The institutionalization of the minimum wage and the government's much trumpeted 'New Deal' for the un-employed are, for example, underpinned by a philosophy of public intervention which differs markedly from Thatcherite thinking. Citizens are to be helped (trained) to help themselves, and the undergirding ethic is equality of opportunity. As Gordon Brown has put it:

> We argue for equality not just because of our belief in social justice but also because of our view of what is required for economic success. The starting point is a fundamental belief in the worth of every human being. We all have an equal claim to social consider-ation by virtue of being human. And if every person is regarded as of equal worth, all

deserve to be given an equal chance in life to fulfil the potential with which they are born. (Quoted in Routledge, 1998, 320)

The quotation signals the ethical understanding of state and community underpinning these interventions which is clearly demarcated from some of the utilitarian and individualist strains found in Conservative discourse in the 1980s.

But Marquand and others are right to emphasize that we may also need to look beyond the most familiar traditions of the left to understand some of the ideological influences upon Labour. Most obviously, liberalism, or at least aspects of this dense heritage in the British context, has been proposed as a more suitable genesis for the thinking of the current government. Freeden highlights particularly Blair's attempts to lay claim to the political heritage of such figures as David Lloyd George, L. T. Hobhouse, William Beveridge and John Maynard Keynes. John Gray, on the other hand, sees in New Labour the triumph of the politics of liberal individualism – in both the economic and social domains. And Sir Samuel Brittan sees the distinguishing feature of Labour's current practice that it has 'fully accepted competitive markets, private enterprise and the profit motive as the motor of the country's economy', though he is less enamoured by what he perceives as its socially illiberal ethos (Brittan, 1999). Several critics have noted the 'Gladstonian' aspects of the constitutional reform agenda unveiled by the government and the proclamation of an ethical foreign policy.

It is equally valid to consider the impact of aspects of conservative thinking, in part through the immediate influence of Thatcherite conservatism. Clearly there are also one-nation strains in New Labour's attempt to represent Britain as an imaginary political community in which distinctions of class and culture matter less than ever before, and in the appeal to the nation to rally together beyond sectional divisions. Some commentators have been ready to interpret the apparently 'authoritarian' and socially conservative register struck by Labour ministers, and notably the Home Secretary, Jack Straw, on a range of issues as evidence of the continued hegemony of conservative discourse.

In addition, some of these aspects of Labour's public talk, and occasionally its behaviour, may well make sense in relation to aspects of the intellectual pedigree of the left and Labour's governmental history. Thus Labour figures have frequently voiced socially conservative themes, as well as on occasions more liberal, cosmopolitan values. Wilson and Callaghan were often opposed to what they termed the permissive society and presented Labour as the guardian of 'traditional' moral values. Callaghan was a socially conservative Home Secretary and as Prime Minister attempted to shift education back to educational basics away from fashionable 'liberal' thinking. [...] Much of Labour's current familial conservatism can be detected further back in the party's history. Moreover, the juxtaposition of a model of community with emphasis upon individual responsibilities as a supplement to rights can be seen as representing a revival of earlier forms of socialist communitarianism, and ethical socialism. New Labour's response to certain contemporary dilemmas can be usefully read in terms of the redeployment of strands of ethical socialist thought. Certainly there are many clues in the public discourse and writing of leading New Labour figures (via the theologian John MacMurray) that the ethical socialist tradition has been mobilized in fairly conscious ways by Labour. Whilst it may be more reassuring for those disappointed by the record of Labour in office to place blame on the capitulation to alien ideologies, a less comfortable reading may actually force us to face those elements of its agenda that have their origins in some aspects of the left's own ideological heritage. Equally, the formation of the Labour party cannot be understood without reference to liberal thought and politics. Socialist and especially social democratic ideology in Britain has enjoyed a symbiotic and mutually sustaining relationship with liberal thought, as evidenced through figures like John Stuart Mill who constituted important bridgeheads between these different traditions but also in terms of the political ambitions of early Labour politicians. To discover liberal motifs, particularly from the collectivist and progressivist 'churches' of the early century, in the words and thought of Labour figures and factions, even on the left of the spectrum, should no longer be the occasion for surprise. Some Labour figures are now prepared to give a public voice to this common heritage (Freeden, 1999).

Conclusions

[...]
[...] Labour's current trajectory cannot be reduced to an echo of Thatcherism, as if the prior histories of the party were wiped clean in 1979. Not only does such an argument underplay the complexity of Labour's transformation but it simultaneously leads to a misreading of the party's political and ideological centre-of-gravity. A roughly coherent political framework, hewn from an eclectic mix of traditions, has been developed under Blair's leadership of the party and it amounts to something other than Thatcherism Mark II. Crucial elements of it are the notion that public expenditure should be increased, though within the framework of 'value-for-money' and as the public sector itself is modernized, as well as a commitment to an active state designed to equip the nation for the 'new economic paradigm' (commonly labelled the information economy) within which it is suggested that we now live. Equally Blair and his allies have sought, in ideological terms, to transcend some of the antinomies of recent political discourse (markets vs the state, or justice vs liberty) though frequently one detects the prevalence of one ideological tradition over others in different domains – conservatism in social policy, liberalism (of a nineteenth-century vintage) in terms of the international economy, as well as a distinctly Whiggish attitude towards the modernization of some of the constitutional and institutional features of the state. For all these different emphases, Blair and his allies feel confident that Britain now offers a 'model' of sorts, outside the social market model favoured by some continental social democrats. Though it is a long way from social democracy as we have known it, and looks a lot like the politics of Christian Democracy practised in other European party systems, this model is clearly not neo-liberal in any straightforward sense.

REFERENCES

Bale, T. (1997) 'Sacred Cows and Common Sense: the Symbolic Statecraft and Political Welfare of the Labour Government' (unpublished Ph.D. thesis, University of Sheffield).
Bevir, M. (1999) *The Logic of the History of Ideas* (Cambridge: Cambridge University Press).

Bevir, M. and Rhodes, R. A. W. (1999) 'Studying British Government: Reconstructing the Research Agenda', *British Journal of Politics and International Relations*, Vol. 1, pp. 215–39.

Blair, T. (1996) *New Britain: My Vision of a Young Country* (London: Fourth Estate).

Brittan, S. (1999) 'A Wrong Turning on the Third Way?' *New Statesman*, 1 January.

Callaghan, J. (1987) *Time and Chance* (London: Collins).

Castells, M. (1996) *The Rise of the Network Society* (Oxford: Blackwell).

Cm 4310 (1999) *Modernising Government* (London: HMSO).

Coates, D. (1980) *Labour in Power? A Study of the Labour Government 1974–1979* (London: Longman).

Crewe, I. (1983) 'How Labour Was Trounced All Round', *The Guardian*, 14 June.

Freeden, M. (1999) 'True Blood or False Genealogy: New Labour and British Social Democratic Thought', *Political Quarterly*, Vol. 70, pp. 1–16.

Giddens, A. (1998) *The Third Way: The Renewal of Social Democracy* (Cambridge: Polity).

Gould, P. (1998) *The Unfinished Revolution: How the Modernisers Saved the Labour Party* (London: Little, Brown).

Grant, W. and Marsh, D. (1977) *The CBI* (London: Hodder & Stoughton).

Hay, C. (1999) *The Political Economy of New Labour: Labouring under False Pretences?* (Manchester: Manchester University Press).

Hirst, P. (1997) *From Statism to Pluralism, Democracy, Civil Society and Global Politics* (London: UCL Press).

Hobsbawm, E. (1998) 'The Death of Neo-Liberalism' in: *Marxism Today Special Issue* (London: Marxism Today).

Lindblom, C. E. (1977) *Politics and Markets* (New York: Basic Books).

MacIntyre, A. (1981) *After Virtue: A Study in Moral Theory* (London: Duckworth).

Marquand, D. (1998) 'The Blair Paradox', *Prospect*, May, pp. 19–24.

Poulantzas, N. (1976) *State, Power, Socialism* (London: Verso).

Przeworski, A. (1985) *Capitalism and Social Democracy* (Cambridge: Cambridge University Press).

Routledge, P. (1998) *Gordon Brown: A Biography* (London: Simon and Schuster).

Sanders, D. (1996) 'Economic Performance, Management Competence, and the Outcome of the Next General Election', *Political Studies*, Vol. 44, pp. 203–31.

Sassoon, D. (1997) *Looking Left: Socialism after the Cold War* (London: I. B. Tauris).

Stones, R. (1990) 'Government–Finance Relations in Britain 1964–7', *Economy and Society*, Vol. 19, pp. 32–55.

Whiteley, P. (1983) *The Labour Party in Crisis* (London: Methuen) (1997).

Wickham-Jones, M. (1996) *Economic Strategy and the Labour Party: Politics and Policy-making, 1970–83* (London: Macmillan).

Wilson, H. (1974) *The Labour Government, 1964–70* (London: Weidenfeld & Nicolson).

8

The Blair Paradox

David Marquand

One year after new Labour's landslide victory, the purpose, nature and significance of the famous Blair project are as mysterious as they were on that magic May morning when the last government was sent packing. We know what the new regime is not; we don't yet know what it is. Patently, it is not socialist. It is not even social democratic or social liberal. It has abandoned the tradition once exemplified by such paladins of social democracy as Willy Brandt, Helmut Schmidt, Ernest Bevin and Hugh Gaitskell. It has also turned its back on Keynes and Beveridge. Its contempt for the French socialists is palpable; it believes it has nothing to learn from the German SDP and it seems more at home with Clinton's suburbanised New Democrats than with any left-of-centre European party.

More significantly still, it is manifestly unshocked by the huge and growing disparities of income engendered by the late 20th century capitalist renaissance. Like the Thatcher governments before it, New Labour espouses a version of the entrepreneurial ideal of the early 19th century. It disdains traditional elites and glorifies self-made meritocrats, but it sees no reason why successful meritocrats should not enjoy the full fruits of their success: it is for widening opportunity, not for redistributing reward. By the same token, it has no wish to undo the relentless hollowing out of the public domain or to halt the increasing casualisation of labour – white collar as well as blue collar – that marked the Thatcher and Major years. The notion that public goods should be provided by public authorities, animated by an ethic of public service to which market norms are alien, appears to be as strange to it as to its predecessors. It is more tender to the employers than to the trade unions, more anxious to court Rupert Murdoch than the Guardian, and more wary of the European social model than of the contemporary American mixture of hyper-individualism and social authoritarianism.

Yet the widely held notion that New Labour stands for the continuation of Thatcherism by other means is hopelessly wide of the mark. There are at least four crucial differences between the new regime and the old. Thatcherism was exclusionary; New Labour is inclusionary. Margaret Thatcher was a warrior; Tony Blair is a healer. Where she divided, he unites. Where she spoke of "enemies within," he speaks of "the people." The Thatcherites saw themselves as a beleaguered minority, surrounded by insidious, relentless and powerful enemies. There were always new battles to fight, new obstacles to uproot, new heresies to stamp out. New Labour, with the same, not particularly impressive, proportion of the popular vote behind it, speaks and acts as though it embodies a national consensus – a consensus of the well-intentioned, embracing rich and poor, young and old, suburbs and inner cities, black and white, hunters and animal rights campaigners, successful and unsuccessful. In place of the Thatcherite cold shower, it offers a warm bath, administered by a hegemonic people's party appealing equally to every part of the nation. This may have nothing in common with social democracy, but it is the nearest thing to christian democracy that modern British politics have known. And christian democracy is light years away from Thatcherism.

The second difference is more complicated. Like its predecessor, the new regime is for individual achievement, not collective action. But it has a radically different conception of the forces that empower achievers. For the Thatcherites, the vehicle of mobility was the undistorted market. Let market forces rip, they thought, and talent would automatically command its market price. The only role for the state was to eliminate the obstacles to the free play of market forces – including, of course, the obstacles presented by traditional elites. For New Labour, talent has to be nurtured before it arrives at the marketplace; and state intervention has to nurture it. Investment in human capital is the key, both to individual opportunity and to national competitiveness; only the state can ensure that the investment is adequate and fairly distributed. A meritocratic society is one in which the state takes action to raise the level of the talents – particularly the talents of the disadvantaged – which the market proceeds to reward. First, the state levels the playing field. Only then does the game commence.

The social vision is closer to Thatcherism than to any other tendency in postwar British history. Individuals compete. There are winners and losers. Having won in fair competition, the winners are entitled to their gains; indeed, they occupy the most honoured places in the social pantheon. As for the losers, their duty is to lick their wounds and return as soon as possible to the fray: New Labour has no patience with whingers or shirkers. But the political vision is far from Thatcherite. Underpinning the individualistic, mobile, competitive society is a dirigiste workfare state which would have warmed the cockles of Beatrice Webb's heart.

That leads on to a third, more paradoxical, difference. Like the Thatcher and Major governments, the Blair government looks across the Atlantic for inspiration, not across the Channel. Its rhetoric is American; the intellectual influences which have shaped its project are American; its political style is American. More important still, it shares the prevailing American view of the global economy, and of the relationships between states and markets within the global economy. Like the New Democrats, New Labour takes globalisation as a given and seeks to run with what it believes to be the grain of the global marketplace. That is why it is suspicious of the European social model, why it shares its predecessor's commitment to flexible labour markets and low social costs and why it sees the French socialists and German social democrats as suspect deviationists rather than as fraternal exemplars.

Unlike the Thatcherites, however, it also takes the European Union as a given, and seeks to run with the grain of European integration – including monetary integration. The paradox is that, as the Thatcherites correctly spotted, part of the purpose of the EU is to Europeanise a solidaristic model of the society and economy, drawn partly from the continental social democratic tradition and partly from the (also continental) tradition of catholic social thought. By the same token, part of the purpose of monetary union is to defend that model against the pressures of the global marketplace, to create a supranational space in which to protect the European social market from creeping Americanisation. New Labour, in short, is facing both ways. It is for Americanisation. Although it has not said so in so many words, it is also for the supranational space. How it will behave if and when it enters the space remains a mystery.

The fourth difference is more paradoxical still. The central theme of the Thatcher revolution lay in a combination of market freedom and state power – with the second as the necessary condition of the first. In theory the Thatcherites were for a minimal state. In practice, they assumed that centralisation was the only possible vehicle for marketisation; that if they were to hobble or crush the manifold institutional and cultural obstacles to their free-market utopia, they would have to make the maximum possible use of the powers which the ancient British doctrine of absolute and inalienable parliamentary sovereignty confers on the government of the day. This, of course, was the great paradox of Thatcherism. The new wine of the free market was to be poured from the old bottles of the British ancien regime. An individualistic economy was to go hand in hand with an authoritarian polity. But the paradox was inescapable. In ten years, the Thatcher governments transformed the political economy and the public culture. The new, low-tax, business-friendly, union-spurning, Murdoch-courting Labour party is a tribute to that transformation. In a more pluralistic polity, with the checks and balances that most modern democracies take for granted, nothing of the sort would have been possible.

New Labour, by contrast, has embarked on the most far-reaching programme of constitutional reform attempted in this country this century. Ironically, the Thatcherites deserve part of the credit. Old Labour was as committed to the doctrines and practices of Westminster absolutism as were the Conservatives. But in the Thatcher years, when Labour found itself on the receiving end of a ferocious centralism, far exceeding anything it had ever attempted itself, it underwent a deathbed conversion. Slowly at first, but with mounting enthusiasm as time went on, it embraced most of the constitutional agenda originally put forward by the SDP–Liberal Alliance, and later given a more radical twist by Charter 88. And the point of that agenda is to dismantle the ancien regime: to create institutional and legal checks and balances which will make it impossible for future governments to impose their will on the society and economy in the way that the Thatcher governments did.

To be sure, New Labour's constitutional commitments contrast sharply with its approach to governance. Its workfare state comes straight out of the old Fabian stable of top-down social engineering. It rests on the premise that government at the centre not only can, but should remake society to fit an a priori grand design. To succeed, the policies that emanate from it will have to be pushed through with as much centralist zeal as the Thatcherites displayed 15 years ago. Beneath the new regime's inclusive style and hegemonic ambitions it is not difficult to detect a propensity for arm twisting and heresy hunting. Alastair Campbell makes Bernard Ingham look, in retrospect, like a relaxed and cuddly champion of journalistic diversity. The Prussian discipline which Blair and his associates have imposed on the parliamentary Labour party exceeds anything attempted by the Conservatives. Blair himself is as adept in the exercise of power as Thatcher was, as convinced that he has a direct line to the hearts of the British people and as determined to ensure that the channels of communication between the people and their elective dictator are not clogged up by ambitious cabinet colleagues or recalcitrant intermediate institutions.

But that merely underlines the paradox in New Labour's constitutional programme. [...] The combination of devolution for Scotland, Wales and Northern Ireland, elected mayors, domestication of the European Convention on Human Rights, freedom of information, House of Lords reform and a referendum on proportional representation points the way towards a profound transformation of the British state. More important still, the process of constitutional change will almost certainly generate a dynamic of its own, carrying the transformation further than its authors intended or expected.

[...]

The implications of all this are startling. The Blairites' right hand seems not to know – dares not find out – what its left hand is doing. The Thatcher paradox – liberal economics combined with Tory politics – has been followed by the Blair paradox: economic continuity combined with political discontinuity. That second paradox, I believe, holds the key to the mysteries that still envelop the new regime. Its origins lie in the confusions and contradictions of the Thatcher years. In the name of economic liberalism, the Thatcher governments made war on traditional institutions and traditional elites. The victims of the Thatcher blitzkrieg included, not only such bastions of traditional Labourism as trade unions and local authorities, but the elite universities, the BBC, the noblesse oblige Tory grandees, the bench of bishops, the higher ranks of the civil service – all the interlocking networks that made up the old establishment. But, as I have pointed out, the war was waged by and through the traditional, incorrigibly elitist institutions of the central state. And in waging it, those same institutions undermined the conditions for their own existence. The combination of free-market wine and ancien regime bottles was unsustainable. The bottles blew up.

It is not difficult to see why. The state-imposed marketisation of the Thatcherites was a contradiction in terms. As Tory traditionalists have always known, the strong state of the ancien regime drew its strength from memories and rituals rooted in history and embedded in a dense network of institutions. The values that nurtured it were hierarchical, not popular; the authority on which it relied was sacral, not secular. But, as Marx saw long ago, free-market capitalism is quintessentially populist and inherently subversive of traditions and rituals. It scorns history, hollows out institutions and undermines hierarchies: in the marketplace the customer is king and Jack's pound is as good as his master's. And so the capitalist renaissance which the Thatcherites helped to instigate destroyed the moral foundations of the institutions through which they had done so – and this made it increasingly difficult for them to mobilise consent for the remains of their project.

The Blair government is the legatee of this process of institutional and cultural evisceration. By May 1997, the ancien regime was in disarray. The fundamental doctrine of absolute parliamentary sovereignty was under threat – from Brussels, from Strasbourg, from Luxembourg, from uppity judges at home. The only slightly less fundamental doctrine of ministerial responsibility had been effectively nullified, as ministers made it possible for themselves to pass the buck for unpopular decisions to unaccountable agencies at arm's length from Whitehall. So, too, had the accompanying assumption, dating from the Northcote–Trevelyan reforms of the 19th century, that responsible ministers were to be sustained by a disinterested, professional civil service without ideological affiliations. The complex understandings and practices that had shaped the relationship between central and local government had been trampled on. Public support for the system was waning steadily as accusations of sleaze in high places reached fever pitch.

On a deeper level, the essentially imperial structure of status, authority and consent which had carried the ancien regime through two world wars, the coming of democracy and the installation of the welfare state had crumbled along with the empire itself. An Eton education, even a First in Greats, had become something to apologise for. Monarchy-baiting had become one of the favourite sports of an awesomely vulgar tabloid press. Julian Critchley's garagistes had taken over the Tory party; expensively educated mandarins ranked lower in the status hierarchy than uncouth utility chiefs; Barings was brought down by a thrusting young Cockney without a university degree. Britain had at last experienced the long-awaited, long-delayed bourgeois revolution. It had become a land fit for Richard Branson.

Politically and socially, there was no going back. Embourgeoisement was irreversible; and the new bourgeois Britain could be governed successfully only through a bourgeois state. The ancien regime could not be put together again. The only way to stem the drain of legitimacy which had helped to undo the Thatcherites was to reconstruct the state on lines appropriate to a modest, post-imperial, late 20th century European country of the second rank. This is what Blair and his colleagues are now doing: this is what they have to do if they are to root the state which they aspire to govern in popular consent. I am not sure that they have grasped the inner meaning of their constitutional agenda. Before the election, they often gave the impression that they saw it only as a sop for disaffected left-wing intellectuals. But their intentions scarcely matter. What matters is that the gap between the society and the state can be closed in no other way. Like the Thatcher paradox before it, the Blair paradox is inherent in the historical conjuncture that brought the government to power.

[. . .]

9

The Great Moving Nowhere Show

Stuart Hall

What is the political character of the Blair regime? Is New Labour a radically new response to the core political issues of our time? Is its perspective as broad in sweep, modern in outlook and coherent as Thatcherism's neo-liberal project, only different – because it is breaking decisively with the legacy and logic of the Thatcher years? Or is it a series of pragmatic adjustments and adaptive moves to essentially Thatcherite terrain? Since taking office, New Labour has certainly been hyperactive, setting policy reviews in place here, legislating and innovating there. A careful audit of the achievements and failures of these early years remains to be made. But that is for a different occasion. Here, we want to stay with 'the big picture'. Where is New Labour really going? Does Mr Blair have a political project?

Thatcherism, from which Mr Blair has learned so much, certainly did have a project. Its aim was to transform the political landscape, irrevocably: to make us think in and speak its language as if there were no other. It had a strategy – an idea of where it wanted to get to and how to get there. Mrs Thatcher had no fondness for intellectuals: the word 'ideas' did not trip lightly off her tongue. Nevertheless, everything she did was animated by a social 'philosophy'. From a reductive reading of Adam Smith, she learned to see individuals as exclusively economic agents. From Hayek, she learned that the social good is impossible to define and that to try to harness markets to social objectives led down a one-way slippery slope to the nanny state, misguided social engineering, welfare dependence and moral degeneration – 'There is No Such Thing As Society'. From the Monetarists she learned market fundamentalism: markets are 'good' and work mysteriously to the benefit of all; they are self-instituting and self-regulating entities; market rationality is the only valid mode of social calculation, 'market forces must prevail!'

What is more, she armed herself with a decisive analysis of the points of historical change which had created the opening to Thatcherism. But she did not, like some versions of the 'Third Way', simply project the sociological trends on to the political screen. She never supposed Thatcherite subjects were already out there, fully formed, requiring only to be focus-grouped into position. Instead, she set out to produce new political subjects – Entrepreneurial Man – out of the mix of altruism and competitiveness of which ordinary mortals are composed. Above all she knew that, to achieve radical change, politics must be conducted like a war of position between adversaries. She clearly identified her enemies, remorselessly dividing the political field: Wets v. Drys, Us v. Them, those who are 'with us' v. 'the enemy within'.

[…]

[…] It was clear from the outset that Mr Blair saw himself in the Thatcherite mould and he has worked hard to model himself on her style of leadership. And with some success! Recent polls suggest the electorate is impressed with 'what they regard as the strong Thatcherite style', though they also seem unsure whether this is more than 'better gloss, more PR and spin' and, more worryingly, they doubt that New Labour 'will make a real difference and force a clean policy break with the Tory years' (*Guardian*, September 28 1998).

Mr Blair has also modelled his ambitions to make everything in Britain 'New' on Thatcherism's project of national self-renewal. Consequently, these days, no New Labour spokesperson opens his/her mouth, nor journalist reports the event, without reference to 'the Blair project'. It is New Labour, not the intellectuals, who put this 'meta-political' question on the agenda. It is Blair who talks of New Labour in apocalyptic terms – 'one of the great, radical, reforming governments of our history', 'to be nothing less than the model twenty-first century nation, a beacon to the world', 'becoming the natural party of government'. ('Natural parties of government' are those whose ideas lead on all fronts, carrying authority in every domain of life; whose philosophy of change has become the common sense of the age. In the old days we used to call them 'hegemonic'.) Mr Blair is definitely into 'the vision thing'.

New Labour's latest bid to give 'this vision thing' historic credibility and so to capture and define 'the big picture' is the 'Third Way'. This comes in several shapes and sizes. There is the intellectual's version of the 'Third Way' offered by Anthony Giddens, Mr Blair's most influential intellectual, which sketches out a number of significantly novel sociological shifts which seem to have major political consequences. Many of these one would be happy to agree with or to debate further. After all, economic globalisation is a reality and has transformed the space of operations and the 'reach' of nation states and national economies. There is a new individualism abroad, due to the growing social complexity and diversity of modern life, which has undermined much of the old collectivism and the political programmes it underpinned. Many problems do present new challenges or assume new forms not well covered by the old political ideologies. We do need to broker a new relationship between markets and the public good, the individual and the community. These sociological shifts are part of the great historical rupture – the onset of late-late-modernity – which Thatcherism first mastered politically but certainly did not originate or set in motion. This is where Marxism Today's 'New Times' analysis and its call for the reinvention of the left began, all those years ago. So much is indeed shared territory.

But when we move from the intellectual to New Labour's more political and strategic version of the 'Third Way', we are less on the terrain of political strategy and more, as Francis Wheen recently observed, in some 'vacant space between the Fourth Dimension and the Second Coming'. The 'Third Way' has been hyped as 'a new kind of politics'. Its central claim is the discovery of a mysterious middle course on every question between all the existing extremes. However, the closer one examines this via media, the more it looks, not like a way through the problems, but a soft-headed way around them. It speaks with forked, or at the very least garbled, tongue. It is advanced as a New International Model to which centre-left governments around the world are even now rallying. However, when it is not rapturously received, it suddenly becomes, not 'a Model', just a 'work in progress'. Can it be both heroic and tentative? It cannot make up its mind whether its aim is to capture 'the radical centre' or to modernise 'the centre-left' (and should not therefore be surprised to find young voters placing its repositioning as clearly 'centre-right'!). It claims to draw from the repertoires of both the New Right and Social Democracy – but also to have transcended them – to be 'beyond Right and Left'. These shifting formulations are not quite what one would call a project with a clear political profile.

In so far as one can make out what it is claiming, does it offer a correct strategic perspective? The fact – of which the 'Third Way' makes a great deal – that many of the traditional solutions of the left seem historically exhausted, that its programme needed to be radically overhauled and that there are new problems which outrun its analytic framework, does not mean that its principles have nothing to offer to the task of political renewal on the left. Welfare reform is only one of many areas where there is a continuing debate between two clearly competing models, drawing on if not identical with, the two great traditions that have governed political life: the left-of-centre version, looking for new forms in which to promote social solidarity, interdependence and collective social provision against market inequality and instability; and the neo-liberal, promoting low taxes, a competitive view of human nature, market provision and individualism. Can the 'tough decisions' on welfare which New Labour have been 'taking' for 18 months really be 'beyond Left and Right'? Or is that a smoke-screen thrown up to evade the really hard questions of political principle which remain deeply unresolved?

One of the core reasons for the 'Third Way''s semantic inexactitude – measured by the promiscuous proliferation of such troubling adverbs as 'between', 'above' and 'beyond' – is its efforts to be all-inclusive. It has no enemies. Everyone can belong. The 'Third Way' speaks as if there are no longer any conflicting interests which cannot be reconciled. It therefore envisages a 'politics without adversaries'. This suggests that, by some miracle of transcendence, the interests represented by, say, the ban on tobacco advertising and 'Formula One', the private car lobby and John Prescott's White Paper, an ethical foreign policy and the sale of arms to Indonesia, media diversity and the concentrated drive-to-global-power of Rupert Murdoch's media empire have been effortlessly 'harmonised' on a Higher Plane, above politics. Whereas, it needs to be clearly said that a project to transform and modernise society in a radical direction, which does not disturb any existing interests and has no enemies, is not a serious political enterprise.

The 'Third Way' is hot on the responsibilities of individuals, but those of business are passed over with a slippery evasiveness. 'Companies,' Tony Blair argues in his Fabian pamphlet *The Third Way*, 'will devise ways to share with their staff the wealth their know-how creates.' Will they? The 'Third Way' does observe accelerating social inequality but refuses to acknowledge that there might be structural interests preventing our achieving a more equitable distribution of wealth and life-chances.

[...] The 'Third Way''s discourse [...] is disconcertingly devoid of any sustained reference to power.

[...]

It therefore seems most unlikely that the shifting indecisions and ambiguous formulations of the 'Third Way' offer us clear guidelines for assessing the underlying thrust of the Blair political project. For an answer to our original question, we will need to look at the Blair performance overall, sifting the strong tendencies from the ebb and flow of everyday governance, trying to disinter from its practice its underlying political logic, philosophy and strategic direction.

In the global context, New Labour has brought a sweeping interpretation of globalisation, which it regards as the single most important factor which has transformed our world, setting an impassable threshold between New Labour and Old, now and everything that went before. This is crucial because, in our view, it is its commitment to a certain definition of globalisation which provides the outer horizon as well as the dubious legitimacy to Mr Blair's whole political project.

New Labour understands globalisation in very simplistic terms – as a single, uncontradictory, uni-directional phenomenon, exhibiting the same features and producing the same inevitable outcomes everywhere. Despite Giddens's strictures, New Labour does deal with globalisation as if it is a self-regulating and implacable Force of Nature. It treats the global economy as being, in effect, like the weather. In his speech to the Labour Party conference, Mr Blair portrayed the global economy as moving so fast, its financial flows so gigantic and so speedy, the pace at which it has plunged a third of the world economy into crisis so rapid, that its operations are now effectively beyond the control of nation states and probably of regional and international agencies as well. He calls this, with a weary finality, 'the way of the world'. His response is to 'manage change'. But it seems that what he really means is that we must 'manage ourselves to adapt to changes which we cannot otherwise control' – a similar sounding but substantively very different kettle of fish.

[...]

New Labour appears to have been seduced by the neo-liberal gospel that 'the global market' is an automatic and self-instituting principle, requiring no particular social, cultural, political or institutional framework. It can be 'applied' under any conditions, anywhere. New Labour therefore seems as bewildered as every neo-liberal hot-gospeller that Japanese bankers just don't actually behave like Wall Street bankers, and that if you dump 'the market' into a state-socialist society like Russia without transforming its political institutions or its culture – a much slower and more complex operation – it is likely to produce, not Adam Smith's natural barterers and truckers, but a capitalist mafia. [...]

Since globalisation is a fact of life to which There Is No Alternative, and national governments cannot hope to regulate or impose any order on its processes or effects, New Labour has accordingly largely withdrawn from the active management of the economy ('In the long run, Keynes is dead!'). What it has done, instead, is to set about vigorously adapting society to the global economy's needs, tutoring its citizens to be self-sufficient and self-reliant in order to compete more successfully in the global marketplace. The framing strategy of New Labour's economic repertoire remains essentially the neo-liberal one: the deregulation of markets, the wholesale refashioning of the public sector by the New Managerialism, the continued privatisation of public assets, low taxation, breaking the 'inhibitions' to market flexibility, institutionalising the culture of private provision and personal risk, and privileging in its moral discourse the values of self-sufficiency, competitiveness and entrepreneurial dynamism.

[...]

On the domestic front, the policy repertoire seems at first sight more diverse, but has tended to follow the same tendential groove. The main emphasis has been thrown on to the supply side of the equation. There have been many commendable social-democratic interventions. But its key watchwords – 'Education and Training, Training and Education' – are driven, in the last analysis, less by the commitment to opportunities for all in a more egalitarian society, and more in terms of supplying flexibility to the labour market and re-educating people to 'get on their bikes' when their jobs disappear as a result of some unpredictable glitch in the global market. New Labour does not and cannot have much of an industrial economic policy. But it can and does expend enormous moral energy seeking to change 'the culture' and produce new kinds of subjects, kitted out and defended against the cold winds that blow in from the global marketplace.

To this source also we must trace the remoralisation of the work ethic, and the restoration of that discredited and obscene Victorian utilitarian distinction between 'the deserving' and 'the undeserving' poor. The New Deal subsidises training and Mr Blunkett attacks class sizes and expands nursery places for lone parents willing to seek employment – very commendable, and about time too. New Labour will not, however, intervene to ensure that there are jobs, though its entire welfare reforms are riveted to work and paid employment. Since it must depend on the private sector to provide them, it can only morally exhort. Hence the paradox of Jack Straw holding parents exclusively responsible for their children's misdemeanours while Welfare-to-Work insists that anyone who can move and wants to draw a benefit must leave their children, get up off their sick beds, overcome their disability, come back out of retirement and work. Not since the workhouse has labour been so fervently and single-mindedly valorised.

[...]

Mr Blair represents his welfare reforms as a continuation of the spirit of Beveridge, but this is simply not the case. For Beveridge understood that welfare systems reflect and have profound effects on the wider social framework. He knew that the principle of 'social insurance' was not only efficient but a way of underwriting citizenship; that 'universalism', despite its costs, was essential to binding the richer sections of society into collective forms of welfare. He anticipated Galbraith's argument that the whole system would be in danger as soon as the rich could willingly exclude themselves from collective provision by buying themselves out. Why should they go on paying for a service they had ceased to use? This potential 'revolt of the elites' is, of course, the critical political issue in welfare reform. The establishment of a two-tiered system, with the richer sectors buying themselves into private provision, is what helps to fix in stone the political threshold against redistribution. It destroys the public interest in favour of private solutions dictated by wealth inequalities and must drive what is then left in the residual 'public' sector to the bottom, perpetually in crisis and starved of investment, and propel those who are left out to the margins.

This 'law' is already manifest in education – though New Labour systematically refuses to confront it. Buying the children out of public education and into the selective private system has become a habitual middle-class pastime, which New Labour's own leaders have indulged as lightheartedly as any other ordinary, unreflective, Thatcherite, possessive individual. 'Targeting', 'selectivity', and 'means testing', which Mr Blair has surreptitiously slid into place as his great 'principles of reform', are destined, as surely as night follows day, to deepen already existing inequalities, to increase marginalisation and social exclusion, to divide society into two unbridgeable tiers and further fragment social integration and reciprocity. [...]

It is deeply characteristic of the whole style of the Blair project that Great Debates are announced which do not actually take place. Instead of a clear and open laying-out of the alternatives, we have a massive public relations and spinning exercise, and policy forums to speak over the heads of the much-abused 'experts and critics', direct to selectively chosen members of the Great British Public. There may be an open invitation to participate, to join the consultation. But this openness is effect-ively closed by Mr Blair's own already-settled conviction that he is Right – what Hugo Young called 'his unfreighted innocence, wide-eyed rationality and untroubled self-belief'. When in difficulties, the party faithful – about whom he is a less than devoted admirer – are summoned to hear the message, not to state their views. The Labour Party, as an organisation within which these profound matters of strategy may gain, through debate, some broader resonance in terms of the everyday lives and experiences of ordinary folks, and genuinely be modified or win consent, has been ruthlessly emasculated. A terrifying and obsequious uniformity of view has settled over the political scene, compounded by a powerful centralisation of political authority, with twenty-something Young Turks beaming out ill-will from ministerial back-rooms, the whole caboodle under surveillance from Millbank and cemented in place by a low-flying authoritarianism.

The Labour benches have, with a few honourable exceptions, been the most bedazzled by the hope of preferment, the most obsequious of all. Critics, welcomed at the front door, are systematically discredited through innuendo and spin-doctored at the back door as being trapped in a time warp, if not actually barking mad. Anyone who does not pass the loyalty test is labelled with the ritual hate-word, 'intellectual', gathered into one indiscriminate heap – those who called for the reinvention of the Left while Mr Blair was still, metaphorically, in his political cradle lumped in with Trotskyist wreckers – and the whole shooting-match branded as 'Old Labour'. 'Bring me the head of Roy Hattersley!'

10

Corporate Populism and Partyless Democracy

Anthony Barnett

[…]

Corporate populism is first of all corporate, in the sense that it is modelled on the behaviour of corporations. Blair's is a committed administration which is determined to make its mark. In this it bears comparison with the Attlee government of 1945 to 1950 rather than the hapless Wilson and Callaghan administrations of the sixties and seventies. There is more than an incidental point of resemblance here. Attlee was obsessed with businesslike efficiency and the delivery of clear decisions, as Amy Baker's new study shows.[1] His way with a series of nationalizations, including even the formation of the National Health Service, could be compared to Blair's approach to constitutional reform. Some initiatives were excellent; others less well-conceived. Each industry was nationalized separately and was run by familiar management in top-down fashion. No joining-up was permitted between, for example, the new electricity, gas and coal utilities. There was no element of popular democratization to give legitimacy to the new public corporations. They were justified as a piecemeal set of separate modernizations. The result was a complex of bureaucracies against which the Conservatives were eventually able to turn public prejudice.

Today, Downing Street is also obsessed with businesslike decision-making. Only, the model of business has changed. Attlee was dissatisfied with the way Churchill conducted affairs of state. Yet if the private sector had presided over mass unemployment and low investment in the thirties, the state had emerged from the test of war intact, with a reputation for delivery. Thus while Attlee wanted decisions to be taken much more efficiently, he could regard British government and its mandarin culture as the natural home of such efficiency.

New Labour did not inherit this tradition. On the contrary, by the end of the Thatcher years, it was companies that were seen as successful agents of modernization and job creation, while government was held to be wasteful and inert, driven by procedures not outcomes. New Labour looked to modern business management to teach it how to deliver, Blair comparing himself to a chief executive. By setting targets, policing delivery, insisting on outcomes, advocating joined-up administration, Ministers project themselves as a businesslike team. Theirs is not a pluralist vision of the state. At the same time they have to 'sell' or market their achievements. They understand that the way a policy is projected is an essential part of the policy, much in the way that the design of a consumer durable is today part of the product itself – no one creating software would treat its appearance as a neutral function separate from its performance. Hence New Labour's determination to end the civil service tradition of issuing non-partisan press releases about new policy initiatives. Finally, just as no major business restricts its market in advance to a minority, but instead strives for universal popularity and brand loyalty, so New Labour seeks to sell its product to everyone.

Readers can judge for themselves whether the concept of corporate populism tallies as a description of the inner workings and attitudes of the Blair administration. He and his team regard running Britain as like being in charge of a major media corporation. In my view this is a concept that helps to explain:

- The positive motivation of its members, their 'can do' activism, legislative ambition, concern for application of policy on the ground, and embrace of opportunity and risk.
- Their wish for universal, focus-group-monitored, appeal; in Albert Hirschman's terms they strive for brand loyalty while pre-empting exit and voice.
- Their inability to comprehend the strength of 'un-businesslike', 'old-fashioned' popular sentiments, such as Welshness, Englishness or support for Ken Livingstone.
- Their dismissive yet erratic attitude towards traditional, non-market institutions such as the British constitution.
- Their attachment to the media-entertainment complex as the key channel for communications strategies, and consequent by-passing of the political party as an antiquated debating machine.
- Their embrace of wealth-creators and big, especially international business, combined with willingness to encourage initiatives that short-circuit ineffective local government on the ground – experiments that out-source services, prevent waste and help people into work and off welfare.
- Their commitment to a unified civil service, flying in the face of the logic of devolution.
- Their resolute centralism and commitment to a single, strategic intelligence in possession of the 'big picture', controlling the image, ensuring consistency.
- Finally, the concept explains why – for all the tactical skill and market research brought to it – the project will go wrong, because a country is not like a company and cannot be run as if it were.

Blair and Co. have been seduced by the absolute sovereignty offered them by the British state. [...] They have yet to understand that the kind of central power it represents is intrinsically outdated. [...]

NOTE

1 Amy Baker, *Prime Ministers and The Rule Book*, London 2000.

Part II

Prudent for a Purpose? New Labour's Economic Policy

Whatever the long-term judgements, it is beyond doubt that New Labour has restored the party's reputation for economic competence. In political terms, not only did this lay the foundations for the general election victory of 1997, it also ensured Labour's second term. Although Gordon Brown has so far proved himself the prudent 'Iron Chancellor', it is easy to forget just how difficult was Labour's journey back to respectability. A crucial element in understanding why it was that Labour succeeded in marginalizing the Conservatives can be found in its approach to business. Labour assiduously courted big business from the moment Blair became leader. The aim was to prove that the party had shed its image of socialism and 'tax and spend'. In its place was a new, low-taxation approach that promised not to interfere with the activities of the private sector. Nowhere was the policy more clearly set out than in Labour's 'Business Manifesto', published just before the 1997 poll.

Gordon Brown's early period as Chancellor was marked by several radical moves, including granting independence to the Bank of England to set interest rates, the introduction of new Comprehensive Spending Reviews and other innovations such as the 'pre-Budget' speech. But, above all, Labour's first term was dominated by the heavy hand of Brown's promise that the government would retain the spending commitments of the previous government for its first three years in office. Critics were appalled at the restrictions on spending this would impose, but, as the Chancellor's Mansion House speech of 1998 and the academic underpinnings provided by Ed Balls, the Chancellor's foremost economic adviser, demonstrate, economic policy was heavily determined by the need to project an image of cautiousness and prudence. Balls's article is, on the surface, a technical academic piece. But its discussion of the principles of transparency, trust and stability give an excellent insight into the new mind-set of the Treasury as Brown has engineered it.

If Labour's approach is designed primarily for domestic consumption, it is also capable of being exported to those left-of-centre parties in other countries who wish to learn from its success. It proved irresistible to social democrats such as Gerhard Schröder, especially the new emphasis on supply-side policies, intervention in the labour market to promote 'flexibility', and an end to the deficit spending which had formerly been used to prop up ailing welfare systems. Blair and Schröder's declaration, *Europe: The Third Way/Die Neue Mitte*, had some success in domestic terms for both leaders. In a broader European context, however, it sometimes fell on deaf ears, especially in France, where a brief but significant return to interventionism under Lionel Jospin was simultaneously under way.

Indeed, the relevance of what might be dismissed as an 'Old Labour' approach to the economy has resurfaced in Britain. Will Hutton, whose 1995 book, *The State We're In*, was a hugely influential critique of Thatcherite neo-liberalism, has challenged a number of deficiencies in Labour's economic policy. He calls for a return to some of the tenets of Keynesianism and criticizes Labour for failing to grasp the opportunity to define a new economic orthodoxy. In an important sense, the dismay of writers such as Hutton is illustrative of the success of New Labour in sticking to its guns. Fears expressed in the tabloid press prior to 1997 that the left would emerge from the woodwork to take over economic policy were completely misplaced. Many had sensibly forecast that Hutton's fairly moderate brand of social democracy would be an influence on New Labour during its first term, but this too turned out to be unfounded. Nowhere has this been more keenly felt than on the left and centre-left of the trade union movement, where many are appalled by the government's proposals for part privatization of the public services. As numerous speeches by trade unionist leaders testify, allowing the private sector to take control of large areas of the public sector is perceived as a step too far, even for New Labour. In many respects the period since the 2001 election marks a new phase of animosity between the trade unions and the Labour leadership, and signals the importance of an issue that will rumble on through the second term and beyond.

No appraisal of the economic record of a government would be complete without asking the fundamental question: did things get better? The litmus test approach is at its strongest when it comes to economic policy. On most of the post-1980s mainstream indices of economic success, New Labour scores highly – keeping house prices high, taxes, interest rates and unemployment (relatively) low. But the extent to which this is the result of sound economic policy, and not just the overspill effects of a late-1990s economic boom, is open to question. Equally, the mark-sheet is only complete once the measures are extended to cover issues around inequality and welfare.

11

Safety First: The Making of New Labour

Paul Anderson and Nyta Mann

More important than the opening to the centre in politics created by Blair's election and the changing of Clause Four was the opening they provided to business. Labour of course had supporters in the boardrooms of Britain before 1994–5. It was never the party of most business people, but from the 1940s a significant minority backed it out of belief in its approach to economic management, sheer opportunism, sentimental attachment to their humble roots or a mixture of all three. In the early 1980s, however, the party lost many of its business supporters as it swung to the left, opposed the Tories' assault on the trade unions and apparently consigned itself to perpetual opposition. Although some stayed with Labour – notably the tycoon Robert Maxwell, a former Labour MP, who exerted a profound and corrupting influence over the party through his ownership of the *Daily Mirror* and its sister papers – they were small in number.

Even after the post-1987 policy review, despite its best efforts to persuade business that it was on its side, Labour found it difficult to get the endorsement of business people outside a tiny group of loyalists – the most important of whom was Clive Hollick, the multi-millionaire managing director of MAI Group. A close ally of Neil Kinnock, Hollick played a crucial part in the creation of the Institute for Public Policy Research (IPPR), the party-loyalist think-tank, in 1988 and was given a peerage by Kinnock in 1991. Other key business supporters in the early 1990s included Greg Dyke, chief executive of London Weekend Television, Swraj Paul, the Indian-born steel magnate who received a peerage from Blair in 1996, Harsh Kumar, an Indian-born commodities trader, and Chris Haskins, chairman of Northern Foods. Business took a growing interest in Labour the more the party looked likely to win power. But the pre-1992 'prawn cocktail offensive' of City lunches mounted by John Smith and his front-bench economics team at best merely persuaded companies that Labour was not as dangerous as it used to be.

Things began to change after 'Black Wednesday' in September 1992, the subsequent collapse of the Tories' standing in the opinion polls and Smith's confrontation with the unions over OMOV: by 1994, business had its feelers out to Labour both directly and through lobbyists. But it was Blair's election and Clause Four that really made the difference. All of a sudden, senior figures in the business world wanted to be part of the Labour milieu again, not merely to discover what the party would do to them and to lobby for their firms' particular interests but also to proffer general advice. Labour's embrace of capitalism under Blair might have been unequivocal – but it was by no means clear that the *sort* of capitalism that Labour favoured was the one that the business world wanted.

The issues were brought into sharp focus in early 1995 by Will Hutton, the economics editor of the *Guardian*, in his best-selling book *The State We're In*. It was a passionate critique of the ills of the British model of capitalism, and it is impossible to summarize adequately in a paragraph. The core of its argument was that Britain had declined relative to other economies because of the long-term economic dominance of the City of London, with its obsession with short-term dividends and lack of concern with long-term investment – a process exacerbated by the attempt of the Tory government since 1979 to 'roll back the frontiers of the state' in social and economic policy and allow free rein to market forces. What is more, the Tories' deregulatory drive and social spending cuts had made Britain much more unequal: we were now living in a '30/30/40 society' (the bottom 30 per cent in dire poverty, the middle 30 per cent in insecurity and the top 40 per cent in affluence), which was not only unjust but bad for economic efficiency and social cohesion. The fetishism of the market had also led to an ossification and devaluation of British democracy. What the country needed, Hutton concluded, was nothing less than a 'reconstruction of the state and the economy': a written constitution, reform of the financial system to encourage long-term investment, reassertion of the state's role in managing and regulating the economy, a 'social partnership' model of industrial relations and a revitalization of the welfare state. In other words, 'stakeholder capitalism' on the German social market model, although with a moderately expansionist Keynesian macroeconomics underpinning it.[1]

Hutton's case was embraced wholeheartedly by much of the Labour-supporting intelligentsia, and he had high hopes that it would be taken on by the Labour leadership. But for Tony Blair and Gordon Brown it was anathema. Not only was Hutton a Keynesian, and thus at odds with Labour's thinking as it had been since 1989 [...] he was also far too keen on corporatist involvement of trade unions in company affairs and on regulation of the labour market. The 'German model' was not performing well in terms of growth, and its lack of 'labour market flexibility' – in other words, its high social costs, high wages, strong unions and employment protection – was under fire from business and *laissez-faire* economists for making it uncompetitive in the now-globalized economy. From 1995 through to the 1997 election, Blair and Brown did all they could to distance themselves from Hutton's ideas. Blair's message to business, repeated *ad nauseam* in speeches to local chambers of commerce and to business conferences, was that a Labour government would do nothing to undermine the flexible labour market created by the Tories in the 1980s. Although Blair referred to the idea of a 'stakeholder society' in Singapore in January 1996 and the phrase appeared repeatedly in Labour propaganda in the run-up to the 1997 general election, he made it plain that this did not mean that he was emulating Hutton. For Hutton, 'stakeholder capitalism' signified a society in which firms have obligations, codified in law, not just to their shareholders but also to some combination of their suppliers, bankers, consumers and workers, as well as responsibilities to the environment and to local communities. Blair's 'stakeholder society' was one in which companies go about their business as usual but in which every citizen has a stake – which could mean anything, but was usually taken as having something to do with the importance of everyone having a funded second pension. [...]

More substantially, in April 1995 the IPPR, with Clive Hollick acting as front man, launched a Commission on Public Policy and British Business, along similar lines to the Commission on Social Justice set up by John Smith in 1992, 'to investigate the competitive position of the British economy and the role that public policy should play in it'. The commission, chaired by George Bain, the principal of the London Business School, was heavily weighted towards business: apart from Hollick, it included Bob Bauman, chairman of British Aerospace, Sir Christopher Harding, chairman of Legal and General, David Sainsbury, chairman of the supermarket chain, and George Simpson, the managing director of GEC, along with a selection of management gurus and academics, the most significant of them John Kay, next to Hutton the best known advocate of 'stakeholding'. Only John Monks, the general secretary of the TUC, represented the 'other side' of industry. Although the IPPR went out of its way to insist that the commission was not a Labour Party body, the very involvement of the IPPR was a signal that its findings would be taken seriously by Blair – as indeed they were. The January 1997 launch of the commission's report, *Promoting Prosperity: A Business Agenda For Britain*, was turned into a bizarre spectacle by deputy prime minister Michael Heseltine, who insisted on inviting himself on to the platform, denouncing the IPPR as a front for the Labour Party and defending the Tory government's record of deregulation. Largely as a result, the content of the report and Blair's response to it were eclipsed. But both spoke volumes about New Labour's relationship with business.

The report was moderately critical of the performance of what Hutton had called 'British capitalism'. There were too many unsuccessful companies and too many underachieving people. Investment was in short supply and government policies changed too often. The report backed a host of New Labour policies: a (low) minimum wage, tougher competition policy, improvements in education and training, investment in the transport infrastructure, tax incentives for long-term investment and strict adherence to a tight fiscal and monetary regime. In addition, the Bank of England should be given independence and Britain should join [the] EMU in the first stage if a majority of other EU countries did the same. But the report also made it clear that big changes were not required in the way the system worked. It gave wholehearted endorsement to the Tory market liberalizations of the 1980s and argued for only the lightest of touches to 'foster stakeholding'.[2]

Speaking at the launch, Blair gave this approach strong support. 'Over the past two years, I have addressed over 10,000 individual business people,' he said. 'It has not just been about collecting endorsements and support. It has been about building a genuine new partnership with business for the future. Today I offer business a new deal for the future. The deal is this: we leave intact the main changes of the 1980s in industrial relations and enterprise. And now, together, we address a new agenda for the twenty-first century: education, welfare reform, infrastructure, leadership in Europe. We want to keep more flexible labour markets. Our proposals for change, including the minimum wage, would amount to less labour market regulation than in the USA. Our aim is not to create inflexible labour markets or try merely to regulate for job security but to make people more employable in the labour market by enhancing their skills, talents and mobility...In the USA it would never occur to question the commitment of the Democrats to business. It should be the same here with New Labour.'[3]

The participants in the IPPR commission were by no means the only enthusiasts for New Labour in the business world. British Telecom negotiated a deal with the party to cable every school in the country in return for being allowed into the cable entertainment business, which Blair revealed at the 1995 Labour conference. David Simon, chairman of BP, now Lord Simon, the minister for trade and competitiveness in Europe, gave Blair the idea of putting a ten-point 'performance contract' at the centre of his speech to the 1996 Labour conference. Alec Reed, chairman of the employment company Reed, declared that it would be 'a tragedy' if Blair did not become prime minister';[4] Cob Stenham, chairman of Arjo Wiggins Appleton, said that 'serious and forward-looking business people should back New Labour'. Matthew Harding, the insurance broker and vice-chairman of Chelsea football club, gave a £1 million donation to Labour just before he died in a helicopter crash in late 1996; Bob Gavron, the printing magnate, handed over £500,000. In late 1996, Labour announced that its donations from business had topped £6 million. It was subsequently revealed that Trevor Chinn, chairman of Lex Services, Britain's biggest motor dealer, and the industrialist Emmanuel Kaye were among the donors to a 'blind trust' that was funding Blair's private office. Anita Roddick, chief executive of the Body Shop, came out for Labour around the same time, as did Terence Conran, the restaurateur and founder of Habitat: both starred in a Labour party election broadcast.

Most important of all, though, were the media magnates – in particular Rupert Murdoch, boss of the global media empire that included Britain's biggest-selling daily newspaper, the *Sun*, since the mid-1970s one of the Tories' most loyal friends in Fleet Street. When Blair won the Labour leadership, Murdoch was a hate figure for the left because of the *Sun*'s virulent campaign against Labour right through to the 1992 general election. But Blair knew that Murdoch was interested in making money above all else, and that he had never had any qualms about using his papers to support nominally centre-left parties as long as they were business-friendly and orthodox in their foreign policy prescriptions. Equally important, there were some small indications that Murdoch was thinking of switching his allegiance in British politics away from the Tories. In 1992, he had helped to pay for a study of media regulation by the IPPR. More recently, both the *Sun* and *The Times* had become much more critical of John Major's Tory government. Soon after Blair became Labour leader, the media mogul was quoted by the German news magazine *Der Spiegel* as stating: 'I could even imagine myself supporting the British Labour leader, Tony Blair.'

Informal contacts between Murdoch and Blair followed, then dinner, then an invitation to Blair to address the 'leadership conference' of NewsCorp, Murdoch's giant multinational conglomerate, on an Australian island in July 1995. Blair accepted readily and treated his audience to a wide-ranging speech in which he declared his enthusiasm for market forces and the family. 'The old solutions of rigid economic planning and state control won't work,' he intoned. 'What is more, during the sixties and seventies the left developed, almost in substitution for its economic prescriptions, which by then were failing, a type of social individualism that confused, at points at least, liberation from prejudice with a disregard for moral structures. It fought for racial and sexual equality, which was entirely right. It appeared indifferent to the family and individual responsibility, which was wrong ... My politics are simple, not complex. I believe you can have a country of ambition and aspiration with compassion and a sense of duty to others. The individual prospers best within a strong, decent, cohesive society. These are the real ends of the left of centre. The means of achieving them will, of course, vary from generation to generation and should be pragmatically, not ideologically, driven.'[5]

Blair insisted that he made no Faustian pact with Murdoch to lay off his business interests in government in return for the support of his papers. 'No policy was traded – indeed, the burden of the speech was an attack on the new right,' he wrote in a scathing piece in the *Guardian*.[6] But it was noticeable that after Blair's trip, Labour became much less enthusiastic for strict regulation of the media, particularly on cross-ownership, and that the Murdoch press became much more enthusiastic about Blair. Labour's long-standing promise of a Monopolies and Mergers Commission investigation into Murdoch's media interests was quietly dropped, and Labour opposed the Tory government's proposals for tighter rules on newspaper groups owning television companies, claiming that they would be unfair to the Mirror Group and hinting that it was in favour of complete deregulation. The deal reached by Labour with British Telecom in 1995 to allow it into the cable entertainment industry was very much in Murdoch's interests because of his role as a supplier of television programmes, and Labour was noticeably quiet about the danger of Murdoch establishing monopolies in various aspects of digital television. The *Sun* and its Sunday sister paper, the *News of the World*, came out unequivocally for Labour in the 1997 election, and although the *Sunday Times* stayed Tory while *The Times* took the bizarre position of backing Eurosceptics of left, right and centre, neither gave Labour much trouble. In the middle of the election campaign, Gerry Robinson, the chairman of both Granada and BSkyB, the satellite television company largely owned by Murdoch, was unveiled by Labour as one of its key supporters in the world of business. Another BSkyB director, Dennis Stevenson, now chief executive of Pearson, the media conglomerate that owns *The Economist* and the *Financial Times* (with Greg Dyke as head of its television operation), was appointed by Blair as head of Labour's independent review on increasing the use of information technology in schools.

Blair also put himself out to make his peace with the mid-market Tory tabloids in the *Express* and *Mail* stables, belonging respectively to United News and Media and Associated Newspapers. With the *Daily* and *Sunday Express*, now merged as a seven-day paper, Blair got nowhere until some time after Hollick's MAI Group took over United News and Media in early 1996. By the time the election campaign started, however, the *Express* was at best lukewarm in its Toryism, while its downmarket tabloid sister paper, the *Daily Star*, backed Labour. With Associated, the story was more colourful. In October 1995, Sir David English, the former editor of the *Daily Mail* who had become editor-in-chief of Associated, wrote a piece in the *Spectator* in which he revealed that Blair had long been a welcome lunch guest at the company – even when Neil Kinnock was Labour leader and the shadow cabinet was boycotting the *Mail* and its sister papers for their vicious coverage of the Labour Party. English had been impressed by Blair's forthright views – and had recently discussed the possibility of the Associated papers coming out for Labour at the next election with his proprietor, Lord Rothermere. '"Could such a thing even be possible?" I wondered. "Well, it certainly would not be impossible, David," he replied, having recently come from a two-hour one-to-one with the Labour leader. So, could Associated Newspapers come out for Labour? It is too early to say. We may or we may not.' Six months later, Rothermere told Sue Lawley on *Desert Island Discs*: 'I think that some of my newspapers might be sympathetic to Tony and others will be sympathetic to John Major.' When it finally came to the crunch, the *Daily Mail* and the *Mail on Sunday* remained Conservative for the 1997 election, but the *Evening Standard* backed Labour – and three weeks after the election Rothermere announced that he would be voting with Labour in the Lords.

In power, New Labour's enthusiasm for business has remained undimmed. As well as the ministerial role for David (now Lord) Simon of BP and the advisory role for Dennis Stevenson of Pearson and BSkyB, the government took on Peter Davies, head of the Prudential insurance empire, to chair an advisory group on tackling youth and long-term unemployment, and Martin Taylor, chief executive of Barclays Bank, to head a taskforce on social security reform. Alan Sugar, the founder of the consumer electronics company Amstrad, was signed up to talk to government business seminars for young entrepreneurs; Bob Ayling, chairman of British Airways, was given a place on the committee organizing the millennium celebrations. Labour's millionaire industrialist MP, Geoffrey Robinson, proprietor of the *New Statesman*, got the number three job in the Treasury, paymaster general; Malcolm Bates, chairman of Pearl Assurance, was drafted in to review the private finance initiative set up by the Tory government to attract private capital to public projects; and Alex Trotman, chairman of Ford in Britain, was recruited to advise on creation of a 'university for industry'.

NOTES

1   Will Hutton, *The State We're In* (Jonathan Cape, 1995).
2   Commission on Public Policy and British Business, *Promoting Prosperity: A Business Agenda For Britain* (Vintage, 1997).
3   Tony Blair, speech at launch of report of Commission on Public Policy and British Business, 21 January 1997.
4   *Daily Mirror*, 22 November 1996.
5   Tony Blair, speech to NewsCorp Leadership Conference, Hayman Island, Australia, 17 July 1995.
6   Tony Blair, 'The Labour Party, New Labour, New Life for Britain', *Guardian*, 24 July 1996.

12

Labour's Business Manifesto: Equipping Britain for the Future

The Labour Party

This manifesto sets out how a new Labour government will work with business. It outlines our policies to back Britain's businesses and help them to compete and deliver healthy growth, good profits, rising living standards and more jobs.

Britain is a nation brimming with talent and potential. At their best our people demonstrate an unrivalled inventiveness and creativity. But too often in the past politicians have failed business and industry and squandered that potential. Unsound economic policies have led to repeated cycles of boom and bust. The old battles – public versus private, employee versus employer and state versus market – have prevented the development of a shared sense of national economic purpose about the need to create wealth.

A new Labour government will provide the vision and strong leadership needed to unlock Britain's potential and turn it into real achievement. At the heart of its approach will be a new partnership with business. It is not a question of 'picking winners'. What government should do, and a new Labour government will do, is create the dynamic and supportive environment in which business can prosper and thrive. An environment in which entrepreneurs with good business ideas have a real prospect of success and well-run established businesses can look to the future with confidence.

Over the past two years we have talked to business about what needs to be done to get the environment right. From macro-economic stability and education reform to more effective backing for science and technology and cutting red tape, we have published detailed proposals showing how government and industry working together can improve our competitiveness.

[...] We set out our business manifesto for a competitive Britain. It is not exhaustive. It does set out our priorities – the basics we need to get right for business to be successful.

- First, macro-economic stability with inflation low and government spending under control.
- Second, a dynamic economy with higher investment, modernised infrastructure and competitive markets.

- Third, stable and co-operative relations between employees and employers and a flexible labour market.
- Fourth, improved education and skills.
- Fifth, a tax and benefit system which rewards work, encourages enterprise and promotes investment and saving.
- Sixth, leadership by Britain in Europe.

We are ambitious for business and for Britain. We set ourselves the objective of putting Britain at the heart of the emerging international economy. We want it to be seen as a great place to do business and the best place from which to compete internationally. We have great strengths. With vision and leadership, and a real partnership between government and business, Britain will succeed.

Business needs stability to succeed. Too often in the past, British business has suffered from short-term inflationary dashes for growth which have led to long-term damage to business confidence.

No Risks with Inflation

A new Labour government will match the current inflation target. Our inflation target will be set to achieve underlying inflation of 2.5 per cent or less. Interest rates will be set to meet that target. We will take no risks with inflation. Low and stable inflation and sustained growth go hand in hand. We will reform the Bank of England and the Treasury so that we can deliver our commitment to low inflation. The Treasury will receive advice from a new council of economic advisers to make policy-making more effective, open and accountable. For the Bank of England, we propose a new monetary policy committee to decide on the advice which the Bank of England should give to the Chancellor. The Court should also be reformed to reflect a wider range of interests, including those of industry.

A Tough Approach to Government Spending and Borrowing

We will meet the 'golden rule' of spending. Over the economic cycle, a Labour government will only borrow to finance public investment and not to fund public consumption. And the ratio of government debt to GDP will be kept stable on average over the economic cycle at a prudent and sensible level.

We will keep a firm grip on public spending. On spending, the first question any incoming government should ask about public spending is the question any management team would ask when taking over a business – not how much more money we can spend but how we can use existing spending better to meet our priorities. We will work within the already announced ceilings for departmental spending for the first two years of a Labour government. Labour's first Budget will not reopen overall spending allocations for the 1997–98 financial year. These are the figures upon which departments are already planning, and will continue to plan. For 1998–99, each departmental minister will reorder spending so it meets our priorities of investment, employment and opportunity. Each department will save in low-priority areas to spend in high-priority areas.

Supporting this process will be a comprehensive spending review. It will immediately examine the allocation of total spending across departments and investigate how we can reshape the distribution of public spending now and into the next century.

Public Sector Pay

Labour will take a firm and fair approach to public sector pay. Decisions will be made with a view to retain, recruit and motivate staff. But these must be made within tough cash limits. Under Labour, all public sector pay agreements must be financed from within the agreed departmental cash limits. Just as we will resist every other unreasonable demand on the public purse we will resist unreasonable public sector pay demands.

[...]

A new Labour government wants a tax and benefit system which encourages work and enterprise, promotes long-term saving and ensures fairness. There will be no return to the penal marginal rates of tax which existed under Labour and Conservative governments in the 1970s. As a signal of our commitment to encourage work, there will be no increase in the basic or top rate of income tax throughout the next Parliament.

[...]

Stability and Co-operation

The key to orderly and effective industrial relations is to establish a fair and effective balance between rights and responsibilities that will promote partnership, not conflict, at the workplace. This is the principle that will inform our whole approach to industrial relations. The Conservatives are scaremongering when they claim a Labour government would turn the clock back, reverse trade union immunities to allow secondary industrial action, and alter the rules on picketing. There is not a word of truth in any of this. The existing laws on industrial action, picketing and ballots will all remain unchanged.

13

'Prudence will be our Watchword': Chancellor's Speech at the Mansion House, 1998

Gordon Brown

Fifty years of our economic history from 1945 was marred by a succession of sterile and self-defeating conflicts between state and market, managements and workforce, public and private sectors. And I believe that we should not only set aside for good these old battles, but think of a Britain where public and private sectors are not just in some temporary truce but where public and private sectors are constructively working together to meet nationally important and defined objectives. For the challenge for all of us now is to play our part in equipping Britain for the 21st century. So this evening I want to chart the course ahead, not for a few months or even a year or two, but for the long term, and in doing so to explain the building blocks.

First, monetary stability that allows businesses and families to make their plans for the long term. Second, long-term fiscal stability that delivers sustainable public finances. [...] And, third, a drive for higher levels of investment, skills and productivity, through three major reform programmes – structural reforms in labour markets, product markets and capital markets. And finally a commitment to open trade and policies for constructive engagement in the developed world's largest market, the European Union. [...]

First, stability. In today's deregulated, liberalized financial markets, the Keynesian fine-tuning of the past, which worked in relatively sheltered, closed national economies and which tried to exploit a supposed long-term trade-off between inflation and unemployment, will simply not work. Neither can stability be delivered in wholly deregulated markets through a rigid application of fixed monetary targets, as was attempted in the 1980s.

When there are ever more rapid financial flows across the world that are unpredictable and uncertain, the answer is to ensure stability through establishing the right long-term policy objectives and to build credibility in the policy through well-understood procedural rules that are followed for monetary and fiscal policy. Stability is enhanced if there is an openness and transparency that keeps markets properly informed and ensures that objectives and institutions are credible.

We know more than most that Britain has been subjected to the instability of boom and bust and constantly changing policies. That is why [...] we had to set out new long-term monetary and fiscal objectives, to ensure these would be met by adopting rules based on open institutions and a commitment to openness and transparency.

First, the right objectives: price stability through a pre-announced inflation target and sustainable public finances through applying the Golden Rule, that over the economic cycle current spending should at least cover consumption. In other words, a balanced current budget combined with a prudent approach to public debt. Second, unambiguous procedural rules: a new system of monetary policy-making, at the heart of which are the independence of the Bank of England and an open letter system. And a commitment to proper procedures in fiscal policy by legislating a fiscal stability code and a pre-announced commitment to prudence. And, third, transparency in policy-making: an open system of decision-making in monetary policy through the publication of minutes, a system of voting and full reporting to Parliament; and in fiscal policy an open and transparent system under which government allows its actions to be subject to full scrutiny, and ensures that key fiscal assumptions are independently audited.

And I believe people now understand that clear long-term objectives, well-understood procedures and openness and transparency are the way to stability for national governments in a modern global marketplace. The new system has in my view already given greater credibility to monetary policy-making.

[...]

We have the chance to create, for the first time in decades, a continuous circle of low inflation, low long-term interest rates and high levels of investment – the best platform for growth and prosperity. So while I do not comment on the month-to-month decisions of the monetary policy committee, I do believe that the whole country should support early action on inflation to prevent the recurrence of stop–go and to achieve economic stability. [...]

Stability requires not only low and stable inflation, but sustainable public finances. I believe that the prudent management of the public finances is the primary responsibility of the Treasury. [...]

It was controversial in 1976 when one Labour Prime Minister said we could not spend our way out of a recession. I say tonight we cannot simply spend our way through a recovery either. So 'prudence' will be our watchword.

[...]

There have been two pressures on past governments which they have found difficult to resist. The first is a fault of previous Labour governments, to spend in the first two years and then to have to cut back in their remaining years with all the instability that this causes. Our tough decisions have ensured that we have used our first years not to spend imprudently but to put the public finances on a sustainable footing. But there is a second temptation for politicians – another form of stop–go – to raise spending in an election year so there is more public spending on what is electorally attractive. Decisions made not as a result of the economic cycle but of the electoral cycle.

It has been suggested that this is my plan for the years to come, the election war chest thesis. Nothing can be further from the truth. Of course, politicians enjoy winning elections. From my own admittedly limited experience, I find that I like winning elections. And from rather more experience I can tell you I hate losing them.

But I have to say that our fiscal rules have been specifically designed to preclude party political manipulation of the public finances for electoral purposes. We have today locked in stability for a whole Parliament and we have done it to create the best environment for investment and for high and stable levels of growth and employment.

[...]

[...] Where it is necessary, modernisation, wholesale modernisation and nothing but modernisation will be my policy. On product markets the way forward is not stifling competition by over-regulation or pursuing a free-for-all devoid of anti-trust, anti-monopolies legislation. It is to vigorously pursue a pro-competition agenda that involves opening up competition in financial services, telecommunications, energy – removing barriers that still thwart open trade. We also need to consider modernising our capital markets. [...] The challenge for Britain is to create a stronger venture capital industry and to help venture capital do more to encourage the high-risk, early stage and start-up companies.

So we need a new approach in Britain to risk-taking that will increase the number of entrepreneurs and raise the growth and survival rate of small businesses. We must destroy the barriers that hold us back – fiscal, regulatory, economic, cultural – as a matter of urgency. And we will consider the measures we must take.

We must also engage in far-reaching reform of our labour markets not just in employment policy but in welfare, education and taxation and social security policy. The way forward is neither old style regulation nor a crude form of deregulation, which leaves the unskilled without the training or education essential for employ-ability. The way forward is one that recognises that bringing out the best in people by policies that ensure opportunities for all is the best route to prosperity in the modern world. So we need a modern employment policy that does not offer welfare irrespective of work, but is built on a system of matching rights with responsibilities, an active welfare state which provides new opportunities for work and a tax and benefit system that makes work pay. [...]

So stability, long-term prudence, and a dynamic supply side are key building blocks for prosperity. [...]

My themes therefore: our economy founded on a platform of monetary stability; sound finances through prudence and investment in reform; a national drive for higher productivity through economic reform and a new purpose in Europe. Taken together, this reform agenda offers a new and radical way forward that helps equip our country for the new century, one that realises, for a new world, the great British qualities – the virtues of hard work, creativity, fair play and openness – and does so in a modern non-dogmatic way.

It is a new way for our country that creates a society that has both sound finances and good public services. No longer a false choice between those who say you can have prudence but only at the cost of running down public investment and good public services and those who say you can have public services but only if you pay over the odds. Neither should we throw money at problems nor walk away from them. It is by breaking with the past and by modernising our approaches that [...] prudence and investment in reform can become the foundation for good efficient public services and a modern infrastructure.

There is a new way for our country's economy too that creates an economy that is both enterprising and fair. No longer a false choice between those who say that if you have enterprise it is at the cost of fairness, or those who say let us have fairness even if it kills off enterprise. Instead, by a modern approach to opportunity to all that draws on the best of British values, we have enterprise and fairness together. [...]

A modern Britain, founded on lasting British values, the values of the British people; built on a determination to make Britain a more prosperous country for all its citizens; driven forward by the energies of a new generation willing, like our predecessors, to reject failed dogmas and to modernise and reform – a Britain ready to fulfil its role in the new world and to realise the potential of its people.

14

Open Macroeconomics in an Open Economy

Edward Balls

[...] In just a few short months, the new Government has made a number of changes in the institutions and practice of economic policy making in Britain:

- independence for a reformed Bank of England;
- a new structure of financial regulation;
- new fiscal rules and a five year deficit reduction plan;
- a major corporate tax reform;
- a windfall tax on the privatised utilities;
- a New Deal for the young people and the long-term unemployed;
- reform of the financing of higher education;
- a new capital fund to rebuild schools;
- a UK Action Plan for Employment and Flexibility in Europe;
- publication of Lord Currie's EMU paper and a new Advisory Taskforce; and
- new impetus for debt relief – the Mauritius Mandate.

That list is, by no means, exhaustive, and there is more to come:

- the Bank of England Bill;
- the first National Assets Register;
- a Pre-Budget Report and economic consultation process;
- capital gains tax reform;
- consultation on the new Individual Savings Account;
- tough legislation on competition policy;
- the Taylor review of taxes and benefits; and
- the Low Pay Commission's report on the minimum wage.

[...] The institutional changes which have been introduced since 1 May at the Treasury and the Bank of England, in some cases only a few days after election day, add up to what is now probably one of the most open and accountable systems of economic policy making in the world. [...]

[...] [T]he changes in both the world economy and our economic understanding of it over the past twenty years mean that policymakers must adjust to new ways of making decisions. Gone are the days of fixed policy rules announced in public and of private deliberations behind closed finance ministry doors, with little or no justification or explanation about policy decisions or mistakes.

[...] [I]n a world of global capital markets in which policy-making by fixed rules has been discredited in theory and practice, governments must take a different route to ensure macroeconomic credibility. Credibility in modern open economies requires three ingredients:

- a reputation for following sound long-term policies;
- maximum openness and transparency; and
- new institutional arrangements which guarantee a long-term view.

[...]

Delivering on these objectives depends not simply on one policy pillar, but three – delivering macroeconomic stability, tackling the supply-side barriers to growth and delivering employment and economic opportunities to all.

[...] The violent boom-bust economic cycles of the past twenty or so years – more extreme than in any other major developed economy – have had a serious negative impact, not simply on jobs during the recessions, and on long-term interest rates because of higher inflation expectations, but on the employability of the long-term unemployed, the capacity of the economy and the willingness of companies to make long-term investment commitments. As Keynes might say now, there is nothing so damaging for the 'animal spirits' of business investors than repeated cycles of boom then bust. [...]

[...] [W]hile stability is the first pillar of New Labour economics, supply-side action to make the economy more dynamic and remove barriers to growth is the second pillar. That means understanding that the proper role for government in economic policy making goes well beyond macroeconomic policy making. It means a new role for government – not picking winners or responding to market failures by trying to replace the market in its entirety, but using the proper role of government to tackle short-termism and market failures by making markets work more dynamically and encouraging investment in the broadest sense – not just in machines, but in technology and innovation, skills and infrastructure – the fuel for growth in the modern economy.

[...]

The third pillar of the new Government's economic policy – the key to ensuring stability and growth is translated into high and stable levels of employment as well as rising incomes for those in work – is to actively promote employment opportunity and reform the welfare state so that it promotes work not dependency. The centrepiece of the first Budget was a new approach to employment opportunity for young people, the long-term unemployed, lone parents and the disabled – on a scale and in a manner never attempted before. [...]

Four Principles of Open Macroeconomic Policy

[...]

Stability through constrained discretion

The first principle is the simplest way I could think of to embody the pro-stability but post-monetarist intellectual consensus upon which modern macroeconomic policy-making is based. [...]

[...] [S]tability and low inflation is a necessary condition for achieving and sustaining high and stable levels of growth and employment, but achieving stability requires the discretionary ability for macroeconomic policy to respond flexibly to different economic shocks—constrained, of course, by the need to meet the low inflation objective or target over time.

[...]

Credibility through sound long-term policies

The rapid globalization of the world economy has made achieving credibility more rather than less important, particularly for an incoming left-of-centre government which has been out of power for two decades. This process of globalization has many dimensions – technological change, capital market liberalization and the growth and global reach of international trade – all of which have profound implications for domestic economic policy. No sensible discussion of New Labour's economic policy could avoid a lengthy discussion of how technological change and the growth of world trade have affected labour market outcomes. While macroeconomic policy errors are one central cause of the rise and persistence of unemployment in the 1980s, the concentration of long-term unemployment among the unskilled demonstrates that changes in the global pattern of demand and supply are another.

For macroeconomic policy making, there can be no doubt that the most significant change in the world economy is the globalization of international capital markets which began before the collapse of the Bretton Woods system of global fixed exchange rates and, spurred on by liberalization and technological change, has accelerated apace since.

The power of 'the markets' is always and everywhere: dollar slumps on bad trade news, D-Mark rises on good inflation news, or, as the *Wall Street Journal* once reported in its headline, Dow-Jones falls on no news. Global capital markets have intensified the 'time inconsistency' problem. In a closed economy, the issue is whether governments can fool their electorates into believing higher growth is sustainable for a while before domestic price inflation rises and the value of their real wages falls. But in an open economy, with capital mobility, discretion also gives the government the ability to fool international investors into believing that growth will be sustained before the exchange rate – and therefore the profitability of their investments – falls.

[...]

But governments which pursue, and are judged by the markets to be pursuing sound monetary and fiscal policies, can attract inflows of investment capital at higher speed, in greater volume and at a lower cost than even ten years ago. Witness the huge investment flows into Latin America, China and South-East Asia over the past decade. Or the rapid convergence of long-term interest rates in Europe as more and more southern European economies have increased their perceived probability of joining EMU.

Moreover, if governments are judged to be pursuing sound, long-term macroeconomic policies and institutional procedures, then they can use discretionary monetary, or indeed fiscal, policy to deal with macroeconomic shocks which need to be accommodated in the short term. It was the fact that German economic policy making institutions were judged to be credible in the long-term that enabled the Bundesbank to accommodate the supply-shock of unification and effectively ignore its favoured money supply targets. It was the fact that Alan Greenspan, as chairman of the US Federal Reserve, had such accumulated credibility that he was able to cut interest rates hard and early at the end of the 1980s without destabilising the financial markets.

[...] [I]n a world of rapidly mobile capital, governments can have policy credibility *and* maintain policy discretion if they pursue, and are seen to be pursuing, monetary and fiscal policies which are well understood and sustainable over the long term and where problems are spotted and tackled promptly rather than disguised while clinging to intermediate indicators to prop up credibility.

[...]

Credibility through maximum transparency

At the heart of the 'time inconsistency' problem is imperfect information – about the true state of the macroeconomy and, more importantly, about the true motivations of policymakers.

[...]

The problem is that the suspicion that the government is manipulating information or policy for short-term motives is as damaging to credibility and the economy as evidence that it has done so. Even if macroeconomic errors begin as mistakes rather than deliberate deception, the more suspicion there is about motivation, and the greater the asymmetry of information between government and the investing public, the higher short-term cost that is paid in lost credibility and the heavier the blow to credibility when things go wrong.

[...]

So [...] the greater the amount of transparency about government objectives and the reasons why decisions are taken, the more information about outcomes that is published as a matter of routine, and the more checks on the ability of government to manipulate the flow of information, the less likely is it that investors will be suspicious of the government's intentions, the greater the flexibility of policy to react to real crises and the easier it is to build a consensus for difficult decisions. [...]

Credibility through pre-commitment

[...] [W]e live in a dynamic world in which reputation matters. [...]

[...] The problem is that a government can get away with cheating once, by claiming that discretion is needed to respond to a shock when all that is intended is a short-term pre-election dash for growth. For it does so at the cost of its reputation in the future. You can only fool people once. But once you have, the public and markets expect it again, and again.

[...]

[...] [T]he more institutional arrangements can demonstrate that policy is truly trying to achieve its declared objectives, and the more difficult it is for the government to cheat by breaking promises or aiming for different objectives, the more the public and investors will believe that decisions are being taken for sound long-term reasons.

15

Europe: The Third Way/ Die Neue Mitte

Tony Blair and Gerhard Schröder

Introduction

[...] Social democracy has found new acceptance [...] because, while retaining its traditional values, it has begun in a credible way to renew its ideas and modernise its programmes. It has also found new acceptance because it stands not only for social justice but also for economic dynamism and the unleashing of creativity and innovation. The trademark of this approach is the New Centre in Germany and the Third Way in the United Kingdom. Other social democrats choose other terms that suit their own national cultures. But though the language and the institutions may differ, the motivation is everywhere the same. Most people have long since abandoned the world view represented by the dogmas of left and right. Social democrats must be able to speak to those people.

Fairness and social justice, liberty and equality of opportunity, solidarity and responsibility to others – these values are timeless. Social democracy will never sacrifice them. To make these values relevant to today's world requires realistic and forward-looking policies capable of meeting the challenges of the 21st century. Modernisation is about adapting to conditions that have objectively changed, and not reacting to polls.

Similarly, we need to apply our politics within a new economic framework, modernised for today, where government does all it can to support enterprise but never believes it is a substitute for enterprise. The essential function of markets must be complemented and improved by political action, not hampered by it. We support a market economy, not a market society. [...]

I Learning from Experience

Although both parties can be proud of our historic achievements, today we must develop realistic and feasible answers to new challenges confronting our societies and economies. This requires adherence to our values but also a willingness to change our old approaches and traditional policy instruments. In the past, the promotion of social justice was sometimes confused with the imposition of equality of outcome. The result was a neglect of the importance of rewarding effort and responsibility, and the association of social democracy with conformity and mediocrity rather than the celebration of creativity, diversity and excellence. Work was burdened with ever higher costs. The means of achieving social justice became identified with ever higher levels of public spending regardless of what they achieved or the impact of the taxes required to fund it on competitiveness, employment and living standards. Decent public services are a vital concern for social democrats, but social conscience cannot be measured by the level of public expenditure. The real test for society is how effectively this expenditure is used and how much it enables people to help themselves. The belief that the state should address damaging market failures all too often led to a disproportionate expansion of the government's reach and the bureaucracy that went with it. The balance between the individual and the collective was distorted. Values that are important to citizens, such as personal achievement and success, entrepreneurial spirit, individual responsibility and community spirit, were too often subordinated to universal social safeguards. Too often rights were elevated above responsibilities, but the responsibility of the individual to his or her family, neighbourhood and society cannot be offloaded on to the state. If the concept of mutual obligation is forgotten, this results in a decline in community spirit, lack of responsibility towards neighbours, rising crime and vandalism, and a legal system that cannot cope. The ability of national governments to fine-tune the economy in order to secure growth and jobs has been exaggerated. The importance of individual and business enterprise to the creation of wealth has been undervalued. The weaknesses of markets have been overstated and their strengths underestimated.

II   New Programmes for Changed Realities

[...] The politics of the New Centre and Third Way is about addressing the concerns of people who live and cope with societies undergoing rapid change – both winners and losers. In this newly emerging world people want politicians who approach issues without ideological preconceptions and who, applying their values and principles, search for practical solutions to their problems through honest well-constructed and pragmatic policies. Voters who in their daily lives have to display initiative and adaptability in the face of economic and social change expect the same from their governments and their politicians.

In a world of ever more rapid globalisation and scientific changes we need to create the conditions in which existing businesses can prosper and adapt, and new businesses can be set up and grow. New technologies radically change the nature of work and internationalise the organisation of production. With one hand they de-skill and make some businesses obsolete, with another they create new business and vocational opportunities. The most important task of modernisation is to invest in human capital: to make the individual and businesses fit for the knowledge-based economy of the future. Having the same job for life is a thing of the past. Social democrats must accommodate the growing demands for flexibility – and at the same time maintain minimum social standards, help families to cope with change and open up fresh opportunities for those who are unable to keep pace. We face an increasing challenge in reconciling environmental responsibility towards future generations with material progress for society at large. We must marry environmental responsibility with a modern market-based approach. In environmental protection, the most modern technologies consume fewer resources, open up new markets and create new jobs. Public expenditure as a proportion of national income has more or less reached the limits of acceptability. Constraints on 'tax and spend' force radical modernisation of the public sector and reform of public services to achieve better value for money. The public sector must actually serve the citizen: we do not hesitate to promote the concepts of efficiency, competition and high performance.

[...]

For the new politics to succeed, it must promote a go-ahead mentality and a new entrepreneurial spirit at all levels of society. That requires a competent and well-trained workforce eager and ready to take on new responsibilities; a social security system that opens up new opportunities and encourages initiative, creativity and readiness to take on new challenges; a positive climate for entrepreneurial independence and initiative. Small businesses must become easier to set up and better able to survive; and we want a society which celebrates successful entrepreneurs just as it does artists and footballers – and which values creativity in all spheres of life. Our countries have different traditions in dealings between state, industry, trade unions and social groups, but we share a conviction that traditional conflicts at the workplace must be overcome. This, above all, means rekindling a spirit of community and solidarity, strengthening partnership and dialogue between all groups in society and developing a new consensus for change and reform. We want all groups in society to share our joint commitment to the new directions set out in this Declaration. [...]

We want to see real partnership at work, with employees having the opportunity of sharing the rewards of success with employers. We support modern trade unions protecting individuals against arbitrary behaviour, and working in co-operation with employers to manage change and create long-term prosperity. In Europe – under the umbrella of a European employment pact – we will strive to pursue an ongoing dialogue with the social partners that supports, not hinders, necessary economic change.

III   A New Supply-side Agenda for the Left

The task facing Europe is to meet the challenge of the global economy while maintaining social cohesion in the face of real and perceived uncertainty. [...] The past two decades of neo-liberal laissez-faire are over. In its place, however, there must not be a renaissance of 1970s-style reliance on deficit spending and heavy-handed state intervention. Such an approach now points in the wrong direction. Our national economies and global economic relationships have undergone profound change. New conditions and new realities call for a re-evaluation of old ideas and the development of new concepts. [...] The main elements of this approach are as follows.

A robust and competitive market framework

Product market competition and open trade is essential to stimulate productivity and growth. For that reason a framework that allows market forces to work properly is essential to economic success and a pre-condition of a more successful employment policy. [...]

A tax policy to promote sustainable growth

In the past social democrats became identified with high taxes, especially on business. Modern social democrats recognise that in the right circumstances, tax reform and tax cuts can play a critical part in meeting their wider social objectives. [...]

Demand and supply-side policies go together – they are not alternatives

In the past social democrats often gave the impression that the objectives of growth and high unemployment would be achieved by successful demand management alone. Modern social democrats recognise that supply-side policies have a central and complementary role to play. [...]

Modern economic policy aims to increase the after-tax income of workers and at the same time decrease the costs of labour to the employer. The reduction of non-wage labour costs through structural reform of social security systems and a more employment friendly tax and contribution structure that looks to the future is therefore of particular importance. The aim of social democratic policy is to overcome the apparent contradiction between demand- and supply-side policies in favour of a fruitful combination of micro-economic flexibility and macro-economic stability. To achieve higher growth and more jobs in today's world, economies must be adaptable: flexible markets are a modern social democratic aim. Macro-economic policy still has a vital purpose: to set the conditions for stable growth and avoid boom and bust. But social democrats must recognise that getting the macro-economics right is not sufficient to stimulate higher growth and more jobs. Changes in interest rates or tax policy will not lead to increased investment and employment unless the supply side of the economy is adaptable enough to respond. To make the European economy more dynamic, we also need to make it more flexible. Companies must have room for manoeuvre to take advantage of improved economic conditions and seize new opportunities: they must not be gagged by rules and regulations. Product, capital and labour markets must all be flexible: we must not combine rigidity in one part of the economic system with openness and dynamism in the rest. [...]

Sound public finance should be a badge of pride for social democrats

In the past, social democrats have all too often been associated with the view that the best way to promote employment and growth is to increase government borrowing in order to finance higher government spending. We do not rule out government deficits – during a cyclical downturn it makes sense to let the automatic stabilisers work. And borrowing to finance higher government investment, in strict accordance with the Golden Rule, can play a key role in strengthening the supply side of the economy.

However, deficit spending cannot be used to overcome structural weaknesses in the economy that are a barrier to faster growth and higher employment. Social democrats also must not tolerate excessive levels of public sector debt. Increased indebtedness represents an unfair burden on future generations. It could have unwelcome redistributive effects. Above all, money spent on servicing high public sector debt is not available to be spent on other priorities, including increased investment in education, training or the transport infrastructure.

From the standpoint of a supply-side policy of the left, it is essential that high levels of government borrowing decrease and not increase.

IV　An Active Labour Market Policy for the Left

The state must become an active agent for employment, not merely the passive recipient of the casualties of economic failure. People who have never had experience of work or who have been out of work for long periods lose the skills necessary to compete in the labour market. Prolonged unemployment also damages individual life chances in other ways and makes it more difficult for individuals to participate fully in society. A welfare system that puts limits on an individual's ability to find a job must be reformed. Modern social democrats want to transform the safety net of entitlements into a springboard to personal responsibility. For our societies, the imperatives of social justice are more than the distribution of cash transfers. Our objective is the widening of equality of opportunity, regardless of race, age or disability, to fight social exclusion and ensure equality between men and women. People rightly demand high-quality public services and solidarity for all who need help – but also fairness towards those who pay for it. All social policy instruments must improve life chances, encourage self-help and promote personal responsibility. With this aim in mind, the health care system and the system for ensuring financial security in old age are being thoroughly modernised in Germany by adapting both to the changes in life expectancy and changing lifelong patterns of employment, without sacrificing the principle of solidarity. The same thinking applies to the introduction of stakeholder pensions and the reform of disability benefits in Britain. Periods of unemployment in an economy without jobs for life must become an opportunity to attain qualifications and foster personal development. Part-time work and low-paid work are better than no work because they ease the transition from unemployment to jobs. New policies to offer unemployed people jobs and training are a social democratic priority – but we also expect everyone to take up the opportunity offered.

But providing people with the skills and abilities to enter the workforce is not enough. The tax and benefits systems need to make sure it is in people's interests to work. A streamlined and modernised tax and benefits system is a significant component of the left's active supply-side labour market policy. We must [m]ake work pay for individuals and families. The biggest part of the income must remain in the pockets of those who worked for it. [We must] [e]ncourage employers to offer 'entry' jobs to the labour market by lowering the burden of tax and social security contributions on low-paid jobs. We must explore the scope to lower the burden of non-wage labour costs by environmental taxes. [We must] [i]ntroduce targeted programmes for the long-term unemployed and other disadvantaged groups to give them the opportunity to reintegrate into the labour market on the principle of rights and responsibilities going together. [We must] [a]ssess all benefit recipients, including people of working age in the receipt of disability benefits, for their potential to earn, and reform state employment services to assist those capable of work to find appropriate work. [We must] [s]upport enterprise and setting up an own business as a viable route out of unemployment. Such decisions contain considerable risks for those who dare to make such a step. We must support those people by managing these risks.

The left's supply-side agenda will hasten structural change. But it will also make that change easier to live with and manage. Adapting to change is never easy and the speed of change appears faster than ever before, not least under the impact of new technologies. Change inevitably destroys some jobs, but it creates others. [...]

Adjustment will be the easier, the more labour and product markets are working properly. Barriers to employment in relatively low productivity sectors need to be lowered if employees displaced by the productivity gains that are an inherent feature of structural change are to find jobs elsewhere. The labour market needs a low-wage sector in order to make low-skill jobs available. The tax and benefits system can replenish low incomes from employment and at the same time save on support payments for the unemployed.

V Political Benchmarking in Europe

The challenge is the definition and implementation of a new social democratic politics in Europe. We do not advocate a single European model, still less the transformation of the European Union into a superstate. We are pro-Europe and pro-reform in Europe. People will support further steps towards integration where there is real value-added and they can be clearly justified – such as action to combat crime and destruction of the environment as well as the promotion of common goals in social and employment policy. But at the same time Europe urgently needs reform – more efficient and transparent institutions, reform of outdated policies and decisive action against waste and fraud.

We are presenting our ideas as an outline, not a finalised programme. [...]

[...] We invite all social democrats in Europe not to let this historic opportunity for renewal pass by. The diversity of our ideas is our greatest asset for the future. Our societies expect us to knit together our diverse experiences in a new coherent programme.

Let us together build social democracy's success for the new century. Let the politics of the Third Way and the Neue Mitte be Europe's new hope.

16

New Keynesianism and New Labour

Will Hutton

[…]

New Labour's Achilles heel is that, because it has no economic theory which is critical of capitalism, it is wide open to simple business definitions of the public interest because it has no other reference point. The private finance initiative in the NHS, competition policy, or the reform of corporate law are all, for example, cast in terms of what business wants: there is no intellectual framework that can offer any contrary ballast. The great advantage Keynesian economic theory offered social democrats was that it provided a non-Marxist critique of capitalism along with a workable economic and social programme, and allowed them to conceive the public interest as rather more than the interplay of private interests in a free market. Keynesian axioms defined the post-war common sense, and gave the left then as strong a position as the right today. It was incontestable that there was a structural mismatch between the motivations of savers and investors, which self-evidently the price mechanism alone could not solve – and this was the proximate reason for capitalism swinging between boom and bust. The issue was what the state should do to solve this embedded problem, and so legitimised government action. The way forward, to manipulate the budget deficit so that it compensated for shortfalls and excesses of demand, also allowed higher public spending and taxation – and thus gave the wherewithal to finance ambitious social programmes. Tony Crosland could argue that Keynesianism solved the growth issue and gave the state a growth dividend simultaneously; social democrats could pursue their social goals without socialising the means of production. Even the Conservative Party became part of this new social democrat consensus.

But new Labour has felt compelled to junk Keynes wholesale, and accept the new right consensus that budget deficit manipulation only disturbs the natural rhythms of the economy, and because all government debt eventually becomes monetised, is necessarily inflationary. High public spending and high taxation crowd out private spending and place an illegitimate burden on companies and individuals alike; there is some natural limit, around forty per cent of GDP, which should be the cap to the public sector's role. Even the welfare state and universal social insurance have proved counterproductive, changing individuals' natural proclivity to work and instead offering an incentive to idleness and the refusal of work opportunities. Government action should be avoided if at all possible.

The 'Third Way' has been cast within these assumptions. But all are contestable. Keynesian theory has moved on as well, and 'New Keynesianism', retaining core Keynesian insights, offers as vigorous a criticism of the dynamics of the market economy as it did fifty years ago. In the last five years of his life Keynes became increasingly preoccupied with the inter-relationship between the international trade and financial system and their impact on the policy options of any one national economy. He saw the structure of the international financial system, with its bias towards over-rewarding surplus countries and over-penalising deficit countries that inevitably accompanies the short-termism of financial markets, as a locus of economic instability in its own right. Deficit countries were forced into excessive economic retrenchment, while surplus countries could indefinitely avoid the inflation in their price level that might help deficit countries to regain competitiveness. The task was to inbuild automatic stabilisers into the international system, so that deficit countries could ameliorate the vortex of self-reinforcing downward ratchets in demand and surplus countries were forced into recycling their surpluses.

The launch of the Bretton Woods system of fixed but adjustable exchange rates along with the IMF and World Bank were a tribute to his thinking – and it is that tradition that New Keynesians are increasingly revisiting. There has also been a resurgence in interest in how, even supposing complete rationality by economic agents, there are inevitable proclivities for market systems to malfunction because prices do not convey enough information to do otherwise. For example conservative advocates of free market economics suppose that prices are necessarily flexible as buyers and sellers haggle, and that it is only interventions by governments, monopolists and trade unions that cause inflexibility. However, New Keynesians like Greg Mankiw have demonstrated that it is perfectly rational for buyers and sellers to change their prices infrequently, and that if the speed of price change varies between markets, then that alone can be a cause of economic instability. Equally, buyers and sellers may be perfectly rational, but simply have differential access to information – and that can change their bargaining strategies.

A new generation of Keynesian theorists use game theory to demonstrate how strategies by market actors are interdependent with the strategies of those with whom they bargain as they try to gain advantage. In *Just Playing*, Professor Ken Binmore argues that the gains from co-operation between market actors, in all imaginable variants of game strategy, are so overwhelming that he claims to have found a new justification of John Rawls' famous advocacy of the social contract as reflecting basic human instincts for fairness. And, lastly, there is a new interest in growth theory. Free market economists are forced to argue that if markets are efficient then growth emerges as a by-product of factors that are exogenous to the market system – the rate of population growth, for example, or the rate of technological change. New Keynesian economists such as David Romer are not prepared to treat growth as exogenous to the market system, and have made great strides in showing how public investment in education, training, transport and science can have extraordinary spillover effects on productivity growth. Endogenous growth theory, much pilloried after its brief advocacy by Gordon Brown when in opposition, is a New Keynesian advocacy of the power of public initiative in pump-priming productivity growth.

This body of theory is the political economy that must underpin any reconceptualising of social democracy. Four clear inter-related themes emerge. The first is that the first condition for any successful social democratic regime is an international economic architecture that permits countries to forge and sustain their own unique social contracts. After the financial mayhem on the periphery of the world economy over the last eighteen months, and the threat it poses to the prosperity of the western heartlands, this has never been more self-evident. Market systems do not create their own stable architecture; they ricochet from hope to despair. Although there is now a new consensus that fixed exchange rate regimes, whether in Asia or Latin America, have to be abandoned for floating rates, little is solved thereby. Countries adopted fixed exchange rates to attract inward direct investment flows, the accompanying technologies and to achieve low inflation: without them they may be less prone to financial panics and sudden withdrawals of capital, but they will find that the pace of sound economic development sharply slows as inward flows of capital and technology decelerate. The Keynesian anxiety to design an international financial system which allows a fair distribution of global economic growth is never more urgent.

Secondly a much more subtle critique of capitalism is opened up along with a redefined role for the state. If prices are inevitably sticky, information held differentially and there is a tendency for market valuations, especially those in the financial system, to overshoot, then the regulatory task is to construct mechanisms of information diffusion and accountability that support and supplement the price mechanism. The issue becomes building a legal and financial constitution in which capitalism can be saved from its own tendency to create monopolies in which markets are cornered, where there is excessive short-termism and incredible rewards to insiders in the know. This is the justification for economic stakeholding; embedding in the warp and weft of capitalism incentives to behave fairly and honourably towards workers, customers, suppliers and investors alike – and where such behaviour is reciprocated.

Thirdly there is a key role for the state in trying to lift the growth of productivity by doing the job the markets do not do spontaneously themselves – addressing externalities and creating public goods. This is the argument for increasing investment, for example, in education where the social rates of return are high, and even to a degree in training where if the returns are lower and more questionable they clearly exist. Public investment in transport, science, research and development and even health brings high economic and social returns as well. The public sector's role is to lead and finance this investment itself; the use of private finance and public/private partnerships of necessity has to be sparing. After all, the private sector neglects these areas precisely because the financial returns are so diffuse and it is hard for the private sector to capture them.

And lastly there is the Keynesian case for setting out and specifying the social contract. The vague formulation of the [T]hird [W]ay – rights should be matched by obligations – needs to be more tightly drawn into a framework in which collaboration by all parties produces a better outcome than individual decision-making. If there is an obligation to search for work and undertake training, for example, that should accompany social security entitlements, then it needs to be clear what responsibility falls to the state to make sure that work is findable. In other words, if there is a case for weak and powerless individuals to take a greater responsibility for their own circumstances, then the state has to take a greater responsibility for ensuring that they have a greater chance of success than at present.

As it stands, the Third Way has become a de facto means of the state reducing its obligations and shifting the burden of risk onto those least able to bear it, while only offering limited help in compensation. This may be a legitimate position for the right, but it is no part of any conceivable social contract. The social contract approach should be generalised across the gamut – from pensions to education.

Apologists for new Labour will argue that there are traces of all these themes in its thinking, and so there are, but they are not built into a coherent political story. New Labour does not argue for membership of the euro as part of a new international financial architecture; does not portray welfare reform as part of a new and humane social contract; does not argue that the state should take a lead role in financing public investment because it raises growth; and does not take a determined position in refashioning corporate law or the banking system to make good embedded shortcomings in the price mechanism. It cannot, because it distrusts the New Keynesian political economy that underlies such an array of propositions, preferring instead to trust the conservative political economy of its opponents. In the short run this has been successful; but in the long run there is no future in creating a progressive coalition that is not progressive. And there is no liberal social democratic position possible that does not incorporate the political economy of Keynes: a truth that new Labour is set to discover the hard way.

17

President's Speech to the TUC Congress, September 2001

Bill Morris

As we welcome our Prime Minister, we are aware that Labour's greatest achievement during its first term of office was to replace the failed economics of the past by laying the foundations of a strong and stable economy for the future.

Of course we recognise that problems still exist; indeed, the TUC was the first among those to identify the 'two-speed' economy. Whilst the service sector continues to flourish, during the past year it is a tragedy that 100,000 jobs have been lost in manufacturing. Today, our call is for action, urgent action, and action now! *(Applause)*

Only a partnership between government, the trade unions and, indeed, business can address the structural problems which have prevented the British economy from matching our competitors' levels of productivity. Reversing the trends on productivity would be a real and lasting achievement for our generation.

The importance of a strong economy, of course, cannot be overstated. But it is not an end in itself. Economic wealth is a means to an end . . . and that end must for us be social justice.

It is on the theme of social justice that I wish to focus today. I believe that having established its credentials for economic competence, Labour must now demonstrate in its second term that it is also the champion for social justice. By delivering social justice, it means delivering on the public services.

For far too long the quality of our public services has been neglected as part of the political debate. But it is now back where it belongs – right at the top of our agenda.

In the debate we make no apologies for our contribution. We are triple stakeholders. We are the taxpayers who fund the services. Our members work at the very sharp end in delivering those services, and we are also consumers of those services.

The people know that public services cannot be fixed by spin or by presentation, but fixed only by real improvements through real investments in real services.

I have to say to you that, as far as we are concerned, the simplistic sound-bytes about 'what works is what works best' is no longer acceptable. For us, public services are not an optional extra. The quality of our public services defines not just the quality of our lives but it also defines the moral state of our nation. That is what it also defines!

The policy-makers need to acknowledge that a society which largely depends on the private sector to deliver public services would be a very different kind of society indeed from that which is required to create equality of opportunity and social justice. It would be a society in which financial imperatives took precedence over social goals. A society where the priorities would be shareholder values rather than social needs.

For us, we say that any reform must therefore proceed on the basis that the public sector is as much about social values and citizenship as it is about delivering services. So, whilst accepting the realities of a market economy, we reject emphatically the notion of a market society. We reject that because it has no place. *(Applause)*

So let it be understood that our ideology will not constrain us from defending our public services and defending our members.

Colleagues, delivering on social justice also means delivering on employment rights.

As we survey the political landscape, we are able to say that this Government have delivered on many aspects of fairness at work, but our agenda this week highlights, through the TUC priorities, a number of areas which need to be further addressed. These include: fair and equal pay; genuine 'work-life balance' for both men and women; lifelong learning opportunities; and a decent pension for all.

In the field of trade union recognition, we believe that we have to see a change in the culture of exclusions and opt-outs. That culture leaves thousands of British workers without any protection or rights. Again, we say, access to justice cannot depend on how many people are on the pay-roll.

It cannot be right that British workers have to deliver first-class labour market flexibility, but have to settle for second-class employment rights. Those two do not add up.

Yesterday, social justice was our dream. Today, social justice is our challenge. Tomorrow, let social justice be our achievement. Thank you. *(Applause)*

18

Did Things Get Better? An Audit of Labour's Successes and Failures

Polly Toynbee and David Walker

Luck and judgement in about equal measure secured the Blair Government's sterling performance. Labour's luck embraced the swift recovery of East Asia and Brazil from recession in 1998 and the continuing mega-strength of the United States, sucking in goods and capital like a vacuum-cleaner. Labour's judgement lay in horse-whispering the right words in the direction of the City and business, which together rode above trend growth, which in turn pumped extra revenues into Gordon Brown's pocket. The right words were *right*. New Labour had to swear repeatedly on the bible of neo-liberalism while Gordon Brown set out to achieve the residual aim of socialism – a more equal society – by stealth.

He certainly covered his tracks. No one seemed to notice how his 1997 changes in pension fund contributions accomplished what one writer in the *Financial Times* called 'one of the greatest raids on corporate cashflow in history'. It and other measures pushed taxes on private companies from 3.5 per cent of GDP in 1998–9 to 3.9 per cent in 2001–2, not a bad feat in a world where globalization was supposed to forbid one-country hits on the private sector. [...]

From 1997 to 2001 the economy boomed. The proportion of those aged between eighteen and sixty-five in work grew spectacularly. By early 2001 at 75 per cent the employment rate was pushing towards its previous peak under Ted Heath in the early 1970s and was getting nearer the 77 per cent in work in the United States – the more people in work, the more likely the economy to grow. One count, the Labour Force survey, said fewer than 1.5 million people were out of work by year's end 2000; another, the count of those claiming social benefits, put the total by early 2001 at under 1 million. In the year to April 2000, average gross earnings were nearly £22,000 per employee, male, that is – women on average earned 38 per cent less; Labour did not change the gender gap.

True, another arm of the growth machine – output per employee – still looked shrivelled. No miracle cure hove in sight for UK productivity. A telling gap remained between what an average worker produced in the UK relative to other countries, especially those allegedly bloated welfare states of France and Germany – though, typically, Brown chose to point the contrast with the free-enterprise United States.

When it comes to the economy politicians can be more credulous than medieval monks, and Thatcher and Tory Chancellor Nigel Lawson had spied miracles round every corner. As for Brown, his favourite colour was amber. Perhaps caution was just as well when large, old holes in the fabric needed explaining: the UK balance of payments deficit, growing under Labour in response to the upward movement of the economic cycle, regional imbalance, under-investment by both firms and the state, and prevalent human under-performance.

Having purged itself of socialism Labour was left with no overarching economic philosophy. In a 1995 lecture Blair said government's role in the modern economy was limited to keeping inflation low while improving human capital. As for public spending, Labour's rap was straight from the Tory groove: 'how much' mattered less than 'what on'. In a Blair speech in Singapore in 1996 'stakeholding' came to brief life: the economy had to be run for the many not the few in conditions of trust between business and government as unemployment was tackled, small business encouraged and everyone made to feel 'part of the same team'.

Stakeholding then died the death, to be replaced by the equally dreamy Third Way. Pollyanna would have loved its offer of basic minimum rights for individuals at work as Government and industry worked together, enhancing the dynamism of the market not undermining it. Labour's manifesto mixed historical obligation to the unions with modernization. But the key to Labour's tenure was Brown's famous pre-election pledge on income tax: neither the basic nor the top rate of tax would increase.

It was a defining moment: the spectre of defeat in 1992 was laid to rest and a revolution wrought in the way Labour was perceived. But the Big Question now dangles before us. How far, in the electoral circumstances of early 1997, was Brown's heroic gesture necessary? After he made it, polling gurus were telling Mill-bank that Labour rated 11 per cent more than the Tories on measures of public trust on matters fiscal. Tory recovery was believed to be still possible and the pledge was a prophylactic – Labour practised safe tax. There is a sad syllogism in the making here. Brown's pledge won Labour not just the election but business confidence, but Brown's pledge prevented Labour satisfying the people because it was linked with no spending increases for two years and dissatisfied people may think twice about endorsing Labour again. So Brown may have jeopardized Labour's second term, for among the consequences of his pledge was his bid to pay for spending by indirect taxes (petrol duty for example).

Yet on the pledge hung so many intangibles, market confidence, City expectations, the absence of the capital flight which, literally and figuratively, tipped earlier Labour Governments into pandemonium. In the remaking of Labour it may have been a talisman, but it was also an albatross.

[...]

Gordon Brown's Mouthful

All things considered, any government in power since 1997 would have enjoyed a benign environment. As for Labour, the party came to office shriven of the ideological sins which revisionists since Neil Kinnock believed made them unelectable

As well as sloughing off old commitments, the Blairites had a theory of what a progressive government should seek to do with and to capitalism.

At the heart of New Labour beliefs was the phrase put into Gordon Brown's mouth by his adviser Ed Balls in 1994. 'Neo-classical endogenous growth theory' accepted there was little the modern state could do to alter economic destiny. It should not even try to intervene to disturb the ownership of capital (a windfall tax excluded) or change commercial or property relations at large. In keeping with the theory, Labour proved reluctant to confront the boardrooms, despite mounting evidence of fat-cats thickening their whiskers with corporate cream. Income Data Services sampled the chief executives of FTSE 100 companies and found their basic salaries improved from £463,000 in 1998–9 to £490,000 a year later; total remuneration packages, as they say, went up from £684,000 to £843,000. Reform of corporate governance – the question of whether shareholders had any real power over executives and their pay – was deferred.

Instead, the job of the state was to foster technological innovation, improve labour force education and skills, enforce tight rules on competition – and preach truth and beauty (Brown, son of the manse, loved to sermonize). The state, in other words, was to be capitalism's better self. Above all the state had to mind its own business. From this flowed the headline commitments made prior to the 1997 election and Brown's golden rules. A government which forbade itself to tax should have no trouble with the other rules for fiscal prudence invented by Brown. There would be no borrowing to finance spending, unless it was long-term investment (calculations to be made over the economic cycle rather than in any given year).

Similarly, over the medium run the state's indebtedness was to be kept stable as a proportion of GDP. Here Brown excelled himself, repaying past borrowing hand over fist and making the UK a European exemplar of prudent housekeeping. Margaret Thatcher had been fond of that kind of household analogy. If the UK were a mortgaged house worth £200,000, under Brown that mortgage was reduced to £80,000 with a prospect of getting it down further to just over £60,000: most financial advisers would suggest it was time to borrow a bit more.

Labour also promised to stick to the Tories' target for price inflation, 2.5 per cent a year or less. It did – inflation was falling below 1.0 per cent by the end of 2000, on the common or HICP (harmonized indices of consumer prices) measure, well below Euroland's 2.3 per cent. But inflation had been on target for the two years prior to the election. In 2001 the proverbial man from Mars might have looked at the price data and said the downward curve was continuous and it was hard to identify exactly when Labour was elected.

Inflation mattered less anyway. A long-run transformation in UK economic capacity seemed to be under way, leading some commentators to talk about the new disinflationary age. Growth no longer had to be pinched off to secure price stability. The productive potential of the UK economy was growing faster than actual growth. And all this was occurring at a time when the longer-term unemployed were being absorbed back into work, lacking skills and so not much able to improve productivity. Part of the explanation was investment: UK spending on information and communications technology was proportionately the same as in the US.

This was a propitious background to New Labour's experiment in central banking. In Brown's coup of 6 May 1997, the Bank of England was set an inflation target and given control over short-term interest rates in order to achieve it. Decisions were entrusted to a new monetary policy committee (MPC), a majority of its members appointed by the Chancellor. On the money supply, only bankers' decisions would command 'the necessary confidence' – Brown said. This was a clever tactic which succeeded in reassuring the markets that Labour's conversion to Thatcherism was genuine – after all, this was the step at which both she and Nigel Lawson had balked. It was also capitulation to the doctrine that democratically elected politicians are incapable of an entire class of economic decisions. If not interest rates, why should politicians take decisions on tax or (this became Stephen Byers's policy) corporate mergers? Labour left open the question of accountability. The Commons Treasury committee sought to interrogate appointees but its criteria were vague. Perhaps temperament was the key attribute. According to economist Sir Alan Budd, a displaced member, optimists differed in their assessment of inflation prospects by as much as 1 per cent. The Liberal Democrats, confusingly, sought both more independence for the members of the MPC and more politicization of their appointments.

The political bonus from giving the Bank this autonomy was huge – once the imperialist governor Eddie George had been persuaded not to resign over losing supervision of the banks. Labour could claim a new historic identity as the low inflation party. At a stroke, Brown exorcized the ghosts of Montagu Norman, Philip Snowden, Lord Cromer and Denis Healey. But of course he was also tying his own hands. After his July 2000 spending plan and his pre-budget reports in November, where was his guarantee the Bank would not judge his spending 'excessive' and push up interest rates, nullifying the political benefit? It was a point he tried to put to pensioners and hauliers but not an easy one to get over.

[...]

How Labour Shrunk the State

Labour had no *a priori* thoughts about how big government should be. It was thus by accident rather than the result of deliberate decision that by April 2001 the state should be smaller as a proportion of GDP than in April 1997. Government spending fell from 41.2 per cent in John Major's last year (1996–7) to 37.7 per cent in 1999–2000. In the final year of Brown's planning period, 2003–4, this key ratio was to reach only 40.6 per cent. It had been as high as 44.1 per cent under Major and even under that epitome of moderation, Roy Jenkins, was 41.8 per cent (in 1969–70). New Labour, in other words, did nothing to reposition the UK in the league table showing how big governments are; it remained some way beneath France and Germany but above Japan and the US. Brown said what mattered more than the size of the state was its creation of general conditions for business.

The commitment to spend at Tory levels plus Brown's personal ascendancy in the cabinet gave the Treasury the commanding heights. First, it ordered a 'comprehensive review' of spending – not so dissimilar, it turned out, from the Tories' 'fundamental' reviews. The Treasury made a further bid for control over the minutiae of spending by publishing in 1998 a set of Public Service Agreements (PSAs) with departments and agencies. Many of them were specious, with falsely precise quantities attached. They were also far from fundamental: they accepted the structure of government as was, failing for example to question the political rationale of the Ministry of Agriculture. The broad shares of spending claimed by defence, despite cuts, and crime remained broadly the same – so much for prioritizing health and education.

A second, slimmed-down edition of the PSAs was published, to steer the period 2001–4. Were they really intended to make government more transparent or were they just a device for putting the frighteners on the rest of Whitehall? If the former, said the Committee on Public Accounts, let us monitor them; the Treasury refused. But Blair's seizure of the health issue seemed to say the PSAs were irrelevant – health would get the money because political exigency demanded it, not because of some abstruse measure of efficiency. Besides, for all the Treasury's supremacy, Whitehall departments were not so easily cowed. Brown ordered up a National Asset Register, a sort of Domesday Book of what the state owned. Little was subsequently heard of it. Similarly ambitious plans to rebase Whitehall accounts on resources consumed rather than cash spent – enacted in 2000 – were scaled back. Existing accounting conventions will continue along with considerable confusion over who (the National Audit Office, Treasury, Public Accounts Committee, Audit Commission?) is actually responsible for ensuring the state gets maximum bang for its buck.

But the Treasury had the aggregates firmly in its paws. Within Tory totals, Brown quickly did some small-scale swopping around, announcing that from the contingency reserve it was pulling down £1 billion extra for schools and £1.2 billion for health, to start in April 1998. House-building by councils was modestly expanded, paid for from recycled receipts from previous sales under the right to buy. The March 1998 budget allocated health a further £500 million, schools £250 million and transport £175 million. This was not 'new' money but the product of under-spending elsewhere.

The July 1998 spending announcement was dangerously oversold. First, its money would be spent only from April 1999; its planning period was 1999–2002. Second, it was basically a health and education review, with 75 per cent of extra spending 1998–9 and 2001–2 going in their direction. It sought to reverse the pattern under the Tories of cutting capital spending. Over the four years from 1997 public investment is supposed to have grown by 12.1 per cent a year in real terms – which meant a huge pick-up since capital spending by the state fell by nearly 5 per cent a year from April 1997 to March 1999. Little wonder that the Government was embarrassed by reports in spring 2000 that the spending was not being delivered – departments and councils had lost the habit.

Then came Brown's apotheosis as spender, the July 2000 announcement, following another review. This one was even less comprehensive, more a collection of bids which, for once, the Treasury was willing to concede – from April 2001 onwards, albeit within the rather conservative framework of keeping total public spending to the 2.5 per cent a year increase 'allowed' by the growth in the economy. One of its most significant elements was the switch to investment. Even pre-empted by the health commitments, it made for a bulging package with net public investment to rise from £8 billion to £20 billion a year, scaffolds up and holes in the roads for years.

PFI v. PPP

Capital spending was also subject to the vagaries of the Private Finance Initiative (PFI), born of the Tories but rechristened by Labour Public-Private Partnerships.

According to the theory, computers for the Inland Revenue, a new Treasury building, hospitals and schools would be built and financed by private consortia in return for a string of future payments which would cover both the cost of capital and management charges. It was big money. Net investment by the state in 1999–2000 was supposed to be £6.4 billion, with private money contributing a further £3.8 billion of projects.

Since 1997 contracts have been signed for 150 projects worth over £12 billion, including thirty-five hospitals, 520 schools and four prisons. Crudely put, the state got 'free' capital spending in exchange for pledging current spending in future. A lot of it: PFI-type payments to the private sector would rise from £3.5 billion every year from 2004–5 to 2012–13.

Some of the nation's best accountancy brains were appalled at the open-endedness of the promise, especially because the state could surely afford to borrow in order to invest. In 2001 UK Government debt is 39.4 per cent of GDP, already one of the lowest EU proportions, with a plan to cut it further, to 33 per cent – while Germany's is 59.5, France's 57.1. There were doubts, too, about whether the private sector did it better. A report by the Industrial Society said the PPP insisted on by John Prescott to finance expansion of the London Underground gave poor value (there were safety worries too). PFI deals in the health service were said by expert critics to have cut the number of available beds and diverted money from the clinical front line. For some companies it was a one-way ticket to income. For example, Andersen Consulting supplied a new system for handling National Insurance but – said the National Audit Office – it ran late, paid the wrong amounts to a lot of claimants and cost taxpayers an extra £53 million. Andersen ended up paying just £4.1 million in compensation. Similarly the computers which got the Passport Agency into so much trouble in 1999 were supplied by Siemens Business Services, which ended up paying a paltry fine.

Without PFI, Labour ministers pleaded, these schemes would not have got going. But that is only true if you accept the Brownian premise that Labour could not 'afford' to borrow to invest. And he could.

[…]

Brown the (Residual) Socialist

Brown strove to keep a progressive political reputation – his briefers portrayed him as the true keeper of the flame of equality. The experts assented. Over the four years the Institute for Fiscal Studies registered a small drop in post-tax income for the best-off tenth of households and a significant gain – 9 per cent – for the poorest tenth: more to come after April 2001. Every little helped, though dour Gordon preferred not to talk about a stealthy increase (from April 2001) in National Insurance for higher earners. At the same time, the redistributionist raised the earnings threshold at which lower-paid people would pay NI.

As for wealth: the trend in the Tory years had been towards more concentration in the upper deciles, i.e. the rich were getting richer. Wealth is hard to measure; pensions for example are in the form of claims to be made in the future. The only current figures are for 1997, when the most wealthy 10 per cent had £63,000 of assets on average versus a notional £100, or more likely nothing, for the bottom 10 per cent. During his reign, Brown did not make it any harder to inherit money. His tinkerings with capital gains may have made accumulation easier for possessors of assets. When the tally is made it could well be that the trends of the early to mid 1990s continued.

[...]

Labour gets a gold star for rectifying the UK's finances. The public sector, as the economists put it, had emerged from the 1992 recession unbalanced, spending out of kilter with taxing and borrowing. That was put right by Kenneth Clarke's spending restraint and tax increases followed – seamlessly – by Gordon Brown. But Clarke cynically admitted that the promises made by the Tories before the 1997 election would not have been kept – especially its plans to restrain spending yet further. So Brown probably kept spending tighter than the Tories would have done, though according to past patterns no doubt they would have spent very differently – tax cuts before services. Needing money, he kept taxing too, albeit stealthily.

The Organization for Economic Cooperation and Development (OECD) judged the UK under Blair to possess an 'enviable' record. The UK economy, said this fount of neo-liberal thinking, was less prone to boom and bust than it had been under Thatcher in the 80s. Low inflation was entrenched. The rate of unemployment compatible with stable prices fell.

So Labour realized – temporarily? – Tony Crosland's old dream of floating the public services on an expanding economy. Of course growth is never reliable. Collapse in the Far East in 1997 had threatened a global slowdown. But by Easter 1998 the worst was over and the curves ticked upwards again. Brown's macro-economic stewardship was not magical but, in the circumstances, was sound enough.

Wise owls say Chancellors always misjudge where precisely they sit on the economic cycle. Spending is to rise hugely during the first five years of the century. If total demand is not to rise faster than the trend rate of growth, about 2.5 per cent a year, then private consumption will have to be kept to a growth rate of some 2 per cent a year, less than half the rate it was growing during the two years to April 2001. In layman's terms that means – whisper it – taxation. [...]

Part III

Realizing Citizenship? Labour and Public Services

One of New Labour's most puzzling contradictions has been its failure to capitalize on the success of its economic policy by expanding and improving the public services. This is all the more perplexing for a party with a long and distinguished history in this area. In many respects, this predicament was inherited from the Conservatives, who had failed to properly invest in the welfare system for most of the 1980s and 1990s. However, the problem is also caused by raised expectations: the electorate expects the welfare state to function 'better' under Labour, and they have therefore been doubly disappointed. The Budget of 2002, announced as this book was going to press, promised significant extra funds for the NHS and education, but it is by no means certain that this will repair New Labour's reputation for public sector failure. The 'public services' covers a potentially vast area of public policy. With this in mind, we have decided to focus on discussion of the general principles underpinning New Labour's approach, along with some examples drawn from community, health and education policy.

New Labour's thinking on welfare has been expressed at two radically different but equally important levels. First, there are the general guiding principles. The 'Third Way' is about the future role of the welfare state in a post-social democratic era, as Tony Blair has made clear on any number of occasions. Of equal importance is placing Labour's new approach in the context of old traditions of arguing about the role of the state. Comparisons between Blair and Brown and the post-war revisionists have flowed thick and fast. Yet there are also critics who suggest that Labour has lost sight of its noble ideal – the pursuit of equality, and that Hugh Gaitskell and Tony Crosland would not have dared go so far as to completely deny the importance of redistribution. It is in this context that Gordon Brown's contributions to the debate should be understood.

If New Labour has downgraded equality, what is its replacement? Julian Le Grand defines the approach as 'CORA' – 'community', 'opportunity', 'responsibility' and 'accountability'. He attempts to put some flesh on the fragile bones of the Third Way, arguing that 'unlike social democracy, it is not egalitarian', and that it contains 'no special commitment to the public sector, to public expenditure or even to the mixed economy'. This kind of argument was bound to inflame those who had looked to the new Government to repair some of the damage they believed had been inflicted by years of underfunding. Once it became clear that neither radical welfare reform nor significant increases in public expenditure were on the agenda, dissenting voices emerged. These were typified by a letter to the *Financial Times* signed by dozens of social policy and sociology researchers from British universities, challenging the relative intellectual failure of New Labour's ideas on the welfare state.

The second level of expression for ideas on the public services is the realm of policy documents. These provide some idea of how ideas are implemented at ground level. A new Social Exclusion Unit, established in the Cabinet Office and operating under the scrutiny of Blair and Brown, was given the task of producing fresh thinking on poverty and welfare dependency and their corrosive effects on local communities. Here we may see the resonance of New Labour phrases like 'no rights without responsibilities'. For in setting out how communities would be reinvigorated by the Government, the emphasis is as much on state encouragement of more 'responsible' personal behaviour as on the economic conditions necessary for equality of opportunity. Similar principles flow through education policy, and here the emphasis on results, meeting targets and producing 'excellence' is promoted in defiance of critics who dwell upon the thorny issue of funding. Labour's answer, when it comes to the public services, is to set out what it believes to be limited and achievable 'pledges' – on class sizes, for example. This approach covers the rest of the public sector, as complex policy on spending is replaced by such confident claims as that there will be 'more nurses and doctors'.

The Government has embarked upon a programme of modernization of the NHS's internal administrative structures, introducing new innovations like NHS Direct – a phone and Internet advisory service, trailed in the Department of Health's 1997 White Paper. It was also determined to dismantle the worst elements of the internal market introduced under the Conservatives, but critics such as Will Hutton point to the fact that rules governing the role of the private sector in capital projects such as hospital building were relaxed under the Private Finance Initiative, storing up potential future problems. The long-term significance of Labour's welfare reforms is explored in two pieces. In a useful summary of the main trends, Stephen Driver and Luke Martell discuss the 'post-Thatcherite' settlement as it relates to welfare. In a richly theoretical piece, Nick Ellison, borrowing from a famous political economist, argues that Labour has shifted its approach to welfare from a social democratic to a 'social Schumpeterian' perspective.

19

The Third Way: New Politics for the New Century

Tony Blair

We seek a diverse but inclusive society, promoting tolerance within agreed norms, promoting civic activism as a complement to (but not a replacement for) modern government. An inclusive society imposes duties on individuals and parents as well as on society as a whole. Promoting better state and civic support for individuals and parents as they meet their responsibilities is a critical contemporary challenge, cutting across our approach to education, welfare, and crime reduction.

Strong communities depend on shared values and a recognition of the rights and duties of citizenship – not just the duty to pay taxes and obey the law, but the obligation to bring up children as competent, responsible citizens, and to support those – such as teachers – who are employed by the state in the task. In the past we have tended to take such duties for granted. But where they are neglected, we should not hesitate to encourage and even enforce them, as we are seeking to do with initiatives such as our 'home-school contracts' between schools and parents.

Criminal justice is critical to the Third Way. It was essential for Labour to break free from the view that social considerations weakened personal responsibility for crime and disorder. Hence my call for a government that was 'tough on crime and tough on the causes of crime'. [...]

The Old Left sometimes claimed that the state should largely subsume civil society; the New Right believes that if the state retreats from social duties, civic activism will automatically fill the void. The Third Way recognises the limits of government in the social sphere, but also the need for government, within those limits, to forge new partnerships with the voluntary sector. Whether in education, health, social work, crime prevention or the care of children, 'enabling' government strengthens civil society rather than weakening it, and helps families and communities improve their own performance. Volunteering; school governorships; fostering and adoption; public health; young offender programmes – all demonstrate the state, voluntary sector and individuals working together. New Labour's task is to strengthen the range and quality of such partnerships.

This is the basis on which to sustain and improve a healthy civil society for the new century. The welfare state is one of the great creations of this century. It lifted many people out of poverty, and offered new opportunities to millions. To provide for those at the bottom is in some ways the essence of the good society. But the ways in which we help people need to change. It is essential that we offer adequate services, not just cash benefits; that we give greater emphasis to partnership between public and private provision; that we recognise the need to relate subsidies to need, particularly where – as with university fees – a failure to do so would result in fewer opportunities and lower quality provision all round. We must also recognise the implications for the welfare state of change in labour market and family patterns – for example the strain on contributory benefits that arises from regular and/or prolonged spells of unemployment. And there are new needs to be met, such as long term care for the elderly.

To emphasise, as I do, the importance of the family is not to believe that we can recreate a nostalgic version of family life in the Fifties. This is as unreal and misguided as calling for the return of the smokestack industries. The traditional structure of the family – full time employment for men, full time housework for women – could not survive the demand for equality between men and women. The life of any family and any community depends on accepting and discharging the formal and informal obligations we owe to each other. The politics of 'us' rather than 'me' demands an ethic of responsibility as well as rights. This is the foundation of social solidarity on which any successful society depends. Some marriages and relationships will not be for life. But people's need to be able to make commitments, and to abide by them, has not changed.

[...]

The era of 'big government means better government' is over. Leverage, not size, is what counts. What government does, and how well, not how much, is the key to its role in modern society.

Taxation goes to the heart of the Third Way. In the Eighties the issue of tax was more important than any other in holding back the Left. Contrary to the belief of the Right, this was not because the middle classes wanted tax cuts at any price. Rather, it flowed from a perception of the Left as invariably the champion of higher, indiscriminate and often ineffective public spending. We seemed to want to throw money at every problem, with little if any concern for the efficiency with which public resources were spent. One of the strongest claims of the Third Way is that tax must be kept under control and that all public spending is 'money for results and reform'. That is why I place such emphasis on the modernisation of public services, to go with the substantial investment they need to succeed. The National Health Service is the largest employer in Europe: we are determined that it does not become a bloated bureaucracy. There will be no return to the old centralised command and control systems, which stifled innovation and responsibility, and we reject the creation of bureaucratic and pointless internal markets. Instead we favour partnerships at local level, with investment tied to targets and measured outcomes, with national standards but local freedom to manage and innovate. [...]

Whitehall also needs to be far more discriminating in its intervention. 'Intervention in inverse proportion to success' is the philosophy underpinning our education reforms: Ministers have been given tough powers to intervene in the case of failing schools and education authorities, but they are increasing the autonomy of the majority doing a good job. We are applying the same principle to the NHS and local government. In all areas, monitoring and inspection are playing a key role, as an incentive to higher standards and as a means of determining appropriate levels of intervention. A new pragmatism is growing in the relations between the public and private sectors. The emphasis must be on goals not rules, and monitoring achievements not processes.

[...] We want to revitalise the ethic of public service. Public servants must do more than administer services; their job is to generate greater public value from our stock of public assets.

20

Equality – Then and Now

Gordon Brown

[...]

[...] [A]fter 20 years in which New Right ideology which has worshipped inequality has dominated the political landscape, it is now more important than ever that we argue the case for equality from first principles.

Today, we argue for equality not just because of our belief in social justice but also because of our view of what is required for economic success. The starting point is a fundamental belief in the equal worth of every human being. We all have an equal claim to social consideration by virtue of being human. And if every person is to be regarded as of equal worth, all deserve to be given an equal chance in life to fulfil the potential with which they are born.

[Tony] Crosland took issue with the old view – used to justify inequality in educational opportunity – that intelligence was a fixed quantity, something given in limited measure in the genetic make-up of the new-born child. Crosland was right. Intelligence cannot be reduced to a single number in an IQ test taken at the age of 11. People cannot be ranked in a single hierarchy and talent cannot be regarded as fixed. So people should not be written off at 7, 11 or 14 or indeed at any time in their life. It is simply a denial of any belief in equality of opportunity if we assume that there is one type of intelligence, one means of assessing it, only one time when it should be assessed and only one chance of succeeding.

But we have still to act on the consequence of recognising these facts: that people have a richness of potential to be tapped, that their talents take many forms – skills in communication, language, and working with other people as well as analytical intelligence – that these talents can develop over a lifetime, and that to get the best economy we need to get the best out of people's potential. And if we are to allow each person to develop that potential which exists within them, it is clear that we need to develop a more demanding view of equality of opportunity than a one-off equality of opportunity up till age 16.

So I believe that everyone should have the chance to bridge the gap between what they are and what they have it in themselves to become. But what is right on ethical grounds is, in the 1990s, good for the economy too. In our information-age economy, the most important resource of a firm or a country is not its raw materials, or a favourable geographical location, but the skills of the whole workforce. And so prosperity for a company or country can be delivered only if we get the best out of all people, and that cannot happen without continuous and accessible equality of opportunity.

Indeed, I would suggest that Britain's economic weakness is not attributable to a neglect at the top of the educational pyramid, but has arisen because we have given insufficient attention in education and employment policies to the latent and diverse potential of the population as a whole. In the industrial age, the denial of opportunity offended many people but was not necessarily a barrier to the success of the economy. Today, in an economy where skills are the essential means of production, the denial of opportunity has become an unacceptable inefficiency, a barrier to prosperity.

And once we take this view that what matters on ethical and economic grounds is the equal right to realise potential, we reject – as Anthony Crosland did – both an unrealisable equality of outcome and a narrow view of equality of opportunity. Indeed, we reject equality of outcome not because it is too radical but because it is neither desirable nor feasible.

Crosland himself wrote of 'the rent of ability', recognising that incentives for effort are essential in any economic system: greater incomes for some justified by the contribution they make to the society as a whole. Indeed I would go further: predetermined results imposed, as they would have to be, by a central authority and decided irrespective of work, effort or contribution to the community, is not a socialist dream but other people's nightmare of socialism.

It denies humanity, rather than liberates it. It is to make people something they are not, rather than helping them to make the most of what they can be. What people resent about Britain is not that some people who have worked hard have done well. What angers people is that millions have been denied the opportunity to realise their potential. It is this inequality that must be addressed. Just as we join Crosland in rejecting an unattainable equality of outcome, so we refuse to narrow our horizons to a limited view of equality of opportunity.

There was an old idea of equality of opportunity in which it meant a single chance to get your foot on a narrow ladder, one opportunity at school till 16 followed by an opportunity for 20 per cent to go into higher education. And for millions of people in Britain it has meant that if you missed that chance it was gone forever. It is the equal opportunity only to become unequal: as Crosland wrote, 'only a few exceptional individuals hauled out of their class by society's talent scouts, can ever climb'. It is in the words of Tawney the invitation for all to come to dinner in the sure knowledge that circumstances would prevent most people from attending.

Whether done on the basis of birth or academic qualifications, the potential of all is clearly denied when we entrench the privilege of a few. So Crosland correctly concluded that a narrow equality of opportunity was not enough if we were to prevent the entrenchment of unjustifiable privilege, and sought a broader view of equality that complemented rather than conflicted with the importance he attached to personal liberty. He proposed what he called a democratic view of equality – one that sought to prevent the permanent entrenchment of privilege from whatever source it came. This more demanding view of equality of opportunity – democratic equality – had, as he said in *The Conservative Enemy*, 'revolutionary connotations'.

So what, in the 1990s, does this concept of democratic equality mean for me?

First, it demands employment opportunity for all because work is central not just to economic prosperity for Britain but to individual fulfilment. And there must be a permanent duty on government to relentlessly pursue this objective.

Secondly, we must as a society ensure not just a one-off educational opportunity in childhood, but continuing and lifelong educational opportunity for all – second, third, and even fourth chances so that people are not written off if they fail at school and are not left behind by the pace of technological change.

Thirdly, life-long opportunity must be comprehensive, extending beyond education and employment, involving genuine access to culture – and, most importantly, a redistribution of power that offers people real control over the decisions that affect their lives.

While Crosland did write about industrial democracy, he said less about the state or about an equal right to participate in the decisions that affect our lives. In the 1940s people accepted services handed down from the state – for example, housing. They now want to make their own choices over their own lives and rightly see themselves as decision-makers in their own right and they want a government that will enable them to make decisions for themselves and give them power over their lives. So the issue for socialists is not so much about what the state can do for you but about what the state can enable you to do for yourself.

Political reform is central to this: it must enable people to have the chance to participate in decisions that affect them. This is about more than the concept of a classless society, it is about power and therefore about a truly democratic society. Proponents of democratic equality must also – even in a global marketplace – address wealth and income inequalities. I believe that these inequalities can be justified only if they are in the interests of the least fortunate.

Crosland took his stand against inequalities of social status and wealth. He viewed the question of income inequalities as of lesser importance, but he thought that great inequalities of wealth, and particularly inherited wealth, could not be justified as a source of enormous social and economic advantage. But Crosland also saw the distinction between the private ownership of property that simply furthered privilege and the private ownership of property that allowed people control over their lives. So he was ahead of his time on the Left in wanting a more general diffusion of property among the entire population. Indeed, he was right to say in *The Conservative Enemy* that 'If the property is well-distributed, a property-owning democracy is a socialist rather than a conservative ideal.'

Democratic equality means we tackle unjustifiable inequalities, but it also, of course, pre-supposes a guaranteed minimum below which no one should fall. Our minimum standards must include a minimum wage, a tax and benefit system that helps people into work, the best possible level of health and social services for all and the assurance of dignity and security for those who are retired or unable to work through infirmity.

21

The Third Way Begins with CORA

Julian Le Grand

[...] [I]s the Blair government simply a new right administration, basically pursuing the Thatcherite agenda albeit perhaps with a more compassionate facade? Alternatively, is it aiming at a kind of sixties social democracy, but with a nineties hard edge? Or is it the operational arm of a real alternative philosophy: one that cannot be located on the old left and new right spectrum, and indeed is not even part of that spectrum? [...]

[...] [I]n many of the government's actions there is clearly a belief in the value of community, especially local communities. This is apparent in much of its dealing with local government, where it is encouraging community-building of various kinds; in the move towards elected mayors in London and probably soon in other major cities, in the drive for devolution for Scotland and Wales; and in the stress on the importance of local actions in the new public health green paper. New Labour councils are emphasising the importance of communities within their areas, often by taking action against what they regard as anti-social activities: witness the tough council tenants' agreement in Oldham where tenants have to keep their gardens 'neat and tidy', are only allowed certain kinds of pets that have to be kept under control, and have to 'look after children properly'.

But the belief in the value of community goes wider than that. Along with many others, the government clearly believes that the individualistic competition of the Thatcher years was socially destructive, and that it needs to be replaced by a spirit of co-operation and consultation.

The white paper on the NHS emphasises the damage that it considers the internal market did to the health service and stresses the importance of co-operation, not only between purchasers and providers, but between GPs, between hospital trusts, and between health bodies and local authorities. The public health green paper talks of a contract between people and government, and of partnership between individuals and local organisations to improve all our health. The importance of social cohesion is emphasised in the very title of the Social Exclusion Unit: not a poverty or inequality unit, nor even a social justice one, but a government body intended to focus on the processes by which people are included or excluded from the wider community.

[...] [A]pparent in many government actions is a strong emphasis on accountability. Community organisations, local governments, health authorities, schools and hospitals are to be encouraged to act more vigorously and more boldly – but they are to be held accountable to their local communities for their actions. The consultation paper Modernising Local Government suggests a number of ways of making local governments more accountable to their communities, including annual elections, maximising electoral registration and making more use of citizens' juries, focus groups and deliberative opinion polling.

And local organisations will also have to be accountable to the national community, as represented by the central government. Since last year's white paper on education, the Department for Education and Employment has set literacy and numeracy targets for schools. They are now also to be confronted with 'Pandas': performance and assessment reports that will include benchmark targets related to the family background of their pupils. Schools that consistently fail to meet these and other targets will be closed or hit squads will be sent in.

In the NHS health authorities and hospitals are also going to have to operate within a national 'performance framework'. Performance will be judged against centrally set indicators. Thirty-seven of these have been suggested, covering an enormous range: to pick five at random, they include deaths from all causes, conception rates for girls aged 13–15, inappropriately used surgery, length of stay in hospital and emergency psychiatric readmission rates. In addition, two central bodies are being set up to oversee the use of medical procedures: the National Institute for Clinical Effectiveness (Nice), to determine what should be used; and the Council for Health Improvement (Chimp, or, as some prefer to call it, Nasty) to make sure that doctors use it. If hospitals consistently fail to perform adequately, the hit squads will again be at the door.

[In addition] and obviously related to the notion of community accountability, there is a strong belief in individual responsibility. This is implicit in the harder attitude emanating from the Home Office towards criminal and other forms of antisocial behaviour, and in the emphasis on parents' responsibilities for their children's misdemeanours. It also seems to underlie the drive for changes to the welfare state, impelled not only by costs but also by a desire to reduce benefit *dependency* and to encourage individuals to take more responsibility for their own actions. As Tony Blair put it in a recent interview on welfare reform with the *Sun*, the government's view is that Britons need to 'stop wringing their hands and start taking more responsibility for their own lives'.

Related to responsibility is the importance of opportunity. Again this is a crucial element of the welfare debate. Unemployed young people, single parents and the disabled are to be given the opportunity to work; opportunities they will have a responsibility to take up and for which they may suffer penalties if they do not.

So there it is: not 'liberty, equality, fraternity', but 'community, accountability, responsibility and opportunity'. Rearranging the order a bit, the initials yield the acronym Cora: a worthy rival to Mrs Thatcher's Tina (There Is No Alternative). For this is a real alternative.

22

Government Must Reconsider its Strategy for More Equal Society

Ruth Lister and others

Sir, We welcome the announcement over the summer of the establishment of a Cabinet Office unit, headed by the prime minister, to address the scourge and waste of social exclusion which disfigures British society and distorts its economy. As the unit starts its work, as professors of social policy and sociology, we wish to encourage public debate about its focus.

In setting out the unit's tasks, Peter Mandelson, minister without portfolio, emphasised policy co-ordination, which is welcome. However, he indicated that the question of the adequacy of benefit levels was on the agenda only for those incapable of paid work and, even for them, would have to wait; the wider issue of redistribution appeared to be ruled out altogether. We would urge the government to think again, otherwise it will be trying to tackle social exclusion with one hand tied behind its back.

'Welfare to work' and education are at the heart of the government's strategy. Unfortunately, ministers have created a false dichotomy between this approach and directly improving the living standards of those experiencing poverty. Yet, research suggests that the effectiveness of education reforms could be undermined by unacceptably high levels of child poverty and that impoverished benefits claimants are not the best recruits for 'welfare to work' programmes. Moreover, such reforms will take time to have an effect; their impact on poverty and exclusion is uncertain, and, in the meantime, families are struggling to survive on inadequate benefits.

We agree with Mr Mandelson that redistribution is not the only route to 'a more equal society'. However, ministers seem to have erased it from the map altogether, despite evidence of the massive redistribution from poor to rich achieved by the Tories. If people have been impoverished and excluded through acts of social and fiscal policy, then there is no need to seek complicated causes and remedies for their poverty and exclusion. Putting money (back) into the pockets of those with insufficient money may not be the answer in all cases; but it would help. Once it is done, the equally serious long-term work on structural change, education and skills can be tackled more effectively by the social exclusion unit.

23

Bringing Britain Together: A National Strategy for Neighbourhood Renewal

Cabinet Office Social Exclusion Unit

The Problem

Over the last generation, this has become a more divided country. While most areas have benefited from rising living standards, the poorest neighbourhoods have tended to become more rundown, more prone to crime, and more cut off from the labour market. The national picture conceals pockets of intense deprivation where the problems of unemployment and crime are acute and hopelessly tangled up with poor health, housing and education. They have become no go areas for some and no exit zones for others. In England as a whole the evidence we have suggests there are several thousand neighbourhoods and estates whose condition is critical, or soon could be.

These neighbourhoods are not all the isolated high rise council estates of popular stereotype. Many are publicly owned, but others are privately rented or even owner occupied. Some are cut off on the edge of cities but others can be found close to wealthy suburbs and prosperous city centres. Some consist of very traditional housing designs that would sell for six figure sums elsewhere.

Why It Came About

There is no simple explanation of why things have got this bad and why so many neighbourhoods are not working.

Major economic and social changes have played a large part. The decline in traditional industries, the availability of unskilled jobs, and the rise of male and youth unemployment, have had disproportionate effects in some parts of the country. Many poor communities show the scars of the weakening of family structures, with more divorce and more children born outside marriage.

But past Government policies have also often contributed to the problem. Poor housing design has had a big impact, weakening communities and making neighbourhoods less safe. And policies on housing allocation, rents and benefits have tended to concentrate the poor and unemployed together in neighbourhoods where hardly anyone has a job.

There have been many initiatives aimed at tackling the broader problems of poor neighbourhoods from the 1960s onwards: the Urban Programme, then the Urban Development Corporations and Task Forces in the 1980s, and the Single Regeneration Budget in the 1990s. All tried new approaches and all had some successes. But none really succeeded in setting in motion a virtuous circle of regeneration, with improvements in jobs, crime, education, health and housing all reinforcing each other.

There are many reasons for this failure. They include the absence of effective national policies to deal with the structural causes of decline; a tendency to parachute solutions in from outside, rather than engaging local communities; and too much emphasis on physical renewal instead of better opportunities for local people. Above all, a joined up problem has never been addressed in a joined up way. Problems have fallen through the cracks between Whitehall Departments, or between central and local government. And at the neighbourhood level, there has been no one in charge of pulling together all the things that need to go right at the same time.

Why It Matters

The failure to get to grips with the problems of the poorest neighbourhoods represents a costly policy failure. Public money has been wasted on programmes that were never going to work and generations of people living in poor neighbourhoods have grown up with the odds stacked against them. We are all paying for this failure, whether through the direct cost of benefits and crime, or the indirect costs of social division and low achievement.

What Can We Do About It?

What should be the objective of public policy? Consultation responses from over two hundred individuals and organisations, and the Social Exclusion Unit's own visits to many poor neighbourhoods, have confirmed that the goal itself is simple. These neighbourhoods are places where unemployment is endemic; crime, drugs, vandalism are rife; and public and private-sector services are second-rate or completely absent. The goal must be to reduce that gap between the poorest neighbourhoods and the rest of the country and bring them for the first time in decades up to an acceptable level.

A National Strategy for Poor Neighbourhoods

Delivering this goal requires a huge effort to re-think policies that have failed, and to make Government initiatives work in the poorest places. It will mean learning the lessons of the past and:

- investing in people, not just buildings;
- involving communities, not parachuting in solutions;
- developing integrated approaches with clear leadership;
- ensuring mainstream policies really work for the poorest neighbourhoods;
- making a long-term commitment with sustained political priority.

This Report sets out the steps towards a national strategy for tackling poor neighbourhoods. A good start has been made in the Government's first year of office. The New Deals for the unemployed, lone parents and the disabled, together with the Government's actions on failing schools, crime reduction and public health, already represent a watershed in terms of starting to address the key causes of social exclusion rather than just dealing with its effects. [...]

[...] New funding programmes will support the regeneration of poor neighbourhoods, focusing in particular on the New Deal for Communities, but also including the next round of the Single Regeneration Budget and Sure Start. The New Deal for Communities will begin in up to 17 pathfinder districts, with more areas able to bid in later years. It will provide funds to develop and implement local community-based plans covering everything from jobs and crime to health and housing. It will ensure that dynamic local leaders have the power and resources to turn their community around. The New Deal for Communities Pathfinders will serve as a showcase for more successful ways of turning neighbourhoods around. They will also represent a major shift of power and responsibility down to the neighbourhood level.

[...] [T]he third strand of the national strategy [is] to fill in the missing bits of the jigsaw and ensure that policies reach effectively into the very poorest neighbourhoods; the most intractable 'joined up' problems of poor neighbourhoods are tackled; and policies reinforce each other and add up to a coherent strategy.

In this new third strand, 18 cross-cutting action teams will work on a fast-track to tackle remaining policy problems and gaps. This work will involve no fewer than ten Whitehall Departments, and draw in many outside experts. The New Deal for Communities Pathfinders will be able to reflect the early output of these teams.

The work of the teams falls under five broad themes:

- getting the people to work: concentrated unemployment has done more damage than anything else in the poorest communities. The priorities are: to maximise the potential of the New Deal in these areas; to tackle barriers to work such as poor skills and discrimination; and to investigate innovative approaches to help people back into the labour market, through benefit flexibilities, work experience and encouraging business start-ups;
- getting the place to work: if housing is poorly managed or unlettable, or crime and anti-social behaviour are not tackled, community support systems can easily crumble. We need to get to grips with what drives area abandonment, make good neighbourhood and housing management the norm, develop a watertight framework for tackling anti-social neighbours, and clarify how community wardens can best complement the police in combating crime;
- building a future for young people: if improvements are to last we need to focus on the next generation. The Sure Start programme will provide more integrated help for young children at risk of social exclusion; it will need to be supplemented by better ways of motivating children to learn at school and providing older children with better alternatives to the attractions of crime and drugs;

- access to services: in too many poor neighbourhoods services such as shops and banks have disappeared. As a result the poorest often face the highest prices. Many don't have access to affordable food and basic financial services and are being left behind by information technology. The Report sets out an agenda for working with the private sector to find better solutions;
- making the Government work better: every level of government needs to improve the way it tackles joined up problems of social exclusion. That means being more strategic, setting clearer goals, getting better information on what's happening, acting on the evidence, and spreading and learning from good practice.

The whole process will be co-ordinated by the Social Exclusion Unit. The Unit will lead some teams and be represented on all of them. Each team will have a champion Minister. Hilary Armstrong, the Minister for Local Government and Housing, will oversee the process as a whole. All policy decisions will be cleared through the relevant Cabinet Committees. There will be interim reports in April and July 1999 and the whole programme of policy development work will be completed by December 1999 when the Government will put together the outcome of all the reports into a coherent national strategy. The aim will be that not only should Government Departments commit themselves to this, but also local authorities, and other key public agencies as well as business, the voluntary sector and others working in poor communities.

The Social Exclusion Unit's remit covers England only, but the analysis underlying the report, and the priority accorded to solving the problems identified, is shared by the Scottish, Welsh and Northern Ireland Offices. The Government will pursue vigorous action to address the issues in all four countries using measures appropriate to each situation.

Action to tackle the problems of poor neighbourhoods is long overdue. On top of the policies that have already been put in place in the Government's first year, and the new money announced in the Comprehensive Spending Review, this report sets out the most concerted attack on area deprivation this country has ever seen. It is an ambitious agenda for turning round the neighbourhoods that don't work, with policies that do.

24

Excellence in Schools

Department for Education and Employment

Tackling the Problems we Face

[...] [T]oo many of our children are failing to realise their potential:

- in the 1996 national tests only 6 in 10 of 11 year-olds reached the standard in maths and English expected for their age;
- achievement at 14 shows a similar picture, with well over a third of 14 year-olds not achieving the level expected for their age in English, maths or science;
- over half of our 16 year-olds do not achieve five or more higher grade GCSEs, two-thirds of them do not achieve a grade C in maths and English, and 1 in 12 achieves no GCSEs at all; and
- international comparisons support the view that our pupils are not achieving their potential. For example, our 9 and 13 year-olds were well down the rankings in the maths tests in the Third International Maths and Science Survey, the most recent international study.

OFSTED estimates that 2–3% of schools are failing, 1 in 10 have serious weaknesses in particular areas and about a third are not as good as they should be. The national debate on standards over the last two years which current Ministers when in Opposition helped to initiate has already focused attention on literacy and numeracy, and is beginning to bear fruit, but there is far to go.

The problem with our education system is easily stated. Excellence at the top is not matched by high standards for the majority of children. We have some first-class schools and our best students compare with the best in the world. But by comparison with other industrialised countries, achievement by the average student is just not good enough.

These problems have deep and historic roots. We failed to lay the foundations of a mass education system at the end of the 19th century as our competitors – France, Germany and the USA – were doing. They recognised that a strategy for national prosperity depended on well-developed primary and secondary education for all pupils, combined with effective systems of vocational training and extensive higher education. By contrast, mass education was neglected, and governments were content to rely on private schools to provide the elite entry to universities and the professions.

Our progress in the 20th century has been slow. A mass education system did not come about until after the Second World War. The school-leaving age remained at 15 until the 1970s and the focus was still on selecting a small proportion of young people for university. That determined the structure of the school system: selection at 11 followed by further specialisation at 16 for those who stayed on.

The demands for equality and increased opportunity in the 1950s and 1960s led to the introduction of comprehensive schools. All-in secondary schooling rightly became the normal pattern, but the search for equality of opportunity in some cases became a tendency to uniformity. The idea that all children had the same rights to develop their abilities led too easily to the doctrine that all had the same ability. The pursuit of excellence was too often equated with elitism.

It was right in the 1980s to introduce the National Curriculum – albeit that it was 20 or 30 years too late. It was right to set up more effective management systems; to develop a more effective inspection system; and to provide more systematic information to parents. These changes were necessary and useful. We will keep and develop them. But they were not and are not enough in themselves. We face new challenges at home and from international competitors, such as the Pacific Rim countries. They do not rely on market forces alone in education and neither should we. It is time now to get to the heart of raising standards – improving the quality of teaching and learning.

Our Policy Principles

We have consistently made clear that there will be unrelenting pressure on schools and teachers for improvement. But we recognise that successful change will not result from pressure alone. Those whose task it is to work day in, day out to raise standards also need to have access to external expertise and to have their achievements celebrated. Under this Government, there will be the right balance of pressure and support which will enable us, together, to rise to the challenges of the new millennium. This is the animating idea behind this White Paper. It informs each of the six principles on which our approach to policy will be based.

Principle 1: Education will be at the heart of government

Our first principle is to ensure that education must be at the heart of government. The Prime Minister has made it clear that education is the Government's number one priority. The first Queen's Speech announced *two* education bills: one to provide the resources to implement the Government's class size pledge, the other to advance the standards agenda set out in this White Paper. The Department for Education and Employment (DfEE) has higher status than ever before. Other departments of government whose work impacts on education will contribute to our drive for educational success. Already education has taken centre stage and it will remain there through this Parliament and beyond. A clear sign of this is our pledge that over the lifetime of the Government we will increase the proportion of national income spent on education as we decrease it on meeting the bills of past social and economic failure.

Principle 2: Policies will be designed to benefit the many, not just the few

Our second principle is that, in deciding our priorities, we shall put in place policies that benefit the many, not just the few. Hence, for example, the shift of resources as a matter of urgency from the Assisted Places Scheme to the reduction of class sizes for all 5, 6 and 7 year-olds. Our policies will be designed to achieve early success rather than later attempts to recover from failure. This explains the emphasis we have placed on nursery education for all 4 year-olds and on raising standards in the three 'Rs' at primary level. As a matter of urgency, the Government will reduce the extent of early failure in the system by encouraging best practice and effective monitoring with speedy intervention where necessary.

Principle 3: Standards matter more than structures

The preoccupation with school structure has absorbed a great deal of energy to little effect. We know what it takes to create a good school: a strong, skilled head who understands the importance of clear leadership, committed staff and parents, high expectations of every child and above all good teaching. These characteristics cannot be put in place by altering the school structure or by legislation and financial pressure alone. Effective change in a field as dependent on human interaction as education requires millions of people to change their behaviour. That will require consistent advocacy and persuasion to create a climate in which schools are constantly challenged to compare themselves to other similar schools and adopt proven ways of raising their performance.

Principle 4: Intervention will be in inverse proportion to success

The main responsibility for improving schools lies with the schools themselves. Where schools are evidently successful, we see no benefit in interfering with their work, although all schools need to be challenged to improve. Schools need a constant supply of good data about how their performance compares with that of other schools, a clear understanding of the Government's strategic priorities and recognition of their achievement. We will of course seek to celebrate success and learn from it but, where a school has problems, intervention is essential to protect the pupils. Ideally intervention should be preventive and early, so that severe failure is avoided. The Government intends to put in place arrangements for targeted interventions by LEAs or the DfEE, informed by OFSTED, that are appropriate to the scale of the problem.

Principle 5: There will be zero tolerance of underperformance

Our aim is excellence for everyone. If this is to be more than rhetoric, then persistent failure must be eradicated. Hence our commitment to zero tolerance of underperformance. We shall seize every opportunity to recognise and celebrate success in the education service, and we shall put in place policies which seek to avoid failure. But where failure occurs, we shall tackle it head on. Schools which have been found to be failing will have to improve, make a fresh start, or close. The principle of zero tolerance will also apply to local education authorities. Our policy will be driven by our recognition that children only get one chance. We intend to create an education service in which every school is either excellent, improving or both.

Principle 6: Government will work in partnership with all those committed to raising standards

Government will lead the drive to raise standards and create the right framework, but it cannot succeed alone. It must work in partnership with all those who have a part to play in improving the quality of education: parents, teachers and governors, local authorities, churches and business. Parents are a child's primary educator and our partnership approach will involve them fully. We want to put the years of division, conflict and short-term thinking behind us.

We will be alert to new ways of working with others to raise standards: new forms of Public/Private Partnership; new forms of collaboration between local and central government; new ways of involving parents in education; new relationships between private and state schools; and new ways of involving volunteers and working with voluntary organisations. Our literacy and numeracy targets for 11 year-olds [...] for example, are not just targets set by the Government to hold the education service to account; but targets set by the Government and the education service together, for which both are jointly accountable.

Through our new Standards and Effectiveness Unit [...] in the DfEE, we have already begun to enhance the capacity of the education service to recognise and spread best practice. The new partnership for change which we are building through our new Standards Task Force [...] will improve the quality of relationships between the different areas of the service. The creation of the General Teaching Council [...] will give teachers a new opportunity to bring their professionalism to bear and we will work with teachers to develop their skills.

Our Policy Focus

In each chapter of this White Paper our proposals will be underpinned by the principles we have set out here. There is no instant or single solution, but the standard of teaching in schools is of critical importance. All of our key proposals will be linked to effective training and support of new and existing teachers. Raising standards will be a long and sometimes hard process. The key lies in combining a range of initiatives to drive up standards in our schools:

- Every child should get the basics of literacy and numeracy right early on through good teaching in early years education and primary schools, supported by smaller classes [....]
- All schools will be challenged to improve and must take responsibility for raising their own standards, using proven best practice with the right balance of pressure and support from central and local government [....]
- We must modernise comprehensive secondary education for the new century – recognising that different children move at different speeds and have different abilities [....]
- We must improve the quality of teaching through a new deal for teachers, with pressure to succeed matched by support for good teaching and leadership [....]
- Parents and local communities should be fully and effectively involved in the education of children [....]
- We must develop effective partnerships at local level to help schools work together towards the common goal of higher standards [....]

We are setting challenging targets which we expect to be met. In return we recognise that effective support also requires investment. That is our deal with parents, pupils and teachers. Growth will be dependent on the availability of resources, but as they become available, they will be targeted on meeting our overall strategic objectives.

In the meantime, we will redirect existing resources so that we can begin to work towards our priorities. The Grants for Education Support and Training will, for example, be refocused to meet our literacy, numeracy and school improvement priorities. We also intend through imaginative Public/Private Partnerships to begin to improve the condition of school buildings which, as a result of over a decade of neglect, is unacceptable. This will take time but we will make a start.

25

The New NHS: Modern, Dependable

Department of Health

A New Start

In paving the way for the new NHS the Government is committed to building on what has worked, but discarding what has failed. There will be no return to the old centralised command and control systems of the 1970s. That approach stifled innovation and put the needs of institutions ahead of the needs of patients. But nor will there be a continuation of the divisive internal market system of the 1990s. That approach which was intended to make the NHS more efficient ended up fragmenting decision-making and distorting incentives to such an extent that unfairness and bureaucracy became its defining features.

Instead there will be a 'third way' of running the NHS – a system based on partnership and driven by performance. It will go with the grain of recent efforts by NHS staff to overcome the obstacles of the internal market. Increasingly those working in primary care, NHS Trusts and Health Authorities have tried to move away from outright competition towards a more collaborative approach. Inevitably, however, these efforts have been only partially successful and their benefits have not as yet been extended to patients in all parts of the country.

This White Paper will put that right. It builds on the extensive discussions we have held with a wide range of NHS staff and organisations. It will develop this more collaborative approach into a new system for the whole NHS. It will neither be the model from the late 1970s nor the model from the early 1990s. It will be a new model for a new century.

Six Key Principles

Six important principles underlie the changes we are now proposing:

- first, to renew the NHS as a genuinely **national** service. Patients will get fair access to consistently high quality, prompt and accessible services right across the country;

- but second, to make the delivery of healthcare against these new national standards a matter of **local** responsibility. Local doctors and nurses who are in the best position to know what patients need will be in the driving seat in shaping services;
- third, to get the NHS to work in **partnership**. By breaking down organisational barriers and forging stronger links with Local Authorities, the needs of the patient will be put at the centre of the care process;
- but fourth, to drive **efficiency** through a more rigorous approach to performance and by cutting bureaucracy, so that every pound in the NHS is spent to maximise the care for patients;
- fifth, to shift the focus onto quality of care so that **excellence** is guaranteed to all patients, and quality becomes the driving force for decision-making at every level of the service;
- and sixth, to rebuild **public confidence** in the NHS as a public service, accountable to patients, open to the public and shaped by their views.

Keeping What Works

There are some sound foundations on which the new NHS can be built. Not everything about the old system was bad. This Government believes that what counts is what works. If something is working effectively then it should not be discarded purely for the sake of it. The new system will go with the grain of the best of these developments.

The Government will retain the separation between the planning of hospital care and its provision. This is the best way to put into practice the new emphasis on improving health and on meeting the healthcare needs of the whole community. By empowering local doctors, nurses and Health Authorities to plan services we will ensure that the local NHS is built around the needs of patients. Hospitals and other agencies providing services will have a hand in shaping those plans but their primary duty will be to meet patients' requirements for high quality and easily accessible services. The needs of patients not the needs of institutions will be at the heart of the new NHS.

The Government will also build on the increasingly important role of primary care in the NHS. Most of the contact that patients have with the NHS is through a primary care professional such as a community nurse or a family doctor. They are best placed to understand their patients' needs as a whole and to identify ways of making local services more responsive. Family doctors who have been involved in commissioning services (either as fundholders, or through multifunds, locality commissioning or the total purchasing model) have welcomed the chance to influence the use of resources to improve patient care. The Government wishes to build on these approaches, ensuring that all patients, rather than just some, are able to benefit.

Primary and Community Services

Most people look first to their family doctor or local pharmacist for advice on health matters. Dentists, optometrists and ophthalmic medical practitioners also provide essential care to meet everyday needs.

Community health service staff offer a range of services for people wherever they are, in their homes, schools, clinics and even in the streets. These services include health visiting, school nursing, chiropody, occupational, speech and language therapy. Services such as district nursing, community psychiatric nursing and physiotherapy can enable people with short or long term disability to be cared for in their own homes.

Other specialist staff such as midwives provide care across hospital and community settings.

Finally, the Government recognises the intrinsic strength of *decentralising responsibility for operational management*. By giving NHS Trusts control over key decisions they can improve local services for patients. The Government will build on this principle and let NHS Trusts help shape the locally agreed framework which will determine how NHS services develop. In the future the approach will be interdependence rather than independence.

Discarding What has Failed

The internal market was a misconceived attempt to tackle the pressures facing the NHS. It has been an obstacle to the necessary modernisation of the health service. It created more problems than it solved. That is why the Government is abolishing it.

Ending fragmentation

The internal market split responsibility for planning, funding and delivering healthcare between 100 Health Authorities, around 3,500 GP fundholders (representing half of GP practices) and over 400 NHS Trusts. There was little strategic coordination. A fragmented NHS has been poorly placed to tackle the crucial issue of better integration across health and social care. People with multiple needs have found themselves passed from pillar to post inside a system in which individual organisations were forced to work to their own agendas rather than the needs of individual patients.

To overcome this fragmentation, in the new NHS all those charged with planning and providing health and social care services for patients will work to a jointly agreed local Health Improvement Programme. This will govern the actions of all the parts of the local NHS to ensure consistency and coordination. It will also make clear the responsibilities of the NHS and local authorities for working together to improve health.

Health Improvement Programme

An action programme led by the Health Authority to improve health and healthcare locally will involve NHS Trusts, Primary Care Groups and other primary care professionals, working in partnership with the local authority and other local interests. [...]

Ending unfairness

The internal market created competition for patients. In the process it created unfairness for patients. Some family doctors were able to get a better deal for their patients, for financial rather than clinical reasons. Staff morale has been eroded by an emphasis on competitive values, at odds with the ethos of fairness that is intrinsic to the NHS and its professions. Hospital clinicians have felt disempowered as they have been deliberately pitted against each other and against primary care. The family doctor community has been divided in two, almost equally split between GP fundholders and non-fundholders.

In the new NHS patients will be treated according to need and need alone. Cooperation will replace competition. GPs and community nurses will work together in Primary Care Groups. Hospital clinicians will have a say in developing local Health Improvement Programmes.

Ending distortion

The market forced NHS organisations to compete against each other even when it would have made better sense to cooperate. Some were unwilling to share best practice that might benefit a wider range of patients in case they forfeited competitive advantage. Quality has been at best variable.

In the new NHS, there will be new mechanisms to share best practice so that it becomes available to patients wherever they live. A new national performance framework for ensuring high performance and quality will, over time, tackle variable standards of service.

Ending inefficiency

Under the internal market, the Purchaser Efficiency Index was the only real measure of performance. But it distorted priorities and – to the universal frustration of NHS staff – institutionalised perverse incentives which got in the way of providing efficient, effective, high quality services. In addition, budgets for emergency care, waiting list[s for] surgery and drug treatments were artificially divided, reducing flexibility.

In the new NHS, the Purchaser Efficiency Index will be replaced by better measures of real efficiency as part of a broader set of performance measures. They will assess the NHS against the things which count most for patients, including the costs and results of treatment and care. National reference costs will allow NHS Trusts to benchmark their performance. And partitioned budgets will be unified so that total resources can be matched locally against the needs of patients, ensuring more efficient and appropriate care.

Internal Market Bureaucracy

Evidence shows that:

- one fundholder with a contract worth £150,000 received 1,000 pieces of paper per year;
- a Health Authority in the south processed 60,000 invoices per year representing 8% of its healthcare budget;
- an inner city Trust contracted with over 900 funds and sent out 40,000 invoices per year.

Ending bureaucracy

The internal market sent administrative costs soaring to unsustainable levels. In recent years effort and resources have been diverted from improving patient services. With so many players on the field, transaction costs in the NHS inevitably spiralled.

This White Paper will cap management costs and cut the number of commissioning bodies from around 3,600 to as few as 500. The Government has already taken steps to reduce transaction costs and along with the changes in this White Paper £1 billion in administration will be saved over the lifetime of this Parliament for investment in patient services.

Ending instability

The internal market forced NHS Trusts to compete for contracts that at best lasted a year and at worst were agreed on a day-to-day basis. Such short-term instability placed a constant focus on shoring up the status quo rather than creating the space to plan and implement major improvement.

This White Paper will scrap annual contracts. Instead, the new NHS will work on the basis of longer-term three and in some cases five year funding agreements that will allow clinicians and managers to focus on ways of improving care.

Unacceptable Variations

At its best, the NHS leads the world. But the degree of local variation means that individual patients cannot be sure of receiving that best:

- the death rate from coronary heart disease in people younger than 65 is almost three times higher in Manchester than in West Surrey;
- emergency readmissions to hospital are 70% higher in one area than in another;

- the proportion of women aged 25–64 screened for cervical cancer varies from 67% to 93% in different areas;
- the number of hip replacements in over 65s varies from 10 to 51 per 10,000 of the population;
- the number of outpatients seen within 13 weeks of written GP referral varies from 71% to 98%;
- the number of outpatients admitted for elective treatment who have waited less than 3 months since a decision to admit varies from 56% to 82%;
- the percentage of drugs prescribed generically varies from below 50% to almost 70%;
- the percentage of consultant episodes carried out as day cases varies from below 50% to almost 70%.

Ending secrecy

Under the internal market hospitals became 'self-governing trusts' run as businesses, focused on finance, and required to compete with each other for short-term contracts. Increasingly NHS Trust Boards meeting in secret made it hard for local people to find out what their local hospital was planning and how it was performing. GP fundholders could make significant purchasing decisions without reference to the local community.

In the new NHS, all NHS Trusts will be required to open up their board meetings to the public. They will have new statutory duties on quality and on working in partnership with others. Comparative information on NHS Trust performance will be published. Openness and public involvement will be key features of all parts of the new NHS.

These developments will place the traditional values of the NHS into a modern setting. They will be backed by the Government's commitment to extra investment in the NHS, year on year. But that extra money has to produce major gains in quality and efficiency. Otherwise the health service will simply not keep pace with the needs of the public it is there to serve. The NHS has to make better use of its resources to ensure that it delivers better, more responsive services for patients everywhere. It has to share best practice and eliminate poor performance so that patients have a guarantee of excellence.

26

How Big Money is Stitching Up the NHS

Will Hutton

Within 10 years most new British hospitals could be owned by companies quoted on the Stock Exchange. They would be contracted to the National Health Service to provide health care, but their ultimate objective would be rather different – to maximise profits.

Britain is witnessing the largest hospital building programme since the birth of the NHS 50 years ago. It should be cause for celebration, but the cost – in jobs, beds, poorer service and public money – may be higher than politicians have ever imagined.

One of the largest projects is the new University College Hospital. The old UCH, sandwiched between two of London's busiest roads, Gower Street and Tottenham Court Road, is – like so much of the NHS – a hospital in crisis. Its medical facilities are ageing. Its financial deficit is climbing. The clinical and organisational costs of operating across its scattered sites have risen inexorably since its forced polygamous marriage three years ago to the Middlesex, Elizabeth Garret Anderson, the National and the Eastman Dental Hospital. It urgently needs to consolidate onto fewer, more manageable sites and invest in equipment. The news that within the next three months the green light will at last be given to the £160 million first phase of a new hospital (with an uncosted second phase to come) has not brought delight and relief. Rather it is where the problems begin.

Medical and nursing staff await the announcement with foreboding. For University College London Hospitals (UCLH) – the generic name for all the hospitals linked in this part of London – is to be rebuilt under the Private Finance Initiative, under which the NHS pays a fee for 30 years to a private consortium which will build, own and run the hospital on the NHS's behalf.

Introduced by the Conservative Party to transfer the financing of public investment from the state to the private sector in the drive to lower public borrowing, the PFI has come into its own under New Labour. More than 30 hospitals, together worth more than £2.5 billion, are being built with private finance.

Advocates of the PFI see it as a neat way of circumventing Treasury rules that in effect limit all but the most desperately needed public investment, so that via a kind of gigantic hire purchase deal the state can build more hospitals on the never never. But Britain has not discovered the philosopher's stone of getting something for nothing. PFI hospitals have meant fewer beds, fewer staff, fewer operating theatres and higher overall costs. Some analysts call it the de facto privatisation of the NHS.

UCLH [...] is set to swell the PFI's ranks. The new PFI hospital will have a third fewer beds, 28 per cent fewer nurses and a fifth fewer operating theatres than the facilities it replaces. None the less it will still have to boost its revenue by increasing the 'throughput' of patients by more than a quarter: performance levels never yet achieved in Britain. And, despite being one of Europe's leading teaching and research hospitals, the new complex will have no lecture or seminar rooms and no research facilities. Many consider the price too high. Consultant Professor Gus McGrouther is so concerned that he is moving his burns unit to another London hospital. He is understood to believe that the new UCLH will be too small and too oriented to quick clinical throughput to service complex and time-consuming burns cases properly.

A climate of anxiety means that no consultant or doctor will talk on the record, but there is widespread concern that the character of UCLH will change. Relations between staff and management are plagued by lack of trust. Last September UNISON balloted everybody who worked in the hospital, including nurses and clerical staff, and won 70 per cent support – albeit on a low turnout – for a one-week strike to support the claim that NHS terms and conditions would continue to apply to everyone in the new hospital. The strike was challenged on the basis that it was illegally political.

Phil Thompson, regional officer for UNISON, says: 'We are dismayed that the trust has used the courts against us. None of this would have happened if the PFI had not been used as a means of funding the new hospital.' Until now the hospital has been able to sustain an open admissions policy, treating everybody from street-dwellers to the patients of rich GPs alike. That policy will have to be reviewed as the demand for quick throughput and tough financial targets takes its grip. As successive support functions are contracted out to external suppliers – a process that will accelerate with semi-privatisation under the PFI – staff will find it harder than ever to maintain the sense of shared purpose and community that enables the hospital to carry on in the face of dwindling resources. And, McGrouther says, there is no point in having a teaching hospital with 'no tutorials and no lecture rooms'.

Nobody I spoke to wants the new hospital stopped; even the unsatisfactory PFI hospital would be better than the existing complex. The senior medical staff recognise that the trust management has probably negotiated as good a deal as possible within its financial constraints. For its part, the management confronts some of the pessimism head on. For example, the trust's finance director and project leader, Peter Burroughs, says that the new hospital will have 40 intensive care beds compared to the current 30, and if there are fewer operating theatres they will be better. He says stories that the hospital will have no teaching and research facilities are wrong. There will be closer links with the university to compensate, he says, and the number of bed reductions is being greatly overstated.

Medical staff are unimpressed. As one senior consultant remarked wryly, you can only do one operation at a time in any one theatre, and for all the talk of teaching and research facilities there is scant sign of them on the plans. It is also a matter of public record that UCLH, including the National, has 875 acute beds (not including private beds); the new PFI hospital on this basis will have 585.

There is a general air of resignation, even at the top. The PFI may not be the best way to finance a hospital, but it is what the Government wants and that is what UCLH will get. Managements have to make the best of it.

UCLH is not alone. In a forthcoming paper for the journal Public Money and Management, Declan Gaffney and Professor Alyson Pollock of University College's School of Public Policy have examined the plans of seven new hospitals around the country being built under PFI schemes. Their review of bed numbers shows a fall by 28 per cent on average; from 5,185 beds today to 3,795.

Workforces and operating theatres are also being sharply reduced. PFI schemes, they say, are more expensive, lower the NHS's service capacity and so force the hospitals in question to raise their targets of patient throughput to unrealistic levels in order to maintain their revenue. 'Inevitably there will be pressure on PFI hospitals to change their case mix and select patients carefully if they are to maintain their income,' argues Pollock.

The reality is that the ambitious targets will not be met. Gaffney and Pollock believe that the burden of higher costs to service the PFI contracts will create unsustainable deficits for the hospitals. Already the Department of Health has had to give PFI schemes 'transitional' help.

As hospitals' losses rise, so regional NHS offices will be compelled to bail them out by diverting resources from other parts of their health budget. Bankruptcy is not an option; politically it is impossible and, in any case, the NHS is legally obliged to rescue any contractor owed money.

The whole purpose of the PFI is to offload government borrowing and risk onto the private sector, but the private sector regards itself as accepting very little risk. It can issue bonds to build hospitals on the very best, triple-A credit ratings, as if it were the public sector, then look to make between 15 and 20 per cent on the shareholders' funds it introduces to the schemes – typically around 10 per cent of the total.

The cost of private-sector finance is thus £1.5 m–£2 m more for every hundred million borrowed annually than if the NHS borrowed itself. The capital costs of PFI hospitals are on average 72 per cent higher than pre-PFI projections. That is partly because the projects are more comprehensive – rather than patching and extending existing buildings, the PFI is building new ones – but extra financing costs account for a third of the increase.

The notion of public-private partnerships to finance and build hospitals is not bad in itself: in general, the private sector is more innovative than the public sector. The difficulty comes with British public accounting rules, the ideological zeal to promote private over public activity, and the way the NHS has been forced to organise its internal cash flows so that it apes the private sector. All combine to make the PFI – at least as applied to hospitals – expensive and hostile to the stated values of the health service.

The Department of Health says that the contracts with the PFI hospitals are so robust that no such danger arises; but no contract on earth can take into account every possible twist and turn in the future. When there is some unanticipated development, the private sector will have only one yardstick with which to respond. Profit.

The heart of the problem is twofold. The capital cost of PFI hospitals is higher than if they were in the public sector partly because of the way they have to be financed; and the trusts are being given no extra cash to pay for the higher costs. The only way to square the circle is to shrink the hospitals and their staffs, and at the same time ask them to increase their throughput of patients so that revenue does not fall. It is a double whammy.

The Government's argument is that the 'capital charge', which the hospitals now pay to the Treasury as a kind of rent for hospital assets, will simply be paid to the PFI consortiums instead. In fact capital charges, in effect a tax on the use of hitherto free NHS assets, were introduced by the Conservatives specifically so that NHS Trusts would end up not caring whether they paid the Treasury or the private sector for the use of hospital services. The alleged increased efficiency of the private sector in managing the assets will produce additional savings, so that – hey presto! – the trust will be able to pay the PFI consortiums. But what Gaffney and Pollock show is that the capital costs of the PFI schemes are so high that the annual payments are well above the annual 'capital charges' the trusts now pay to the Treasury, and what additional efficiency means in practice is reducing the size of the hospital.

The stress on UCLH can be seen from a cursory glance at its published figures and what we know about the structure of its PFI deal. Much of the £16 m savings that it says it will create to pay the private consortium comes simply because the new hospital will be smaller. As Burroughs says, 90,000 square metres of hospital is cheaper to heat and light than 130,000 sq m. That cannot be denied, but having up to 1,000 fewer staff and 190 fewer beds begins to cut into the bone, especially when the throughput of patients must be increased. Next year the Trust Board predicts that the hospital's deficit will climb to £16 m, a deterioration which will accelerate if the rate at which patients are treated cannot be increased sufficiently.

UCLH's problems are replicated elsewhere. In Swindon the £140 m PFI hospital could only go forward with a £40 m subsidy and again much reduced bed numbers. In West Kent the extra costs of the Dartford and Gravesham PFI scheme meant not only reduced bed numbers but the relocation of a child resource centre. The physical disability and mental health services had to be abandoned. In Birmingham, if the PFI hospital is approved it will be at the expense of a neighbouring hospital. In West Herts the plan for a new PFI hospital depends on the closure of the four local acute hospital sites and a 50 per cent reduction in acute beds. And so it goes on. As Pollock says: 'The implications for local residents are very serious. Most affected will be the elderly and vulnerable groups.'

None of this is inevitable. If the NHS could borrow itself rather than through the private sector, it would transform the costs and lay the basis for public-private partnerships on an equal basis. Hospital capacity could be planned on projections of patient need rather than the needs of a PFI deal. As it is, false savings are being generated out of shrunken clinical budgets and smaller hospitals to pay contractors for assuming risks that they do not consider are risks anyway. It is a gigantic delusion – which threatens not just the clinical capacity of the NHS, but the principles on which it rests. Extraordinarily, we are privatising our new hospitals and shrinking the NHS at our own expense, with little or no public debate.

27

New Labour: Politics after Thatcherism

Stephen Driver and Luke Martell

[…] [W]hat should social policy aim to do? This goes to the heart of the New Labour welfare agenda. For postwar social democracy, social policy was seen primarily in terms of counterbalancing free market capitalism. Social policy was about promoting social justice; and social justice involved strong notions of distributive justice which required practical measures to redistribute income and wealth. Moreover, redressing economic and social inequality was also seen as the most effective way of dealing with social problems: the causes of crime and anti-social behaviour were at root socio-economic. Most social democrats accepted that the welfare state could co-exist with an economy based on private property, especially a mixed economy in which there was a large element of state ownership, planning and macro-economic management. But New Labour's commitment to a market economy (rather than a mixed economy) has shifted the debate, and has in large part been made possible by its social policy. Here the Commission on Social Justice marks a significant development in New Labour thinking.

Social justice and economic efficiency

The Commission on Social Justice was established by John Smith in 1992. Headed by Lord Borrie and run by the Institute for Public Policy Research (IPPR) with David Miliband as its secretary, the commission provided a focus for rethinking Centre-Left social policy within mainstream Labour politics. Published in 1994, the final report's themes quickly became familiar New Labour ones. At the core of the report is the idea that welfare should be supportive of both social justice and economic efficiency: they are 'two sides of the same coin'.[1]

In certain important aspects, the report's focus on social justice reaffirms familiar social democratic themes. There are commitments to civil and political liberties and to basic needs; poverty, inequality and discrimination remain central concerns. But in other respects the report marks a step away from postwar social democracy in the distinction it draws between 'levellers', those people it suggests who are only concerned about the distribution of wealth, and 'investors', who are concerned about the conditions for promoting wealth creation in a market economy. To the writers of the report – investors not levellers – the pursuit of social justice need not necessarily be at the expense of economic efficiency – and vice versa. Social justice is conceived of as a widespread (and more equal) distribution of individual 'life chances': what has been dubbed 'endowment egalitarianism'. Traditionally, such opportunities have been seen by the Left as reflecting the class divisions in society; and these divisions as rooted in the unequal distribution of property, wealth and income. So, for the Left, something had to be done about the class structure of society and the market system which reflected that structure. They had either to be abolished (socialism), or their effects had to be counterbalanced by the state intervening in the market and redistributing wealth (social democracy).

The *Social Justice* report, however, takes a rather different view. Inequalities in individual opportunities are rooted in the stock – or lack – of individual skills and abilities, and the environment within which such abilities can be enhanced and used. In post-Fordist style, the report argues that competition and capital mobility in the new global economy create a demand for investment in new labour skills and flexibility. [...] [G]overnments may no longer have the power to manage demand to boost employment, but they can shape the supply side of the economy in such a way as to make the country more attractive to international investors and individuals more employable at higher rates of pay. In so doing, the sum total of economic activity is made greater. Social policy, then, is the means to provide labour with the flexibility it needs to find jobs in the global economy. If governments do this, not only will they bring about a more just society but they will also further the interests of the economy. And if governments fail to do this by making the right investments in welfare, they will precipitate a downward and destructive spiral of low skills, few opportunities, poor economic performance and social disintegration.

In trying to compete in the new global economy, moreover, new patterns of work will challenge the assumptions of the old welfare state – such as male full-time, lifelong working. These combined with social and cultural changes in the status and employment of women give rise to demands for a welfare system capable of dealing with the decline of lifetime employment, two-parent families and male breadwinners. Proposed measures such as 'lifelong learning', welfare to work and reform of the tax and benefits system are intended to 'promote personal autonomy and choice', giving individuals the 'confidence and capability' to manage their own lives.[2]

The central message from the Commission on Social Justice was a significant one for Labour's modernizers. The welfare state could be a help, not a hindrance, to economic development. Social justice, it turned out, could be good for business. Many of the policy ideas, such as 'lifelong learning', welfare to work and tax and benefit reform, have found their way into New Labour social policy – although some, such as the reduction of working hours, have not.

Even some who broadly welcomed the report suggested that the interdependence between the market and the welfare state, between efficiency and equality, was overplayed by the commission.[3] Leaving aside the real problem of linking them in a global economy environment, it leaves the Left vulnerable to the charge that social justice is an instrumental value and not one which was being argued for on its own merits. After all, what if social justice does not promote economic efficiency, which it might often not? What then is the commission and Labour left with? And even if the marriage of economic efficiency and social justice does pay in the longer term, who will pay for the social problems a country like Britain faces in the short term?

Social justice in practice: welfare to work

The main influence of the Social Justice Commission on New Labour can be seen in its welfare-to-work programme. Gordon Brown, the main architect of the programme, offered in 1994 a broad view on what the welfare state should be about:

> We must look hard at our own welfare system to ensure that it provides pathways out of unemployment and poverty rather than trapping people in persistent dependency. For the risks and insecurities that the welfare state was set up to combat have changed dramatically over fifty years and the welfare state has to keep up with the times. The welfare state must be about supporting people as they respond to these challenges – extending their choices and opportunities; acting as a trampoline rather than as a safety net.[4]

Trampoline, not safety net, is the positive metaphor which Labour's welfare policies in general, and welfare to work in particular, seek to portray. The broad idea behind the programme is a simple one. The welfare state should not passively deal with those who become unemployed for whatever reason. Rather, it should actively assist them back into the labour market by providing education, training and work experience opportunities. 'Unless we get our education system right', wrote Blair on the day the government's 1997 education White Paper was published, 'our children will not be prosperous and our country will not be just.' Education, Blair said, should be 'at the heart of government'.[5] More investment in education and training had already become part of party policy during the Policy Review, despite the unease many on the Left felt for government training schemes. Much of Labour's claim that its welfare-to-work programme is more than just another training scheme to massage the unemployment figures rests on the emphasis on the transfer of benefit payments to education and training as well as job search programmes. In the 1997 manifesto there are commitments to 'Lifelong Learning', individual learning accounts enabling public money to be combined with contributions from individuals and from employers so as to allow the individual to buy training packages.[6] Labour proposes a University for Industry to encourage adult skills training. Labour supports proposals to extend and reform vocational qualifications made by Sir Ron Dearing in 1996, including the widening of A-levels. Without Labour's education and training policies there is little 'plus' to its 'flexibility plus'.

The first pieces of New Labour's welfare-to-work programme were in place within two years of Blair becoming leader.[7] In the 1997 manifesto the welfare-to-work policy for 250,000 young people was one of the party's five 'election pledges'. The final details of the programme were announced by Brown in his first budget in July 1997. The four options for the young unemployed are: a private sector job; work with a voluntary sector employer; a job with a 50,000-strong environmental task force; or full-time study on an approved course. Employers are given a £60 per week rebate for six months to encourage them to take on the young unemployed. Despite criticism from within the Labour Party on earlier plans to cut benefit levels by 40 per cent, David Blunkett announced that young people who refused one of the four options would lose all their benefit for the first two weeks if they were without 'just cause'. After two weeks claimants will receive benefits at 60 per cent of the full rate. Those who refuse one of the four options a second time will have their benefit stopped for a month.[8] Employers will be required by government to offer either on-the-job training or day release for study on accredited courses.

In addition to the plans for the young unemployed, Brown announced measures for the long-term unemployed, for single parents and for the disabled – again policies which had been previewed by Labour in opposition. Under one scheme employers receive a subsidy of £75 per week for taking on those unemployed for more than two years. In addition, the government offers firms a £750 per head training subsidy. Lone parents with children in the second year of full-time education are offered advice and counselling on employment and training opportunities at job centres. In addition, Brown announced plans to train 50,000 young people as childcare assistants and for changes in benefit rules to make childcare more affordable for single parents. Money from the National Lottery goes towards setting up after-school clubs. Finally, plans were unveiled to help those on disability and incapacity benefit to find training and employment. As expected, Brown announced that the welfare-to-work programme was to be financed from a 'windfall tax' on the privatized utilities raising £5.2 billion.

The welfare-to-work measures announced by Brown are not entirely novel to Britain. In 1996 the Conservative government launched 'Project Work', a programme of interviews, 'job search' and compulsory work experience for those unemployed for more than two years. Refusal to take part in the programme led to a withdrawal of benefits. The idea of welfare to work is well established abroad. Labour (and the Commission on Social Justice before) has been able to draw on a number of schemes from across the world.[9] In Australia the Labor government's welfare reforms included a voluntary programme of training, childcare allowances and after-school clubs to help single mothers back to work (the Jobs, Education and Training, or JET, scheme); and the Job Compact programme, where the employment service found the unemployed jobs with the private sector. The United States has also provided much food for thought for Labour's welfare reformers. Bill Clinton was elected as president in 1992 on a promise to 'end welfare as we know it'. Welfare, the Clinton Democrats argued, rewarded idleness, created dependency and trapped the poor in poverty. Instead, government should help people help themselves: welfare to work.[10] One of Clinton's most controversial proposals was to stop benefits after two years in return for a guaranteed subsidized private sector job or a place on a government community service. Clinton also proposed extending the Jobs Opportunities and Basic Skills programme, set up in 1988, to provide basic education and training for the unemployed. Clinton's grand hopes for welfare reform foundered on the rocks of a Congress which went Republican in the mid-term elections in 1996. But the 'tough love' welfare strategy continued, often at state level, as Clinton allowed states to experiment in welfare reforms. One such scheme, Greater Avenues for Independence (GAIN) in California, which offers job search, education, training and work experience opportunities to the unemployed on an individual basis, crops up in Labour policy documents as an example of 'world's best practice'.[11]

There is another side to Labour's welfare-to-work programme: making work pay. There are two elements to Labour's policy: the minimum wage and the reform of the tax and benefits system to make taking a job more attractive to the unemployed. A minimum wage has long been Labour policy. New Labour argues that a legal floor to wage levels is necessary because low pay is unfair and the unemployed need incentives to take jobs. After the election the new Labour government established a Low Pay Commission under George Bain to recommend both the level of the minimum wage and any exemptions from it. In November 1997 Labour published a bill to establish the minimum wage, likely sometime in 1999. It supported a flat rate for the whole economy and all economic sectors, although it left the details of rates and whether young people and trainees would be exempt to the Bain commission. However, reports suggested that the Labour government had made clear to the Low Pay Commission that the rate should 'have regard to the wider social and economic implications' and that young people be exempt or be covered by lower rates.[12] Tackling social exclusion for New Labour includes a recognition that low paid jobs are better than no jobs at all.

Reform of the tax and benefits system is the other area where New Labour hopes to reward those who want to work. Reducing the disincentives against the unemployed taking work has long been talked about by Labour.[13] The Conservative government reduced the real value of benefits and introduced the means-tested Family Credit as an in-work benefit. Labour's 1997 manifesto stated that it would 'examine the interaction of the tax and benefits system so that they can be streamlined and modernized, so as to fulfil our objectives of promoting work incentives, reducing poverty and welfare dependency, and strengthening community and family life'. The manifesto makes reducing the starting rate for tax a 'long-term objective'. This would reduce the marginal cost of employment in lower paid work for the jobless.

Soon after their victory at the polls, Labour set up a review of the tax and benefits system chaired by the chief executive of Barclays Bank, Martin Taylor. Again, New Labour appears to be looking abroad for inspiration – in this case, to the USA. Part of Clinton's plan to reform welfare was to 'make work pay'. This meant increasing the Earned Income Tax Credit (EITC).[14] EITC was introduced in 1975, and it attempts to reduce the disincentives of taking work by giving tax credits rather than benefit handouts to poor working families. EITC is a form of tax rebate which rises to a set ceiling as earnings increase and then is withdrawn gradually as that level is exceeded. The hope in Britain is that the unemployed will take low-paid jobs because work will pay more than life on the dole: they will not lose all the extra income by paying high marginal taxes. And the government will be seen to be rewarding work, not welfare. Speaking after the 1997 budget, Brown said that EITC was superior to Family Credit: 'EITC would be unlike Family Credit in that the more you worked the more you would receive from the tax credit system. By contrast, with Family Credit, there is a cut off point so there is almost an incentive not to work.'[15] In his Autumn 1997 'green budget' Brown announced that the Taylor review would look at transforming the Family Credit benefit payment into a tax credit.

[...]

Labour's Communitarianism: From Social Democracy to Social Authoritarianism?

The charge of social authoritarianism is often thrown at New Labour. Out with Old Labour's liberal approach to the criminal justice system has gone its more general sixties permissiveness. Under the influence of North American communitarianism and English ethical socialism, Labour modernizers have reacted to what they perceive as the rights-claiming and 'anything goes' culture of the period. The basis for the charge of social authoritarianism can be found in the character of the communitarianism New Labour espouses.[16]

First, Labour's communitarianism is strongly laced with ideas of reciprocity: helping the poor and unemployed gain that stake in society is conditional on them doing something about their own condition. The welfare-to-work programme involves significant elements of compulsion and makes rights to welfare more conditional on the 'responsibilities' of welfare recipients. Secondly, alongside welfare to work is an emphasis on moral entreaty to cure society's ills: 'The only way to rebuild social order and stability', wrote Blair, 'is through strong values, socially shared, inculcated through individuals, family, government and the institutions of civil society.' Blair went on to deny that this meant a 'lurch into authoritarianism or attempt to impose a regressive morality'.[17] Yet, thirdly, this does involve a politics based on a conformist idea of the 'strong community'. Labour espouses firm, even punishable, ideas about the duties and obligations citizens owe the community. Labour's communitarianism is about there being common duties and values to which we all adhere. And, fourthly, there is regressiveness. The content of these duties and values, what Blair has called the 'new social morality', is heavily marked by conservative values, crowding out the more progressive and pluralist ethics of much recent Centre-Left thinking. On family policy, schooling and law and order, New Labour has taken policy positions which are marked by conservative values – on the role and shape of the family in society; on teaching methods; and on the causal explanatory chains for criminal acts. Progressive values on such matters get proportionately less space, especially when *both* main parties now increasingly shun them. Fifthly, there is something prescriptive about New Labour's approach as well. In a way no longer thought possible for the economy, New Labour in government looks set to be interventionist on social matters. The 'strong community' looks dirigiste. There is a reliance on legislative solutions to what are presented as ethical threats. Whatever the problem – bad behaviour in schools, noisy neighbours, children on the streets in the late evening – New Labour seems poised to reach for the legal pen. In their first days of government it was prescriptive moral verdicts on issues such as cigarette advertising, the sale of alcoholic soft drinks and curbs on handguns and foxhunting which aroused some of the cries of bossy social authoritarianism. And New Labour appears to see few problems when it comes to legislating for individual behaviour, yet has fought shy of doing the same for corporate responsibility: this will be left to voluntary solutions.

Labour modernizers deny the charge of social authoritarianism. Tony Wright acknowledges that:

> Some people may feel uneasy about Labour's emphasis on community and responsibility, thinking that at best it is irrelevantly nostalgic and at worst dangerously authoritarian. If understood properly, it is neither. It does not deny the importance of experiment and diversity, or the fact that the community is made up of a plurality of communities, nor does it involve the state poking around in people's private lives where it has no business. But it does involve a challenge both to the possessive individualism of the New Right and to the thin rights-based liberalism of some of the Old Left: neither can provide the basis for a new politics of community and responsibility which redraws the balance between rights and duties, individual purposes and shared purposes, me and we.[18]

New Labour policy may also be seen to remain within the boundaries of a modern liberal tolerant and progressive society. When speaking on the family, Blair always adds the qualifications that he does not want a return to 'Victorian hypocrisy about sex, to women's place being only in the kitchen', or to politicians 'preaching to people about their private lives'. Leading Labour modernizers, such as Patricia Hewitt, present progressive views on family policy. Jack Straw remains a liberal on many social questions, such as race relations, the gay age of consent and the ban on gay and lesbian people in the military. Blair accepts that abortion is a matter of conscience.

For those who defend New Labour against the charge of social authoritarianism, legislating on moral issues is what governments are for. The real issue here may not be that Labour has got too moralistic at the expense of liberal permissiveness (within limits moralism is what governments are for) but that it has become more conservative and less progressive in the *content* of its moralism. Defenders might also argue that Labour was elected on a popular vote to pursue a moral agenda. Or they could argue that Labour's *social* authoritarianism does not match the *political* authoritarianism of Lady Thatcher's partial use of government power against left-wing opposition in the trade unions and local government. Labour may in practice mix centralized presidential leadership and social moralism, but does so in combination with democratic reforms which will increase devolution of power, accountability and transparency.

NOTES

1 Report of the Commission on Social Justice, *Social Justice: Strategies for National Renewal* (Vintage, London, 1994), p. 97. See also Gordon Brown, *Fair is Efficient* (Fabian Pamphlet 563, Fabian Society, London, 1994).
2 *Social Justice*, p. 113; see also Gosta Esping-Andersen, 'Equality and work in the post-industrial life-cycle', in David Miliband (ed.), *Reinventing the Left* (Polity, Cambridge, 1994), and his *The Three Worlds of Welfare Capitalism* (Polity, Cambridge, 1990).
3 See Chris Pierson, 'From words to deeds: Labour and the just society', *Renewal*, 3,1 (1995), pp. 45–55; Stuart White, 'Rethinking the strategy of equality: an assessment of the report of the Commission on Social Justice', *Political Quarterly*, 66,3 (1995), pp. 205–10.
4 Brown, *Fair is Efficient*, p. 22.
5 Tony Blair, 'Why schools must do better', *The Times* (7 July 1997).
6 In terms of employer contributions, these would be voluntary in nature: the 1995 policy proposal to charge a training levy on employers has disappeared from Labour policy. See *A New Economic Future for Britain* (Labour Party, London, 1995), p. 20. In October 1997 there were suggestions that the forthcoming White Paper on Lifelong Learning would extend individual learning accounts to all students. See *Times Higher Education Supplement* (10 October 1997).
7 *A New Economic Future for Britain*; *Getting Welfare to Work* (Labour Party, London, 1996).
8 'Workshy young face huge cut in benefits', *The Times* (4 July 1997).
9 See *Getting Welfare to Work*, pp. 3, 9–10.
10 For early Clinton reforms, see Simon Crine, *Reforming Welfare: American Lessons* (Fabian Society, London, 1994).
11 *Getting Welfare to Work*, p. 9.
12 'Beckett seeks minimum wage exemption for young people', *The Times* (25 September 1997).
13 See *A New Economic Future for Britain*; *Getting Welfare to Work*.
14 See Crine, *Reforming Welfare*.

15   Quoted in *The Observer* (6 July 1997).
16   See Stephen Driver and Luke Martell, 'New Labour's communitarianisms', *Critical Social Policy*, 17,3 (1997), pp. 27–46.
17   Tony Blair, in Giles Radice (ed.), *What Needs to Change: New Visions for Britain* (HarperCollins, London, 1996), p. 8.
18   Tony Wright, *Why Vote Labour?* (Penguin, Harmondsworth, 1997), pp. 78–9.

28

From Welfare State to Post-Welfare Society? Labour's Social Policy in Historical and Contemporary Perspective

Nick Ellison

[...]

If Labour's difficult years in Government during the 1970s brought home lessons that could perhaps have been learned in the 1960s, the result, so far as social policy was concerned, was that Labour began to recognise just how impossible it was to combine economic growth with commitments to ever-increasing social spending. Not surprisingly, in view of the fact that this realisation effectively removed its central raison d'être, the Party imploded as 'left' and 'right' joined battle over the nature of future 'socialist' objectives. But, however inevitable this process of internal struggle actually was, it was very much an internal affair. Looking inwards delayed the realisation that the ultimate demise of welfare collectivism had not been entirely due to the Party's failure somehow to do better, but was partly attributable to broader structural forces which began to have a noticeable impact on society and economy from the mid-60s onwards. A developing understanding of the nature of these forces for change has been an important element in the Party's attempt to redefine 'social democracy' over the past 15 years.

Looking back, it is plain now that the endemic weakness of the British economy, which Labour (and Conservative) Governments had to confront, owed a good deal to changing global conditions with which Britain was not best placed to deal. Deindustrialisation, mass unemployment and changes to both the labour market and labour process, have affected Governments across the industrial world as they try to adapt to the demands of 'globalisation'.[1] In Britain's case 'deindustrialisation' – the trend away from male manufacturing employment – began in the mid-1950s, becoming an absolute decline a decade later.[2] Subsequent increases in service-sector employment have not only failed to soak up sufficient amounts of labour to prevent endemically high unemployment, but have led to a greater proportion of casual and part-time jobs which are lower paid, with lower rates of unionisation.

[...]

Far from attempting to stem the tide of change, Conservative Governments embraced it. Welfare arrangements were altered in an effort to accommodate moves towards labour market flexibility, the hope being to 'sell' Britain as a low-wage, low cost economic competitor in the world market. In Jessop's phraseology, Britain began the process of moving from a 'Keynesian welfare state' to a 'Schumpeterian workfare state', the jargon tracing a shift from the beneficent paternalism of the welfare collectivist era to a developing sense of 'welfare' as a set of practices designed to foster the new enterprise culture.[3] Simple amounts of expenditure are less significant here than the nature of the reorganisation of welfare provision and delivery in the wake of the state's abandonment of any attempt to balance economic and social needs. Even though spending on many services has generally increased in real terms over the past 18 years, the ways in which these services are organised have been progressively altered, key changes dating from the 1987 Conservative election victory.[4] In a prevailing context of privatisation and 'marketisation', reforms in health and education reflect a preoccupation with the use of internal competition to drive up standards according to quality criteria defined by the central state. 'Purchaser-provider' splits in these areas have taken rather different forms, but both have seen a greater accent on provider accountability to service users[5] even as the central state has set punitive cash limits for service provision. In social security, emphasis has shifted from a welfare collectivist concern for 'relative equality' between claimants and the rest of society to a Schumpeterian preoccupation with the maintenance of downward pressure on benefit levels and ever-tighter eligibility criteria – all in the name of preventing 'welfare dependency'.

Now, while these changes fundamentally challenged Labour's welfare collectivist ethic, it would be wrong to suggest that the Party has simply been a passive onlooker as ideas about the role and nature of social policy have been transformed around it. For one thing, Labour was already beginning to amend its traditional assumptions in the late 1970s, as mentioned, but much clearer instances of new thinking began to emerge from the left-of-centre academic fringe in the early 1980s. Even by the time of the 1983 general election, surely the Party's darkest hour, sympathetic social policy experts were beginning to argue that 'all is not well in the welfare state as we know it – and not just because of Mrs Thatcher's cuts'.[6] By the mid-to-late 1980s, market socialists associated with the Fabian Philosophy Group were advocating a rather different approach to welfare provision based on greater user empowerment.[7] A new emphasis was placed on 'liberty' rather than on the 'equality' of traditional welfare collectivism, the central principle being 'democratic equality', defined as 'a more equal distribution of primary goods to secure a fair value of liberty'.[8] Importantly, the now-common suggestion that citizenship duties should be expected as a condition of the receipt of individual welfare rights and benefits also emerged from market socialist circles.[9]

The Labour Party itself paid little formal attention to these ideas until after the 1987 election defeat. But, stung by the scale of the Conservative victory rather than the fact of defeat itself, the Party embarked upon a two-year policy review during which time it began to accept two important modifications to its traditional welfare collectivist position. First, there was formal acknowledgement that the role of the state should be limited, Neil Kinnock commenting in the review's main published document that 'there is a limit to what the modern state can and should do'.[10] In economic terms Labour had seemingly abandoned its belief that the state should attempt to manipulate economic outcomes. The only form of 'intervention' now considered feasible was 'market management' through medium term supply-side policies, the aim being to promote long-term economic stability. Second, this recognition of 'the efficiency and realism which markets can provide'[11] found an echo in the acceptance of individual liberty, as opposed to social equality, as the primary goal of social policy. *Meet the Challenge, Make the Change* made it clear that citizens 'had to take responsibility for their own lives and fulfil their obligations to others',[12] leading one critic to suggest that social policy now existed purely in the highly constrained context 'of a monetarist rationale for restraining welfare expenditure in order to foster economic growth'.[13]

In fact, this judgement was premature. Despite the rhetoric, the policy review produced some fairly traditional proposals for welfare. Commitments remained to raise spending on an NHS still free at the point of need, to maintain and extend the comprehensive education system and to raise social security benefits to more adequate levels while ensuring that the income maintenance system became more accessible to service users.[14] In reality, then, the 1992 election marked a half-way stage. Labour had only partly abandoned its welfare collectivist ethos, the commitments to increased social spending, accompanied by promises to raise direct taxation indicating that a prospective Labour Government was still some way from fully endorsing Schumpeterian workfarism.

The position changed rapidly after the Conservatives unexpectedly won a fourth term. If Labour under Kinnock's leadership had begun the process of moving towards a 'post-welfare' ideology on broadly Schumpeterian lines, further changes were in store. The Commission on Social Justice (CSJ) appointed by the late John Smith in the wake of the 1992 election defeat, together with the changes in both ideology and Party structure which have followed Tony Blair's election as leader after Smith's untimely death, mark the two most significant stages on the way to what may be called the Party's present 'social Schumpeterian' stance.

The Commission on Social Justice

In its final report, the Commission on Social Justice (CSJ) made a case for a conception of social justice defined as a hierarchy of four ideas. First, a free society needs to be founded upon the equal worth of all citizens expressed in equality before the law, political and civil liberties and so on. Second, all citizens are entitled to have their basic needs for food, income, shelter and health met by the state. Third, in order to ensure self respect and equal citizenship there must be the widest possible access to opportunities and life chances and fourth, to achieve the first three conditions it is important to recognise that not all inequalities are unjust, but that those that are should 'be reduced and where possible eliminated'.[15]

These four main ideas translate into a number of policy options intended to close the prevailing 'justice gap'. In short, 'fair taxation', the widening of access to wealth, and a 'modern form of full employment' set in an economic framework which encourages 'long term investment in people, ideas and infrastructure' provide the basis for a conception of citizenship grounded in responsibilities as well as rights.[16] This policy framework is set in a context of increasing structural change in society, economy and polity. Looser patterns of employment have to be accepted, for example, not just to match the changing requirements of business but to meet the difficulties posed by a less stable family environment. Employment flexibility will be necessary if childcare and care of the elderly are to be undertaken without having to resort to total dependence on the welfare state. In addition, new pension arrange-ments and methods of funding them will be needed to accommodate changing attitudes to 'retirement', particularly as the number of older people in the population expands.

The mechanisms for achieving these objectives reflect Schumpeterian arrange-ments, the emphasis being placed upon matching economic with social 'investment' to 'empower' individuals and communities in the context of an emphasis on economic growth. Economic investment in labour, technology, education and training, child care and community resources to ensure high productivity and full employment, and social investment to secure freedom from poverty, a more equitable distribution of wealth, strong families and flexible welfare provision are expected to create a society based on individual opportunity and strong community.[17] In practical terms, the state's role is to encourage positive attitudes to employment by paying unemployment benefit to part-time workers and facilitating the transition from welfare to work. The state here is enabling rather than paternalistic. Eschewing traditional ideas of the top-down conferment of social rights, the CSJ wanted to equate guaranteed basic rights to education and training, to a guaranteed minimum income, fair taxation and so on with corresponding duties, particularly to work where work is available – this injunction being rather curiously extended to mothers with children over five years of age[18] – but also to employers who should provide good working conditions, fair wages and employee partnership arrangements.

Leaving aside for the moment the question of their feasibility, it is important to note that these ideas signal a further stage in the abandonment of welfare collectiv-ism. Although the CSJ's proposals were labelled as a 'fairly traditional social demo-cratic strategy', this judgement is based on the view that 'the overall ambition remains one of redressing social ills through growth'[19] which on the basis of the analysis here is too broad to be particularly useful. The point, surely, is that the role of the state has been transformed from a guarantor of social rights to relatively passive social actors to one of an enabler and supporter of active individuals, and where necessary a 'coercive' force, reminding individuals of their duties where they choose to remain inactive. In this way, while a flavour of the old formula of economic growth specifically for social welfare remains, the CSJ nevertheless placed a much greater burden of responsibility for redress on individuals themselves.

Labour under Blair

This social Schumpeterian position has been given an added boost by a new Labour leadership able to capitalise on earlier Party reforms. Blair's successful 'transform-ation' of the Party would have been unthinkable without the prior initiatives taken by Kinnock and Smith. The new leader built upon Kinnock's reforms of Labour's policy-making apparatus[20] and Smith's successful attempt to reduce the power of the trade union bloc vote at Conference – both leadership-friendly measures – by jettisoning Clause Four of Labour's constitution, thereby ending any ambiguity about Labour's stance on economic ownership. Each of these internal measures is intimately connected to the new ideas which emerged during the Policy Review and the deliberations of the CSJ in so far as they have reduced the sources and strength of 'old' Labour opposition to them.

Relatively unencumbered by historical baggage, then, Labour under Blair has continued to develop the ideas discussed by the CSJ. What has emerged is a dual strategy, one part of which elevates economic stability above all else as 'the essential platform for sustained growth',[21] but the other part of which stresses the potential for the creation of a more 'organic' sense of society and social obligation as meeting the needs of both society and individuals – the spirit of the idea being encapsulated in Blair's phrase 'social advance and individual achievement'.[22] Pride of place is given to greater productivity in the free market, Government's role being conceived in the enabling terms of investing in an educated and skilled workforce, creating opportunities for employment, new businesses and so on. Social spending commitments must if possible enhance, but certainly not inhibit, this overriding goal and for this reason a 'carrot and stick' approach appears to be the hallmark of contemporary social policy. Where individuals act responsibly to make the most of educational opportunities, to find work – to 'get on' – the state will support their efforts through effective social provision and the extension of social rights, enabling them to feel they have a 'stake' in society. Where they are not judged suitably responsible, however, the state can get tough: claimants may be refused benefit, juvenile offenders, the voluntarily homeless and others may find themselves subject to the rigour of 'zero-tolerance'. In short, where individuals make the most of their 'stake' the aim is to draw them in to an extended web of belonging; where they do not, there will be penalties.

[...]

This [...] is social Schumpeterianism at work: the traditional welfare element – the top-down attempt to confer equality for its own sake – is underplayed, while 'quality' and 'relevance' are promoted in the name of social and economic efficiency.

NOTES

1 A much used and abused term (see Paul Hirst and Grahame Thompson, *Globalisation in Question*, Polity, 1996). There seems to be little disagreement about the fact of rising economic competition on an international scale as increasing numbers of countries begin to enter the world market. The fact that emerging economies can compete with the older industrial societies on labour costs and labour processes has plainly affected the latter's approach to economic policy-making. That said, the further argument that 'globalisation' is contributing to a decline in the power of the nation-state is a more contentiously fought issue. For contrasting views see Hirst and Thompson, and Susan Strange, *The Retreat of the State*, Cambridge University Press, 1996.

2 See John Allen and Doreen Massey, *The Economy in Question*, Sage, 1988; Sean Glynn and Alan Booth, *Modern Britain: An Economic and Social History*, Routledge, 1996.

3 Bob Jessop, 'The Transition to Post-Fordism and the Schumpeterian Workfare State', in Roger Burrows and Brian Loader (eds), *Towards a post-Fordist Welfare State?*, Routledge, 1994, pp. 24–5.

4 See Christopher Pierson, 'Continuity and Discontinuity in the Emergence of the "Post-Fordist" Welfare State', in Burrows and Loader.

5 Although there is a good deal of debate about who constitutes a 'user'. In education, for example, as noted in Peter Taylor-Gooby and Robyn Lawson (eds), *Markets and Managers: New Views on the Delivery of Welfare*, Open University Press, 1993, pupils, parents and/or employers and industry could legitimately be placed in this category, but their interests are likely to be very different.

6   Howard Glennerster quoted in Pete Alcock, 'The Labour Party and the Welfare State', in Martin J. Smith and Joanna Spear (eds), *The Changing Labour Party*, Routledge, 1992, p. 143.

7   Typically through 'weighted' voucher systems to provide a redistributionary element to user 'choice' in education and a much more powerful tribunal system for rights enforcement in areas not susceptible to the use of vouchers. See Julian Le Grand and Saul Estrin (eds), *Market Socialism*, Clarendon Press, 1989.

8   Raymond Plant, *Equality, Markets and the State*, Fabian Tract 494, Fabian Society, p. 7.

9   See Raymond Plant, 'Social Rights and the Reconstruction of Welfare', in Geoff Andrews (ed.), *Citizenship*, Lawrence and Wishart, 1991; Geoff Mulgan, 'Citizens and Responsibilities', in Andrews.

10   Labour Party, *Meet the Challenge, Make the Change*, Labour Party, 1989, p. 6.

11   Labour Party, *Looking to the Future*, Labour Party, 1990, p. 6.

12   Labour Party, *Meet the Challenge*, p. 6.

13   Alcock, p. 139.

14   Labour Party, *Meet the Challenge*, p. 52.

15   Commission on Social Justice, *Social Justice: Strategies for Renewal*, Vintage, 1994.

16   Commission on Social Justice, *Social Justice in a Changing World*, IPPR, 1993, pp. 25–9.

17   Commission on Social Justice, *Social Justice: Strategies for Renewal*, pp. 102–4.

18   Commission on Social Justice, *Social Justice: Strategies for Renewal*, p. 240.

19   Christopher Pierson, 'Doing Social Justice: The Case of the Borrie Commission', in Joni Lovenduski and Jeffrey Stanyer (eds), *Contemporary Political Studies*, Vol. II, PSA, 1995, p. 846.

20   See Eric Shaw, *The Labour Party since 1979: Crisis and Transformation*, Routledge, 1994.

21   Labour Party, *New Labour Because Britain Deserves Better*, Labour Party, 1997, p. 11.

22   Tony Blair, *Socialism*, Fabian Tract, Fabian Society, 1994, p. 7.

Part IV

Modernizing the United Kingdom? Labour's Constitutional Agenda

In 1997, the Labour government embarked upon the biggest programme of constitutional reform in British history. Many of the proposals had been developed while
the party was in opposition. Yet, once in government, it soon became obvious that
constitutional change was more difficult in practice. Almost as soon as the first
initiatives – devolution referendums for Scotland and Wales – were announced, the
government was criticized for lacking a coherent overall vision of where the machinery of democracy was headed. This criticism remains forceful, especially given
the ambivalence and delay over reform of the House of Lords and the electoral
system. In spite of this, the fact remains that there have been some remarkable
innovations. Here, New Labour's claim to novelty is justified. Such has been the
scale and pace of change that it is easy to forget that the last eighty years or so have
not witnessed much in the way of constitutional change of any kind. As our extracts
demonstrate, since 1997, Labour has tackled some of the thorniest issues of British
democracy. Its success rate, however, has been mixed.

The Modernizing Government agenda, launched by the 1998 White Paper, was in
large part a reaction to the fragmented Whitehall machinery that Labour inherited
from the Conservatives. Under the 'Next Steps' initiative, started in the late 1980s,
many executive agencies were split off from their 'parent' departments at the centre,
and run on 'business-like' lines. But Labour's plans for reform did not involve
dismantling them and simply reinstating the 'public service ethic' characteristic of
the British civil service. Instead, they chose to work with the system, but emphasized
what has become known as 'joined-up government': intra-agency co-operation and
co-ordination from the centre by newly empowered bodies like the Cabinet Office.
Much of this was made possible by the application of new information and communications technology, as 'e-government' itself became a major plank of public sector
managerial reform.

Scottish devolution had been a long time in the making for Labour. Similar
comment could be made about the incorporation of the European Convention on
Human Rights (first drafted in 1950) into domestic law – a move that may turn out

to have a lasting impact on the legal system. The significance of introducing a new mayor and elected assembly for London is less certain. The political context of the proposals centred upon the challenge to New Labour's hegemony of the former left-wing Labour dissident, Ken Livingstone. But it is easy to lose sight of the fact that the proposals did not seriously threaten the balance of power – either in London itself or in the relations between local and national government.

By far the most controversial constitutional issue for New Labour is electoral reform. Promised a referendum before the 1997 election, the Liberal Democrats were left out in the cold by the Cabinet's refusal to countenance the Jenkins Report. Although Jenkins did his best to produce recommendations that the government would find acceptable, his inclination towards proportional representation was difficult to mask. His main principles and recommendations have so far been the closest Britain has come to changing its electoral system since 1917, but they failed to find favour with the Labour government, particularly then Home Secretary Jack Straw. Because Britain's electoral system, the Single Member Plurality System (SMPS), distorts the relationship between votes and seats, the substantial growth of third and fourth parties since 1970 has been disguised. This suits both Labour and the Conservatives, and it particularly suits Labour at the present time, being the party in government. Electoral systems often have as dramatic an effect on electoral outcomes as do electoral preferences and the votes cast for each party. Tony Blair, like Margaret Thatcher and John Major before him, led his party to victory under an electoral system where a party with the largest minority of the votes cast, some 42–44 per cent, secures a reliable parliamentary majority, some 60–64 per cent of the seats in the House of Commons. In 2001, if Commons seats were allocated in strict proportion to vote share, Labour would have had 269 MPs, not 412, the Conservatives 211 instead of 166, and the Liberal Democrats 122 instead of 52. Under SMPS Labour has a 'winner's bonus' of 134 seats. In this regard, setting normative judgements to one side, it is not difficult to see that should Labour approach the question of electoral reform instrumentally, it will see little wrong with the present arrangements.

Part of the unfinished business of constitutional reform remains the future of the House of Lords. The failure to confront the supremacy of the House of Commons is illustrative of the limits of New Labour's constitutionalism. Those in favour of a fully elected second chamber have found much to criticize in the government's proposals for reform. New Labour remains wedded to the government being able to govern, subject to the usual democratic checks and balances, and provided it commands the support of the Commons, even if only by being able to rely on the support of the largest minority of voters at a general election.

The final, and perhaps most pressing, constitutional question facing New Labour in government involves the Northern Ireland peace process. The difficult work of rooting the 1998 British–Irish agreement in the practical context of Northern Irish politics has proved a key issue for Labour, but there is also a high degree of continuity across the Major and Blair governments. Not only does this remind us that the politics of the British constitution have wide implications, but it also highlights the incredible complexities of the Northern Ireland issue, and the relatively imaginative record of New Labour in trying to address them.

29

Modernising Government

The Cabinet Office

Modernising government is central to the Government's programme of renewal and reform. In line with the Government's overall programme of modernisation, Modernising Government is modernisation for a purpose – to make life better for people and businesses. Modernising Government is a long-term programme of improvement. But the Government is putting forward a new package of reforms now:

- A commitment to ensure that public services are available 24 hours a day, seven days a week where there is a demand, for example by the end of 2000 everyone being able to phone NHS Direct at any time for healthcare advice.
- Joined-up government in action – including a clear commitment for people to be able to notify different parts of government of details such as a change of address simply and electronically in one transaction.
- A new drive to remove unnecessary regulation, and a requirement on Departments preparing policies which impose new regulatory burdens to submit high quality Regulatory Impact Assessments and to consult the Cabinet Office in advance.
- A new target of all dealings with government being deliverable electronically by 2008.
- New 'Learning Labs' to encourage new ways of front-line working by suspending rules that stifle innovation.
- Taking a more creative approach to financial and other incentives for public service staff, including a commitment to explore the scope for financial reward for staff who identify financial savings or service improvements.
- Within Whitehall, a new focus on delivery – asking every Permanent Secretary to ensure that their Department has the capacity to drive through achievement of the key government targets and to take a personal responsibility for ensuring that this happens. Bringing more people in from outside and bringing able, younger people up the ladder more quickly.

To ensure that government is both inclusive and integrated, we have three aims in modernising government:

- Ensuring that policy making is more joined up and strategic.
- Making sure that public service users, not providers, are the focus, by matching services more closely to people's lives.
- Delivering public services that are high quality and efficient.

We are centring our programme on five key commitments:

- Policy making: we will be forward looking in developing policies to deliver outcomes that matter, not simply reacting to short-term pressures. We will:
  - identify and spread best practice through the new Centre for Management and Policy Studies.
  - bring in joint training of Ministers and civil servants.
  - introduce peer review of Departments.
- Responsive public services: we will deliver public services to meet the needs of citizens, not the convenience of service providers. We will:
  - deliver a big push on obstacles to joined-up working, through local partnerships, one-stop shops, and other means.
  - involve and meet the needs of all different groups in society.
- Quality public services: we will deliver efficient, high quality public services and will not tolerate mediocrity. We will:
  - review all central and local government department services and activities over the next five years to identify the best supplier in each case.
  - set new targets for all public bodies, focusing on real improvements in the quality and effectiveness of public services.
  - monitor performance closely so that we strike the right balance between intervening where services are failing and giving successful organisations the freedom to manage.
- Information age government: we will use new technology to meet the needs of citizens and business, and not trail behind technological developments. We will:
  - develop an IT strategy for Government which will establish cross-government co-ordination machinery and frameworks on such issues as use of digital signatures and smart cards, websites and call centres.
  - benchmark progress against targets for electronic services.
- Public service: we will value public service, not denigrate it. We will:
  - modernise the civil service, revise performance management arrangements, tackle under-representation of women, ethnic minorities and people with disabilities and build the capability for innovation.
  - establish a public sector employment forum to bring together and develop key players across the public sector.

This long-term programme of modernisation for a purpose will move us towards our central objective in modernising government: better government to make life better for people.

Vision

Government matters. We all want it to deliver policies, programmes and services that will make us more healthy, more secure and better equipped to tackle the challenges we face. Government should improve the quality of our lives. Modernisation is vital if government is to achieve that ambition. Government must face the challenge of the times, and embrace the opportunity it offers:

- We live in an age when most of the old dogmas that haunted governments in the past have been swept away. We know now that better government is about much more than whether public spending should go up or down, or whether organisations should be nationalised or privatised. Now that we are not hidebound by the old ways of government we can find new and better ones.
- Information technology is revolutionising our lives, including the way we work, the way we communicate and the way we learn. The information age offers huge scope for organising government activities in new, innovative and better ways and for making life easier for the public by providing public services in integrated, imaginative and more convenient forms like single gateways, the Internet and digital TV.
- We must unleash the potential within the public service to drive our modernising agenda right across government. There is great enthusiasm and determination within the public service to tackle the problems which face society, to do the job better.
- Distinctions between services delivered by the public and the private sector are breaking down in many areas, opening the way to new ideas, partnerships and opportunities for devising and delivering what the public wants.

Modernisation is a hallmark of the Government. We are rebuilding the National Health Service. We are raising standards in education. We are modernising our constitution and local government. We are reforming our welfare system so that it will truly and fairly address the needs of our society. We are tackling crime in new ways. We are modernising our defence capability and Armed Forces. We have a new, positive relationship with our partners in Europe. But modernisation must not stop there. To achieve these goals we must modernise the way government itself works:

- The way we devise our policies and programmes.
- The way we deliver services to individual citizens and businesses.
- The way we perform all the other functions of a modern government.

Modernisation, though, must be for a purpose: to create better government to make life better for people. Just as the Government is pursuing the aims of investment for reform and money for modernisation in the way it decides on spending programmes, so too must modernisation of government be a means to achieving better government – better policy making, better responsiveness to what people want, better public services.

People want government which meets their needs, which is available when they need it, and which delivers results for them. People want effective government, both where it responds directly to their needs – such as in healthcare, education and the social services – and where it acts for society as a whole, such as protecting the environment, promoting public health and maintaining our prison and immigration services and defence capability. To achieve that, the Government's strategy is one in which the keystones of its operations are inclusiveness and integration:

- *Inclusive*: policies are forward looking, inclusive and fair.
- *Integrated*: policies and programmes, local and national, tackle the issues facing society – like crime, drugs, housing and the environment – in a joined up way, regardless of the organisational structure of government.

The Government is putting these principles into practice by aiming to:

- provide public services of the highest quality, matching the best anywhere in the world in their ability to innovate, share good ideas, control costs and above all to deliver what they are supposed to.
- ensure that government is responsive to the user and is, from the public's point of view, seamless.
- make certain that citizens and business will have choice about how and when to access government services – whether from home via interactive TV, via call centres, via one-stop shops or, indeed, post offices, libraries, banks or supermarkets.

People are exercising choice and demanding higher quality. In the private sector, service standards and service delivery have improved as a result. People are now rightly demanding a better service not just from the private sector, but from the public sector too.

The Government is committed to public service. But that does not mean public services should stand still. Public servants must be the agents of the changes citizens and businesses want. We will build on the many strengths in the public sector to equip it with a culture of improvement, innovation and collaborative purpose. Public sector staff need to respond to these challenges, working in partnership to deliver this programme.

Some parts of the public service are as efficient, dynamic and effective as anything in the private sector. But other parts are not. There are numerous reasons for this, and some are common to many governments around the world:

- *Organisation*: because institutions tend to look after their own interests, public services can be organised too much around the structure of the providers rather than the users. This can be evident in their opening hours, their locations, the demands they make of citizens; the help they do and do not provide when they are needed; and the extent to which they link up with other service providers to offer services in packages that are relevant to people's lives.
- *Inertia*: although the public can express its dissatisfaction with its public service through the ballot box, this can be a blunt instrument, removing whole local or central governments intermittently and often not addressing the underlying reasons why things are wrong. The risk is that particular parts of the public sector can therefore be left to fail for too long.
- *Inputs not outcomes*: the system in Whitehall and elsewhere – in particular the importance attached traditionally to the annual spending negotiations – has meant that Ministers, Departments and units have often been forced to devote much of their effort to maximising their funding rather than considering what difference they can make in the form of actual results or outcomes.
- *Risk aversion*: the cultures of Parliament, Ministers and the civil service create a situation in which the rewards for success are limited and penalties for failure

can be severe. The system is too often risk averse. As a result, Ministers and public servants can be slow to take advantage of new opportunities.

- *Management*: over the past 20 years, various management changes within the public service have improved value for money and quality in the way services are delivered by organisations. But too little attention has gone into making sure that policies, programmes and services across the board are devised and implemented in ways that best meet people's needs, where necessary by working across institutional boundaries.

- *Denigration*: public servants are hard-working and dedicated and many are as innovative and entrepreneurial as anyone outside government. But they have been wrongly denigrated and demoralised for too long. There has been a presumption that the private sector is always best, and insufficient attention has been given to rewarding success in the public service and to equipping it with the skills required to develop and deliver strategic policies and services in modern and effective ways.

To help counter some of these difficulties, the Government is working in partnership – partnership with the new, devolved ways of government in Scotland, Wales and Northern Ireland, and partnership with local authorities, other organisations, and other countries.

Devolution is a crucial part of the Government's modernisation programme. It is a stimulus to fresh thinking about the business of government. All parts of the United Kingdom stand to benefit from it. We are setting up three new devolved administrations in Scotland, Wales and Northern Ireland. We will also, in time, move towards elected regional assemblies in England. This White Paper sets out commitments on behalf of the Government of the United Kingdom. We hope the devolved administrations will join us in taking the programme forward. We want to co-operate with them in areas which straddle our respective responsibilities.

Local government is responsible for a quarter of public expenditure on services, including education, social services, police, housing and public transport. We have worked very closely with the Local Government Association and other bodies in preparing this White Paper. Local government must be an equal partner in our drive to modernise government. We want to encourage initiatives to establish partnerships in delivering services, by all parts of government in ways that fit local circumstances; and to establish common targets, financial frameworks, IT links, management controls and accountability mechanisms that support such arrangements. We will continue to involve other groups too, including business and the voluntary sector. We will continue to work closely with the public sector trade unions to achieve our shared goals of committed, fair, efficient and effective public services.

There is no such thing as a 'typical' citizen. People's needs and concerns differ: between women and men for example, between the young and the old; and between those of different social, cultural and educational backgrounds and people with disabilities. Some of these concerns have not been given sufficient recognition in the past. We must understand the needs of all people and respond to them. This, too, is a crucial part of modernising government.

We are exchanging ideas with other countries on policy making, on delivering services and on using information technology in new and innovative ways. We are learning from each other.

Modernising government means identifying, and defeating, the problems we face. It means freeing the public service so that it can build on its strengths to innovate and to rise to these challenges. It means raising all standards until they match the best within and outside the public service, and continue improving. It means transforming government, so that it is organised around what the public wants and needs, rather than around the needs or convenience of institutions.

This White Paper sets out our programme for modernising government. It does not pretend to have all the answers. This is a large project and we live in a fast-moving world. The Government is therefore presenting an agenda for progress. We explain what we think the current problems and challenges are, where we have made a start in tackling them, and how we plan to take our work forward in the future. We are centring our programme on five key commitments:

- Policy making: we will be forward looking in developing policies to deliver results that matter, not simply reacting to short-term pressures.
- Responsive public services: we will deliver public services to meet the needs of citizens, not the convenience of service providers.
- Quality public services: we will deliver efficient, high quality public services and will not tolerate mediocrity.
- Information age government: we will use new technology to meet the needs of citizens and business, and not trail behind technological developments.
- Public service: we will value public service, not denigrate it.

30

Foreword to *Scotland's Parliament*

Donald Dewar

The Government's aim is a fair and just settlement for Scotland within the frame-work of the United Kingdom – a settlement which will be good both for Scotland and the United Kingdom. The Scottish Parliament will strengthen democratic control and make government more accountable to the people of Scotland.

Scotland will remain firmly part of the United Kingdom. Westminster will continue to be responsible for those areas of policy best run on a United Kingdom basis. These include foreign affairs, defence and national security and macro-economic and fiscal matters. It follows that the UK Government will continue to act in many areas of public life in Scotland but in future it will be the Scottish Parliament – working within the framework of the United Kingdom – which will be responsible for much of the business of government in Scotland.

The Scottish Parliament will reflect the needs and circumstances of all of the people of Scotland regardless of race, gender or disability. Scotland will no longer be the only democratic country with its own legal system but no legislature of its own. With its new responsibilities, the Scottish Parliament will be in a position to encourage vigorous sustainable growth in the Scottish economy. Policies on health, housing and education will respond more directly to Scotland's needs. The Parliament will work to protect and develop our unique environment and natural and built heritage and to enrich our cultural inheritance.

Like many others, I have campaigned long and hard for a Scottish Parliament over the years. I have never doubted the importance of the issue or the difference that a Parliament will make. This reform will not in itself solve the problem of resources or banish the dilemmas of government. What it can do is connect and involve people with the decisions that matter to them. It can bring a sense of ownership to political debate and a new confidence to our affairs. The argument for change has been sustained through the difficult days. Now is the time for decision.

There should be no further delay. This White Paper sets out in practical detail the Government's plans to translate our manifesto commitments into a sound and durable constitutional settlement. It will be widely welcomed throughout Scotland. A referendum will be held on 11 September. The people of Scotland will make their choice. I am confident that there will be a resounding vote in favour of both propositions.

31

Human Rights Act 1998

An Act to give further effect to rights and freedoms guaranteed under the European Convention on Human Rights; to make provision with respect to holders of certain judicial offices who become judges of the European Court of Human Rights; and for connected purposes.

Be it enacted by the Queen's most Excellent Majesty, by and with the advice and consent of the Lords Spiritual and Temporal, and Commons, in this present Parliament assembled, and by the authority of the same, as follows:
[...]

Legislation

3   *Interpretation of legislation*

(1)   So far as it is possible to do so, primary legislation and subordinate legislation must be read and given effect in a way which is compatible with the Convention rights.

(2)   This section:
   (a)   applies to primary legislation and subordinate legislation whenever enacted;
   (b)   does not affect the validity, continuing operation or enforcement of any incompatible primary legislation; and
   (c)   does not affect the validity, continuing operation or enforcement of any incompatible subordinate legislation if (disregarding any possibility of revocation) primary legislation prevents removal of the incompatibility.

4   *Declaration of incompatibility*

(1)   Subsection (2) applies in any proceedings in which a court determines whether a provision of primary legislation is compatible with a Convention right.

(2)   If the court is satisfied that the provision is incompatible with a Convention right, it may make a declaration of that incompatibility.

(3)   Subsection (4) applies in any proceedings in which a court determines whether a provision of subordinate legislation, made in the exercise of a power conferred by primary legislation, is compatible with a Convention right.

(4)   If the court is satisfied:
    (a)   that the provision is incompatible with a Convention right, and
    (b)   that (disregarding any possibility of revocation) the primary legislation concerned prevents removal of the incompatibility,
it may make a declaration of that incompatibility.

(5)   In this section "court" means:
    (a)   the House of Lords;
    (b)   the Judicial Committee of the Privy Council;
    (c)   the Courts-Martial Appeal Court;
    (d)   in Scotland, the High Court of Justiciary sitting otherwise than as a trial court or the Court of Session;
    (e)   in England and Wales or Northern Ireland, the High Court or the Court of Appeal.

(6)   A declaration under this section ("a declaration of incompatibility") –
    (a)   does not affect the validity, continuing operation or enforcement of the provision in respect of which it is given; and
    (b)   is not binding on the parties to the proceedings in which it is made.

5   Right of Crown to intervene

(1)   Where a court is considering whether to make a declaration of incompatibility, the Crown is entitled to notice in accordance with rules of court.

(2)   In any case to which subsection (1) applies:
    (a)   a Minister of the Crown (or a person nominated by him),
    (b)   a member of the Scottish Executive,
    (c)   a Northern Ireland Minister,
    (d)   a Northern Ireland department,
is entitled, on giving notice in accordance with rules of court, to be joined as a party to the proceedings.

(3)   Notice under subsection (2) may be given at any time during the proceedings.

(4)   A person who has been made a party to criminal proceedings (other than in Scotland) as the result of a notice under subsection (2) may, with leave, appeal to the House of Lords against any declaration of incompatibility made in the proceedings.

(5)   In subsection (4): "criminal proceedings" includes all proceedings before the Courts-Martial Appeal Court; and "leave" means leave granted by the court making the declaration of incompatibility or by the House of Lords.

Public authorities

6   Acts of public authorities

(1)   It is unlawful for a public authority to act in a way which is incompatible with a Convention right.

(2)   Subsection (1) does not apply to an act if:

(a) as the result of one or more provisions of primary legislation, the authority could not have acted differently; or

(b) in the case of one or more provisions of, or made under, primary legislation which cannot be read or given effect in a way which is compatible with the Convention rights, the authority was acting so as to give effect to or enforce those provisions.

(3) In this section "public authority" includes:

(a) a court or tribunal, and

(b) any person certain of whose functions are functions of a public nature,

but does not include either House of Parliament or a person exercising functions in connection with proceedings in Parliament.

(4) In subsection (3) "Parliament" does not include the House of Lords in its judicial capacity.

(5) In relation to a particular act, a person is not a public authority by virtue only of subsection (3)(b) if the nature of the act is private.

(6) "An act" includes a failure to act but does not include a failure to:

(a) introduce in, or lay before, Parliament a proposal for legislation; or

(b) make any primary legislation or remedial order.

7 Proceedings

(1) A person who claims that a public authority has acted (or proposes to act) in a way which is made unlawful by section 6(1) may:

(a) bring proceedings against the authority under this Act in the appropriate court or tribunal, or

(b) rely on the Convention right or rights concerned in any legal proceedings,

but only if he is (or would be) a victim of the unlawful act.

[...]

Remedial action

10 Power to take remedial action

(1) This section applies if:

(a) a provision of legislation has been declared under section 4 to be incompatible with a Convention right and, if an appeal lies –

(i) all persons who may appeal have stated in writing that they do not intend to do so;

(ii) the time for bringing an appeal has expired and no appeal has been brought within that time; or

(iii) an appeal brought within that time has been determined or abandoned; or

(b) it appears to a Minister of the Crown or Her Majesty in Council that, having regard to a finding of the European Court of Human Rights made after the coming into force of this section in proceedings against the United Kingdom, a provision of legislation is incompatible with an obligation of the United Kingdom arising from the Convention.

(2)   If a Minister of the Crown considers that there are compelling reasons for proceeding under this section, he may by order make such amendments to the legislation as he considers necessary to remove the incompatibility.

(3)   If, in the case of subordinate legislation, a Minister of the Crown considers:

(a)   that it is necessary to amend the primary legislation under which the subordinate legislation in question was made, in order to enable the incompatibility to be removed, and

(b)   that there are compelling reasons for proceeding under this section,

he may by order make such amendments to the primary legislation as he considers necessary.

[...]

Schedules

Schedule 1

The Articles

Part I
The Convention

Rights and Freedoms

Article 2
Right to life

1.   Everyone's right to life shall be protected by law. No one shall be deprived of his life intentionally save in the execution of a sentence of a court following his conviction of a crime for which this penalty is provided by law.

2.   Deprivation of life shall not be regarded as inflicted in contravention of this Article when it results from the use of force which is no more than absolutely necessary:

(a)   in defence of any person from unlawful violence;

(b)   in order to effect a lawful arrest or to prevent the escape of a person lawfully detained;

(c)   in action lawfully taken for the purpose of quelling a riot or insurrection.

Article 3
Prohibition of torture

No one shall be subjected to torture or to inhuman or degrading treatment or punishment.

Article 4
Prohibition of slavery and forced labour

1.   No one shall be held in slavery or servitude.

2.   No one shall be required to perform forced or compulsory labour.

3.   For the purpose of this Article the term "forced or compulsory labour" shall not include:

(a)   any work required to be done in the ordinary course of detention imposed according to the provisions of Article 5 of this Convention or during conditional release from such detention;
(b)   any service of a military character or, in case of conscientious objectors in countries where they are recognised, service exacted instead of compulsory military service;
(c)   any service exacted in case of an emergency or calamity threatening the life or well-being of the community;
(d)   any work or service which forms part of normal civic obligations.

ARTICLE 5
RIGHT TO LIBERTY AND SECURITY

1.   Everyone has the right to liberty and security of person. No one shall be deprived of his liberty save in the following cases and in accordance with a procedure prescribed by law:

(a)   the lawful detention of a person after conviction by a competent court;
(b)   the lawful arrest or detention of a person for non-compliance with the lawful order of a court or in order to secure the fulfilment of any obligation prescribed by law;
(c)   the lawful arrest or detention of a person effected for the purpose of bringing him before the competent legal authority on reasonable suspicion of having committed an offence or when it is reasonably considered necessary to prevent his committing an offence or fleeing after having done so;
(d)   the detention of a minor by lawful order for the purpose of educational supervision or his lawful detention for the purpose of bringing him before the competent legal authority;
(e)   the lawful detention of persons for the prevention of the spreading of infectious diseases, of persons of unsound mind, alcoholics or drug addicts or vagrants;
(f)   the lawful arrest or detention of a person to prevent his effecting an unauthorised entry into the country or of a person against whom action is being taken with a view to deportation or extradition.

2.   Everyone who is arrested shall be informed promptly, in a language which he understands, of the reasons for his arrest and of any charge against him.

3.   Everyone arrested or detained in accordance with the provisions of paragraph 1(c) of this Article shall be brought promptly before a judge or other officer authorised by law to exercise judicial power and shall be entitled to trial within a reasonable time or to release pending trial. Release may be conditioned by guarantees to appear for trial.

4.   Everyone who is deprived of his liberty by arrest or detention shall be entitled to take proceedings by which the lawfulness of his detention shall be decided speedily by a court and his release ordered if the detention is not lawful.

5.   Everyone who has been the victim of arrest or detention in contravention of the provisions of this Article shall have an enforceable right to compensation.

ARTICLE 6
RIGHT TO A FAIR TRIAL

1.   In the determination of his civil rights and obligations or of any criminal charge against him, everyone is entitled to a fair and public hearing within a reasonable time by an independent and impartial tribunal established by law. Judgment shall be pronounced publicly but the press and public may be excluded from all or part of the trial in the interest of morals, public order or national security in a democratic society, where the interests of juveniles or the protection of the private life of the parties so require, or to the extent strictly necessary in the opinion of the court in special circumstances where publicity would prejudice the interests of justice.

2.   Everyone charged with a criminal offence shall be presumed innocent until proved guilty according to law.

3.   Everyone charged with a criminal offence has the following minimum rights:

(a)   to be informed promptly, in a language which he understands and in detail, of the nature and cause of the accusation against him;
(b)   to have adequate time and facilities for the preparation of his defence;
(c)   to defend himself in person or through legal assistance of his own choosing or, if he has not sufficient means to pay for legal assistance, to be given it free when the interests of justice so require;
(d)   to examine or have examined witnesses against him and to obtain the attendance and examination of witnesses on his behalf under the same conditions as witnesses against him;
(e)   to have the free assistance of an interpreter if he cannot understand or speak the language used in court.

ARTICLE 7
NO PUNISHMENT WITHOUT LAW

1.   No one shall be held guilty of any criminal offence on account of any act or omission which did not constitute a criminal offence under national or international law at the time when it was committed. Nor shall a heavier penalty be imposed than the one that was applicable at the time the criminal offence was committed.

2.   This Article shall not prejudice the trial and punishment of any person for any act or omission which, at the time when it was committed, was criminal according to the general principles of law recognised by civilised nations.

ARTICLE 8
RIGHT TO RESPECT FOR PRIVATE AND FAMILY LIFE

1.   Everyone has the right to respect for his private and family life, his home and his correspondence.

2.   There shall be no interference by a public authority with the exercise of this right except such as is in accordance with the law and is necessary in a democratic

society in the interests of national security, public safety or the economic well-being of the country, for the prevention of disorder or crime, for the protection of health or morals, or for the protection of the rights and freedoms of others.

ARTICLE 9
FREEDOM OF THOUGHT, CONSCIENCE AND RELIGION

1. Everyone has the right to freedom of thought, conscience and religion; this right includes freedom to change his religion or belief and freedom, either alone or in community with others and in public or private, to manifest his religion or belief, in worship, teaching, practice and observance.

2. Freedom to manifest one's religion or beliefs shall be subject only to such limitations as are prescribed by law and are necessary in a democratic society in the interests of public safety, for the protection of public order, health or morals, or for the protection of the rights and freedoms of others.

ARTICLE 10
FREEDOM OF EXPRESSION

1. Everyone has the right to freedom of expression. This right shall include freedom to hold opinions and to receive and impart information and ideas without interference by public authority and regardless of frontiers. This Article shall not prevent States from requiring the licensing of broadcasting, television or cinema enterprises.

2. The exercise of these freedoms, since it carries with it duties and responsibilities, may be subject to such formalities, conditions, restrictions or penalties as are prescribed by law and are necessary in a democratic society, in the interests of national security, territorial integrity or public safety, for the prevention of disorder or crime, for the protection of health or morals, for the protection of the reputation or rights of others, for preventing the disclosure of information received in confidence, or for maintaining the authority and impartiality of the judiciary.

ARTICLE 11
FREEDOM OF ASSEMBLY AND ASSOCIATION

1. Everyone has the right to freedom of peaceful assembly and to freedom of association with others, including the right to form and to join trade unions for the protection of his interests.

2. No restrictions shall be placed on the exercise of these rights other than such as are prescribed by law and are necessary in a democratic society in the interests of national security or public safety, for the prevention of disorder or crime, for the protection of health or morals or for the protection of the rights and freedoms of others. This Article shall not prevent the imposition of lawful restrictions on the exercise of these rights by members of the armed forces, of the police or of the administration of the State.

ARTICLE 12
RIGHT TO MARRY

Men and women of marriageable age have the right to marry and to found a family, according to the national laws governing the exercise of this right.

ARTICLE 14
PROHIBITION OF DISCRIMINATION
The enjoyment of the rights and freedoms set forth in this Convention shall be secured without discrimination on any ground such as sex, race, colour, language, religion, political or other opinion, national or social origin, association with a national minority, property, birth or other status.

ARTICLE 16
RESTRICTIONS ON POLITICAL ACTIVITY OF ALIENS
Nothing in Articles 10, 11 and 14 shall be regarded as preventing the High Contracting Parties from imposing restrictions on the political activity of aliens.

ARTICLE 17
PROHIBITION OF ABUSE OF RIGHTS
Nothing in this Convention may be interpreted as implying for any State, group or person any right to engage in any activity or perform any act aimed at the destruction of any of the rights and freedoms set forth herein or at their limitation to a greater extent than is provided for in the Convention.

ARTICLE 18
LIMITATION ON USE OF RESTRICTIONS ON RIGHTS
The restrictions permitted under this Convention to the said rights and freedoms shall not be applied for any purpose other than those for which they have been prescribed.

PART II
THE FIRST PROTOCOL

ARTICLE 1
PROTECTION OF PROPERTY
Every natural or legal person is entitled to the peaceful enjoyment of his possessions. No one shall be deprived of his possessions except in the public interest and subject to the conditions provided for by law and by the general principles of international law.

The preceding provisions shall not, however, in any way impair the right of a State to enforce such laws as it deems necessary to control the use of property in accordance with the general interest or to secure the payment of taxes or other contributions or penalties.

ARTICLE 2
RIGHT TO EDUCATION
No person shall be denied the right to education. In the exercise of any functions which it assumes in relation to education and to teaching, the State shall respect the right of parents to ensure such education and teaching in conformity with their own religious and philosophical convictions.

ARTICLE 3
RIGHT TO FREE ELECTIONS
The High Contracting Parties undertake to hold free elections at reasonable intervals by secret ballot, under conditions which will ensure the free expression of the opinion of the people in the choice of the legislature.

Part III
THE SIXTH PROTOCOL

ARTICLE 1
ABOLITION OF THE DEATH PENALTY

The death penalty shall be abolished. No one shall be condemned to such penalty or executed.

ARTICLE 2
DEATH PENALTY IN TIME OF WAR

A State may make provision in its law for the death penalty in respect of acts committed in time of war or of imminent threat of war; such penalty shall be applied only in the instances laid down in the law and in accordance with its provisions. The State shall communicate to the Secretary General of the Council of Europe the relevant provisions of that law.

32

A Mayor and Assembly for London

Department of the Environment, Transport and the Regions

A New Style of Governance

[...]

This government was elected with a mandate to modernise Britain and bring our political and administrative arrangements up to date. This document sets out new arrangements for running London which are innovative, relevant and forward looking.

Since the abolition of the GLC in 1986, London has lacked strategic direction and leadership. Londoners and London organisations have complained about confused responsibilities, duplication of effort, conflicting policies and programmes and a general sense of drift. No one was in charge or able to speak up for London. This has led to a city of stark contrasts. On the one hand it is one of the most competitive in Europe, a beacon of enterprise, creativity and culture. Yet on the other it is beset with problems of congestion, pollution and social deprivation. In short, it is a city full of energy, but where the big issues do not get sorted out. It does not have to be like this. There is a better way.

A new and radical approach to governing London is long overdue. There needs to be a new style of politics, a style which is modern in its outlook, inclusive in its approach, relevant to Londoners and, above all, democratic and accountable. Our aim is to increase public confidence in the democratic process, engender enthusiasm and restore Londoners' pride in their city.

At the heart of our proposals for London is a directly elected executive Mayor with the power to make a real difference to London on the issues that matter to Londoners. A Mayor with strategic responsibilities where they are needed, who will tackle the issues and change things for the better.

The Mayor

Whilst there is no recent history in this country of strong executive mayors, else-where in the world they have made a positive difference to the lives of their citizens and the communities they serve. The capital needs leadership. It also needs someone who will work with the grain of London, bringing the people, the boroughs, the private and voluntary sectors together to tackle the real issues. In developing these proposals for London we have drawn on international experience, but the arrangements set out here are tailor-made for London – a London solution to London's problems.

The Mayor will have sweeping new powers over transport and economic development and will have two powerful organisations – Transport for London (TfL) and the London Development Agency (LDA) – bringing together expertise on these issues. Two new democratic authorities – a Metropolitan Police Authority (MPA) and a London Fire and Emergency Planning Authority (LFEPA) – closely linked with the Mayor, will be responsible for the work of the police and the fire and emergency planning services. These will follow the models outside London, but reflecting London's unique arrangements, will build in roles for the Mayor and the Assembly. On planning and the environment the Mayor will have a direct role, setting a new planning strategy for London and with power to tackle the major threats to London's environment and its long-term sustainability. The Mayor will work closely with cultural and sporting organisations to build on the capital's success and with the health sector to promote the health of Londoners.

The nature and extent of the Mayor's responsibilities will allow vital connections to be made between transport and the environment, regeneration and crime prevention, economic development and the culture, leisure and tourism sectors. Policy will not be made in separate boxes but will be developed in an integrated way, ensuring that the same core objectives underpin all activities and that sustainable, efficient and effective action is taken by whoever is best placed to act.

We shall require the Mayor to propose an overall vision for London, defining clear policy objectives and setting benchmarks against which to measure success. The Mayor will draw up detailed strategies, set budgets and appoint people to run key services. The Mayor will be able to undertake research or employ consultants to analyse problems and find solutions. Taskforces involving relevant London organisations will be created to tackle pressing issues. With a mandate from up to 5 million electors, the Mayor will have exceptional influence, going well beyond the specific statutory and financial powers of the Office, yet remain accountable to Londoners. As its public face, the Mayor will promote London at home and overseas, attracting inward investment, major sporting and cultural events. We expect the Mayor to become a high profile figure who will speak out on London's behalf and be listened to. Londoners will all know who their Mayor is and have an opinion on how he or she is doing. This will change the face of London politics.

The Mayor will have a range of powers, duties and responsibilities designed to ensure that the programme on which he or she was elected can be delivered. The Mayor's office will be at the heart of a powerful administrative machine, staffed by a small number of political advisers and high quality officers. The Mayor will have a wide range of expertise at his or her disposal, including secondees from other organisations, and will be able to set the pace. We expect intense competition to fill these high profile and challenging jobs – leading the battle against congestion, air pollution, crime and poverty; working with partners to promote business competitiveness; speaking up for London internationally and attracting major sporting and cultural events – whatever policies the Mayor is elected by Londoners to deliver.

The Assembly

With such a powerful elected Mayor, it is essential that there is another democratic-ally elected forum where other political views or interests can be aired, where London-wide issues can be debated openly, and where people with special skills, expertise and experience of London can give their views. But it must be much more than a talking shop; it must also be able to scrutinise the activities of the Mayor and other bodies and provide vital public accountability. There will, therefore, be a separately elected Assembly alongside the Mayor.

A prime duty of the Assembly will be to hold the Mayor to account on London's behalf. It will scrutinise all of the Mayor's activities, those of the two new authorities and the bodies responsible for transport and economic development. It will also be able to initiate scrutinies of other issues of its choice which it judges to be of importance to London. These powers [...] will allow the Assembly to question the Mayor and the Mayor's staff, to hold public hearings on issues of importance to them and to have access to relevant people, papers and technical expertise.

The Assembly will have a key role in setting the GLA's budget. It will work closely with the Mayor on the budget and strategic priorities. As part of this process, the Assembly will develop proposals for action to tackle those issues it considers to be important. The Mayor will be obliged to consider these and respond to the Assembly. At the end of the process, the Assembly will be able to agree or reject the Mayor's budget, if it commands a sufficient majority.

Assembly members will also play an important role on the new independent authorities for policing and for fire and emergency planning, bringing a greater democratic accountability into the delivery of these public services than has been the case hitherto. There will be a clear separation between scrutiny and other functions to preserve propriety and accountability.

Open and partnership working

The Mayor and Assembly will be required to consult widely and work closely with London organisations – boroughs, the private sector and voluntary bodies – in a new inclusive style of politics. There will be open hearings where evidence will be taken, question times in which they can respond to views put to them and where strategies and policies can be debated, and an annual State of London debate. Major decisions made by the Mayor will be available to the Assembly and the public, with reasons.

It will be for the GLA to decide how best to consult. This might include the creation of a consultative forum. We are attracted by the ideas put forward by the London Voluntary Service Council (LVSC) for a civic forum involving all sectors of society debating issues of interest and making proposals to the Mayor and Assembly. We expect the Mayor and the Mayor's staff to develop close links with groups representing different sectors – ethnic minorities, trade unions, young people, small businesses – and to listen to their views and take action where needed.

A successful Mayor will create a good working relationship with key London organisations in the public, private and voluntary sectors to tackle problems and promote London's strengths. The contributions of London organisations and the community at large will be crucial. There can be no going back to the days of confrontation and parochialism. Everyone has a role to play in forging London's future success. London will now have the governance structures it needs to maintain and build on the climate of partnership working which has become a feature of life in the capital in recent years, and it is up to Londoners together to make them work effectively.

These new arrangements will modernise and significantly improve the governance of London. They are not changes for change's sake but real improvements which will add value and fill the democratic and organisational deficits which have held London back. These arrangements will give power to the people. Londoners will be able to choose the person in charge of their city and be sure that he or she is publicly accountable for their actions.

[...]

The London boroughs and the City of London

London boroughs and the City of London, with some minor exceptions, will continue to be responsible for the delivery of local services. But we expect them to work closely with the Mayor and the Assembly to ensure that there is good local information available to inform strategic decisions and to assist in the delivery of agreed London-wide policies. They will have a full part to play in transforming the way London is run and the Mayor and the Assembly will work closely with them and consult them on relevant issues.

[...] [W]e do not propose to abolish the City Corporation. In reaching this decision we were relying upon the assurance that the Corporation would continue its work in promoting inward investment and financing studies for the benefit of London as a whole, and had accepted that it must respond to the need to improve its electoral arrangements. The Corporation has produced its own proposals for reform which have been the subject of consultation and discussion with those who live in the City and the variety of bodies which operate there. These proposals involve both reforming the existing franchise in order to prevent abuse and the extension of the electoral system to give a wider variety of bodies and organisations voting rights within the square mile.

We shall continue to maintain an interest in the Corporation's proposals for reforming its franchise as they develop.

Cost

The cost of running the GLA is expected to be about £20 m per annum. Most of this will be met by central government from existing resources, but Londoners will contribute a small amount, for example about 3p per week for those with a Band D council tax bill. Overall, there will be no increase in total public expenditure. Generally, the GLA will be subject to the same financial regime as local authorities in England.

[...]

Conclusion

London is on the verge of a new and exciting era in its history. Londoners will once again be in control of their city and have a say in its future. Thus equipped, the nation's capital will be able to take full advantage of the opportunities and meet the challenges which the twenty-first century will bring. That is good not just for London, but for Britain as a whole.

33

The Jenkins Commission Report on the Voting System

Jenkins Commission

Introduction

The remit which we were given by the government in December 1997 was to recommend the best alternative 'system or combination of systems' to the existing commonly-called 'First Past the Post' system of election to the Westminster Parliament. In doing this we were asked to take into account four not entirely compatible 'requirements'. They were (i) broad proportionality; (ii) the need for stable government; (iii) an extension of voter choice; and (iv) the maintenance of a link between MPs and geographical constituencies.

Fortunately the 'requirements' were none of them absolute. Otherwise our task would have been not merely difficult (which it certainly has been) but impossible. Proportionality may be 'broad' not strict. 'Stable government' in the context is necessarily a relative term, for the only way to ensure it absolutely (at least until the régime blows up) would be by avoiding elections altogether, which would make our enquiry otiose. Voter choice is at once important and imprecise. And it is 'a link' and not 'the link' between MPs and geographical constituencies which has to be respected. This semi-flexibility has made it possible for us to aim at a point which comes near to reconciling all four criteria.

It must be stressed that there is no question of our being asked to impose a new electoral system upon the British public. What we are asked to do is to recommend the best alternative system which will then be put to the British electorate in a referendum. There has been some suggestion from the opponents of any electoral change (see for instance the House of Commons debate on 2 June 1998) that we should have been given the opportunity to consider the virtues of the present system and to adjudicate between it and all alternatives. But this is surely a misconceived argument for it would have given us a power which we do not have and do not seek. The one proposition which is guaranteed a place upon the referendum ballot paper is the maintenance of the status quo. Our role is merely to recommend what the alternative should be.

Nevertheless it has in practice been inevitable that when considering the advantages and disadvantages of any new system we should have been constantly measuring them not only against each other, but also against what exists today and in the course of that we necessarily had to deploy arguments both for and against the existing system. It is further the case that none of us are electoral absolutists. We all of us believe that any system has defects as well as virtues. Some systems are nonetheless much better than others, and we have endeavoured to seek relative virtue in an imperfect world.

The Meaning of Representation

Before we get into the comparison of the merits of different systems we think it right to set out certain assumptions which have lain behind our work. These relate first to our concept of 'fairness' in electoral outcomes; second to the place of political parties; and third to the role of Members of Parliament, who are an important outcome of any electoral system.

Fairness and the role of parties

First, 'fairness', which is an important but imprecise concept. Fairness to voters is the first essential. A primary duty of an electoral system is to represent the wishes of the electorate as effectively as possible. The major 'fairness' count against First Past the Post is that it distorts the desires of the voters. That the voters do not get the representation they want is more important than that the parties do not get the seats to which they think they are entitled. Parties should, like the electoral system, be servants rather than masters, although in their case it is necessarily to a segment rather than to the whole which they appeal. If they aspire to be parties of government, however, that segment needs to be a wide one, and if the nation as a whole is to function well they need also to show some respect for the opinions of their opponents. Parties should not elevate themselves into mystical entities, enjoying special rights of their own. That way lies what can be described as the 'tabernacle' approach to politics, by which all virtue lies with those within the sacred temples and all those outside are eternally damned. Such an approach is almost certainly a recipe for parties getting above themselves, being intolerantly dogmatic when they are successful, and degenerating into narrow sects when they are not. It is also a recipe for the 'blame the other side for everything' confrontational style of politics, which has done much to reduce respect for the functioning of the House of Commons and for politicians generally, and which in the quite recent past has also encouraged a confrontational mood in industry, although that is less of a problem today than it was a couple of decades ago.

It is also the case that the near unanimous opinion which was expressed to the Commission in its consultative hearings around the country was a distrust of any electoral system which increased the power of party machines. While we do not deceive ourselves that the limited number who attended these meetings can be regarded as a representative cross-section, this persistent current of opinion, coming as it did from those who were hostile to any change as well as from the committed reformers and some who were more neutral, made a strong impression upon us.

Allowing for this, however, it is important not to be carried too far by a fashion-able current and to pretend that representative democracy can function without parties. Within the Commission's own electoral systems context it is impossible not to use the results for parties as the principal criterion for measuring 'unfairness'. The basic evil is unfairness towards voters but its manifestation is unfairness to various groups, of which some (women, ethnic minorities) are not specifically political, but with parties nonetheless being the principal beneficiaries or losers. In saying this we are not unmindful of the argument that, in justifying fairness, what is sometimes called 'proportionality of power', as well as proportionality of representation, should be taken into account. Just as the gross and persistent under-representation of a substantial minority cannot be justified, so it would be undesirable to correct that by giving to the minority such a permanent hold upon hinge power that neither of the larger groupings could ever exercise independent power without the permission of the minority. That would substitute one distortion for another. But a balance can be struck. If in the catch-phrase (and somewhat misleading like all such phrases) we avoid the tail wagging the dog this should and can be done without all dogs having their tails cut off.

Within a wider context it is also the case that any Parliament endeavouring to function without any party organisation would be an inchoate mass, incapable not merely of giving effective sustenance to government (and thus meeting the second of our terms of reference requirement) but even of organising its own business, from electing a Speaker to deciding which issues should be debated on which day. As, in addition, parties are mostly sustained by those with a spirit of public service, we do not see our role as being either on the one hand to denigrate parties or on the other to increase the already very considerable powers which are exercised by these necessary tools of democracy.

The role of the Members of Parliament

The role of Members of Parliament can now be broadly regarded as four-fold: to represent their constituencies; to provide a pool from which most of the holders of ministerial office are chosen; to shape and enact legislation; and to enable the party in power to sustain the central planks of its legislative programme whilst yet being held to account for its executive action.

The House of Commons fulfils the first two of these distinct but overlapping roles with marked effectiveness. There is no doubt that most of its members work hard in their constituencies and once elected regard themselves as representing the entire electorate within their constituency regardless of which party individual electors supported at the polls. This convention has been rightly valued down the years by almost all MPs. The workload of members within their constituencies has grown, as is illustrated by an explosive increase over the years in the size of their postbags. In contrast to the not so very distant past, members are expected to spend a lot of time in their constituencies. Our clear impression is that most members take this constituency responsibility very seriously and discharge it well. With devolution, this constituency role will not be so obvious for members in Scotland (in particular), Wales and Northern Ireland, since many of the issues a member has traditionally dealt with will be handled at devolved level.

Similarly few governments have not been able to recruit from the House of Commons a ministerial team which contains several stars and maintains a general level of competent and devoted public service. This is not contradicted by the fact that nearly all governments have found it necessary to bring in a few people not previously in Parliament for some ministerial posts. This has become notably so for Law Officers, Scottish ones for some time past, more recently for English ones as well.

By sharp contrast it is difficult to be at all sanguine about the performance of the House of Commons as a legislature. There is a mass of complex legislation each session. The tasks imposed on the relevant civil servants and parliamentary draftsmen are demanding. There is no doubt that in the past much legislation has been hastily conceived, and that imprecise ministerial instruction or sheer pressure of time have resulted in inadequate thought being given to the precise form in which legislation is brought forward. We hope that the increasing trend towards pre-legislative scrutiny will contribute to an improvement in the draft legislation presented to Parliament.

Legislation is not very effectively scrutinised in the House of Commons. In most cases, government MPs are expected to and do support the first and each subsequent versions of a bill equally faithfully. Usually only amendments which are introduced by the Government have much chance of success. The theory that any government always knows best or will assuredly get it right first time is not easy to sustain. Nor does the career structure of parliamentary politicians encourage many backbench MPs to concentrate on the painstaking, low-profile work of improving the quality of legislation. A lot is left for a revising second chamber to do.

Inevitably perhaps, the competing responsibilities of MPs do not assist them in the task of coping with the large and complex burden of legislative business. We believe nonetheless that there is considerable scope for some members to concentrate more fully and more critically on the legislative process and for there to be amongst the mix of members some who have appropriate expertise and temperament to undertake the grinding and often unnoticed slog of improving the quality of our laws. For on those laws depend the legal foundation and economic and social balance of our society.

The fourth, and for many the most central, role of the House of Commons is to ensure that the executive is held fully accountable for its actions. This task is hard when governments elected by minority votes can command large majorities. Fortified by the whipping system, by the natural loyalty to their leader of most MPs and by an equally natural desire on the part of many for political preferment, this can lead to what Lord Hailsham in 1976 memorably described as 'elective dictatorship'. He was speaking during a period of Labour government, which had been supported by only 39% of the electorate, but which was nonetheless pushing through what appears in retrospect at any rate to be some of the last gasps of a dogmatic desire for nationalisation – of the ports and of the aircraft industry.

A decade or so later, however, a Conservative government, with only a few percentage points more of electoral support behind it, pushed through first the disciplined enactment of the poll tax, and then, within the same parliament, its equally disciplined repeal. This was followed in the 1990s, in the last years of a government moving towards heavy electoral defeat, by further measures of privatisation, from the railways to the Stationery Office, of questionable popularity. In view of this record it may be thought that some greater diffusion of power through the encouragement amongst MPs of more independence and more concentration upon the legislative process would be desirable. Insofar as a reformed electoral system could assist in this direction that would be a mark in its favour.

Recommendations and Conclusions

The Commission's central recommendation is that the best alternative for Britain to the existing First Past The Post system is a two-vote mixed system which can be described as either limited AMS or AV Top-up. The majority of MPs (80 to 85%) would continue to be elected on an individual constituency basis, with the remainder elected on a corrective Top-up basis which would significantly reduce the disproportionality and the geographical divisiveness which are inherent in FPTP.

Within this mixed system the constituency members should be elected by the Alternative Vote. On its own AV would be unacceptable because of the danger that in anything like present circumstances it might increase rather than reduce disproportionality and might do so in a way which is unfair to the Conservative party. With the corrective mechanism in operation, however, its advantages of increasing voter choice and of ensuring that in practice all constituency members (as opposed to little more than half in recent elections) have majority support in their own constituencies become persuasive. Lord Alexander would, however, prefer to retain FPTP for constituency elections. [. . .]

The Commission recommends that this system should be implemented throughout the United Kingdom.

The Commission recommends that the second vote determining the allocation of Top-up members should allow the voter the choice of either a vote for a party or for an individual candidate from the lists put forward by parties. They should therefore be what are commonly called open rather than closed lists.

The Commission recommends that, in the interests of local accountability and providing additional members with a broad constituency link, additional members should be elected using small Top-up areas. The Commission recommends the areas most appropriate for this purpose are the 'preserved' counties and equivalently sized metropolitan districts in England. In Scotland and Wales, we see no reason to depart from the units which are used for the return of additional members to the Parliament in Scotland and to the Assembly in Wales with respectively eight and five Top-up areas. In Northern Ireland there should be two Top-up areas each returning two members. In England the Top-up members would therefore in effect be either county or city-wide members from 65 different areas.

The Commission recommends that the Top-up members should be allocated correctively, that is on the basis of the second vote and taking into account the number of constituency seats gained by each party in each respective area, according to the following method:

- the number of second votes cast for each party will be counted and divided by the number of constituency MPs plus one gained by each party in each area;
- the party with the highest number of second votes after this calculation will be allocated the first Top-up member;
- any second additional member for an area will be allocated using the same method but adjusting to the fact that one party will already have gained a Top-up member.

The Commission recommends that the proportion of Top-up members needed for broad proportionality without imposing a coalition habit on the country should be between 15% and 20%. A decision on the exact proportion of Top-up members should [...] relate to other changes in the pipeline such as the reduction in the number of Scottish seats and the work of the Boundary Commissions.

The Commission recommends that the allocation of Top-up seats to areas should ensure that the ratio of constituency to Top-up members is, as far as is practicable, equal in the four constituent nations of the United Kingdom. The allocation of Top-up members to the areas within each of those parts should ensure that each area has at least one Top-up member with the remainder being allocated to those areas with the greatest number of electors. [...] Northern Ireland should have two Top-up members in two Top-up areas.

The Commission recommends that the right to put forward candidates for Top-up member seats should be limited to those parties which have candidates standing for election in at least half of the constituencies within the Top-up area.

The Commission stresses that all members of the House of Commons whether elected from constituencies or as Top-up members should have equal status in Westminster.

The Commission recommends that Top-up member vacancies, which are unlikely to be more than two or three a parliament, should be filled by the candidate next on the list of the party holding the seat. If there is no available person the seat should remain vacant until the next general election. Constituency vacancies would of course be filled by the normal by-election procedure.

The Commission believes that changes to the existing Rules for the Redistribution of Seats (Schedule 2 to the Parliamentary Constituencies Act 1986) will be integral to the successful implementation of the new system. Bias should be reduced by the use of a single electoral quota for the United Kingdom; and the Boundary Commissions should be given a statutory power to take account of population movement and thus help to keep the result of their work more up-to-date.

Secondary recommendations

The Commission recommends that there should be a properly planned publicly-funded but neutrally-conducted education programme to prepare voters for the decision they will be required to make in the referendum.

The Commission concludes that the education programme and oversight of referendums generally should fall to an independent commission. This role would fall naturally to an Electoral Commission.

The Commission recommends that an independent Electoral Commission should be established to advise Parliament on and have oversight of electoral administration and related matters.

The Commission recommends that the Government should put in place arrangements to review the new system after, say, two general elections.

The Commission recommends that substantial further changes should not be made without a second referendum.

34

Response to the Jenkins Commission Report

Jack Straw

The Secretary of State for the Home Department (Mr Jack Straw): I am glad to open the debate on a question at the heart of our constitutional arrangements. The choice of 5 November – Guy Fawkes day – for this debate is entirely fortuitous. However, it serves to remind us how long Parliament has been central to the life of this nation, and how, over time, this institution has carefully adapted itself to reflect the will of the British people.

[...]

In all the debates about the appropriate electoral system for Westminster, I have personally taken one side of the argument – in favour of first past the post. That will come as no great surprise to hon. Members on either side. I therefore remain unpersuaded of the case for change, although I am always open to higher argument.

I have also long believed there should be a proper, informed debate on the issue. Indeed, at my party's conference in 1995, I spoke on behalf of the national executive committee to urge my party to back a referendum on the voting system for the House of Commons. For it was, and is, my belief that this is an issue that should ultimately be decided by those who matter most in our democracy – the British people.

Following that vote at the 1995 party conference, our election manifesto duly pledged us to create an independent commission to identify the best possible electoral system as an alternative to first past the post. We honoured that pledge within the first few months of taking office. The commission was appointed on 1 December last year, and began its work early this year.

As we discussed in the debate on 2 June, members of the commission were chosen because of their knowledge and expertise, because they were broadly sympathetic to electoral reform, and because they represented a broad spectrum of political views. [...]

[Based on] the likely results of the 1997 election – the one with which we are all most familiar – had the proposed system been in place, and using the median – 17.5 per cent – of the range proposed. That shows that, on this system, Conservative representation would have increased from 165 seats to 168, an increase of three seats. Labour representation would have decreased from 419 seats to 368, a loss of

51 seats, or a reduction. Liberal Democrat representation would have increased by 43 seats from 46 seats to 89. It is estimated that the Scottish nationalists and Plaid Cymru would have increased their representation from 10 seats to 15.
[...]
   [...] Those hon. Members who have carefully followed the proceedings of the European Parliamentary Elections Bill may be reminded of the Belgian system; indeed, it is similar, but not the same. There is one key difference.

Mr Dennis Skinner (Bolsover): It is double Dutch.

Mr Straw: We shall come on to the Flemish-speaking Victor d'Hondt in a moment, because he features in the system.
   Although all the votes, whether cast for individuals or the list as a whole, will be used to determine how many top-up seats a party wins – using the now favourite d'Hondt divisor – it appears, although the report is not entirely explicit on this point –
[...]
   The commission's report is one of the best written official reports that I have read for many years, and our gratitude for that must go to its chairman, Lord Jenkins. The Government would now like to see a widespread debate about the merits of the report within political parties, in Parliament and among the public at large. Today's debate is an important contribution to that.
   As to timing, we have always envisaged that the referendum would be before the next election, and that remains an option. However, plainly, in the light of Lord Jenkins's specific recommendations, this is less certain, because the new system cannot be introduced until the election after next. Nor, in our judgment, is there a need for the Government to come to an early view about the commission's recommendation.
   There are a number of important points of detail in his recommended system which Lord Jenkins has left to be resolved. We have always believed that the referendum, whenever it is held, should be a choice of equals – a choice between first past the post and an explicit alternative. Parliament may take the view that, in order that the British people know exactly what they are being asked to consider, the exact proportion of top-up seats, the way in which the constituency and top-up area boundaries will be determined and the exact method of allocating votes for top-up seats should be determined in advance. It is a matter for Parliament, but if we were to do that, these things would plainly take time.
   As I have already explained, the simple truth is that, with the best will in the world, the Jenkins system could not be in place by the next general election. That is because the system that is envisaged would require the number of constituencies to be reduced from the present 659 to about 530 to 560. Every constituency boundary throughout the United Kingdom would need to be redrawn, a process that would take the Boundary Commission some years. That is because the average number of eligible voters per constituency at present is about 72,000. If that number were increased by between 15 and 20 per cent, the average would increase to between 85,000 and 90,000. There are no constituencies of that size except the one that happens to be at Milton Keynes.
   In opting for the system it did, the commission acknowledged that 'we cannot realistically expect our recommendations to be in operation at a general election in

much less than eight years'. I am not sure that it would necessarily take quite as long as that, but the process certainly could not be completed before the next election.

When we last debated this issue – it was in June, on a Supply Day, when the right hon. Member for Devizes (Mr. Ancram) spoke first – I told the House: 'The plan is that the referendum should take place well before the next election.' – [*Official Report*, 2 June 1998; Vol. 313, c. 190.] I said that in good faith. It was open to the commission to recommend one or other of the well-known options to first past the post – the alternative vote, regional lists of the sort that we intend or propose to have for the European Parliament, and the single transferable vote in multi-Member constituencies.

For each of those, it would have been perfectly possible to legislate for the referendum, to hold the referendum and, if there had been a vote in favour of change, to implement it well before the next election. However, as I told the right hon. Member for Bromley and Chislehurst (Mr. Forth) in response to an intervention, the system that Lord Jenkins has recommended, though ingenious, has no parallel anywhere in the world, so one may be forgiven for not fully anticipating its prospect.

There are two other important reasons why the Government will not rush into holding a referendum. The first is that the Jenkins commission is not the only independent committee headed by an eminent member of another place to have reported recently. The Committee on Standards in Public Life – the Neill committee – recently delivered its report on party funding. The Government have strongly welcomed that report, and, as the House knows, a full day's debate on it will be held next Monday.

The Neill committee made a number of detailed recommendations about referendums, the detail of which we shall want to study carefully before we take steps to provide for a referendum on the voting system for elections to the House of Commons. Obviously, we shall take full account of the feelings of the House next Monday in reaching our conclusions.

The second reason for not jumping to an instant conclusion on the Jenkins report is that the recommendations need to be seen in the context of the Government's wider, far-reaching programme of constitutional reform. We need to see how the new election systems settle down in Scotland, Wales, London and the European Parliament. It is particularly important that we look at the commission's proposals alongside reforms to the House of Lords, which will follow the removal of the right of hereditary peers to sit and vote in the other place. It would not be wise to embark on reform to the House of Commons electoral system until we are more certain of the changes that will take place in the other place.

Mr Edward Leigh (Gainsborough): In 20 years.

Mr Straw: The hon. Gentleman says, in 20 years. We are advancing the programme for the second stage of that reform by establishing a royal commission.

Thus, a great deal of constitutional change is under way, and the British people would not thank us for moving too quickly without thinking carefully about how any changes fit into the whole. We shall want to see how the various changes bed down and how well the new electoral systems for the Scottish Parliament, the Welsh Assembly and the European Parliament work.

My main purpose today is to listen to the debate, but in so doing I wish to make the following points about the context of the debate and how it should be conducted, both here and in the country. First, in this debate, there can and should be no moral or constitutional absolutes. Each of the main British parties has, at various times in its history, or for various purposes, supported both first past the post and proportional representation systems. The Labour party was in favour of proportional representation for the first 23 years of this century, while the Liberals were against. Labour and the Liberals then changed places as the main opposition to the Conservatives, and in doing so changed opinions on PR.

Although the Labour party has not so far advocated a PR system for Westminster since 1923, apart from the alternative vote in 1930, it initiated and approved the introduction in this Parliament of PR for the Welsh Assembly, the Scottish Parliament and the European Parliament. In the 1970s, many Conservatives supported PR for this House. I have a long list of those, including the noble Lord Hurd, Christopher Patten, Lord Lawson, Malcolm Rifkind, Lord Younger and many other luminaries. Indeed, Lord Carr of Hadley, a predecessor of mine as Home Secretary, told his colleagues in the Conservative party in October 1977 that, with a PR system of elections for Westminster, 'the tide of socialism could be halted'. I remind the Conservative party that it supported the introduction of PR in Northern Ireland, including the introduction of a closed list system with d'Hondt divisors for elections to the Northern Ireland forum.

The common thread through all that is that no electoral system can be best for all circumstances. We must seek a system that is most appropriate for the purpose and functions of the bodies in question. My second point flows from that. I am sure that the House will wish to consider the outcome of any change to the electoral system, not some of the more exaggerated claims about fairness and wasted votes. I believe that all sides in this argument seek fairness, but it is important not to disguise self-interest in the outcome of any electoral system by claiming that one side of the argument has a monopoly on morality.

Lord Jenkins was on strong ground when he said in his report: 'fairness in representation is a complex concept'. Indeed it is. For all the claims of 'wasted votes' made by the opponents of PR, and their equally vociferous claims that PR leads not to wasted votes but to wasted elections, there is a simple truth about elections by any system: some people win and some lose – [*Interruption.*] As I spent 18 years rather than 18 months on the Opposition Benches, I had a long time to spot that consequence.

Those who win form a Government who have power over those who lose. Almost certainly, the Government will then do things to which those who lose take great exception. Those who have lost may well feel that, in the event, their vote has had no effect, and was therefore wasted. In one sense they are right, but that is inescapable so long as we determine elections by the weight of votes, however the elections are conducted or the votes counted.

We must ensure that our voting system is as fair as possible, but mathematically there can never be an identity between the proportion of votes cast and seats gained for a party, and the proportion of power that is then obtained. Proportionality must be measured not only between parties at any one point in time, but over time – over many elections. As a result, what is fair or unfair, and what is proportional or not proportional, can lead to many different answers.

[...] It is a testament to the strength of this institution that its members have accepted the need to consider reform when and where necessary. In the 100 years or so after the first Reform Act, successive extensions to the franchise changed the character and position of this place. Many of the reforms to our procedures and rules that have taken place more recently – the introduction of departmental Select Committees and of Wednesday morning sittings, to name just two – have also affected how we operate. It is therefore entirely appropriate for the House to have a full and proper debate on this issue.

There are scores of different electoral systems, and, I suspect, just as many different views on the subject of electoral reform among hon. Members. The Government look forward to hearing some of those views expressed today. We are also keen to see a much wider debate in the country at large. As I have explained, there is no need to rush to a verdict on this issue; nor would it be desirable to do so. The Government want to hear what others have to say about the commission's proposals. The commission has performed a valuable service in setting an agenda for debate. Now let the debate begin.

35

The House of Lords: Completing the Reform

Lord Chancellor's Department

Introduction

The Government intends to complete reform of the House of Lords early in this Parliament, in fulfilment of its election mandate and the *report of the independent Royal Commission* chaired by Lord Wakeham. This White Paper sets out its proposals, on which it is seeking comments.

The most important changes proposed are:

- The hereditary peers will finally cease to have any privileged rights of membership;
- A majority of the members of the new House will be nominated by the political parties, in proportions intended to reflect the shares of the national vote in the previous General Election. There will also be about 120 appointed members with no political affiliation, 120 directly elected members to represent the nations and regions, and a continuing role for Law Lords and Bishops of the Church of England;
- An independent statutory Appointments Commission will have substantial powers. It will appoint the independent members and decide – within certain bounds – how many seats each major political party is entitled to, thereby substantially reducing Government patronage;
- The size of the House will be capped at 600 in statute, with an interim House as close as may be to 750 members to accommodate existing life peers;
- There will be formal commitments to achieving balance and representativeness in the House;
- The link with the peerage will be dissolved.

[...]

The *House of Lords Act 1999* (c. 34) removed most hereditary peers from the House of Lords, stopped the inheritance of a title being an automatic entry ticket to Parliament, and ended the century-long dominance of the House by one political

party. At the same time, the Government established an independent Royal Commission, under the chairmanship of Lord Wakeham, to recommend a composition for a fully reformed Lords appropriate to its constitutional functions as a second, revising chamber. The Royal Commission consulted extensively before reporting. The Commission Report, *A House for the Future*, Cm 4534, January 2000, and issues relevant to reform have since been debated in both Houses of Parliament and beyond. The proposals in this White Paper build on that essential groundwork and complete the work of removing any hereditary basis for the House.
[...]

The Main Government Proposals

The Government accepts the Royal Commission's recommendations for the role of the second chamber. It also endorses many of the Commission's recommendations on membership. Where the Commission sets out options, it has generally based its proposals within the parameters of those options. Its key proposals are as follows:

- The House of Lords should remain subject to the pre-eminence of the House of Commons in discharging its functions;
- No group in society should in future have privileged hereditary access to the House;
- Its principal function should continue to be to consider and revise legislation; to scrutinise the executive; and to debate and report on public issues;
- Membership should be separated from the peerage which would continue as an honour;
- Its political membership should be broadly representative of the main parties' relative voting strengths as reflected in the previous General Election;
- It should be largely nominated including a significant minority of independent members as well as members elected to represent the nations and regions within the UK;
- There should be increased representation of women and those from ethnic minority backgrounds;
- There should be a statutory Appointments Commission to manage the balance and size of the House, to appoint the independent members, and to assure the integrity of those nominated by political parties.

All these elements are consistent with the Government's electoral mandate. They are based closely on the principles and recommendations set out by the Royal Commission. There are however a number of areas where further consideration of the practical effects of certain recommendations has led the Government to consider some modification of the precise recommendations so as to ensure implementation of the Commission's principles in the most effective way possible, as the Manifesto says. Areas where the Government would welcome views are:

- The overall balance between elected, nominated and *ex officio* members, and the balance between political and independent members;

- Whether elections to the Lords should be linked to General Elections, those for the European Parliament, or over time linked to those from devolved and regional bodies within the UK;
- The length of term for elected members;
- The term of appointment;
- What grounds should lead to statutory expulsion from the House;
- Should there be a change from an expenses-based system of remuneration.

The Pre-eminence of the House of Commons

[...]
The House of Commons has [...] long since been established as the pre-eminent constitutional authority within the UK. [...]

This constitutional framework, founded on the pre-eminence of the House of Commons, has provided Britain with effective democratic Government and accountability for more than a century, and few would wish to change it. As the Royal Commission emphasised, 'The House of Commons, as the principal political forum, should have the final say in respect of all major public policy issues' and 'it would be wrong to restore the fully bicameral nature of the pre-1911 parliament' (paragraph 4.7). It is vital that reform of the Lords does not upset this balance but rather, within this context, that it strengthens the capacity of Parliament to legislate, deliberate and hold the Government to account.

Reform of the House of Lords must therefore satisfy one key condition: it must not alter the respective roles and authority of the two chambers and their members in a way that would obscure the line of authority and accountability that flows between the people and those they elect directly to form the Government and act as their individual representatives. Decisions on functions, on authority, and membership of the House of Lords need to be consistent with these settled principles of our democracy.

The Role of the House of Lords

Within the constitutional settlement described above, the House of Lords exercises important functions. It is one of the checks and balances in our constitution. It has the duty, and the power, to press the Government hard to justify its actions, although, save in highly exceptional circumstances, not in the end to frustrate the decided will of the House of Commons.
[...]

There is no case for giving specific new functions to the House of Lords. The Government agrees with the Royal Commission that there is a role for the House of Lords in reviewing the impact of constitutional reform. But this is something which should develop within the existing constitutional framework.
[...]

Nothing in the proposed reform of the House of Lords does, or should, affect Commons financial privilege or the need for the Lords to continue to observe restraint in the way it exercises its still extensive powers.

[...] It therefore proposes no changes to the legislative or conventional framework governing the relationship between the two Houses.

[...]

Nominations and elections

The Government supports the recommendation of the Royal Commission for a House with a majority of nominated members together with a minority elected element. It agrees with the Commission that this approach is best suited to securing a properly representative membership, able to fulfil the functions of the second chamber, while complementing and enhancing, not usurping, the House of Commons.

It is sometimes argued that only direct election can provide legitimacy for the second chamber. This was not an argument accepted by the Commission or by the Government. Only a minority of democracies worldwide have wholly directly elected second chambers. The idea that the directly elected US Senate is the norm against which others should be judged is wrong. It is a component of the interlocking federal arrangements within the USA.

Just as the limited role, powers and functions of the House of Lords do not require its members to be elected to confer legitimacy on it, so also a second chamber constituted on the same elected basis as the first chamber would be superfluous and dangerous. In the case of the UK, where the legitimacy of national Government depends wholly upon elections to, and the support of, the House of Commons, the second chamber does not legitimise Government itself. Its role, rather, is one of a subordinate revising and deliberative chamber, for which direct election has a role to play but is neither a necessary nor a sufficient basis for its membership. The Royal Commission Report, in paragraph 11.6, says: 'regardless of its political complexion, the central objection to a directly elected second chamber is that it would, by its very nature, represent a challenge to the pre-eminence of the House of Commons... we would be strongly opposed to a situation in which the two Houses of Parliament had equivalent electoral legitimacy. It would represent a substantial change in the present constitutional settlement in the UK and would almost certainly be a recipe for damaging conflict.' In paragraphs 11.8–11.12, the Report also sets out a number of other reasons why a wholly directly elected second chamber would not produce the range of members or the level of representativeness required.

A separate basis for composition is necessitated by further considerations. Apart from taxation and the voting of supply, there is no formal separation of functions between Commons and Lords. A parallel elective basis of authority for two chambers with parallel functions would inevitably create strongly competing authorities in the same spheres. This would apply with still greater force if, as is sometimes suggested, the second chamber were wholly elected but on a different electoral system from the House of Commons. Arguments would then arise on the issue of which chamber had the superior democratic legitimacy based on which electoral system was thought superior. Two wholly directly elected chambers within the Westminster system would be a recipe for gridlock and the Government therefore joins the Royal Commission in rejecting this option.

A mainly elected second chamber would have the following, further, practical disadvantages:

- The independent members would virtually disappear. Yet this is an element of the existing House of Lords to which people attach the highest importance;
- Elected politics is becoming increasingly a full-time occupation. Even allowing for the lack of a constituency function for members of the second chamber, the result of moving to a wholly or mainly elected second chamber would be to risk losing the potential the Lords provides to bring to Parliament the expertise and experience of those who are leaders in a wide range of national endeavours, including commerce, the voluntary sector, education, health, the armed forces and the faith communities. Such experience cannot replace or compete with a direct electoral mandate, but it makes a valuable addition to the expertise and competence of Parliament as a whole;
- The larger the elected component, the greater will be the number chosen to represent each geographical unit and the greater, inevitably, will be the competition they pose to MPs in their representational role.

[...]

The Government's proposals

The Government proposes, on the basis of the principles above, the following composition for the House of Lords:

- The membership should be largely nominated, but with a number of safeguards to ensure that it cannot be manipulated by the Government of the day. Those safeguards include:
  - A statutory Appointments Commission. As well as selecting independent members of the House, it would determine the numbers for the political parties and vet their choices for propriety;
  - A requirement that the representation of the political parties should reflect the votes cast in the preceding General Election so far as possible within the constraints of overall size and length of term;
  - A cap on the overall size of the House;
  - Guaranteed numbers or proportions for the non-political membership;
  - An elected element, specifically to ensure that there is adequate regional representation.

Elected representation of the nations and regions

The Government accepts the Royal Commission recommendation that there should be a minority elected element of regional members to represent the nations and regions of the UK.
[...]

Timing of elections

[...]
The Government is attracted to the alternative of holding elections to the Lords on the same day as General Elections. That would ensure a higher turn out. It would mean that the issues taken into account were national or local ones, since people would be voting at the same time for both Houses of Parliament, consistent with the role that both Houses play in considering and giving their consent to the Government's programme and calling it to account. It would also make it far easier to manage the political balance of the Lords as a whole, since the Appointments Commission would not be faced with a shifting balance within the elected membership during the course of each Parliament. Taken together, the Government believes that these are powerful arguments and it seeks views on this alternative to the Royal Commission's proposal. [...]

Independent members

The Government fully supports the Royal Commission's belief in the value that non-politically aligned members of the Lords can bring to the Parliamentary process. They bring a different perspective and expertise from that of members with party political affiliations, which is particularly valuable to a second chamber with the revising, scrutinising and deliberative role of the Lords. Accordingly, the Government accepts the recommendation of the Royal Commission that independent members should form about 20% of the reformed Lords. [...]

Summary of numbers

The effect of these proposals is that, in a House of 600 and with a directly elected component in line with the Government's proposals, the House ultimately would consist of:

- 120 non-party political members appointed by the Appointments Commission;
- 120 directly elected members;
- 16 Bishops;
- at least 12 Law Lords, and, very probably, some other Law Lords between the ages of 70 and 75;
- a balance of not more than 332 nominated political members, where the number available to each political party is determined by the Appointments Commission.

The Appointments Commission

In line with the recommendations of the Royal Commission, the Government proposes to establish a statutory independent Appointments Commission. It will be accountable to Parliament rather than to Ministers. Its members will be appointed by the Queen in response to an Address from the House of Lords, and will be removable only by the same procedure. As in the case of the present Commission, membership will be divided between representatives of the major political parties and independent members, selected in accordance with the rules of the Commissioner for Public Appointments.

The Appointments Commission will have three main functions.

- First, it will determine the overall size and political balance of the House, within parameters laid down by statute. The Government envisages that the maximum size of the House will gradually be reduced to 600 members over the 10 years from the coming into force of the Act. Over that period the Commission will be expected to ensure that the political membership comes fairly closely to reflect[ing] their share of the votes at the preceding General Election. The Government envisages a threshold before a party can qualify for such a proportionate share. There will be over 400 political members of the House. The minimum vote required to qualify for one seat would therefore be 0.25% of the vote. In the Government's view, allowing parties with such a low level of support to claim a seat by right would lead to unacceptable fragmentation in the membership of the House. The Government is minded to set the threshold at 5%, but would be interested in views on the appropriate level. Where a party contests seats in only one part of the United Kingdom, the threshold will be set in relation to its share of the vote in that part only.
- The Appointments Commission will also be required to maintain the independent element at around 20% of the total. The Commission, not the Prime Minister, will decide at each round of appointments how many nominations to invite from each party. The only exception is that the Government believes it right to retain the discretionary right for the Prime Minister to appoint a small number of people – 4 or 5 a parliament – directly as Ministers in the Lords. The Royal Commission thought that the Appointments Commission should not have the power to enforce resignations as part of the rebalancing exercise, since it would cut completely across the desire to encourage members to be independent and authoritative, without concerns for the consequences for their continued membership of the House.
- As recommended by the Royal Commission, the Appointments Commission will be required to ensure that the appointed members are broadly representative of British society. In particular, the Appointments Commission will ensure that at least 30% of new appointees are women and 30% are men, working towards gender balance in the chamber as a whole over time. The Commission will also have regard to the importance of ensuring fair overall representation for both the nations and regions of the UK and from the ethnic minority communities.
- The Commission will itself select the non-political members. It will do so using an open and transparent selection procedure. The Government believes that the interim Appointments Commission deserves praise for the way they have begun the process and endorses their conclusion that the two key criteria for appointment are: experience and capacity to make an effective contribution to the work of the Lords; and a commitment to active participation to do so. The independent members are intended to bring experience and expertise to the House beyond that normally secured by party appointees. The Commission will select them by an open and transparent process.

- The Commission will carry out the propriety checks on those nominated by the political parties. This will be its only involvement in the individual nominations made by the parties. The Government does not accept the Royal Commission recommendation that the Appointments Commission should have the final say over the identity of party nominations. Parties of whatever persuasion must be able to decide who will serve on their behalf. The Commission will of course scrutinise nominations to ensure that those put forward are fit and proper candidates for membership of the Lords.

These roles for the Appointments Commission add up to a radical change in the way the composition of the House of Lords is determined. The present legal position is that the Prime Minister of the day can recommend to the Queen the creation of as many peers as he or she wishes, without regard to political balance or indeed any other considerations. In the future, there will be clear rules about the way in which the political balance of the House is to be determined. Moreover, the interpretation of those rules will be taken out of the hands of the Government. An independent, cross-party body will control the make-up of the House of Lords. The Appointments Commission will also assume responsibility for selecting independent members, thus removing a further source of Government patronage. As a party leader, the Prime Minister will be left with no more power than any other leader. The nominations of the non-Government parties will also no longer need to pass through the Government's hands.

These changes build on the Government's undertaking in the transitional House not to seek more than parity with the main Opposition Party and its establishment of an interim Appointments Commission. The difference is that in the future the rules will be statutory provisions; no other Government will be able to resile from them without the authority of statute.

36

The Nature of the British–Irish Agreement

Brendan O'Leary

The Agreement of 10 April 1998, ratified in referenda in both parts of Ireland on 22 May 1998, is a major achievement. [...]

The Institutional Nature of the Agreement

What kind of institutional Agreement is it? The answer for a student of political science is that it is a consociational agreement, that is, a political arrangement that meets all four of the criteria laid down by Arend Lijphart:

(i)   cross-community executive power-sharing;
(ii) proportionality rules applied throughout the relevant governmental and public sectors;
(iii) community self-government (or autonomy) and equality in cultural life; and
(iv) veto rights for minorities.[1]

A consociation is an association of communities – in this case the communities are British unionist, Irish nationalist, and others. A consociation can be created without any explicit consociational theory to guide it – indeed that has often happened. More often, consociations are the equilibrium outcomes of bargains or pacts between the political leaders of ethnic or religious communities. This Agreement is the product of tacit and explicit consociational thought, and of bargaining, or of what is sometimes called 'pacting'.

But the Agreement is not just consociational, and it departs from Lijphart's prescriptions in important respects that have practical implications for Northern Ireland and for regulating ethnic and national conflict elsewhere: it has important external dimensions; it was made with national, and not just ethnic or religious communities; and it has been endorsed by (most of) the leaders and (most of) the led. Indeed, I suspect it is the first consociational pact to have been immediately popularly endorsed by referendum. To be formulaic: the Agreement envisages an internal consociation built within overarching con/federal institutions; it has imaginative elements of co-sovereignty; it promises a novel model of 'double protection'; and it rests on a bargain derived from diametrically conflicting hopes about its likely long-run outcome, but that may not destabilize it. One supplement must be added to this very lengthy formula. The Agreement is vulnerable both to post-Agreement bargaining and to legalism. Let me justify this phrasing.

The Four Consociational Elements

Executive power-sharing

At the heart of any consociational arrangement is executive power-sharing. The Agreement creates a dual premiership. Indeed, it can be argued that it establishes two quasi-presidential figures in a devolved Northern Assembly: a First Minister and a Deputy First Minister. They have presidential characteristics because, once elected, it is almost impossible to depose them until the next general election – presidentialism means an executive that cannot be destroyed by an assembly except through impeachment, and, in future, I maintain that it will be extremely difficult for the Northern Assembly to remove its dual premiers. [...]

The rules practically ensure that a unionist and a nationalist share the top two posts. The Agreement and UK legislation (the 1998 Northern Ireland Act) make it clear that both posts have identical symbolic and external representation functions. Indeed, they have identical powers; the only difference is in their titles. [...]

Unlike some presidents and most prime ministers, neither the First Minister nor the Deputy First Minister formally appoints the other Ministers to the Executive Committee. Under the plain meaning of the Agreement, these posts should be allocated to parties in proportion to their strength in the Assembly, according to a mechanical algorithm, the d'Hondt rule. The rules are simple in their implied consequences. Any party that wins a significant share of seats, and is willing to abide by the Agreement, has a reasonable chance of access to the executive, a subtle form of what Lijphart calls 'grand coalition government' – though it is a coalition government without a coalition agreement.
[...]

In short, the consociational criterion of cross-community executive power sharing is squarely met in the Agreement.
[...]

Proportionality

Consociational arrangements are built on principles of proportionality. The Agreement meets this test in three palpable ways: on the executive in the manner already discussed; in the elections to the Assembly; and in public sector positions.

All future elections to the 108 member Assembly will use a proportional representation system, the single transferable vote (STV) in six member constituencies – though the Assembly may choose, by cross-community consent procedures, to advocate change from this system later. The Droop quota in each constituency is therefore 14.3 per cent of the vote, which squeezes the very small parties, or, alternatively, encourages them to form electoral alliances.

[...]

Proportionality rules, combined with accommodative incentives, do not stop with the executive, the committee system in the Assembly, or with the electoral system. The Agreement is consistent with past and future measures to promote fair employment and affirmative action in the public sector that will, one hopes, eventually ensure a proportional and non-discriminatory civil service and judiciary. The Agreement also envisages a representative police force. It is the task of the Independent Commission on policing, headed by former Hong Kong Governor Christopher Patten, to ensure the creation of a police service or services that are representative of Northern Ireland. The RUC's mono-national culture and, indeed, its monopoly on policing services must end if the Agreement is to be fully consistent with a consociational model. Democratic consociation cannot exist where those of military age in one community are almost the sole recruitment pool to police all of those in another community. A fully representative, and preferably two-tier model of federal and democratically accountable policing is the best way to ensure that proportional policing supplements the other political institutions of the Agreement.

Communal autonomy and equality

Consociational settlements avoid the compulsory integration of peoples; instead they seek to manage differences equally and justly. To be liberal or social-democratic, such settlements must also protect those who wish to have their identities counted differently, or not as collective identities.

The Agreement leaves in place the new arrangements for schooling in Northern Ireland in which Catholic, Protestant and integrated schools are to be equally funded. In this respect, Northern Ireland is fully consociational and liberal – only the very small minorities of non-Christian religious believers (less than 1 per cent of the population) lack full and equal funding, and it would be generous and just to make such provisions for them where numbers permit. The Agreement also makes new provisions for the educational use, protection and public use of the Irish language – along the lines used for Welsh in the UK – thereby adding linguistic to educational protections of Irish nationalist culture.

Most importantly, the Agreement completes the equalization of both major communities as national communities, that is as British and Irish communities, not just, as is so misleadingly said, as Protestants and Catholics. The European Convention on Human Rights – which is weak on the protection of collective rights and equality rights – will be supplemented by measures that will give Northern Ireland its own tailor-made Bill of Rights, to protect both national groupings as well as individuals. The worst illusion of parties to the conflict and some of its successive managers, based in London, Belfast, or Dublin, was that which held that Northern Ireland could be stable and democratic while being either British or Irish. The Agreement makes Northern Ireland bi-national – and opens up the prospect of a fascinating jurisprudence, not least in the regulation of parades and marches.

[...]

The Agreement does not neglect the non-national dimensions of local politics, nor does it exclude the 'Others' from what I have heard described in Alliance party circles as a squalid communal deal. All aspects of unjustified social equalities, as well as inequalities between the national communities, are recognized in the text of the Agreement, and given some means of institutional redress and monitoring. The Agreement addresses national equality, the allegiances to the Irish and British nations, and social equality, which is to say, other dimensions that differentiate groups and individuals in Northern Ireland: religion, race, ethnic affiliation, sex, and sexuality.

Equality issues, be they national or social, are not left exclusively to the local parties to manage and negotiate, which might be a recipe for stalemate. Instead, under the Agreement, the UK Government has created a new statutory obligation on public authorities: they will be required to carry out all their functions with due regard to the need to promote equality of opportunity in relation to people's religious background and political opinions; and with respect to their gender, race, disabilities, age, marital status and sexual orientation.

[...]

Minority veto rights

The final dimension of a consociational settlement is the protection of minorities through giving them veto rights. The Agreement fulfils this criterion in the Assembly, in the courts, and through enabling political appeals to both the UK and Irish Governments.

The Assembly has cross-community procedures (parallel consent, weighted majority and petition procedures [...]) that protect nationalists from unionist dominance. Indeed, they do so in such a comprehensive manner that, before the election of the First and Deputy First Ministers, there were fears that the rules designed to protect the nationalist minority might be used by hard-line unionist opponents of the Agreement to wreck its initiation and development. (This possibility remains alive, but is somewhat diminished because the weighted majority rule in the Assembly requires a lower level of unionist consent than was required for the election of the First and Deputy First Ministers.) The 'Others' are less well protected in the Assembly – they can be outvoted by a simple majority, and any nationalist-unionist super-majority, and their numbers leave them well short of being able to trigger a petition on their own. However, the 'Others' have not been at the heart of the conflict, so it is not surprising if they are not at the heart of its pacts – though it is not accurate to claim that they are excluded from the Agreement.

[...]

Confederal and Federal Elements of the Agreement

The Agreement is not only internally consociational: it is also confederalizing, and federalizing. This meshing of internal and external institutions marks it out as novel in comparative politics. Let me make it plain why I regard the Agreement as both confederalizing and federalizing, though my emphasis is on the former.

Confederations exist when political jurisdictions voluntarily delegate powers and functions to bodies that can exercise power across all jurisdictions. The Agreement creates two such confederal relationships. The Agreement has subtle federalist dimensions if it is agreed that a federal relationship exists when there are at least two separate tiers of government over the same territory, and when neither tier can unilaterally alter the constitutional capacities of the other.

The all-Ireland confederal relationship

The first relationship is all-Ireland in nature: the North–South Ministerial Council (NSMC). [...]

What was intended by the Agreement was clear. Nationalists were concerned that if the Assembly could outlast the North–South Council, it would provide incentives for unionists to undermine the latter. Unionists, by contrast, worried that if the Council could survive the destruction of the Assembly, nationalists would seek to bring this about. The Agreement is a tightly written contract with penalty clauses. Internal consociation and external confederalism go together. The Assembly and the Council are 'mutually interdependent'; one cannot function without the other. Unionists cannot destroy the Council while retaining the Assembly, and nationalists cannot destroy the Assembly while keeping the Council. If the Assembly does not create the Council, it will in effect destroy itself – enabling, in the extreme case, any citizen in Northern Ireland to argue for the suspension of the Northern Assembly until the North–South Ministerial Council is established.

The North–South Ministerial Council is the means by which nationalists hope to persuade unionists of the attractions of Irish unification; and it will, if established, satisfactorily link Northern nationalists to their preferred nation-state, albeit without the range of ambitions that Northern nationalists would have preferred. Consistent with the Agreement, the Irish Government has agreed to change its constitution to ensure that the North–South Ministerial Council will be able to exercise island-wide jurisdiction in those functional activities where unionists are willing to co-operate.

The North–South Ministerial Council will function much like the Council of Ministers in the European Union, with ministers having considerable discretion to reach decisions, but remaining ultimately accountable to their respective legislatures. The Council will meet in plenary format twice a year, and in smaller groups to discuss specific sectors – say, agriculture, or education – on a 'regular and frequent basis'. Provision is also made for the Council to meet to discuss matters that cut across sectors, and to resolve disagreements. In addition, the Agreement provides for cross-border or all-island 'implementation' bodies – which means the same as 'executive'. These are to be responsible for implementing decisions taken in the six areas specified above.

[...]

The British–Irish confederal relationship

There is a second weaker confederal relationship established by the Agreement. It affects all the islands of Britain and Ireland. Under the new British–Irish Council, the two sovereign Governments, all the devolved governments of the UK, and all the neighbouring insular dependent territories of the UK, can meet, agree to delegate functions, and may agree common policies. This proposal meets unionists' concerns for reciprocity in linkages – and provides a mechanism through which they may in future be linked to the UK even if Northern Ireland becomes part of the Republic of Ireland.

[...]

A UK–Northern Irish federalizing process

The Agreement is the penultimate blow to unitary unionism in the UK – already dented by the 1997–98 referendums and legislative acts establishing a Scottish Parliament and Welsh Assembly. But does the Agreement simply fall within the rubric of 'devolution within a decentralized unitary state'? Arguably not. Two Unions make up the UK: the Union of Great Britain and the Union of Great Britain and Northern Ireland. The constitutional basis of the latter Union is now very distinctly different to the former.

The Agreement is a treaty between two states, and it is based on Irish national self-determination as well as British constitutional convention. The UK officially acknowledges in the Agreement that Northern Ireland has the right to join the Republic, on the basis of a local referendum, and it recognizes, in a treaty, the authority of Irish national self-determination throughout the island of Ireland. Moreover, the Agreement's institutions are being brought into being by the will of the people of Ireland, North and South, and not just by the people of Northern Ireland – recall the interdependence of the North–South Ministerial Council and the Assembly. Consequently, the UK's relationship to Northern Ireland, *at least in international law*, is explicitly federal because the Westminster parliament and executive cannot, except through breaking treaty obligations, and except through denying Irish national self-determination, exercise power in any manner in Northern Ireland that is inconsistent with the Agreement.

This federalizing process will be enhanced if the UK and Northern Irish courts treat Northern Ireland's relationships to Westminster as akin to those of the former Dominions – which had a federal character – as they did in the period of the Stormont Parliament (1921–1972). Moreover, the nature of devolution in Northern Ireland is not closed by the UK's 1998 Northern Ireland Act. The Act has created an open-ended mechanism for Northern Ireland to expand its autonomy from the rest of the UK – albeit with the consent of the Secretary of State, and the approval of Westminster. No such open-ended provision has been granted to the Scottish Parliament or the Welsh Assembly. In short, maximum feasible autonomy while remaining within the Union is viable, provided there is agreement to that within the Northern Assembly. Legalist Diceyians will insist that Westminster's sovereignty in Northern Ireland remains ultimately intact, but, if the Agreement beds down, the political development of a federal relationship between the UK and Northern Ireland is assured for the medium-term – whatever is said in the dry recesses of the Constitution's *ancien régime*.

Irish federalizing processes

The Agreement also opens federalist avenues in the Republic of Ireland – hitherto one of the most centralized states in Europe. The North–South Ministerial Council is seen by nationalists, North and South, as the embryonic institution of a federal Ireland: first confederation, then federation after trust has been built. This stepping-stone theory is most loudly articulated by 'no unionists', but they are not wrong in their calculation that many nationalists see the North–South Council as 'transitional' – Sinn Féin says so; Fianna Fáil says so.

Neither the Irish Government nor its people abandoned Irish unification when they endorsed the Agreement. Indeed, it has become 'the firm will of the Irish nation, in harmony and friendship, to unite all the people who share the territory of the island of Ireland, in all the diversity of their identities and traditions, recognizing that a united Ireland shall be brought about only by peaceful means with the consent of a majority of the people expressed, in both jurisdictions in the island' (from the new provisional Article 3). The amended Irish Constitution therefore officially recognizes *two* jurisdictions that jointly enjoy the right to participate in the Irish nation's exercise of self-determination. Unification is no longer linked to 'unitarism' and is entirely compatible with either full confederation or federation.

[...]

Double protection and co-sovereignty

The subtlest part of the Agreement goes well beyond standard consociational thinking. This is its tacit 'double protection model' – laced with elements of co-sovereignty. It is an agreement designed to withstand major demographic and electoral change. The Agreement promises to entrench the identical protection of rights, collective and individual, on both sides of the present border. In effect, it promises protection to Northern nationalists now on the same terms that will be given to Ulster unionists, should they ever become a minority in a unified Ireland. Communities are to be protected whether they are majorities or minorities, and whether sovereignty lies with the UK or the Republic – whence the expression 'double' protection.

The two states not only promise reciprocity for the local protection of present and future minorities, but have also created two intergovernmental devices to protect those communities. One is the successor to the Anglo-Irish Agreement, the inter-governmental conference that guarantees the Republic's government access to policy formulation on all matters not (yet) devolved to the Northern Assembly or the North–South Ministerial Council. The other is the British and Irish Council. If Irish unification ever occurs, the Republic's government would find it politically impossible not to offer the British government reciprocal access in the same fora.

It is important to note what has not happened between the two sovereign Governments. Formal co-sovereignty has not been established. Unionists claim that they have removed the 1985 Anglo-Irish Agreement in return for conceding a North–South Council. This claim is, at best, exaggerated. Under the new Agreement, the Irish government will retain a say in those Northern Irish matters that have not been devolved to the Northern Assembly, as was the case under Article 4 of the Anglo-Irish Agreement. And, as with that agreement, there will continue to be an intergovernmental conference, chaired by the Irish Minister for Foreign Affairs and the Northern Ireland Secretary of State, to deal with non-devolved matters, and this conference will continue to be serviced by a standing secretariat. The new Agreement, moreover, promises to 'intensify co-operation' between the two governments on all-island or cross-border aspects of rights, justice, prison and policing – unless and until these matters are devolved to the Northern executive. It is true that there is provision for representatives of the Northern Assembly to be involved in the inter-governmental conference – a welcome democratization – but they will not be able to block the two governments from acting within their remits. The Anglo-Irish Agreement fully anticipated these arrangements. Therefore, it is more accurate to claim that the Anglo-Irish Agreement has been fulfilled, than it is to say that it has been removed.

NOTE

1 See, *inter alia*, Arend Lijphart, *Democracy in Plural Societies*, New Haven 1977, and Michael Walzer, *On Toleration*, New Haven 1997.

Part V

Britain in the World, Labour in the European Union

Although Britain has long been an 'awkward' member of the European Union, British political parties, excepting the Conservative Party, are currently more pro-European now than at any other time in modern British history. None more so than New Labour, which has abandoned the past Euroscepticism which led the party to oppose Britain joining the then EEC in 1962 and in 1973 and to advocate withdrawal in 1983. Labour accepts that 'Britain has to be European; not on the margins but right at the centre of Europe...co-operating, engaging and leading' (Labour Party Manifesto, 1997). Previously, it had stated the opposite, opposing continued membership because it would prevent a Labour government from pursuing 'radical, socialist policies for reviving the British economy' (Labour Party Manifesto, 1983).

In replacing the Conservative Party's stance of 'triumphant isolationism' with a policy of 'constructive engagement', Blair-led New Labour' European policy is both 'patriotic' and 'pro-European'. After 1987, in a dramatic reversal of past form, Labour increasingly became the more European of the two major parties, moving toward Europe as the Conservatives moved away from it. As Europe became a Thatcherite bugbear, it became the Labour vogue, leading the party to declare in support of Europe as 'an alliance of independent nations choosing to co-operate to achieve the goals they cannot achieve alone' (Labour Party Manifesto, 1997). Of course, economic imperatives significantly determine Labour's pro-Europeanism, given that Europe forms the largest single market in the world and that up to 60 per cent of British trade is in Europe, 700,000 British businesses currently operate in Europe, and 3.5 million jobs depend directly on British membership of the European Union. For Labour ministers there is 'no alternative' but for Britain to participate in Europe. Withdrawal in any form is thus no longer a serious option.

Currently, monetary union remains the most important European issue facing Labour, and the Blair government has publicly adopted a 'wait and see' stance, effectively ruling out calling for entering the Euro until 'some time in the near future', cautiously moving to a position of joining 'when the time is right', adopting a 'when, rather than if' attitude. As several of the following extracts illustrate,

Labour believes that Britain should join the single currency, but only following a referendum on the issue, when Gordon Brown's five economic tests are met, and, most importantly, when it is considered to be in Britain's national interest to join.

In Blair's words, the government's position on the single currency is plain: '[I]f joining a single currency is good for British jobs and British industry, if it enhances British power and British influence, I believe it is right for Britain.' While aspiring to secure for Britain a position of European leadership unimagined since 1945–50, Labour does not do so out of any Euro-federalist aspiration. Its Europeanism is underpinned by a continuing inter-governmentalism which, continuing functional integration notwithstanding, opposes European federation in the short and medium term. Labour's external policy results from it being a 'British' not just a 'European' political party, its Europeanism being of a qualified inter-governmental character. Despite the internationalist perspective behind a great deal of its 'Third Way' rhetoric, the party favours a Europe of nation-states, but accepts that the pursuit of national economic interests through Europe may ultimately incur a supra-national cost in the form of 'ever closer political union'. Of course, the same could be said of all other EU member states, but this none the less suggests that Labour's contemporary 'Europeanism' should be placed squarely in the context of its continuing 'Britishness'.

In this regard, Tony Blair has made no secret of his belief that while being firmly 'of' and 'for' Europe, Britain has geo-political interests beyond Europe. As well as being pro-European, the Labour government remains strongly, determinedly Atlanticist, eager to work in concert with the United States. As the following extracts make clear, Europe apart, Labour's external policy demonstrates considerable continuity with past policy. However, as has become increasingly clear, recent trends in economic, political and cultural globalization find expression in Labour's policy. Two free-standing complementary perspectives underpin Labour's response. First, economic, political and cultural globalization encourages the internationalization of decision taking. Secondly, national interests and preferences are best pursued through interstate bargaining, particularly within Europe and with the United States, and decisions will be reinforced by the supra-national consequences that follow.

National governments now consider themselves unavoidably – and necessarily – disciplined by a 'global market' in the form of international capital and transnational companies. As such, governments must not only seek some way to assert a degree of influence within the international marketplace, but have increasingly to deal with global problems on a global scale. If, as Blair suggests, 'by working together, nation states can extend their authority... they can effectively tackle problems they are powerless to address on their own... [and] collectively reclaim the sovereignty they lost to globalization, while still reaping its benefits', governments deem themselves obliged to co-operate. Labour accepts the globalization thesis, acknowledging that as national borders become increasingly permeable, the state's ability to govern is diminished. This requires states to co-operate one with another in order to mitigate the effects of globalization, so encouraging the growth of international agencies, supra-national institutions, and perhaps further promoting internationalized systems of governance such as the European Union, the WTO, the UN and NATO.

37

From Hostility to 'Constructive Engagement': The Europeanisation of the Labour Party

Philip Daniels

The Labour Party's Changing Stance on European Integration

Since the early 1960s, Europe has been a source of division and difficulty for the Labour Party. The party's stance on European integration has oscillated between outright opposition and positive support, with each shift in policy shaped by intra-party factional conflicts, domestic political competition and the dynamics of the integration process. Even during periods in the 1960s and 1970s when official party policy favoured Britain's membership of the European Community (EC), the support was not wholehearted and the issue tended to divide the party at all levels. [...]

Labour's difficulties with European integration derived from its commitment to Britain's existing global links, its analysis of the EEC and its focus on the nation-state as the appropriate arena in which to achieve its policy objectives. In the 1950s, the Labour Party shared the Conservatives' concerns that participation in the integration process would undermine Britain's defence and security links with the United States and its important trade relationship with the Commonwealth. The Labour Party also had misgivings about the nature of the EEC which it regarded as a capitalist club for the rich and an insular organisation. Most importantly, Labour feared that British membership of the EEC, whose member-state governments were dominated by parties of the right in the 1950s and 1960s, would frustrate attempts to carry through socialist policies in Britain. Concerns about the loss of national sovereignty inherent in the process of European integration have been a recurrent theme in Labour difficulties over the European issue. For the anti-European left of the party, the retention of national economic sovereignty was the principal factor in their opposition to British membership. On the right of the party too, a small anti-European element opposed membership largely on the grounds that it would under-mine parliamentary sovereignty. [...]

The Evolution of Labour's Pro-European Policy, 1983–97

Between 1983 and 1987, Labour slowly shifted away from outright rejection of Britain's EC membership towards an unenthusiastic acknowledgement that early withdrawal was not a viable policy option. [...]

[...] Tony Blair has continued Labour's pro-European stance in opposition and in government since May 1997. He has emphasised the party's commitment to 'constructive engagement' with the European Union (EU) as the best way to advance Britain's interests. At the same time, the party under Blair has moved cautiously on European issues such as the single currency and institutional reform in order to thwart Conservative attempts to depict Labour as a 'soft touch' or 'Brussels' poodle'. [...]

During the 1980s Labour's approach to Europe moved from deep hostility, through studied inattention to positive acceptance. Labour's shift to a pro-European stance has no clear point of origin. It evolved steadily in the post-1983 period, initially as a political necessity but later embraced by the party as an opportunity to advance its political and economic goals.

[...] Simultaneous and related developments in domestic politics and in the European arena explain the transformation of Labour's position on Europe. The pressures of domestic political competition, a change in trade union attitudes on Europe, the dynamics of the European integration process, and important changes in the party's approach to economic policy and the role of the nation-state are key elements in understanding Labour's new-found Europeanism.

Domestic Political Competition and Electoral Strategy

[...] In general terms, the 'Europeanisation' of the party may be seen as a response to its long exclusion from national office and as a key element of a broader electoral strategy designed to convey the image of a party which is modern, credible and fit to govern. The policy review exercise, launched in 1988, was central to this strategy of programmatic renewal.

Crushing defeats in both the 1983 and 1987 elections convinced the party leadership that a major renewal of policy was essential. Labour's incremental move to a pro-European stance became a fundamental element in this overhaul of party policy. The Labour leadership regarded the 1983 withdrawal commitment as damaging to the party's electoral prospects since it contributed to an image of a party which was out of touch, lacking credibility and dominated by the left. In its moves towards a pro-European position, the party leadership sought to improve its overall image as a party fit to govern and to reflect majority British opinion which favoured continued membership of the EC, but generally showed little enthusiasm for deeper political and economic integration.[1]

The pro-European stance thus became a key element in the Labour Party's move back towards the middle ground of British politics. The gradual embrace of Europeanism helped the party to recapture some of the political ground lost following the formation of the SDP in 1981; it has symbolised the party's shift away from the left-wing programme which characterised its early years in opposition in the post-1979 period; it has enabled the party to highlight and exploit the deep divisions in the Conservative Party over Europe and to claim that the Thatcher and Major governments' self-inflicted isolation in Europe has been damaging to British interests; and its support for the pound's entry into the ERM and, in principle, the single currency has reinforced the credibility of the party's commitment to fiscal discipline and responsible economic management.

[...]

[...] Since the late 1980s Labour has projected an image of a party largely united over Europe and with little significant ideological opposition to Britain's European membership. Labour's approach to European policy during this period has been characterised by a cautious pragmatism. The party has emphasised that 'constructive engagement' with the EU rather than a negative, confrontational approach is the best way to advance British national interests. It has supported key European policy initiatives, such as the 'social dimension'[2] and Economic and Monetary Union (EMU), which have been politically difficult for the Conservative Party. At the same time, however, Labour's positive Europeanism has been balanced by an undertaking to defend British national interests (described by Blair as 'the patriotic case for Europe'[3]) and to oppose the creation of a federal EU, thus making it difficult for the Conservatives to gain a significant electoral advantage over Labour on the European issue.[4] This caution was clearly evident in the run-up to and during the 1997 election campaign: while Labour maintained its essentially pro-European stance, on issues such as the single currency and treaty reform it ensured that there was little ground between it and the Conservative Party.[5]

[...]

Economic Management in the European Context

Changes in Labour's economic policy since the early 1980s have been an important factor in the party's accommodation with Europe. There are several elements in this link between the party's Europeanisation and changes in its economic thinking. First, the acknowledgement across the party that growing economic interdependence imposed significant constraints on national economic strategies made it easier for Labour to come to terms with membership of the EC. Second, a commitment to Europe was a key part of Labour's efforts to enhance its credibility as a party of competent economic management. Third, since the late 1980s there has been a growing congruence between Labour's macro-economic policy and the economic doctrine at the heart of the EU's moves towards EMU.

Economic policy was a central factor in the Labour Party's anti-European position in the early 1980s. The Alternative Economic Strategy (AES), to which the party was committed in the early 1980s, was based on a mixture of protectionism, assistance to national industries, renationalisation and expansionary Keynesian spending programmes. Much of this proposed programme was incompatible with the obligations of EC membership. The 1983 manifesto commitment to withdrawal from the EC was, in part, an acknowledgement that membership would place severe constraints on the implementation of a future Labour government's programme based on the AES.[6] Given the British economy's deep enmeshment in Europe, however, withdrawal from the EC appeared unrealistic and damaging to Britain's long-term economic interests.

The evolution of Labour's pro-European stance has gone hand in hand with the abandonment of the nationalist approach at the heart of the AES and the reshaping of the party's economic policy to one based on acceptance of the market economy, orthodox monetary and fiscal policy, and Britain's full participation in an open, global economy. The Europeanisation of the Labour Party has been eased by the party's acknowledgement of growing economic interdependence and the futility of an economic strategy based on the concept of insulating the domestic economy from the constraints imposed by the international economic context within which Britain operates. [...]

Conclusion

The Labour Party's shift from outright opposition to the EC in the early 1980s to enthusiastic support by the end of that decade for Britain's participation in the integration process represents one of the most significant recent changes in British party politics. [...]

Labour's 'Europeanisation' has been a gradual transition, shaped by the interplay of domestic political developments, changes in party and trade union thinking, and the dynamics of Europe's economic and political integration. In terms of the domestic political context, Labour's embrace of Europeanism forms part of a broader strategy of programmatic and ideological renewal designed to make the party a credible alternative for government. At the same time, Labour has adjusted more readily than the Conservatives to the dynamics of the integration process since the latter half of the 1980s. Policy developments in the EU, such as the social dimension to the single market, have been attractive to the Labour Party and the trade union movement. After a long exclusion from national government, Europe offered a welcome alternative to the Conservative governments' economic and social policies. More importantly, the issue of national sovereignty, which was at the heart of Labour's traditional hostility to the European project and is the basis for Conservative divisions over Europe, has become a much less salient issue for the Labour Party in the 1990s. For example, the party's economic thinking has shifted away from the national protectionism of the early 1980s, to an approach which accepts the close interconnectedness of European economies and the EU as the appropriate context for co-ordinating member states' economic policies. The Labour Party's approach to the single currency clearly exemplifies this change in its economic policy and the declining importance of the sovereignty issue for the party. While the party remains cautious about development towards EMU, its concerns are primarily about the *economic impact* membership of a single currency would have on Britain rather than fears about the political and constitutional implications of joining the single currency.

While domestic political calculations, rooted in an electoral imperative, have been important determinants in Labour's more positive Europeanism, the change in the party's position is not mere political convenience. Labour's repositioning on the European issue reflects important changes in its policies and programme and an acknowledgement that Europe provides the most appropriate framework to pursue many of its policy objectives, particularly in the economic sphere. For Labour, pro-Europeanism became attractive, feasible and consistent with the party's policy goals. The pro-European stance finds support at all levels of the party and internal opposition to Britain's membership of the EU is now negligible. Divisions remain within the party over the scope, pace and direction of European integration. On an issue so wide-ranging, contentious and ever-changing this is to be expected. Nevertheless, the differences over Europe in the Labour Party are not comparable to the major fractures in the Conservative Party over the issue. The Labour leadership's tight grip on the party and policy, established under Kinnock, has been reinforced during Blair's tenure. This makes it highly improbable that an anti-EU position could make much headway within the party. [...]

Nevertheless, the European issue remains potentially difficult for the Labour government. The EU with which it has reached an accommodation is not static and further political and economic integration could reopen divisions in the party and cause domestic political difficulties. In particular, the issue of Britain's participation in a future single currency poses difficult and potentially divisive choices for the Labour government. In choosing to remain outside the first wave of single currency members, the government risks being isolated from the emerging 'hard core' of the EU and its influence diminished as a result. The European issue, the 'rogue elephant' of British politics, retains its potential to divide parties and debilitate governments.

NOTES

1 For a summary of British public opinion on the European issue see N. Nugent, 'British Public Opinion and the European Community', in S. George (ed.), *Britain and the European Community: The Politics of Semi-Detachment* (Oxford: Clarendon 1992), pp. 172–201.

2 Labour's support for the Social Charter, officially announced in Dec. 1989, allowed the party to abandon its support for the closed shop since the Charter guarantees individuals the right not to join a union. Thus, the party was able to remove a contentious domestic issue from its agenda.

3 See *Wherever Next? The Future of Europe* (London: Fabian Society 1996), p. 2.

4 An early indication of party's caution over Europe came in 1990 when the national leadership warned Labour MEPs that their support for a significant strengthening of the European Parliament went well beyond the party's position. See 'Labour MEPs Warned Off Federalism', *Guardian*, 16 March 1990.

5 Labour wants the EU to develop as an organisation based on independent nations co-operating in specific policy areas. It favours rapid completion of the Single European Market, enlargement, reform of the CAP and the common fisheries policy, an enhanced role for regional and local authorities in the EU, and greater openness and transparency in EU decision-making. In the run-up to the June 1997 Intergovernmental Conference it shared the Conservative Party's opposition to any erosion of the national veto on taxation matters, the budget, defence and security, immigration, and treaty reform. In contrast to the Conservative government, however, it supported the extension of qualified majority voting (QMV) to industrial, regional, environmental and social affairs, and a limited extension to the EP's powers of co-decision with the Council of Ministers. While the party pledged to sign up to the Social Chapter, it indicated that it would not support any proposals which would burden business and threaten jobs. See 'Brown says EU social costs would be vetoed', *The Times*, 11 Nov. 1996.

6   'The next Labour government committed to radical, socialist policies for reviving the British economy, is bound to find continued membership a most serious obstacle to the fulfilment of those policies. In particular the rules of the Treaty of Rome are bound to conflict with our strategy for economic growth and full employment, our proposals on industrial policy and for increasing trade, and our need to restore exchange controls and to regulate direct overseas investment.' Reproduced in F. W. S. Craig (ed.), *British General Election Manifestos 1959–1987* (Aldershot: Parliamentary Research Services, Dartmouth 1990), p. 382.

38

New Labour – New Europe?

Kirsty Hughes and Edward Smith

[...] Tony Blair, in his first major European speech as British Prime Minister, called for the creation of a 'people's Europe' and announced that the British government 'shares the goal of a constructive partnership of nations in Europe'.[1] A few weeks later the Chancellor, Gordon Brown, called for Britain to be 'leading in Europe' and rejected 'both the federal way forward and the regulatory way ahead';[2] and [...] the point was reiterated by the Prime Minister, stating that 'we must end the isolation of the last twenty years and be a leading partner in Europe'.[3] These statements have a familiar ring. John Major also famously called for Britain to be 'at the heart of Europe'.[4]

The key question being asked of Britain's approach to Europe under its first Labour government for a generation is whether this is new Labour, new Europe or new Labour, old Britain. The determination of the government to be a leading player combined with a rather typical British unease with supra-national structures (though not the outright hostility of the Conservatives) raises again the question of whether Britain will lead in a direction that no one else wants to take or whether it can promote and gain support for a new approach to the EU.

As yet, the answer to this key question is unclear. Ruling out the prospect of Britain becoming a strong proponent of ever closer union, there remain three potential routes down which Labour may take Britain in Europe – the choice among which will also depend on the decisions, preferences and views of Britain's European partners. First, Britain could act on the rhetoric of the government and indeed play a leading part in promoting a new political vision and role for the EU in the twenty-first century, drawing on the lessons, successes and strengths of its domestic position. Second, it could be a constructive but pragmatic European player, offering elements of new thinking and positive ideas but without an overall vision and without being a dominant player. There are already signs of this approach. Third, Britain could – without replicating the bitter divisions of the preceding Conservative government – be a side player in the EU, left behind as Europe develops in directions it cannot support. There is some evidence in support of each of these three routes, but so far the second is the most appropriate characterization.

In this article, we assess the main elements of Britain's European policy under the Labour government, how it compares with earlier British approaches and how it relates to the challenges Europe faces.

A Change of Approach?

In comparison to the previous administration, the current British government has adopted a new, positive tone in the EU. The importance of the change in both tone and behaviour should not be underestimated. The deep splits in the Conservative Party over Europe – splits that went to the heart of the cabinet – left Britain isolated in the EU, with its influence much reduced even in areas where it had common policy goals with its European partners. [...]

The new government does differ from its predecessor in its overall approach to the EU. Labour is not plagued by serious splits on Europe: there is a broad consensus around the view that Britain should have a major role in the EU. There are dissenters on the single currency but, as discussed further below, these doubts are principally on economic rather than national sovereignty grounds. The three leading figures in the cabinet – Blair, Brown and Cook – all recognize that Britain increases its global status and influence by being a serious, influential EU player. At the same time, both Cook's mission statement[5] and Blair's first major foreign policy statement[6] have made it clear they still see Britain as a global player, particularly given its position as a permanent member of the UN Security Council, and its role in other bodies including the Commonwealth and the G8. There is, therefore, a combination here of a modern approach, recognizing the importance for a medium-sized country like Britain of working with and through the EU, with a more traditional emphasis on Britain's independent global role. It will be important to observe how the balance or tension between these two emphases develops.

The new British government is not an uncritical supporter of all of the current EU structures and policies. The Prime Minister made this clear in his key Malmö speech to the Party of European Socialists Congress, where he criticized both old left and old right approaches, calling for a 'third way' in economic and social policy and criticizing EU institutions for being 'out of touch, out of date, not responsive to the people's needs'.[7] Labour's European rhetoric emphasizes the need to renew and redefine Europe, to create a 'people's Europe', tackling the dominant challenge of European unemployment and making the EU relevant to European publics. [...]

Employment as Top Priority

[...] Labour's main ideas for tackling EU unemployment are, on the one hand, to work to complete the single market – thus improving competitiveness and, so the argument goes, prospects for employment – and, on the other hand, to increase flexibility and employability in labour markets. Labour's signature of the EU social chapter at Amsterdam – applying EU social legislation to Britain in areas such as the working week and maternity rights – has lowered some of the ideological barriers between Britain and its partners erected by the previous government. Labour in power has also been careful to qualify calls for greater flexibility, aware of continental suspicions of the concept. The new buzz word – 'employability' – essentially refers to improving the skills, knowledge and adaptability of job-seekers. Aside from completion of the single market, Labour's main emphasis is on each individual country adopting the right labour market policies (which it considers Britain already to have done); the British government is not arguing for new powers, policy competences or expenditure at the EU level.

Irrespective of the merits of different economic views, it is difficult to argue that Labour's emphasis on completing the single market and transferring employment best practice between member states represents either a radical new departure for EU policy or a radical new British approach to the EU. It would be a major shift if EU member states reorganized their social market systems to take on the main elements of the British system. Not only is this unlikely, but if it were to happen (and some changes are under way), it would be a consequence of individual countries' choices and not of EU policies or developments. Overall, the emphasis on the single market reflects a strong element of continuity in British European policy.

The Single Currency

The Labour government has adopted a positive stance towards economic and monetary union (EMU), albeit one hedged in with provisos. [...]

The government position is now that it is in principle in favour of EMU and that a successful single currency would be good for the EU and for Britain. However, it will recommend that Britain join EMU only if the economic benefits to the country are clear and unambiguous. On the basis of five economic tests – of convergence, flexibility, and the impact on investment, financial services and employment – the government has concluded that joining the single currency is not yet in Britain's economic interests and is unlikely to be so until after the next general election (due at the latest in 2002). On the basis of this stance on EMU, the government is aiming to persuade business to prepare for membership of the single currency and to change public opinion in favour of entry.

While all the public emphasis is being placed on the economic issues, there are central political questions and decisions here. First, it is clear that the longer Britain remains outside the single currency the more political influence in the EU it will lose – there is no prospect of Britain being the 'dominant actor', as Tony Blair intends, while the country is not in EMU. Second, the government cannot take Britain into EMU without winning the referendum on the question that it has promised. The decision to rule out early membership of EMU rests as much on the political calculation that a referendum cannot be won in the next one to two years as on any economic calculations.

[...]

Overall, the new government's strategy represents a substantial change in Britain's approach to the single currency. [...] The decision to join or remain outside the single currency area will be a defining one for Britain's position in the EU. If a renewed integration dynamic develops in the wake of the single currency, Britain may continue to find itself at odds with EU developments; however, a broad EMU does mean that countries participating will have a range of views on further EU development, especially in the context of enlargement, and Britain need not be isolated.

Timing is critical. Joining three years late, in 2002, would not be particularly damaging economically; but, notwithstanding the welcome for its new constructive stance in the EU, Britain's political influence will continue to fall for so long as it does not participate in this key policy. As policy discussions, bargains and coalitions develop around EMU, these will impact on other areas as deals are done. Delay in joining until 2004/5 would leave Britain increasingly marginalized in the EU, in the company perhaps of Denmark and the central and east European applicants/entrants. [...]

Institutions

[...] Labour's approach to institutional issues is different from that of the previous government. At Amsterdam, Britain supported an increase in powers of the European Parliament and supported an extension of qualified majority voting (leaving Germany, to general surprise, as the country blocking some of the proposed extensions). Britain was, however, cautious on both the principle and specifics of flexibility in decision-making, and maintained its traditional position of continued opposition to the integration of the Western European Union into the EU. In the important and rapidly developing policy area of borders and immigration, Britain remains on the outside of the continental consensus – with unanimous agreement of the participating countries necessary if Britain ever did wish to join the Schengen area within which EU citizens may cross national frontiers without passport control. The government returned from Amsterdam proclaiming a British success story both in the measure of agreement reached and in the opt-outs (which it calls opt-ins) and the vetoes it achieved; the failure of Amsterdam to take even the first institutional steps necessary for enlargement did not loom large in the government's view. Overall, while Britain will remain cautious on institutional issues, it is clearly now more in the mainstream and not isolated. [...]

[...] Already there are signs that Labour's domestic constitutional agenda is connecting with European policies. The incorporation of the European Convention on Human Rights into domestic British legislation will mark a further alignment of the British legal system with European norms. As a possible forerunner for proportional representation (PR) in British national elections, the government will apply PR in the British elections to the European Parliament in 1999. Finally, and most importantly, the popular agreement to devolve power to the regional level with a parliament in Scotland and an assembly in Wales may, over time, lead to a substantive shift in attitudes towards transferring powers of governance both up to the EU and down to the regions. This could transform both the politics of Britain in the EU and public attitudes towards the sovereignty question, but what matters is how long it may take.

Public Opinion and the Media

Given the importance in domestic politics in recent years of the bitter and divisive debate over Europe within the Conservative Party and government, it is relevant to ask to what extent Labour's initial European policy approach reflects caution and the aim of slowly building up a new consensus on European issues. On the single currency, this is clearly the case: the government has embarked on a strategy aimed at building up a broad base of support for EMU, changing public opinion and (if possible) sidelining the Eurosceptic media.

On other issues, survey evidence suggests that public opinion, despite recent debates, is not generally hostile to the EU.[8] However, although British membership of the Union continues to be supported, there are widely differing views as to whether there should be more integration or a return to a trade bloc. This disparity of opinion may be problematic in trying to define a new overall approach. [...] [T]his suggests that the government may expect to receive public support for a pragmatic and constructive approach to the EU. It also suggests that there is scope to try to define a more ambitious, overarching political view of the purpose of the EU, building on the areas of policy consensus. The advantages of a pragmatic approach rather than an overall European vision are clear in terms of consensus but not so compelling in terms of influence. Whether the government can find an approach that receives general support in the UK and provides a basis on which the UK can play a serious role in the EU is the challenge.

Conclusion

The Labour government [...] moved rapidly in its first six months in office to establish a more positive and constructive British approach to the EU. There is both substantial continuity in policy with British approaches in the past, notably in the emphasis on the economic aspects of the EU and on economic liberalism, and development of some new policy approaches. While the positive stance on the single currency represents a big shift, the current position nonetheless remains one of maintaining the opt-outs on both the single currency and the border controls. The new government, while showing traditional British reluctance to focus on institutional issues, is much more prepared than the Conservatives to agree to some institutional and social developments, and is more at ease discussing a range of questions, including human rights, the environment and crime, at European level. The issue at the top of Labour's European agenda – jobs – reflects again a fairly traditional British approach with its emphasis on the single market and on responsibility lying with individual member states.

The picture that emerges from this analysis is principally one of Britain playing a constructive and pragmatic role in the EU. However, Labour's aim of being a leading player is severely constrained by Britain's non-participation in EMU; and its rhetoric of a people's Europe needs more policy substance to underpin it. If Britain maintains its EMU opt-out in the medium term, it will find itself once again on the sidelines in Europe. Labour – despite its support for enlargement – has yet to develop an overall political vision of the role and structure of the EU in the twenty-first century. Britain's future role in the EU will depend on when and whether it participates in EMU, what sort of political strategy it does develop, and how strategies towards the EU develop in other member states. [...]

NOTES

1 Speech by the Prime Minister, the Rt Hon. Tony Blair MP, to the Party of European Socialists Congress, Malmö, 6 June 1997.
2 Speech by the Rt Hon. Gordon Brown MP, Chancellor of the Exchequer, to the Royal Institute of International Affairs, 'Britain leading in Europe', 17 July 1997.
3 Speech by the Prime Minister, The Rt Hon. Tony Blair MP, at the Lord Mayor's banquet, London, Guildhall, 'The principles of a modern British foreign policy', 1 November 1997.
4 The Rt Hon. John Major MP, former prime minister, 'The evolution of Europe', *Conservative Party News*, 11 March 1991.
5 FCO Mission Statement, 12 May 1997.
6 Blair, 'The principles of a modern British foreign policy'.
7 Blair, speech, Malmö, 6 June 1997.
8 *British Social Attitudes Survey 1997*.

39

Speech at the Launch of the Britain in Europe Campaign, October 1999

Tony Blair

[...] For months, if not years, there has been a clamour from those opposed to Europe, that has been always shrill and often effective. We are told that Europe is bad for the British economy. That being part of Europe means abandoning our allies in the USA. That Europe is obstinately against reform, dedicated to bloated bureaucracy rather than the needs of European citizens. That being in Europe means losing our identity as the British nation. That as a consequence, Britain should rule out joining the Euro and should prepare to leave Europe altogether.

It is time we took each one of these arguments in turn and demolished them.

Three and a half million British jobs depend on our membership of the EU. Over 50 per cent of our trade is with Europe. British firms daily sell 320 million pounds of goods and services into the European single market. Inward investment flows into Britain as a result of our being part of Europe. The English language, a flexible labour market, a thriving culture are all good reasons for companies choosing Britain as their place of entry to Europe. Last year alone, inward investment created 50,000 new jobs. But it is investment dependent on Britain in Europe.

Europe is not marginal to the British economy. It is fundamental to it and each day becomes more so. To quit Europe would be an act of economic mutilation.

Second, Britain is stronger with the US by reason of being in Europe. Go to the US. Deal, as I have, over the past two years, with issues of trade and investment, war and peace, with our US allies. They value us in our own right. Of course they do. But they value us even more as people who have influence in Europe who can talk to key European allies and who are respected both in the US and in Europe. Likewise, we are stronger in Europe if strong with the US. Stronger together. Influential with both. And a bridge between the two.

Third, we know Europe needs reform and we are fighting for it. [...]

And we make this case, not because we are pro-Europe – though I believe in the ideal of European partnership. We make it because we are pro-Britain. To be part of Europe is in the British national interest. So far from submerging our identity as a nation in some Eurosceptic parody of a Federal super-state, we believe that by being part of Europe we advance our own self-interest as the British nation. This is a patriotic cause. The people here represent a patriotic alliance that puts country before Party. The Britain of the 21st Century should surely be the Britain I grew up believing in: not narrow-minded, chauvinistic or isolationist; but a country open in its attitudes, engaged in the outside world, adventurous in taking on the future's challenges, and having the confidence to know that working with others is a sign of strength not weakness.

[...]

The real denial of our history would be to retreat into isolation from the continent of Europe of which we are part and whose history we have so intimately shaped. I will not and could not lead the country to such a position. In 1975, still a student, I voted yes in the referendum. I believed Britain's destiny was with Europe then. I believe it now. And I am proud to be part of a gathering that stretches across all political parties and none, to make our case to our country.

40

Europe – Superpower, not Superstate: Speech in Warsaw, October 2000

Tony Blair

[...]

[...] British policy towards the rest of Europe over half a century has been marked by gross misjudgements, mistaking what we wanted to be the case with what was the case; hesitation, alienation, incomprehension, with the occasional burst of enlightened brilliance which only served to underline the frustration of our partners with what was the norm. The origins of this are not complex but simple. Post-war Britain saw the issue – entirely naturally – as how France and Germany were kept from going back to war with each other. Britain's initial role therefore was that of a benign, avuncular friend encouraging the two old enemies to work together. Then with gathering speed, and commensurate British alarm, Europe started not just to work together but to begin the institutional cooperation that is today the European Union. At each stage, Britain thought it won't possibly happen and held back. And at each stage it did happen and we were faced with the choice: catching up or staying out.

This was complicated by the fact that for all the other key players, there were compelling reasons for being in: reasons of history, reasons of proximity, reasons of democracy. For Britain, the victor in WWII, the main ally of the United States, a proud and independent-minded island race (though with much European blood flowing in our veins) the reasons were there, but somehow always less than absolutely compelling.

[...]

[...] [T]he circumstances of today mean it is time to overcome the legacy of Britain's past. Two things have changed. From Europe's perspective, Britain as a key partner in Europe is now a definite plus not a minus. Britain has a powerful economy, an obvious role in defence and foreign policy and there is genuine respect for Britain's political institutions and stability. Also, in a world moving closer together, with new powers emerging, our strength with the United States is not just a British asset, it is potentially a European one. Britain can be the bridge between the EU and the US.

And for Britain, as Europe grows stronger and enlarges, there would be something truly bizarre and self-denying about standing apart from the key strategic alliance on our doorstep. None of this means criticisms of Europe are all invalid. They aren't, as I shall say later. But to conduct the case for reform in a way that leaves Britain marginalised and isolated, is just plain foolish for Britain in our national interest.

For Britain, as for those countries queuing up to join the European Union, being at the centre of influencing Europe is an indispensable part of influence, strength and power in the world. We can choose not to be there; but no-one should doubt the consequences of that choice and it is wildly unrealistic to pretend those consequences are not serious. In particular, there is no doubt in my mind, that our strength with the US is enhanced by our strength with the rest of Europe and vice versa.

I have said the political case for Britain being part of the single currency is strong. I don't say political or constitutional issues aren't important. They are. But to my mind, they aren't an insuperable barrier. What does have to be overcome is the economic issue. It is an economic union. Joining prematurely simply on political grounds, without the economic conditions being right, would be a mistake. Hence our position: in principle in favour; in practice, the economic tests must be met. We cannot and will not take risks with Britain's economic strength. The principle is real, the tests are real.

[...]

The most important challenge for Europe is to wake up to [a] new reality: Europe is widening and deepening simultaneously. There will be more of us in the future, trying to do more. The issue is: not whether we do this, but how we reform this new Europe so that it both delivers real benefits to the people of Europe, addressing the priorities they want addressed; and does so in a way that has their consent and support.

There are two opposite models so far proposed. One is Europe as a free trade area, like NAFTA in North America. The other is the classic federalist model, in which Europe elects its Commission President and the European Parliament becomes the true legislative European body and Europe's principal democratic check.

The difficulty with the first is that it nowhere near answers what our citizens expect from Europe, besides being wholly unrealistic politically. In a Europe with a single market and single currency, there will inevitably be a need for closer economic co-ordination. In negotiations over world trade and global finance, Europe is stronger if it speaks with one voice.

In areas like the environment and organised crime, in policing our borders, Europe needs to work together. In foreign and security policy, though nations will guard jealously their own national interests, there are times when it will be of clear benefit to all that Europe acts and speaks together. What people want from Europe is more than just free trade. They want: prosperity, security and strength.

In a world with the power of the USA; with new alliances to be made with the neighbours of Europe like Russia; developing nations with vast populations like India and China; Japan, not just an economic power but a country that will rightly increase its political might too; with the world increasingly forming powerful regional blocs – ASEAN, Mercosur; Europe's citizens need Europe to be strong and united. They need it to be a power in the world. Whatever its origin, Europe today is no longer just about peace. It is about projecting collective power. That is one very clear reason, quite apart from the economic reasons, why the central European nations want to join. So a limited vision of Europe does not remotely answer the modern demands people place on Europe. The difficulty, however, with the view of Europe as a superstate, subsuming nations into a politics dominated by supranational institutions, is that it too fails the test of the people.

There are issues of democratic accountability in Europe – the so-called democratic deficit. But we can spend hours on end, trying to devise a perfect form of European democracy and get nowhere. The truth is, the primary sources of democratic accountability in Europe are the directly elected and representative institutions of the nations of Europe – national parliaments and governments. That is not to say Europe will not in future generations develop its own strong demos or polity, but it hasn't yet. [...]

Europe is a Europe of free, independent sovereign nations who choose to pool that sovereignty in pursuit of their own interests and the common good, achieving more together than we can achieve alone. The EU will remain a unique combination of the intergovernmental and the supranational.

Such a Europe can, in its economic and political strength, be a superpower; a superpower, but not a superstate. We should not therefore begin with an abstract discussion of institutional change. We begin with the practical question, what should Europe do? What do the people of Europe want and expect it to do? Then we focus Europe and its institutions around the answer. How we complete the single market. How we drive through necessary economic reform. How we phase out the wasteful and inefficient aspects of the CAP. How we restore full employment. How we get a more coherent foreign policy. How we develop the military capability we require without which common defence policy is a chimera. How we fight organised crime, immigration racketeering, the drugs trade. How we protect an environment that knows no borders.

[...]

Proposals for Political Reform

First, we owe it to our citizens to let them know clearly what policies and laws are being enacted in their name. The European Council, bringing together all the Heads of Government, is the final court of appeal from other Councils of Ministers unable to reconcile national differences.

[...]

Second, there is an important debate about a Constitution for Europe. In practice I suspect that, given the sheer diversity and complexity of the EU, its constitution, like the British constitution, will continue to be found in a number of different treaties, laws and precedents. It is perhaps easier for the British than for others to recognise that a constitutional debate must not necessarily end with a single, legally binding document called a Constitution for an entity as dynamic as the EU.

What I think is both desirable and realistic is to draw up a statement of the principles according to which we should decide what is best done at the European level and what should be done at the national level, a kind of charter of competences. This would allow countries too, to define clearly what is then done at a regional level. This Statement of Principles would be a political, not a legal document. It could therefore be much simpler and more accessible to Europe's citizens.

I also believe that the time has now come to involve representatives of national parliaments more on such matters, by creating a second chamber of the European Parliament. A second chamber's most important function would be to review the EU's work, in the light of this agreed Statement of Principles. It would not get involved in the day-to-day negotiation of legislation – that is properly the role of the existing European Parliament. Rather, its task would be to help implement the agreed Statement of Principles; so that we do what we need to do at a European level but also so that we devolve power downwards. Whereas a formal Constitution would logically require judicial review by a European constitutional court, this would be political review by a body of democratically elected politicians. It would be dynamic rather than static, allowing for change in the application of these principles without elaborate legal revisions every time. Such a second chamber could also, I believe, help provide democratic oversight at a European level of the common foreign and security policy.

[…]

Conclusion

We need to get the political foundations of the European Union right. These foundations are rooted in the democratic nation state. Efficiency and democracy go together. […] We want a Europe where there are national differences, not national barriers, where we hold many of our policies in common, but keep our distinct, separate identities.

The European Union is the world's biggest single economic and political partnership of democratic states. It represents a huge opportunity for Europe and the peoples of Europe. And as a Union of democracies, it has the capacity to sustain peace in our continent, to deliver unprecedented prosperity and to be a powerful force for democratic values in the rest of the world.

Our task, with the help of the new democracies about to join the EU, is to shape a European Union in a responsive way – in touch with the people, transparent and easier to understand, strengthened by its nations and regions – a European Union whose vision of peace is matched by its vision of prosperity. A civilised continent united in defeating brutality and violence. A prosperous continent united in extending opportunities to all. A continent joined together in its belief in social justice. A superpower, but not a superstate. An economic powerhouse through the completion of the world's biggest single market, the extension of competition, an adaptable and well educated workforce, the support for businesses large and small. A civilised continent through common defence, the strength of our values, the pursuit of social justice, the rich diversity of our cultures.

41

Speech at the Mansion House, June 2001

Gordon Brown

[...] [I]n just a few short years the world has moved from sheltered to open economies; from local to global competition; from national to world wide financial markets; from location, raw materials and indigenous capital as sources of national competitive advantage to skills, knowledge and creativity as what makes a difference.
[...]

So Britain did need a wholly new monetary and fiscal framework that went beyond the crude Keynesian fine-tuning of the fifties and sixties and the crude monetarism of the seventies and eighties and, instead, offered a modern British route to stability. With first, clear policy rules: a symmetrical inflation target and our fiscal disciplines. Second, clearly established procedures: the Code for Fiscal Stability and, most of all, Bank independence [....] And third, an openness and transparency we have not seen in the past.

I believe that as we are tested by events like rising oil prices, exchange rate pressures, and now the US slowdown, our new framework makes us better placed than before to cope with the ups and downs of the economic cycle. [...]

[...] [I]n the euro area a modern route to economic stability is being sought based on a shared recognition that the old fine-tuning cannot work, that in liberalised markets rigid monetary targets cannot on their own deliver stability and that the discretion necessary for effective economic policy is possible only within a framework that commands public and market credibility. And there is, I believe, also a growing understanding that this credibility depends upon clearly defined and publicly understood long-term policy objectives.

So, just like Britain, the euro area has been establishing a framework for economic stability. And, as I said in October 1997, in principle British membership of a successful single currency offers us obvious benefits – in terms of trade, transparency, costs and currency stability. And membership of a successful single currency could help us create the conditions for higher and more productive investment and greater trade and business in Europe.

In 1997, the Government said that, while we recognise the constitutional issue as a factor in the decision, we do not consider it a bar to entry if there is clear and unambiguous evidence of the economic benefits of joining, and if the people have the final say in a referendum. And that commitment to a referendum – if the economic tests are met – is a promise we made in our election manifesto only a few weeks ago.

The 1997 statement also set five economic tests:

- First, sustainable convergence between Britain and the economies of a single currency;
- second, whether there is sufficient flexibility to cope with economic change;
- third, the effect on investment;
- fourth, the impact on our financial services industry; and
- fifth, whether it is good for employment.

These tests are the necessary economic pre-requisites for membership of a successful currency union.

So I reject the view of those who would rule out membership of the single currency on principle. They would refuse to join even if it were in the national economic interest to do so. To rule out membership of the single currency on dogmatic grounds would in my view be damaging for investment, jobs and business generally.

Similarly, I reject those who would urge us to join regardless of the assessment of the five tests. Such a course would risk repeating past failures, would prejudice our stability and would also be damaging for investment, jobs and business generally.

Our approach is, and will continue to be, considered and cautious – one of pro-euro realism. Pro-euro because, as we said in 1997, we believe that – in principle – membership of the euro can bring benefits to Britain. Realist because to short-cut or fudge the assessment, and to join in the wrong way or on the wrong basis without rigorously ensuring the tests are met, would not be in the national economic interest.

Because the Government is determined that we will make the right long-term decisions for Britain, we will not take risks with Britain's hard won stability. So the assessment as to whether it is in the British national economic interest or not will be comprehensive and rigorous. It is only on this basis – taking into account all relevant economic information – that the Cabinet will decide whether to recommend membership to Parliament and then to the British people.

Before any such assessment is started, we must, of course, continue to do the necessary preliminary work for our analysis – technical work that is necessary to allow us to undertake the assessment within two years as we promised. Indeed, since 1997, our strategy has been, as I set out then, to prepare and decide. This has already involved the publication of the draft national changeover plans and the work of our standing committee with business. To prepare and then decide is the approach that we will continue to pursue.

Around the future of the euro there is, of course, an ongoing national debate. But across Europe a debate on the future of Europe is also taking place and Britain must be at the centre of that debate too – a debate on economic reform amidst the challenge of globalisation, enlargement into the East, and the wider Nice agenda to make decision-making in Europe more open, accountable and relevant to the population as a whole. Because this is a time of great change and challenges for the European Union, every country must not only debate its place in Europe but what kind of Europe we want.

Britain's relationship with Europe is a question that every generation in this country has had to ask and answer. And in this generation – for our time – let us remind ourselves why Europe is so important.

It is sometimes said that there are no great causes left. Being part of Europe is itself a great cause – to have granted to us, in our generation, the opportunity to set aside old enmities and feuds, to contribute to a mission that has helped secure half a century of peace in Western Europe, and now the historic task to cement peace and democracy in Central and Eastern Europe as we have done in the West.

At one time the case for Europe was simply peace. But today the case for Europe must be not only that, working together, we can maintain peace but that, working together, we can maximise prosperity. And getting the economic future of Europe right matters for Britain because over three quarters of a million United Kingdom companies now trade with the rest of the European Union. It is a fact that in the 1970s, when we joined Europe, less than 8 billions of our trade was with the rest of Europe. Today it is £132 billions – half our total trade – with 3 million jobs affected.

So Europe is where we are, where we trade, from where thousands of businesses and jobs arise. And we are part of Europe by geography, by history, by economics and by choice. The channel has always been a route to the wider world, not a moat cutting ourselves off from it. And, as a trading nation, the greater the stability in our relationship with our major trading partners, the greater the benefit to us.

I believe that those who seek to renegotiate the very basis of our membership with Europe, even when they simultaneously protest they do not want to leave, put at risk the stability that is so central to modern business and investment decisions. And I believe that government and business must join together in putting the case unequivocally for Britain being in Europe – a stronger Britain on the basis of a strong and secure relationship with Europe.

And as the great debate on Europe's future begins, we should not only put the case for Europe but for a reformed Europe – and for Britain leading reform in Europe. Indeed the more Europe extends its single market, the better it is for Britain and Europe. The more Europe embraces economic and institutional reform, the better it is for Britain and Europe. The more Europe looks outwards, the better it is for Britain and Europe. And the more Europe and America work closely together, the better it is for Britain, Europe and the world.

While the single market encompasses 375 million people today – and potentially nearly 500 million in the future, we have still a long way to go to secure for British business and British consumers the full benefits in commercial opportunities and consumer prices.

So here the economic reform agenda is clear and challenging: it is to complete the single market in utilities, energy, telecoms and financial and professional services that we have argued not just for action plans which signal intent but timetables which signal deadlines.

[...]

Our Government's vision of Europe, as set out by Tony Blair in Warsaw, is not a federalist one but one in which independent nation states work together to shape the decisions. It is one where there is, increasingly, mutual recognition of national standards and solutions based on exchange of information, peer review and benchmarking rather than the central imposition of 'one size fits all'. It is of a market that must, rightly, have a social dimension, but with subsidiarity or national decision-making the way forward. It is of tax competition not tax harmonisation. And as Tony Blair also said, it is of an open and accountable administration subject to the direction of elected ministers, not an unaccountable bureaucracy.

Alliances are being built for reform. The old pressures for tax harmonisation are already now being vigorously pushed back as we argue for the principles of tax competition. Countries are coming together to insist the European budget is brought under control and following Britain's initiative on fraud to set up an independent fraud office, there is a need to expose and tackle waste and fraud vigorously. It is now also accepted that widespread reform of the commission must take place.

So here again the reform agenda is clear and challenging. And right across Europe people now clearly want the debate on integration to be complemented by a debate on accountability. And on these issues relevant to the 2004 IGC the Prime Minister will, during the next year, be setting out our Government's proposals.

I believe that those genuinely committed to advancing Britain's national interest should support rather than dismiss a practical approach to making the reform agenda work. And, perhaps most important of all, the new Europe must be outward looking rather than inward looking.

The first post-war reshaping of Europe into a common market took place in the shadow of war as we moved beyond the old conflicts of the past. The second reshaping of Europe is happening not just as a result of internal forces at work within Europe but in response to vast global changes – not least fast increasing trade and capital flows, between Europe and the rest of the world and the growth of transcontinental companies. In just one decade, direct European investment in the USA has increased more than ten fold, from 20 billion dollars a year to 230 billion dollars a year. And we need only look at the impact of the American slowdown on European economic growth to understand this growing economic interdependence.
[...]

Between them, Europe and America together account for 55 per cent of world trade, 60 per cent of trade in services and – remarkably – 80 per cent of world wealth. But it is more than commerce that binds us. Increasingly, in this age of globalisation, our national goals are shared international goals, our responsibilities are shared responsibilities, and our opportunities are shared opportunities. And, together, Europe and America have an even greater responsibility for world stability and growth, not least as they affect developing countries. So we must think transcontinentally as well as continentally.

If someone had said to any of us 20 years ago that Eastern and Central Europe would soon embrace Western Europe, Russia would start to look westwards, and that in Western Europe the old ideological conflicts between state and market would be resolved such that state and markets work together and that there would be a free flow of capital round the world, all of us would have been astounded to the point of disbelief. But we would have been even more astounded if we were told that at precisely that point of opportunity for the world economy, voices would advocate American disengagement and settle for a Europe that looks inwards.

The end of the Cold War should not be the signal for disengagement or parochialism but for a new and enhanced form of engagement between our continents, where shared interests that could yield mutual benefits lead to a reform agenda that is yet again clear and challenging and as ambitious and wide ranging as:

- the elimination of industrial tariffs;
- open skies;
- the mutual recognition of standards across the professional services;
- common rules of competition;

- eliminating barriers to the establishment of European and US companies in each other's markets;
- and a joint strategy for oil supplies as well as for tackling debt and poverty in developing countries. [...]

In forging that stronger relationship, Britain plays a pivotal role. Britain does not have to choose between America and Europe, but is well positioned as the vital link between America and Europe.

And so this Government believes in a Europe where cooperation is widening and deepening as we extend the single market and embrace economic and institutional reform – not at the expense of the rest of the world but in concert with it.

[...] Winston Churchill said that those who build the present only in the image of the past will miss out entirely on the challenges of the future. I believe that, learning from each other, all of us – businesses and governments working together – can face the great challenges of today's economy not by resisting change but by helping people to cope with it; not by standing still but by radical economic reform; and not by protectionism but by promoting open, competitive markets and international cooperation. It makes for a Britain that is outward looking and open to the world, ambitious to succeed, wholly committed to an enterprise culture and determined to be fully equipped to lead in the 21st century economy.

42

Statement on European Monetary Union to the House of Commons, October 1997

Gordon Brown

[...] Since the end of the Second World War Britain has faced no question more important and more contentious than that of our relationship with Europe. Divisions within governments of both parties, and hence indecision, have made British policy towards Europe, over many years, inconsistent and unclear. The economic consequences of these weaknesses have been a loss of international initiative and influence, recurrent instability and continuing questioning of our long-term economic direction. To break with this legacy, and to establish clear national purpose, which has eluded us for decades, economic leadership is essential, and Britain must now make the difficult decisions on Europe, however hard.

The decision on a single currency is probably the most important this country is likely to face in our generation. [...] So I will deal, in turn, with the question of principle, the constitutional implications of EMU, and the economic tests that have to be met. In each area, I will set down the Government's policy. [...]

Issues of Principle

I start with the question of principle. The potential benefits for Britain of a successful single currency are obvious: in terms of trade, transparency of costs and currency stability. Of course, I stress it must be soundly based. It must succeed. But if it works economically, it is, in our view, worth doing. So in principle, a successful single currency within a single European market would be of benefit to Europe and to Britain. Secondly, it must be clearly recognised that to share a common monetary policy with other states does represent a major pooling of economic sovereignty. There are those who argue that this should be a constitutional bar to British participation in a single currency, regardless of the economic benefits it could bring to the people of this country. In other words, they would rule out a single currency in principle, even if it were in the best economic interests of the country.

That is an understandable objection and one argued from principle. But in our view it is wrong. If a single currency would be good for British jobs, business and future prosperity, it is right, in principle, to join. The constitutional issue is a factor in the decision, but it is not an over-riding one. Rather it signifies that in order for monetary union to be right for Britain the economic benefit should be clear and unambiguous. So I conclude on this question of principle: if, in the end, a single currency is successful, and the economic case is clear and unambiguous, then the Government believes Britain should be part of it.

There is a third issue of principle – the consent of the British people. Because of the magnitude of the decision, we believe – again, as a matter of principle – that whenever the decision to enter is taken by government, it should be put to a referendum of the British people. So whenever this issue arises, under this Government there will be a referendum. Government, Parliament and the people must all agree.

So we conclude that the determining factor as to whether Britain joins a single currency is the national economic interest and whether the economic case for doing so is clear and unambiguous.

The Five Economic Tests

I now turn to the Treasury's detailed assessment of the five economic tests that define whether a clear and unambiguous case can be made. These are:

1   Whether there can be sustainable convergence between Britain and the economies of a single currency.
2   Whether there is sufficient flexibility to cope with economic change.
3   The effect on investment.
4   The impact on our financial services industry.
5   Whether it is good for employment.

Economic cycles

Of these, the first and most critical is convergence: can we be confident that the UK business cycle has converged with that of other European countries so that the British economy can have stability and prosperity with a common European monetary policy? That convergence must be capable of being sustained and likely to be sustained – in other words, we must demonstrate a settled period of convergence. [...]

We will need a period of stability with continuing toughness on inflation and public borrowing. The Treasury's assessment is that, at present, the UK's economic cycle is not convergent with our European partners and that this divergence could continue for some time. To demonstrate sustainable convergence will take a period of years.

Flexibility

To be successful in a monetary union, countries will need even more flexibility to adjust to change and to unexpected economic events once the ability of countries to vary their interest rates and exchange rates has gone and the Euro and a single European interest rate are in place. Flexibility may be particularly important for the UK if there is any risk that our business cycle has not fully converged with those of the other EMU members.

The Treasury assessment of the second test is that, in Britain, persistent long-term unemployment and lack of skills – and in some areas lack of competition – point to the need for more flexibility to adapt to change and to meet the new challenges of adjustment. The Government has begun to implement a programme for investing in education and training, helping people from welfare into work and improving the workings of our markets.

Of course, other European countries need to tackle unemployment and inflexibility to make sure Europe as a whole is able to withstand any shocks that arise. The Government will continue to argue that employability, flexibility and stronger competition policies must be a top priority so that monetary union can be successful.

Investment

The third test is investment: whether joining EMU would create better conditions for businesses to make long-term decisions to invest in Britain. The Treasury assessment is that, above all, business needs long-term economic stability and a well-functioning European single market. It concludes that membership of a successful single currency would help us create the conditions for higher and more productive investment in Britain. But the worst case for investment would be for Britain to enter EMU without proper preparations and without sufficient convergence and with all the uncertainty that would entail.

Financial services

The fourth test asks what impact membership of the single currency would have on our financial services industry. EMU will affect that industry more profoundly and more immediately than any other sectors of the economy.

The Treasury's assessment is that we can now be confident that the industry has the potential to thrive whether the UK is in or out of EMU, so long as it is properly prepared. But the benefits of new opportunities from a single currency could, however, be easier to tap from within the Euro zone. This could help the City of London strengthen its position as the leading financial centre in Europe.

Employment

For millions of people, the most practical question is whether membership of a successful single currency would be good for prosperity and jobs. The Treasury assessment is that our employment-creating measures, and welfare state reform, must accompany any move to a single currency. Ultimately, we conclude that whether a single currency is good for jobs in practice comes back to sustainable convergence. A successful single currency would provide far greater trade and business in Europe. The Treasury assessment is that in vital areas the economy is not yet ready for entry and that much remains to be done. The previous policy of keeping options open, without actively making preparations, has left parts of the economy unprepared. Our overall assessment is that Britain needs both a period for preparation and a settled period of sustainable convergence. Both require stability.

The Government's Conclusions on EMU

Applying these five economic tests leads the Government to the following clear conclusions.

British membership of a single currency in 1999 could not meet the tests and therefore is not in the country's economic interests. [...] The issue then arises as to the period after 1 January 1999. We could simply leave the options open, as before, but with no clear direction either way for the rest of the Parliament. That would be politically easy but wrong. There would be instability, perpetual speculation about 'in or out', 'sooner or later', which would cause difficulties in the financial markets and for business and industry. It would make it harder to prepare for the possibility of a single currency because every step in preparation, every time the issue was discussed, would feed fresh bouts of speculation.

It must be in the country's interest to have a stable framework within which to plan. And we are fortified in this because on the economic tests we have set out, the practical difficulties of joining a single currency in this Parliament all point to the same conclusion. There is no need, legally, formally or politically, to renounce our option to join for the period between 1 January 1999 and the end of the Parliament, nor would it be sensible to do so. There is no requirement under the Treaty for this. What is more, no government can ever predict every set of economic circumstances that might arise.

What we can and should do is to state a clear view about the practicability of joining monetary union during this period. Applying our economic tests, two things are clear. There is no realistic prospect of our having demonstrated, before the end of this Parliament, that we have achieved convergence which is sustainable and settled rather than transitory. And Government has only just begun to put in place the necessary preparations which would allow us to do so. Other countries have for some years been making detailed preparations for a single currency. For all the reasons given, we have not.

Therefore, barring some fundamental and unforeseen change in economic circumstances, making a decision, during this Parliament, to join is not realistic. It is also therefore sensible for business and the country to plan on the basis that, in this Parliament, we do not propose to enter a single currency.

There are those who urge us to seek consent, in principle, in a referendum now or soon, but with a view to entering sometime later. Any serious gap between the referendum and the actual entry date would undermine the conclusions of the referendum.

Because the essential decision is economic, it can be taken only at a time when government and then the people can judge that sustainable convergence has been established. So in our view the interval between the decision to join and our joining must not be unduly protracted.

[...]

We are the first British government to declare for the principle of monetary union. The first to state that there is no over-riding constitutional bar to membership. The first to make clear and unambiguous economic benefit to the country the decisive test. And the first to offer its strong and constructive support to our European partners to create more employment and more prosperity.

The policy I have outlined will bring stability to business, direction to our economy, and long term purpose to our country. It is the right policy for Britain in Europe. More important it is the right policy for the future of Britain. [...]

43

The Blair Government and Europe

Philip Stephens

Any review of Britain's European policy during Tony Blair's first term confronts a paradox. Blair, the most instinctively pro-European Prime Minister since Edward Heath, has begun to rebuild the nation's fractured relationship with its continental neighbours. Yet if he has made Britain's case in Europe with measurable success, he has failed to make Europe's case in Britain.

[...] Blair has led a government that is listened to attentively, if sometimes with irritation, in Brussels, Berlin, Rome – even in Paris. It has built a network of alliances and launched several initiatives – most notably in the fields of defence and economic liberalisation. It has accepted integration where it works and pressed, often with success, for decentralisation where it is sensible. Yet here we meet the paradox. This achievement in rebuilding many of the bridges demolished with glee by Thatcher and with a heavy heart by Major tells only half the story. The government has re-engaged, but the people sulk on the sidelines. At the beginning of 2001, Europe still seems more of a threat than an opportunity to many people in Britain. Blair would claim such was his inheritance after eighteen years in which most things European had been demonised by the Conservatives. And most of the press, weaned on the confrontations of the Thatcher/Major years, is undoubtedly hostile to an approach which sees Europe as a partner rather than an enemy. But the popular mood is a reflection, too, of a leader whose self-confidence and, occasionally, boldness abroad has been matched by ambivalence and hesitation at home. Blair has set out the ambition in unequivocal terms. 'I have a bold aim,' he remarked in a speech at Aachen in the summer of 1999: 'That over the next few years Britain resolves once and for all its ambivalence towards Europe. I want to end the uncertainty, the lack of confidence, the Europhobia.' As his first term approaches its close, he might well reflect now that little has changed.

An Unsentimental European

[...] Overall, Blair's policy since 1997 should be seen as that of a convinced but unsentimental European. He is of that generation of politicians without personal memory of the Second World War and barely conscious of the privations which followed. He has been spared the nightmares of those in a previous generation who never came to terms with the fact that Britain had lost the peace. When Anthony Eden's ignominious Suez failure closed the final chapter on Britain's imperial preten- sions, Blair had not yet begun primary school. In his speech to the French National Assembly in 1998, he recalled that the first vote he had cast had been in favour of joining the Common Market. He did not mention that a decade later he would stand for election as a Labour MP on a platform of withdrawal. So what? Politicians change their minds. Margaret Thatcher memorably argued in 1975 that the sharing of sovereignty with the rest of Europe was vital to the pursuit of Britain's national interest. The purpose here is to stress that Blair's commitment to Britain's place in Europe is practical and pragmatic rather than ideological – though no less strong for that.

The same hard-headed calculations have shaped his attitude to the sharing of sovereignty. Blair has never made any secret of his preference for a Europe that mixes supranationalism with inter-governmentalism over the founding fathers' inte- grationist vision of 'ever closer union'. Like Jacques Chirac, he envisages a united Europe of states rather than a united states of Europe. The continent could be a superpower, he said in Warsaw during the autumn of 2000, but not a superstate. Blair sees sovereignty as the capacity of a nation to promote its security and prosperity rather than as some precious and indivisible jewel. The national interest counts above Westminster's jealous guardianship of its prerogatives.

Thus the government's European strategy begins and ends with power. As frankly as any, Blair has cast the task of the British Prime Minister in terms of maximising the nation's power and influence abroad. Rebuilding relationships in Europe, nour- ishing ties with Washington, intervening in Kosovo or sending gunboats and troops to Sierra Leone – all have been joined in this central purpose. More than that, the policies have been deemed mutually reinforcing. As Blair remarked in his Warsaw speech: 'For Britain, being at the centre of influence in Europe is an indispensable part of influence, strength and power in the world.' And then: 'Europe today is no longer just about peace. It is about projecting collective power.' As for the choice posed by some between Washington and Brussels, it was false. Blair understood early on that to be weak in Europe was to be diminished in the United States. Equally, an intimate relationship with President Bill Clinton was scored as a plus not a minus in the power game in Europe.

[...]

[...] There are two areas in which Blair can credibly claim progress in writing Europe's agenda. In the first – defence – he has done as much as any European leader to make something of the EU's aspiration to build a common foreign and security policy. And thus far at least the European Security and Defence Initiative has managed to balance the goal of an independent European capability with the need to assuage US sensitivities about any rival to NATO. In the area of economic reform, the government can argue with some justice that it was the first to press the case for the Union to swap the old dirigiste agenda of Jacques Delors in favour of something closer to a liberal market model. A shift in priorities at the Cardiff summit in June 1998 foreshadowed the significant change of direction at Lisbon in March 2000. The Lisbon agenda, with an emphasis on economic dynamism, welfare reform, enterprise and innovation, was hailed by Blair as 'a sea change in EU economic thinking'. There was a touch of hyperbole in that description, but it was fair to say the summit marked a decisive break. What Blair missed was the irony. EMU had been, and still is, seen by many in Britain as the route by which the rest of Europe would entrench the social market model of economic management – a recipe, in other words, for sclerosis. The reverse has been true. The principal motor of change in the structure of continental capitalism has been the new competitive pressure created by the euro. A single capital market and the transparency that implies have triggered a transformation in Europe's corporate landscape. There are still voices, notably in Paris, heard calling for more regulation and harmonisation. But they are being drowned out by the realities of the market. Blair has been fortunate in that his exhortations have run with the tide of events.

[...]

Which Way? The Euro

When John Major persuaded his then Chancellor Kenneth Clarke to agree that a Conservative government would swap sterling for the euro only if the people voted yes in a referendum, it was an act of desperation. But Major's last-ditch and ultimately futile attempt to hold together his government in the spring of 1996 was one of those rare decisions that changed the course of history. Within months, Tony Blair had decided that in order to neutralise the issue at the looming general election Labour too had to offer a referendum. The decision on whether Britain would eventually join thus passed from the politicians to a sceptical public – and to a largely hostile media.

Neither Blair nor Brown was a natural enthusiast for the single currency. In the months following the general election both harboured hopes that the starting date might be deferred. Brown discussed with officials the possibility that Britain might actually call for such a delay – a suggestion that was dismissed as naive by Sir Nigel Wicks, the senior official in charge of European affairs at the Treasury. At this point both Prime Minister and Chancellor were also agreed that there was little or no prospect of Britain joining the first wave of EMU in January 1999. The cyclical disjunction between Britain's economy and that of its European neighbours was simply too great. Speaking just a few days after the election, Brown offered a reminder that both he and Blair had said during the campaign that 'it is highly unlikely that we will join EMU at the first date in 1999'. Against that, there was a shared perception that for Britain to remain outside of the single currency in the medium to long term would be to sacrifice vital interests in Europe. This initial coincidence of view came under increasing strain over the following few years.

Brown's announcement in October 1997 that Britain was ruling out participation for the lifetime of the present parliament was badly bungled. Preceded by a series of conflicting leaks from senior ministers and officials, the precise terms of the state-ment were the subject of the intense bargaining and some acrimony between Prime Minister and Chancellor. The behind-the-scenes wrangling also shone a light on the rivalry between Brown and Peter Mandelson, the fiercely pro-European Minister without Portfolio. The Chancellor's instinct was to close off completely the option of joining ahead of another election. With Mandelson's encouragement, Blair insisted on a small escape clause allowing a change of policy in the event of 'unforeseen circumstances'. This intervention inflamed Mandelson's already difficult relationship with Brown, amplifying the tensions between the two which had existed since the 1994 contest for the party leadership. The euro was henceforth another constant source of damaging friction at the top of the government.

The October 1997 statement offered both logic and ambiguity in equal measure. By setting five economic 'tests' for participation, Brown framed the argument in terms of the national economic interest. The new Labour government would take its decision on rational economic grounds – a necessary reassurance for the electorate. On the other hand the only important test of the five – the need for a sustained period of economic convergence – was a statement of common sense. The others – with their vague and rather fatuous exhortations about employment, flexibility, investment and the City – were entirely subjective. These 'tests', one senior Treasury official was to remark, could be 'passed' at any point the Chancellor chose. Of course, the official smiled as he said this, Brown might just as easily choose to fail them.

There was, of course, political substance to the October statement. Brown declared that the government had decided that there was no constitutional bar to Britain's entry. It had settled the political argument. In Brown's words: 'I have said that, if a successful single currency works and is successful, Britain should join it. We should therefore begin now to prepare ourselves so that, should we meet the economic tests, we can make a decision to join a successful single currency early in the next parliament.' Eighteen months later Blair, at Mandelson's prompting, would go further, telling the House of Commons: 'We have stated today as a matter of principle Britain should join a single European currency.'

The cup, though, was as half-empty as it was half-full. Brown's policy, carefully designed to give himself a veto over British participation and to close off debate before an election, became a strategy not for preparation but for inertia. That, the suspicion must now be, was the Chancellor's intention. In an important sense, the October 1997 statement was not so much a policy as a conscious decision not to have a policy unless and until the Chancellor said otherwise. As such it has since exposed both the flimsiness of the government's platform and the divisions within the Cabinet.

The attempt to sustain a neat line between the economics and the politics of EMU is disingenuous. A minimum level of convergence between interest, inflation and exchange rates is clearly a precondition for entry. But the government has sought, vainly, to deny the obvious truth that this is first and foremost a political decision. Blair has said many times that the political principle has been decided in favour. Privately, he has acknowledged that participation in the euro within the lifetime of the next parliament is central to his political ambition to end the ambiguity about Britain's place in the Union. But he has failed to make the political case. The European leaders who in 1997 took the government at its word when it said it expected to hold (and presumably win) a referendum early in the next parliament had by the end of 2000 a decidedly more jaundiced view. A senior German minister was heard to remark that he expected Hungary to be in the euro-zone before Britain. Among the staunch pro-Europeans in the Cabinet, there is a fear he was not that far from the truth.

The potential implications for Blair's European policy, and for relationships within the Cabinet, are immense. Thus far Britain's detachment from the euro has cost it little in terms of political influence. Blair has been given the benefit of the doubt. And the euro's troubles on foreign exchange markets have slowed progress within the euro-zone towards the creation of a political architecture for the single currency. But a strategy which had as its stated intent to 'prepare and decide' instead now risks foreclosing the option of joining. Sensitive to the government's own equivocation and influenced by the relentlessly hostile stance of William Hague's Conservatives and their supporters in the media, public opinion has become more rather than less antipathetic to the replacement of sterling with the euro. About 70 per cent now say they are opposed to entry. In some respects that can be seen as a notable success for the Eurosceptic press. Millions of trees have been felled in the cause of the campaign against the euro by the *Sun*, the *Daily Mail* and the *Telegraph*. But the government must take responsibility for allowing the newspapers to step into a vacuum. The framework established in 1997 and defended ever since by Gordon Brown is essentially passive and defensive. By stipulating that Britain will join 'if' rather than 'when' the economic conditions are met, the government has cast itself almost as a bystander. If by happy chance the British and continental European economies converge, it will join; if not, then it won't. This is not what one might call leadership. It has also allowed the opponents of EMU free rein in the political arena. Blair might well say that the political case for participation is compelling. But that case has to be made – as the Danish government discovered to its cost in the autumn of 2000 when its people voted against joining.

Several of Blair's ministers have recognised the inherent weakness of this position. Peter Mandelson and Robin Cook in particular have sought many times to persuade Blair to emphasise the positive in the 1997 policy. [...] In January 2000 Blair personally quizzed the Chancellor about whether he was seeking fatally to undermine the commitment to eventual membership. Brown assured him that was not the case, but the doubts have lingered. [...]

Whatever Brown's reasons, Blair has been unwilling to over-rule the Chancellor – and to take on the Eurosceptic press. It is striking that of more than half a dozen serious speeches on Britain's place in Europe, only one has been delivered in Britain. Blair has reserved his most interesting thoughts for Aachen, Ghent and, most recently, Warsaw. There have been moments – in his statement on the euro in the House of Commons in February 1999, and at the launch of the Britain in Europe campaign in the autumn of that year – when we have caught a glimpse of the strength of his pro-European conviction. But these have been moments, short interludes in a long story of timidity in the face of public opinion. Europe, or more accurately the euro, the siren voices tell him, could cost him that second election victory. So he goes quiet. This in turn tells us something interesting about the character of the Prime Minister. Popular myth casts him in the role of the command-and-control leader. The reality is that he has never quite understood how powerful he is. He has hoarded that huge parliamentary majority rather than invested it. Blair remains convinced that Britain can and should join the single currency during his second term. It is pivotal to that ambition to end once and for all the ambivalence about Britain's European destiny. In Germany and France, Italy or Spain, Europe is an extension of the national interest. In Britain, it is perceived still as a threat to nationhood. This public scepticism, Blair will tell you, is wide but shallow. The inevitable recovery in the euro's value against the dollar will change perceptions. So too will the introduction of notes and coins. A second Labour election will transform the mood. The battle to persuade the British people that Europe is not some great conspiracy can be won. That is what he says. I think he believes it. Blair has proved himself a pragmatic European, something confirmed again in his approach to the treaty changes before last month's Nice summit. His own suggestions for the future shape of an enlarged Union, with perhaps a second chamber for the European Parliament drawn from national assemblies and a clearer framework for the division of powers between nations and the Union, speak to the same self-interested realism. But in regard to the euro there has been too much wishful thinking, too much timidity. Maybe Blair is right when he says the mood will change after the next election. One thing, though, is certain. This government cannot much longer make Britain's case in Europe unless it can make Europe's – and the euro's – case in Britain.

44

Britain in the World: Speech to The Royal Institute of International Affairs, Chatham House, January 2000

Robin Cook

[…]

It is a curiosity of semantics that the word 'internationalism' produces a favourable reaction, except on the wilder shores of reactionary isolationism. But the word 'globalisation' generally provokes a wary, if not hostile, reaction. If you asked me whether I am in favour of globalisation, I would give broadly the same answer as Tom Friedman. My attitude to globalisation is much the same as my attitude to the dawn. On balance, I think it is a good thing that the sun rises every day. But I also know there is nothing I can do to stop it even if I wanted to. Similarly, the only rational response to globalisation is to pursue strategies that maximise benefits and minimise damage.

What then is the foreign policy that helps deliver the benefits of globalisation and deflect its damage to Britain? The purpose of our foreign policy is to pursue our national interests. In broad terms, those national interests are the four objectives I set out in the Mission Statement for the Foreign Office in this Parliament:

- promoting prosperity through trade and the British economy;
- ensuring the security of the United Kingdom;
- enhancing the quality of life of people through global diplomacy on environment, the drugs trade and cross-border crime; and
- building respect for our values by supporting human rights and freedom.

How the Foreign Office promotes those national interests requires us to understand the modern world, and produce a strategy that relates to the world as it will be in this new century, not as it was in the last.

I propose four guiding principles that can help us shape a foreign policy for the Internationalist century:

- globalisation requires more bridges and fewer barriers;

- the global interest is becoming the national interest;
- the global community needs universal values; and
- the stronger Britain's standing in our own continent, the greater the leverage we will have in the other six.

[...]

Global Interest and National Interest

[...]

The labels of unilateralist and multilateralist have become inverted. It is the parties of the Right, still clinging hopelessly and touchingly to an outdated model of the nation state in isolation, who are the modern unilateralists. It is the parties of the Left of Centre, with their preference for collective solutions, who are better fitted to understand and operate in the modern multilateralist world.

Britain has more to gain than any other single state from an orderly international framework for the global economy. We depend for our living on trade. We export more per head than either the US or Japan. In absolute terms, our trade with the wider world is twice as great as at the zenith of Empire. We have a larger portfolio of overseas investment than any other European nation. We have more to lose from instability in the international markets.

It is fortunate therefore that Britain also has a broader representation than any other state on the multilateral bodies that will help shape the global economy. We are the only state which is a member of the G8, the EU, NATO, and the Commonwealth, and is a permanent member of the Security Council. Britain has a unique opportunity to pursue the national interest through the global interest.

[...]

The Cold War fostered client states whose repressive behaviour was often condoned in return for their loyalty to one or other camp. This was a particular paradox for the West. All too often it found itself in the pursuit of a proclaimed crusade for freedom shoring up regimes for whom freedom was not on the agenda.

By contrast, the age of globalisation is creating more progressive pressures. Regimes which govern their citizens by fear and repression cannot expect the same people to display the creativity and innovation in the workplace which are essential for a knowledge-based economy. Respect for human rights is not a luxury of growth, but the condition of that growth. [...]

We support human rights and democracy for other people because these are values we demand for ourselves. That is why the [...] theme of our foreign policy for the modern age is Diplomacy for Democracy.

[...]

I flatly reject the cynical view that, because we cannot make the world perfect, we should give up on trying to make it better. The obligation on us is not to put everything right, but to do what we can to make a difference. We will therefore take every realistic, responsible step to pursue Diplomacy for Democracy.

[...]

Intervention

The biggest unresolved question in upholding universal values is when is it right for the international community to intervene and who decides that it is right? The United Nations Charter declares that 'armed force shall not be used, save in the common interest'. But what is the common interest, and who shall define it? We need to establish new rules of the road.

The UK has submitted to the UN Secretary-General in response to those questions a set of ideas to help the international community decide when it is right to act.

- first, any intervention is by definition a failure of prevention. Force should always be the last resort;
- second, the immediate responsibility for halting violence rests with the state in which it occurs;
- but, third, when faced with an overwhelming humanitarian catastrophe and a government that has demonstrated itself unwilling or unable to halt or prevent it, the international community should act;
- and finally, any use of force in this context should be collective, proportionate, likely to achieve its objective, and carried out in accordance with international law. [...]

Stronger in Europe, Stronger in the World

Critical Engagement, enlightened self-interest and Diplomacy for Democracy provide a foreign policy through which we can best pursue Britain's national interests. Those national interests girdle the globe. The diplomatic strategy I have outlined is pursued in every continent. But the stronger Britain's standing in our own continent of Europe, the greater the leverage we will have in the other six. This is such a self-evident proposition that it is surprising it needs to be stated. Yet there are a number of people who seem to believe that the UK can project a foreign policy that goes all the way round the world without passing through Europe.

Any sane foreign policy must start by accepting the facts of geography. Europe is where we belong. We cannot opt by political levitation to belong to another continent. As someone once famously said, there is no alternative. As one of her Foreign Secretaries, Lord Carrington, wrote in his memoirs, 'Britain's destiny is Europe'.
[...]
The European Union is one of the most successful models yet devised for coping with an age in which nations are more interdependent than they are independent. It has reinforced mutual respect for the borders between nations. But at the same time, it has dismantled borders as barriers between people and between businesses. Only those who have a psychological need for the comfort blanket of protection from the outside world should fear the result as a threat.
[...]
None of this means the end of the nation state. On the contrary, the age of globalisation has been paralleled by strong assertions of national identity and

culture. A healthy democracy needs the social cohesion provided by national identity if its minority are to accept those elected by the majority as their legitimate representatives. That is why Gerhard Schroeder rightly told his party congress last month that the nation state will be the centre of people's hopes and needs. And why Jacques Chirac has said Europe's future is not a United States of Europe but a United Europe of States.

Conclusion

Last year, I heard Kofi Annan making a moving speech in which he told the UN General Assembly that:

> As the world has changed in profound ways since the end of the Cold War, I believe our conceptions of national interest have failed to follow suit. [We need] a new, more broadly defined definition of national interest. . . . A global era requires global engagement. Indeed, in a growing number of challenges facing humanity, the collective interest is the national interest.

I believe Kofi is right. The new forces of globalisation offer immense prospects for progress. Those prospects will be fulfilled only if we take every opportunity to pursue our national interest through a foreign policy that also meets the international interest.

45

The Doctrine of the International Community, April 1999

Tony Blair

[...]
We live in a world where isolationism has ceased to have a reason to exist. By necessity we have to co-operate with each other across nations. Many of our domestic problems are caused on the other side of the world. Financial instability in Asia destroys jobs in Chicago and in my own constituency in County Durham. Poverty in the Caribbean means more drugs on the streets in Washington and London. Conflict in the Balkans causes more refugees in Germany and here in the US. These problems can only be addressed by international co-operation. We are all internationalists now, whether we like it or not. We cannot refuse to participate in global markets if we want to prosper. We cannot ignore new political ideas in other countries if we want to innovate. We cannot turn our backs on conflicts and the violation of human rights within other countries if we want still to be secure.

[...] [W]e are now in a new world. We need new rules for international co-operation and new ways of organising our international institutions. After World War II, we developed a series of international institutions to cope with the strains of rebuilding a devastated world: Bretton Woods, the United Nations, NATO, the EU. Even then, it was clear that the world was becoming increasingly interdependent. The doctrine of isolationism had been a casualty of a world war, where the United States and others finally realised standing aside was not an option.

Today the impulse towards interdependence is immeasurably greater. We are witnessing the beginnings of a new doctrine of international community. By this I mean the explicit recognition that today more than ever before, we are mutually dependent, that national interest is to a significant extent governed by international collaboration and that we need a clear and coherent debate as to the direction this doctrine takes us in each field of international endeavour. Just as within domestic politics, the notion of community – the belief that partnership and co-operation are essential to advance self-interest – is coming into its own; so it needs to find its international echo. Global financial markets, the global environment, global security and disarmament issues: none of these can be solved without intense international co operation.

As yet, however, our approach tends towards being ad hoc. There is a global financial crisis: we react, it fades, our reaction becomes less urgent. Kyoto can stimulate our conscience about environmental degradation but we need constant reminders to refocus on it. We are continually fending off the danger of letting wherever CNN roves be the cattle prod to take a global conflict seriously. We need to focus in a serious and sustained way on the principles of the doctrine of international community and on the institutions that deliver them. This means:

- In global finance, a thorough, far-reaching overhaul and reform of the system of international financial regulation. We should begin it at the G7 at Cologne.
- A new push on free trade in the WTO with the new round beginning in Seattle this autumn.
- A reconsideration of the role, workings and decision-making process of the UN, and in particular the UN Security Council.
- For NATO, once Kosovo is successfully concluded, a critical examination of the lessons to be learnt, and the changes we need to make in organisation and structure.
- In respect of Kyoto and the environment, far closer working between the main industrial nations and the developing world as to how the Kyoto targets can be met and the practical measures necessary to slow and stop global warming, and
- A serious examination of the issue of third world debt, again beginning at Cologne.

In addition, the EU and US should prepare to make real step-change in working more closely together. [...]

Globalisation

Globalisation is most obvious in the economic sphere. We live in a completely new world. Every day about one trillion dollars moves across the foreign exchanges, most of it in London. [...]

Any Government that thinks it can go it alone is wrong. If the markets don't like your policies they will punish you. The same is true of trade. Protectionism is the swiftest road to poverty. Only by competing internationally can our companies and our economics grow and succeed. But it has to be an international system based on rules. That means accepting the judgements of international organisations even when you do not like them. And it means using the new trade round to be launched at Seattle to extend free trade.

The international financial system is not working as it should. The Asian financial crisis of last year, and the knock-on impact on Brazil, demonstrate that. The fact is that the Bretton Woods machinery was set up for the post-war world. The world has moved on. And we need to modernise the international financial architecture to make it appropriate for the new world. The lesson of the Asian crisis is above all that it is better to invest in countries where you have openness, independent central banks, properly functioning financial systems and independent courts, where you do not have to bribe or rely on favours from those in power.

We have therefore proposed that we should make greater transparency the keystone of reform. Transparency about individual countries' economic policies through adherence to new codes of conduct on monetary and fiscal policy; about individual companies' financial positions through new internationally agreed accounting standards and a new code of corporate governance; and greater openness too about IMF and World Bank discussions and policies.

We also need improved financial supervision both in individual countries through stronger and more effective peer group reviews, and internationally through the foundation of a new Financial Stability Forum. [...]

[...]

International Security

The principles of international community apply also to international security. We now have a decade of experience since the end of the Cold War. It has certainly been a less easy time than many hoped in the euphoria that followed the collapse of the Berlin Wall. Our armed forces have been busier than ever – delivering humanitarian aid, deterring attacks on defenceless people, backing up UN resolutions and occasionally engaging in major wars as we did in the Gulf in 1991 and [...] in the Balkans. Have the difficulties of the past decade simply been the aftershocks of the end of the Cold War? Will things soon settle down, or does it represent a pattern that will end into the future?

Many of our problems have been caused by two dangerous and ruthless men – Saddam Hussein and Slobodan Milosevic. Both have been prepared to wage vicious campaigns against sections of their own community. As a result of these destructive policies both have brought calamity on their own peoples. Instead of enjoying its oil wealth Iraq has been reduced to poverty, with political life stultified through fear. Milosevic took over a substantial, ethnically diverse state, well placed to take advantage of new economic opportunities. His drive for ethnic concentration has left him with something much smaller, a ruined economy and soon a totally ruined military machine.

One of the reasons why it is now so important to win the conflict is to ensure that others do not make the same mistake in the future. That in itself will be a major step to ensuring that the next decade and the next century will not be as difficult as the past. [...]

At the end of this century the US has emerged as by far the strongest state. It has no dreams of world conquest and is not seeking colonies. If anything Americans are too ready to see no need to get involved in affairs of the rest of the world. America's allies are always both relieved and gratified by its continuing readiness to shoulder burdens and responsibilities that come with its sole superpower status. We understand that this is something that we have no right to take for granted, and must match with our own efforts. That is the basis for the recent initiative I took with President Chirac of France to improve Europe's own defence capabilities.

As we address these problems [...] we may be tempted to think back to the clarity and simplicity of the Cold War. But now we have to establish a new framework. No longer is our existence as states under threat. Now our actions are guided by a more subtle blend of mutual self-interest and moral purpose in defending the values we cherish. In the end values and interests merge. If we can establish and spread the values of liberty, the rule of law, human rights and an open society then that is in our national interests too. The spread of our values makes us safer. [...]

The most pressing foreign policy problem we face is to identify the circumstances in which we should get actively involved in other people's conflicts. Non-interference has long been considered an important principle of international order. And it is not one we would want to jettison too readily. One state should not feel it has the right to change the political system of another or foment subversion or seize pieces of territory to which it feels it should have some claim. But the principle of non-interference must be qualified in important respects. Acts of genocide can never be a purely internal matter. When oppression produces massive flows of refugees which unsettle neighbouring countries, then they can properly be described as 'threats to international peace and security'. When regimes are based on minority rule they lose legitimacy – look at South Africa.

Looking around the world there are many regimes that are undemocratic and engaged in barbarous acts. If we wanted to right every wrong that we see in the modern world then we would do little else than intervene in the affairs of other countries. We would not be able to cope. So how do we decide when and whether to intervene? I think we need to bear in mind five major considerations.

First, are we sure of our case? War is an imperfect instrument for righting humanitarian distress, but armed force is sometimes the only means of dealing with dictators. Second, have we exhausted all diplomatic options? We should always give peace every chance [....] Third, on the basis of a practical assessment of the situation, are there military operations we can sensibly and prudently undertake? Fourth, are we prepared for the long term? In [the] past we talked too much of exit strategies. But having made a commitment we cannot simply walk away once the fight is over; better to stay with moderate numbers of troops than return for repeat performances with large numbers. And finally, do we have national interests involved? [...] I am not suggesting that these are absolute tests. But they are the kind of issues we need to think about in deciding in the future when and whether we will intervene.

Any new rules, however, will only work if we have reformed international institutions with which to apply them. If we want a world ruled by law and by international co-operation then we have to support the UN as its central pillar. But we need to find a new way to make the UN and its Security Council work if we are not to return to the deadlock that undermined the effectiveness of the Security Council during the Cold War. This should be a task for members of the Permanent Five to consider once the Kosovo conflict is complete.
[...]

I say to you: never fall again for the doctrine of isolationism. The world cannot afford it. Stay a country, outward-looking, with the vision and imagination that is your nature. And realise that in Britain you have a friend and an ally that will stand with you, work with you, fashion with you the design of a future built on peace and prosperity for all, which is the only dream that makes humanity worth preserving.

Part VI

A New Whitehall Style?
New Labour in
Government

While explained by wider phenomena, principally the political, electoral and socio-economic environment within which the Labour Party found itself in the 1980s and 1990s, the making of New Labour has owed much to a handful of 'politically motivated men'. Tony Blair, Gordon Brown, Peter Mandelson and Alastair Campbell comprised the quartet at the very heart of New Labour. As Andrew Rawnsley suggests, 'They are, in essence, New Labour.' In government, Blair and Brown, Prime Minister and Chancellor of the Exchequer, dominate, Blair being perhaps the most dominant prime minister since 1945 (so far), and Brown certainly the most powerful Chancellor of the Exchequer, ever waiting in the wings as the putative prime minister should Blair ever stumble.

The Blair–Brown duumvirate was first forged during Labour's opposition years, particularly in 1994 when Blair, not Brown, became the modernizing candidate to succeed the late John Smith. It has been the key government relationship, if at times an uneasy and wary one. Alastair Campbell, first Blair's Press Secretary and now his Director of Strategy and Communication, became Labour's spin-doctor-in-chief. The closest adviser to the Prime Minister, perhaps the second most powerful man in Downing Street, he has found himself described as the real 'Deputy Prime Minister'. Often a lightning rod of anti-Blair comment, Campbell has wielded considerable power across government, advising on policy making, not merely on its presentation. Peter Mandelson, twice obliged to resign from the Cabinet, is no longer at the centre of the New Labour cadre, but still retains some shadowy role as a Prime Ministerial adviser.

After eighteen years out of office, Labour found it had a great deal of catching up to do in 1997. Tony Blair was the first Prime Minister since Ramsay MacDonald to enter office with no prior ministerial experience. Not one member of Labour's Shadow Cabinet had been in the Cabinet before, and only a handful had ever been in government. Despite this noticeable lack of experience, however, the incoming Labour government was fully prepared. Although ministers, none more so than the

Prime Minister, had the steepest of learning curves to climb, the leadership of the government knew just how it wanted to govern.

Many commentators suggest that its plan, the style of government to be pursued, reflected a desire to organize government from the prime ministerial centre. It was based upon Blair's centralized leadership of the party in opposition when shadow spokespersons were required to toe the party line, and when discipline was seen as the key to electoral victory. This was the model for Blair's premiership. As Dennis Kavanagh and Anthony Seldon rightly suggest, 'Blair's impatience with the...Shadow Cabinet meant he relied heavily on his personal aides and some supportive shadow ministers....They knew his mind and shared his ideas of what needed to be done. Those who were not "on message" were ruthlessly sidelined.' In opposition and now in government, Blair cultivated a presidential image, aspiring to what Peter Hennessy terms a 'command premiership', based on what was described as a 'change from a feudal system of barons to a more Napoleonic system'. He was determined from the first to run the government from the centre, confident that 'there's only one thing the public dislikes more than a leader in control of his party, and that's a leader not in control of his party' (Tony Blair, *Guardian*, 28 February 2000). Although necessarily sharing power with Gordon Brown, particularly in economic and social policy, and working with other ministers as and when necessary, Blair has sought to lead his government, firmly and always from the front.

Over time, reform of the Whitehall centre has produced considerable changes within the UK executive, but the pace of such changes has quickened under Tony Blair. In particular, the policy reach of Downing Street has been considerably extended through a revamped Cabinet Office. The role of the Treasury has also been expanded beyond public expenditure control, and now embraces an active part in policy making in certain areas (particularly in welfare to work, education and training, and public–private partnerships in health and transport). This trend means that the Whitehall centre – defined by Blair as being his 'own office, the Cabinet Office and the Treasury' – now plays the most significant role in the formation of the government's agenda, particularly in regard to forward planning, strategic thinking and green-lighting department initiatives. As with US Cabinet members, British Cabinet ministers are expected to stick to their Cabinet briefs, and are given less and less opportunity to influence policy beyond their department. Parliament in turn is obliged to be reactive, not proactive, although, as Philip Cowley reminds us, Labour MPs have been for the most part wholly supportive, if at times privately critical, of the government's agenda.

The demands of government invariably require political parties to increasingly revolve around the needs and incentives of the party in public office. Blair's style of government has prompted numerous criticisms, among them the charge of 'presidentialization', an issue to which Michael Foley has turned his hand. Alongside descriptions of excessive prime ministerial power have gone charges of 'control freakery', all firmly bound up in the 'politics of spin' and 'news management', at which the New Labour government has sought to excel. Given the focus of the news media on personalities atop political hierarchies, New Labour constantly intervenes in the twenty-four-hour news cycle, attempting to fashion the news agenda in a direction which favours the government and thereby strengthens it. The New Labour 'product', having been packaged, has to be 'sold', and rapidly defended against all criticism.

As Nicholas Jones, Bob Franklin, Ivor Gaber and Andrew Chadwick suggest, the themes of news promotion and management have lain at the very heart of New Labour in government, dominating its media operations. Because political news agendas are affected by the varied interaction of news media and political parties, Labour attempts on a daily basis to shape the opinion of the news media, and so manage (if not manipulate) the information and opinion the public eventually receive. In so doing, New Labour strategists continually try to reinforce the role of the Prime Minister and other ministers, thereby boosting its leadership by its promotion of the Government and the party.

46

Servants of the People: The Inside Story of New Labour

Andrew Rawnsley

New Labour was the product of traumatic and multiple failures. Tony Blair's rhetoric might be relentlessly futuristic, but he was fixated by the past. This was not surprising. Before 1 May 1997, Labour had not won an election in more than twenty-two years and had not secured a proper parliamentary majority in over three decades. The pact between a success-starved party and the power-hungry group who seized the commanding heights was that the modernisers would deliver office in exchange for taking control. In an especially hubristic surge, Blair described New Labour as 'the political arm of the British people'. Yet the progenitors of this all-embracing self-styled People's Party were tiny in number. Less a mass movement, more a junta who had executed a coup, they were what Harold Wilson once called, in a different context, a 'tightly knit group of politically motivated men'.

The founding axis of New Labour was Tony Blair, whose Thatcherite father would have become a Tory MP had he not suffered a stroke, and Gordon Brown, the son of a socialist Church of Scotland rector. This twinning of opposites was one of the most talented and tortuous couplings that there has ever been in high British politics.

By the standards of politicians, Blair came to the profession exceptionally late. As a schoolboy, he was a conservative rebel, often stretching the rules, rarely breaking them. Contemporaries recalled a charismatic teenager with a particular talent for acting who could nearly always talk his way out of trouble. At university, he read law but wished it had been history, toyed with becoming a priest, and played at being a rock star. Only after he met a Labour activist called Cherie Booth did his inchoate yearnings to achieve something of substance combine with what one biographer calls his 'appetite for applause' to crystallise into political ambition.

Where Blair was the slow convert, Brown was baptised into the faith. His political memory stretched back to the age of eight when his father let him stay up until one thirty in the morning to hear the results of the 1959 election that Labour lost. Brown was a published political author and an elected student rector when Blair was still fantasising about being Mick Jagger.

When these two bright tyros arrived in parliament together in 1983, their potential was soon spotted as exceptional by the third man, Peter Mandelson. A former

Young Communist, trade union researcher and TV producer, Neil Kinnock's director of communications pushed both of them forward. While Mandelson admired Blair, he idolised Brown. Mandelson so pined during separations that he could not bear being on holiday for much more than a day before he started ringing up Brown.

The death of John Smith was the birth of New Labour. The crown of leadership that Brown always assumed would belong to him was taken by the younger Blair. Their relationship survived, but it was ever after strung with tensions which would play out creatively and destructively in government.

The protégé–patron relationship between Blair and Mandelson had been reversed. The bond between Mandelson and Brown turned to hate. Though the truth was not this simple, Brown could never forgive what he saw as Mandelson's vile treachery during the leadership contest when he switched his affections to Blair. Through the election that they were jointly managing and into government, the two men barely exchanged a civil sentence with each other. To further complicate these emotionally racked relationships, though Blair was their chief, he still felt, in crucial respects, subordinate to the other two men, especially Brown.

The triangle became more like a rhomboid with the steady rise in influence of Alastair Campbell. He was already connected with the modernisers before he left his career as a tabloid Labour propagandist to become Blair's press secretary. No group of political animals knew in more intimate detail each other's strengths and vulnerabilities. Campbell was one of the first people to whom Mandelson turned when his father died; when Campbell flirted with death during the alcohol-induced nervous collapse which turned him teetotal, Mandelson was one of the first to come to his side.

To seize control of a party, and then take power over the country, was an immense bonding experience. The ties that both bound and strained this complex cat's cradle of relationships have been decisive in the development of the government. Other characters played large parts in the success of New Labour, and have important roles in this narrative. But it is this quartet who achieved the sensational election victory just as they became the masterminds of the campaign to retain power. They are, in essence, New Labour.

47

The British Presidency: Tony Blair and the Politics of Public Leadership

Michael Foley

Political commentators are rarely lost for words but they can struggle with superlatives. From the inception of Tony Blair's leadership of the Labour party, and especially his accession to the premiership, it quickly became commonplace for him to be described as a pre-eminent and dominant leader. His position was seen to be so unassailable that the customary language of British politics had to be reformulated to accommodate the phenomenon. It was the sheer scale and penetration of Blair's personal authority that confounded convention and defied traditional analysis. Just as Blair appeared to surpass his predecessors, so he also seemed to supersede the normal methods of characterising party leaders and prime ministers. References to his extraordinary command of the Labour party became legion soon after he secured the leadership in 1994. Blair's commitment to modernising the party by democratising the organisation, by distancing himself from the trade unions and by abandoning Clause Four in favour of a more centrist agenda, generated an electoral strategy that was dependent upon the leadership for its identity and direction. The emphasis upon organisation, discipline and cohesion from the top of a party that had not previously been noted for its ability to control division and dissidence, provoked widespread recognition at Blair's personal achievement in transforming Labour into a formidable electoral machine.
[...]

At the outset of the incoming Labour government, great emphasis was laid upon the presentation and co-ordination of policy, on the continued cultivation of the press and in particular the tabloids, and on the need to maintain party discipline and ministerial coherence in the continued campaign of public outreach. The introduction of Millbank's methods, personnel and ethos into Whitehall had many implications, not least for the integrity of cabinet decision making and for the clarity of government policy. [...] The problems associated with spin doctors, unauthorised briefings and strategic leaks were in many respects attributable to the priority given media relations at the centre. The Blair team operated openly on the premise that the

leadership's active engagement and symbolic identification with the public needed to be sustained and developed for the benefit of the government and the party.
[...]

[...] Campbell rapidly acquired the reputation of being the prime minister's 'enforcer'. His status as 'the most powerful unelected politician at the very heart of the British Government'[1] was a reflection of the importance of news management in the Blair administration. Campbell's position was an expression of both his skills and the value attached to them by New Labour, which was an organisation whose origins had lain in public projection and presentation. After a year in government, Campbell's position was so secure that its potential for controversy had been neutralised. As Kevin Toolis noted, his power base was literally that of Tony Blair:

> Blair never moves from Downing Street without Campbell. He never appears on a platform without Campbell nearby. Never makes a speech that Campbell has not read or rewritten. Never walks into an important room without Campbell close behind. Never takes a decision that Campbell has not been consulted on. Never holds a significant meeting that Campbell does not attend or at least know about. Other Cabinet ministers slavishly repeat Campbell's line on the latest twist of Government policy in their broadcast interviews. Not vice versa.[2]

Such a power base was sufficient to quell any political or constitutional objections to the position of Alastair Campbell in the administration. As a result, he quickly became a far more formidable figure than Bernard Ingham had been in Margaret Thatcher's governments. Unlike Ingham, Campbell sat in cabinet meetings, attended party conferences, and was visibly engaged in campaign strategy and electioneering.

For a party that had become leadership centred in its rise to power, Campbell's emancipation from the restraints of previous press secretaries was exemplified by the priority given by the government to keeping as much of the media as possible 'on side'. It also reflected the importance of retaining the government's close identity with the figure and personality of Tony Blair. It was Campbell's role to maintain the status of the leader's brand name upon the government and, by extension, the reputation of the government in the public domain. He was instrumental in ensuring that selected elements of government activity would be seen to be derivative of Blair's leadership.
[...]

Leadership Stretch in Britain

The propulsion of leaders into public arenas and the drive to commit party agendas and programmes to a process of public outreach through the agency of leadership projection has led party leaders to become increasingly differentiated from their colleagues. Leaders are no longer merely party spokespeople, but the ostentatious flagships of their respective fleets. They have no choice. They are simply part of a self-generating and self-intensifying process that compels party leaders to achieve high levels of public attention and recognition by moulding themselves successfully to the channels of political communication that can best provide it. Leaders struggle with one another on a continued basis to be the most effective expression of popular convictions and anxieties. What were once media opportunities to reach a wider audience have now been turned into overriding media obligations to publicise political positions through the effective projection of party leaders as national figures.

[...] It is the electronic media, and particularly television, which lie at the centre of a synergy between the media, the party leaderships and electoral motivations. For example, much of the recent exposure and public attention given to leaders has come as a result of an underlying dynamic between the mass media and party politics. In short, television's inclination to personalise the treatment and presentation of politics has been matched by the willingness of parties to provide their leaders with the prominence and licence to fit the party product to its optimal form of communication. Just as 'the dominance of television helps to presidentialize the message of the parties'[3] so the messengers themselves have become increasingly presidentialised. In turn, in doing so, leaders acquire further public prominence which enhances their television news value to an even greater extent than before. As a result of this process, a leader can improve the security of his or her position in the party, and thereupon claim further executive discretion to exploit the visibility of that position for the party's interests and objectives.

[...]

[...] Blair's iron grip upon his party, combined with his strategic awareness, clear convictions and organised discipline, generated the kind of respect and fear among colleagues and adversaries that Margaret Thatcher had once achieved. In opposition and in government, Blair has had no inhibitions over fostering a cult of personality. [...] The 1997 general election represented the culmination of a three year process to mould the Labour party around the figure and promise of a single individual. 'I listen carefully to colleagues', Blair said, 'but in the end it's like running a business. You can't do it by committee ... and I'm aware of this. If you have made this extraordinary claim that you can lead the country ... if you have put yourself very much up front, as I have, you take the downside. The buck stops with me and that's that.'[4] Blair had long since acknowledged the loneliness of his leadership position, but he had always accepted that it was an integral component of a personal campaign. It was, in essence, 'part of the deal'.[5]

[...] [T]he definition of the New Labour project, the continued identity of the administration, the meaning of the 'third way', and the drive and energy of the government have all been palpably dependent upon the intensive presentation of Blair's persona. Just as the processes of leadership stretch and personalised power have been both actively and unwittingly advanced by the Blair leadership, so the actions of the Labour government have increasingly been refracted through the lens of the prime minister. [...]

This personalising process on the part of Tony Blair has been a key component in the promotion of issues and policies by Number 10. This prime ministerial imprimatur in the presentation of news is typified by the following sample of representative headlines:

Blair apologises to Ireland for potato famine
  Daily Telegraph, 2 June 1997
Blair vows to tackle tearaways
  Daily Telegraph, 14 June 1997

Blair pledge to low paid
    The Guardian, 15 November 1997
Blair acts on 'cronyism culture'
    The Guardian, 13 July 1998
Blair to hire 20,000 for millennium bug army
    The Independent, 30 August 1998
Blair invents secular vicars to save family
    Sunday Times, 27 September 1998
Blair offers advice to parents
    The Guardian, 20 November 1998
Blair sharpens his axe to end 'feudal domination' of Lords
    The Independent, 25 November 1998
Blair reasserts his will to build Lib Dem links
    Financial Times, 11 January 1999
Blair bid to break Ulster peace deadlock
    The Observer, 7 February 1999
Blair promises to end child poverty within 20 years
    The Times, 19 March 1999
Blair pledge to refugees
    The Guardian, 4 May 1999
Blair tells Serbians to overthrow Milosevic's 'corrupt dictatorship'
    The Independent, 5 May 1999
Blair battles to cast Britain in role of world's conscience
    Financial Times, 28 May 1999
Blair puts hunt ban beyond doubt
    The Times, 9 July 1999
Blair tells TUC: I am in charge
    The Times, 15 September 1999
Blair promises to speed 'top to bottom' modernisation of Britain
    The Independent, 28 September 1999
Blair acts after unit's plans are ignored by Whitehall
    The Times, 15 October 1999
Teacher 'excuse culture' attacked by Blair
    The Times, 21 October 1999
Blair backs 30,000 strong Euro army
    Sunday Times, 14 November 1999
Blair's war on drivers
    The Express, 18 November 1999
Blair halts plans for 1.1 m homes in the South
    Daily Mail, 30 November 1999

The personal convictions and experiences of the premier have often been flagged in the launch of policy initiatives and reviews. It has been a feature of the Blair premiership that so many of these initiatives have borne the imprint of the prime minister's personal interest in a new scheme or course of action. Sometimes this has taken the form of the prime minister actively using his position to publicise an issue as a matter of personal concern (e.g. Northern Ireland, education, welfare reform, the NHS and the future of the European Union). [...]

Tony Blair and the British Presidential Dimension

Tony Blair's premiership has disrupted the superstructure of British government. His radicalism has extended beyond the substance of policy to the methods of decision making and administration. In a period when constitutional change has come to represent the defining property of the New Labour government, the status and authority of the prime minister's own position has become the subject of intense speculation. [...] The term 'presidential' conjures up a profusion of associations relating to executive centralisation and personal power. As such, the presidential analogy has an immediate resonance in circumstances of such rapid fluidity. In the case of the Blair premiership, the usage of the presidential frame of reference seems particularly appropriate in reaching an understanding of developments that can be construed as departures from the conventional dynamics and traditional relationships at the heart of British government.

Blair and Labour

The Blair leadership transformed the identity of the party away from its old attachments to trade unionism, public ownership, high taxation and large-scale redistribution towards a centre-left organisation that was attentive to the demands and opportunities of the global market and to the needs of business innovation and investment. Blair's project and Blair's vision came to define the Labour party's brand image in an electoral context that was increasingly interpreted as a marketing exercise in product promotion. Innumerable American parallels were drawn, not just between the policy content of New Labour and the New Democrats, but also between the techniques of presidential campaigning and Blair's drive for the premiership. The strategy of New Labour had been to create a Blair coalition capable of maintaining its core supporters but with the capacity to appeal to traditionally non-Labour voters, especially in 'middle England'. In an increasingly dealigned electorate, depending upon class-based voting, ideological polarities and the social solidarity of the Labour heartlands was no longer a feasible proposition. Through opinion polling, focus groups, think-tank investigations and market research, the Labour party had to transform its entire image in order to break the Conservative hegemony and to reach out for the independents, the switchers, the floaters and the new voters.[6] Blair was the agent of expression and the chief beneficiary of Labour's shift into an openly coalitional party. In place of ideological fervour was an emphasis upon pragmatism. Instead of partisan conflict, there was a cross-party appeal for consensus and inclusive pluralism. References to 'our people' by past Labour leaders were replaced by invocations of 'the people'. This carried the clear implication that representation entailed a collective trust to protect the public interest at the expense of sectional preferences.

Loosening the texture of the party brought with it a proportionate need to tighten the leadership. This entailed changing the agenda of party management. Under normal circumstances, Labour's effectiveness as a party was conditional upon the creation and maintenance of an internal equilibrium between power bases at the highest reaches of the organisation. Under New Labour, party management was centred upon the mobilisation of the party's membership into a common cause to raise public confidence in Labour's potential as a party of government. Blair was determined to use his leadership to draw attention away from the party and to establish his own criteria for the public's evaluation of Labour. Blair was criticised for his iconoclasm, his presumption and his 'permanent revolution' of the party. Within a year of his election as leader, Blair and his advisors were denounced as 'Stalinist'. The Labour back-bencher, Richard Burden, typified the concern felt by many over the party's obsession with eliminating negative images of itself in the rush to appeal to mainstream opinion:

> Labour is drifting towards a US-style party – a ruthlessly effective electoral machine as the vehicle for those who want to go into politics rather than a radical party with a definable ideological base ... Americanisation has seen New Labour actually increasing its demands for internal discipline. Mechanisms for the party to communicate directly with its members may be more extensive than they have ever been. But such communication is essentially 'top down'. Power is increasingly centralised around the leader's office, with immense pressure on everyone else to fall in line.[7]

This type of criticism remained constant throughout Blair's period as leader of the opposition and it has been a marked feature of his premiership. In both cases, it has been prompted by a reaction to an alleged excess of power. It has not been a question of calling upon the party leader to exert leadership or of demanding new leadership. The complaint has been one of too much emphasis upon leadership and too much power lodged in the leadership. [...]

[...] Blair has continued to keep his distance from the party, to exert tighter management of its activities and to remind it of its exalted duty to the British public. His high visibility and continued popularity have reaffirmed the rationale of his authority. Just as the public and democratic manner of his election to party leader in 1994 served to inject his leadership with leverage greater than any other Labour leader, so the associations of his modernisation programme and style of leadership with the election triumph of 1997 have further enhanced his authority. And yet Blair's anxiety over Labour's capacity to lapse back into fissile dissidence has compelled him to continue making changes to the structure of the party in order to retain the leadership's leverage over it. The once formidable NEC has been stripped of many of its powers over the party. In August 1998, it was announced that the party conference would be reorganised to eliminate the recurrence of damaging disputes being aired on the conference floor. What had been conceived as the sovereign parliament of the Labour movement and the arena where the party would monitor and confront a Labour government was now re-engineered to provide a showcase for the Blair administration and a rallying point for the leadership. The prime minister was determined that the party conference should not have the status of an alternative government that had been achieved under previous Labour administrations. [...]

[...] Even after Labour's poor showing in the 1999 elections for the European parliament, which raised serious concerns over the loss of core support in the Labour heartlands, the prime minister rounded on those critics who speculated on the need to bring 'traditional values' back into the party:

> [W]hilst I am leader of my Party and Prime Minister of this country, I will never again have Britain forced to choose between a Labour Party that ignored the import-

ance of business and ambition, and a right-wing Conservative Party which ignored the need for justice and compassion. That is the New Labour message and it will remain 100% proof. We govern for all the people... [...] We were elected to serve the whole country, those who voted for us and those who didn't. That is what we will continue to do.[8]

[...]

[...] To the prime minister, 'governing as New Labour' meant continuing in government what the party had achieved in opposition – namely forming a cohesive support structure for the leadership team whose right to expect consent was based upon the outcomes of a party election and a general election. Andrew Rawnsley explained the logic: 'In the Blairite conception of parliamentary democracy, the role of New Labour MPs is to sustain the Government... New Labour did not get elected by licensing dissent, and it is not going to be re-elected by encouraging the habit now. That is an article of faith with the Prime Minister.'[9] Such an outlook was not born simply out of a political need to keep the prodigious ranks of New Labour MPs closed around the figure of the prime minister. It entailed a more fundamental expectation based upon legitimacy and obligation. Those closest to the prime minister operated on the belief that 'most of the New Labour horde occupying the government benches were not elected on their own wonderful merits, but because they swept to Parliament on Mr Blair's coat-tails'.[10] Even if this could not be shown to be precisely the case, Blair had been primarily responsible for the modernisation, message, campaign and face of the party in the election. In the eyes of his lieutenants and the Labour whips, this was tantamount to Blair having secured power on behalf of his party. In accordance with this concept of parliamentary democracy, MPs were obligated to the leadership and to its judgements and decisions.

NOTES

1   See Peter Oborne, *Alastair Campbell and the Art of Media Management* (London: Aurum, 1999).
2   Kevin Toolis, 'The Enforcer', *Guardian*, 4 April 1998.
3   David Butler and Dennis Kavanagh, *The British General Election of 1987* (Basingstoke: Macmillan, 1988), p. 249.
4   Quoted in Lesley White, 'New Man, Old Boy', *Sunday Times*, 20 April 1997.
5   Quoted in Andrew Marr, 'Two Years Hard Labour', *Independent*, 13 July 1996.
6   Dominic Wring, 'From Mass Propaganda to Political Marketing: The Transformation of Labour Party Election Campaigning', in Colin Rallings et al. (eds), *British Parties and Elections Yearbook 1995* (London: Frank Cass, 1996), pp. 105–24.
7   Richard Burden, 'Pause for Thought', *Guardian*, 11 August 1995.
8   Tony Blair, Speech to the CBI, 2 November 1999.
9   Andrew Rawnsley, 'Relax Prime Minister, it would be good for you and your government to let the page slaves go free', *Observer*, 7 June 1998.
10   Ibid.

48

Tony Blair as Prime Minister

Peter Hennessy

[...]
Tony Blair and his inner group of advisers seemed determined to operate inside
No. 10, once they got there, as they had within the Labour Party – driving policy
and presentation from the centre around a core of delivery musts, and brooking no
serious resistance either from ministerial colleagues or from cumbersome, traditional government mechanics. The one great exception to this was the Chancellor
of the Exchequer-in-waiting, Gordon Brown. For the deal at the heart of the Blair
style was that a command premier would operate alongside a command Chancellor
licensed to dominate across a wide range of economic and domestic policy. It
was plainly going to be a centre-driven administration with the 'centre', as later
defined publicly by Mr Blair, as 'my own office, the Cabinet Office and the Treasury'.[1]
[...]
    [...] Mr Blair's vanguard roared into No. 10 like a through train, greatly impress-
ing the waiting civil servants with their push-and-go and team-like qualities. Similarly, Gordon Brown's very personal coterie hit the ground running in policy terms in
the Treasury, too. [...]
    [...] Blair's inner corps, Jonathan Powell (chief of staff), Alastair Campbell (press
secretary) and David Miliband (acting, later confirmed, head of the Policy Unit),
'came in as a package', said one old No. 10 hand, who had never seen anything quite
like it. 'They had all worked so closely together in opposition on the policy and press
side, they just came in as they were. Within forty-eight hours it was all in place. Very
impressive.'[2] [...]
    Over in the Treasury, the reception of the Brown team (Ed Balls, economic
adviser; Ed Miliband, brother of David and personal adviser to Brown; Charlie
Whelan, press adviser) was warm enough on the afternoon of 2 May when 'officials
lined the staircase of the Treasury's monumental chambers...to cheer...the
new chancellor into office'.[3] But it soon cooled when it swiftly became apparent
that the Brown style would be to work as tightly as possible through his politically appointed temporary civil servants at the expense of the regular officials he
had inherited, with the Permanent Secretary, Sir Terry Burns, and the head of

Information, Jill Rutter, as particular losers. The career Treasury, as it might be called, felt very definitely 'sidelined in favour of the chancellor's personal appointees' in these early days.[4]

From the beginning it was plain that the Blair–Brown axis would dominate economic policy, that the full Cabinet would be nowhere and that its main economic committee (which Brown would lead, the first time a Prime Minister had vacated the chair since 1966) would be scarcely better placed. The decision-taking circle that mattered on economic strategy was described simply by the bilateral meetings between Blair and Brown. [...]

One of the most significant economic decisions of the Blair administration was also taken during the first week of its life – the shifting of responsibility for setting interest rates from what had effectively been a chancellorial/prime ministerial prerogative in consultation with senior figures from the Bank of England and the Treasury, to the Monetary Policy Committee of the Bank of England alone. Sir Alan Budd (who as the Chief Economic Adviser to the Treasury Brown inherited, spent the bulk of Labour's first weekend in office piecing together the mechanics and details of this transition with Terry Burns)[5] was right to stress the boldness of this move, the degree to which it took politics *out* of interest rate setting and put economics *in* as well as the 'wonderful moment of political drama' involved when Brown announced the decision to an unsuspecting world on 8 May 1997. Only two other Cabinet ministers were in the loop of prior knowledge on the shift to an independent Bank of England – the Deputy Prime Minister and Secretary of State for Environment, Transport and the Regions, John Prescott, and the Foreign and Commonwealth Secretary, Robin Cook. Not only was the full Cabinet left unconsulted, it had not even met for the first time when the decision was announced.

[...]

[...] [In] June 1997, the Whitehall editor of the *Daily Mail*, Sonia Purnell, had got hold of a Prime Minister's personal minute on the subject of 'Press Handling'. 'An interesting idea injected into the media', Blair told his ministers, 'will be taken as a statement of Government policy. All new ideas or statements of this sort must be cleared with No. 10.'[6] It would be wrong to see anything clandestine about this approach, for all the confidentiality that attaches to a prime ministerial minute. When the *Ministerial Code*, Blair's updated version of *Questions of Procedure for Ministers*, was published the following month, there it was – openly proclaimed in black and white.

It was the soon to be notorious paragraph 88 of the *Ministerial Code* which became swiftly treated as the classic statement of 'control freakery' and which led Peter Riddell to declare: 'Goodbye Cabinet government. Welcome the Blair presidency' in his *Times* column.[7] Under the heading 'Co-ordination of Government Policy', it reads:

> In order to ensure the effective presentation of government policy, all major interviews and media appearances, both print and broadcast, should be agreed with the No. 10 Press Office before any commitments are entered into. The policy content of all major speeches, press releases and new policy initiatives should be cleared in good time with the No. 10 Private Office; the timing and form of announcements should be cleared with the No. 10 Press Office. Each Department should keep a record of media contacts by both Ministers and officials.[8]

For Peter Preston of the *Guardian*, adherence to 88 would reduce any minister to a 'diminished, drivelling figure'.[9] For Peter Riddell, the Blair version of the old QPM represented 'the biggest centralisation of power seen in Whitehall in peacetime'.[10]

[...]

[...] Whenever you talk to those who live at the 'Blair Centre', they all give you the impression of how powerful everybody else in Whitehall seems to them. They tend to go on to make the case for an even more forceful centre.

[...]

[...] There may not have been a grand design ready for Blair-as-Napoleon or his No. 10 commanders to implement, but the instinct was there. Listen to a member of the 'Blair Centre' not long before the second anniversary approached:

> Do we need a Prime Minister's Department? It's largely an academic debate now because we already have one. It's a properly functioning department with a departmental head [the chief of staff, Jonathan Powell] with a sense of being *the* central machinery of government. We do now, in effect, have a PMD *but* (and it's a crucial 'but'), it is not formalised. This is an advantage because it makes it extremely flexible.
>
> It makes it possible to bring in large numbers of advisers at very short notice. Almost all the people in this structure hold office at the pleasure of the PM. It is *sui generis* – a case apart from the rest of the Whitehall machine. The centre is now not just a person, the Prime Minister and a small staff – it is machinery around him.
>
> The key part of the job is to keep the PM informed – to be the PM's early-warning mechanism on policy developments. And when the government changed, No. 10 became much more central to the presentation of policy. The area where there has been a big increase in staffing is the Press Office and the Strategic Communications Unit. That represents a determination that No. 10 shall not just be *primus inter pares*, but the dominant department in putting forward the message of the government.[11]

[...]

[...] The Blair-style No. 10 was noticeably akin to a French-style *cabinet* and [...] Brown, because of his preferred way of working, was close to running a *cabinet* system, too, not least because Ed Balls acted as the gatekeeper to the Chancellor. 'Officials who wished to persuade the latter had first to carry the former,' as David Lipsey elegantly expressed it.[12] It was important, however, to trace the growth points of special adviserdom in No. 10 within the context of an overall increase from eight to twenty-seven between 2 May 1997 and the end of 1999.

The Policy Unit had grown from eight special advisers under Major to twelve under Blair. By the end of 1999 they had been joined by two career officials. [...] Four of the special advisers worked within the Private Office, which in the postwar period had very largely been a fiefdom of the career Civil Service (Powell; his deputy, Pat McFadden; Anji Hunter, Mr Blair's personal assistant in opposition and government; and Fiona Millar, who ran the social side of the office and assisted Mrs Blair). Ten other special advisers were distributed across what might be called the enhanced communications capacity of No. 10 – the Campbell-led Press Office; the Strategic Communications Unit headed by a career official, Alun Evans (succeeded by Campbell himself in early 2000); and later the Research and Information Unit run by another special adviser, the psephologist and political analyst, Bill Bush.

It was the qualitative, if not the quantitative, increase in special advisers – their prominent position in what one former chief economic adviser to the Treasury called 'the geography of power'[13] – which led one seasoned and balanced Whitehall figure to worry lest 'this is not a way into the American system by the back door'.[14]

[...]

There are several worrying features about excessive prime ministerialism in the conduct of British central government. It cuts against the collective grain, which runs that way for a purpose – as just about the only barrier against undesirable accumulation of power which can all too easily accrue around a single figure under Britain's constitutional arrangements. An excessive focus on the premier can both overburden the Prime Minister (Mr Blair acknowledged publicly that he found the job 'remorseless' just before the Balkans War began) and, in the words an American journalist applied to President Clinton during the conflict, 'threaten to drain the political oxygen available for other projects'[15] if the head of government is faced by too many huge sappers of time and energy simultaneously. Mr Blair had no shortage of these in the spring of 1999. Kosovo and Northern Ireland alone were enough to induce the oxygen starvation effect. The Prime Minister was in danger of wearing himself out, as Roy Jenkins wrote of Mr Gladstone, in 'fighting his endless battle for the victory of activity over time'.[16]

[...]

There is a paradox at the heart of the Blair style, however, which his insider defenders deploy at such moments of serious criticism from experienced figures. How can he be a control freak running a command premiership?, their argument runs. Hasn't he presided over a government which has dispersed more power in its first three years than any in history? And don't forget the Brown factor. Has there ever been a greater degree of *de facto* power-sharing between a Prime Minister and a Chancellor of the Exchequer? To which I think the answer is 'True – but.'

[...]

Power-sharing with his Chancellor of the Exchequer, however, was a matter of daily importance, and the Blair–Brown partnership was as much the bedrock of the government as the Attlee–Bevin axis between 1945 and 1950. We have already seen the centrality of their regular bilaterals to the government's economic policy. But there is much more to it than that. Brown is, in effect, overlord of the economic and domestic front. It is a bi-stellar administration with policy constellations revolving round the two stars in Downing Street. It was an old Cabinet Office hand, Jonathan Charkham, who first alerted me to the policy range encompassed by Brown's Budgets – a scope imaginable only for Prime Ministers before the late 1990s. Mr Charkham saw Brown as comparable to a French Prime Minister with Blair as a kind of Fifth Republic President,[17] an impression powerfully underscored in the Chancellor's speech to the Institute for Fiscal Studies in May 1999.

The *operational* key to Brown's reach, as opposed to his *personal* power as the second biggest beast on the New Labour terrain, was the new wiring of control installed as part of the triennial comprehensive spending reviews. The public service agreements that underpin the implementation of the CSR process ensure that departments only receive their next tranche of finance if the Treasury is satisfied they have already achieved the policy outcomes outlined by their time-table agreed in advance and monitored by the PSX Cabinet Committee which Brown chairs. This leaves Brown with the most detailed power over policy of any Chancellor since 1945, with the Treasury's tentacles exerting an unprecedented sway within departments.

The rival Blair and Brown courts may engage in a good deal of mutual bad-mouthing, and Brown has always been a somewhat solitary, moody and prickly politician, but the two principals make an extraordinarily effective combination. The final stages of the first Comprehensive Spending Review in 1998 was very much a No. 10–Treasury business. There was precious little collegiality about it, despite the existence of PSX (and the Cabinet's Economic Committee, EA, which is supposed to consider issues affecting the government's wider economic policy, rarely meets). As David Lipsey put it: 'the CSR was a triumph for a strong prime minister and a strong chancellor, working together. Nothing illustrates this more clearly than the brutality of its execution. The two just called in ministers and told them how much they were getting. There was no appeal.'[18]

For all the plethora of governmental departments and units active on welfare-to-work questions (including the hugely productive Social Exclusion Unit in the Cabinet Office), the reality is that Gordon Brown's 'command chancellorship' is the ultimate arbiter of what does or does not happen domestically on any serious scale unless the Prime Minister chooses to moderate the Treasury's wishes to some degree.

[...]

[...] The [New Labour] programme has been driven through without regard to the niceties of traditional Cabinet structures, the differences of function between permanent officials and temporary special advisers or any great sensitivity towards Parliament.

Quite apart from the critical question of 'will it work?', the 'revolutionary' adjective could be applied by the turn of the century to certain sustained aspects of the Blair approach, notably the demise of anything approaching a genuine system of Cabinet government. We have seen, too, the tacit abandonment of the robust idea that the Cabinet Office, unlike No. 10, is a shared resource belonging to ministers collectively rather than the Prime Minister exclusively. It has been a question of ever closer fusion since May 1997, though Sir Richard Wilson continued to see himself as the servant of the Cabinet as a whole, as a hyphen linking the Blair Centre with the departmental periphery and a holder of the ring when disputes require resolution.

[...]

[...] [The] bigger, new style of picture [...] links Mr Blair's disdain for the old collegial Cabinet- and Cabinet committee-driven model with the great variety of new approaches to policy advice and policy-making[.].

[...]

[...] Accusations of overmightiness at the centre have long annoyed Tony Blair and his people. Rebutting them at regular intervals has been a recurring feature of his premiership. They are usually allied [...] with observations about the historically unparalleled force, scope and organization of the press, communications and information rebuttal capacities available to him, presided over by the most influential press secretary in Downing Street history, Alastair Campbell.[19]

The most sustained questioning Tony Blair has faced about the 'command premiership' he was expected to and, indeed, has operated since May 1997 came in the interview he gave Michael Cockerell for the BBC2 *Blair's Thousand Days* programme. Mr Cockerell put to him the idea that his individually agreed aims with each Cabinet minister and Permanent Secretary represented an extension of prime ministerial power not seen before. 'It's not that I want everything done via me', Mr Blair replied,

> But we have a programme and it's my job as Prime Minister to deliver it. And so inevitably if you don't have a strong centre... You're not running the government properly. But, I think there's a dichotomy here that is false really because most ministers want the support of the centre in driving their programme through. But the idea that I sort of, you know, for example in Education or in Health, or in the Treasury, you know, just sort of issue edicts or diktats from here [No. 10 Downing Street] that others carry out, I think is absurd.[20]

At this stage, Michael Cockerell brought Mr Blair back to his personal agreements with Secretaries of State and Permanent Secretaries which made them more accountable to him than to any previous Prime Minister. 'I doubt that very much,' said Mr Blair.

> I mean I think most Prime Ministers who have got a strong programme end up expecting their Secretaries of State to put it through; and you've always got a pretty direct personal relationship as Prime Minister, you appoint the Cabinet ministers. I'm not sure – I mean – I don't know about this. I've got a feeling with this thing that if you have a strong idea of what you want to do and believe in pushing it through, then you're, in inverted commas, a 'dictator'. And if you're not, then you're 'weak'. And you know, you pays your money and you takes your choice on that one.
> ...this idea...that...I don't discuss things with ministers...is just not true... People often say in relation to Cabinet government, look I would be pretty shocked if the first time I knew a Cabinet minister felt strongly about something was if they raised it at the Cabinet table. I would expect them to come and knock on my door and say, 'Look, Tony, I've got a problem here. I disagree with this' or 'I disagree with that'. And that happens from time to time. And people do that. And then you sit down and you work it out.
> But, you know, the old days of Labour governments where, I think, the meetings occasionally went on for two days and you had a show of hands at the end of it. Well, I mean, I shudder to think what would happen if we were running it like that.[21]

Allied to this fascinating reply was Mr Blair's assertion that he kept a 'pretty iron grip' on his diary as 'one of the greatest dangers in this job is that you lose the big picture because... if you're not careful, you'd have meetings from six in the morning till midnight, and you might in the end achieve very little'.[22]

There are a number of important and revealing aspects to the Prime Minister's long reply to Michael Cockerell. First, note the stark portrayal of the alternatives. You either have a strong and determined approach to the job or, just like that, you have weakness, indecision and chaos, as if the operating of Cabinet and premiership were an either/or matter, a question of primary colours rather than more subtle and variable shades. Secondly, notice that oversimple parody view of previous Labour styles – Attlee's, Wilson's and Callaghan's – as if they were all the same. Thirdly, note too the similarity to late Mrs Thatcher, the era Nigel Lawson characterized as 'creeping bilateralism' or the 'consent of the victims' in which Cabinet ministers settled for doing individual policy deals with the boss in return for acquiescence in collective meetings of the Cabinet or its committees.[23]

[...]

Summing up the Blair style, Jack Straw said: 'The Prime Minister is operating as chief executive of . . . various subsidary companies and you are called in to account for yourself.' 'A good process,' the Home Secretary added, loyally.[24]

[. . .] Whatever else might be said of him, Tony Blair is a command and control premier with a sense of political mortality.

NOTES

1   Address by the Rt Hon. Tony Blair, MP, Leader of the Labour Party to the Newspaper Society, London, 10 March 1997 (Labour Party Media Office).
2   Private information.
3   David Lipsey, *The Secret Treasury: How Britain's Economy is Really Run* (Viking, 2000), pp. 6–8.
4   Ibid.
5   Ibid.
6   Sonia Purnell, 'Cabinet big guns gagged by Blair', *Daily Mail*, 2 June 1997.
7   Peter Riddell, 'Tories should focus on what really matters', *The Times*, 1 August 1997.
8   Ministerial Code: A Code of Conduct and Guidance on Procedure for Ministers (Cabinet Office, July 1997), p. 30.
9   Peter Preston, 'Not without a Note from the PM, Minister', *Guardian*, 18 August 1997.
10 Riddell, 'Tories should focus on what really matters'.
11 Quoted in Peter Hennessy, *The Importance of Being Tony: Two years of the Blair Style* (Guys and St Thomas Hospital Trust, 12 July 1999).
12 Lipsey, *Secret Treasury*; Philip Webster, 'Brown puts "crony" in top Treasury job', *The Times*, 23 October 1999.
13 Private information.
14 Private information.
15 John Harris, 'Clinton at war, hears history calling', *International Herald Tribune*, 21 April 1999.
16 Roy Jenkins, *Gladstone* (Macmillan, 1995), p. 177.
17 Hennessy, *Importance of Being Tony*, p. 3.
18 Lipsey, *Secret Treasury*, p. 165.
19 For two important but different studies of Blair, Blair's people and the media, see Nicholas Jones, *Sultans of Spin* (Gollancz, 1999), and Peter Oborne, *Alastair Campbell: New Labour and the Rise of the Media Class* (Aurum, 1999). For Campbell's view that journalists are as much spinners of stories as spinned against, see Alastair Campbell, 'A man more spinned against than spinning', *The Times*, 31 January 2000.
20 Tony Blair, interviewed by Michael Cockerell on *Blair's Thousand Days: What makes Tony Tick*, BBC2, 30 January 2000.
21 Ibid.
22 Ibid.
23 Nigel Lawson, *The View From No 11: Memoirs of a Tory Radical* (Bantam, 1992). For the most revealing passage in this 'Consent of the Victims' chapter, see p. 129. For 'Creeping bilateralism', see Lord Lawson and Lord Armstrong of Ilminster, 'Cabinet Government in the Thatcher Years', *Contemporary Record*, 8/3 (Winter 1994), pp. 473–83.
24 Jack Straw, Briefing for the 'Cabinet and Premiership' course, Department of History, Queen Mary and Westfield College, University of London, 19 April 2000.

49

The Powers behind the Prime Minister

Dennis Kavanagh and Anthony Seldon

[...]

When he entered Number Ten as Prime Minister on 2 May 1997 Tony Blair was the first incumbent since his Labour predecessor Ramsay MacDonald in 1924 not to have had any prior government experience. Indeed, only one of Blair's ministers (John Morris) had served in a Cabinet before. The reason for the personal and collective inexperience was that Labour had been in opposition for the previous eighteen years. Since entering the Commons in 1983, Blair and many colleagues had known only the life of opposition.

But Blair also began with some advantages. A new Prime Minister, particularly following a general election success, usually starts out in a strong position. The scale of Labour's election victory in May 1997 was historic, and was seen by many commentators and colleagues as a personal endorsement of the leader. Surveys pointed to a 'Blair effect', the extra voting support which the party gained from having him as leader. Labour's general election campaign concentrated on him, his opinion poll ratings were remarkably high and much of the media treated him favourably as a figure apart from his party and Shadow Cabinet.[1]

[...]

It is important to realise how far politicians' styles of leadership are reactive, despite their claims to be drawing primarily on their own personal beliefs and life experience as the key shapers of their thinking. To Mrs Thatcher, for example, both Ted Heath and Harold Wilson were, in their different ways, negative models. John Major was a contrast to Mrs Thatcher and widely applauded at first for being so. Later criticism of him as weak and indecisive, unable or unwilling to give a clear lead on European issues because of party divisions, provided an additional incentive for Blair to be as unlike Major as possible. It is true that Major was hampered throughout by the attacks from Mrs Thatcher and her acolytes, as well as by large sections of the Conservative press, and the open disdain with which he was treated by party rebels. Although Major could not help his lack of an assured majority in the 1992 Parliament, Blair regarded him as a Prime Minister who lacked authority, in large part because he failed to give leadership. In a parliamentary exchange on 24 April 1995, about Major's decision to restore the party whip to persistent rebels, he boasted: 'There is one big difference. I lead my party. He follows his.' He wanted to be seen as a man who led from the front – successfully appealing to party members to revise the party's Clause IV, distancing the party from the trade union leaders, and slapping down party critics (usually those on the left). In contrast to the massive media coverage afforded to Conservative rebels, Labour dissenters were often marginalised by an aggressive and effective Labour media-management operation. For Blair, being seen to be in charge was as important as actually being in charge. He knew that the authority and public standing of previous Labour leaders had been undermined by internal dissent and damaging leaks by party critics.

Blair also reacted against features of 'old' Labour which he thought weakened the party leader. His project of modernising Labour involved fundamental reform of the party's policies, institutions and ethos to take account of social, economic and political changes in the country. Building on Kinnock's party reforms, the role of Conference, the NEC and constituency parties were altered to make Labour more disciplined and streamlined, and to facilitate Blair's personal leadership. Under him, the party gave presentation and media management a higher priority in order to respond to the opportunities and threats posed by the media's continuous political coverage. Operating in a culture of inner-party democracy, most previous Labour Party leaders had had to possess consensus-building skills, taking account of what the annual party conference or the trade unions would accept. The result had often been fudged policies and Cabinet appointments balanced between left and right factions – all executed in the interests of party unity. Blair, however, regarded the appeasement of activists and bargaining with the NEC and trade union leaders as incompatible with his idea of decisive leadership and having a clear 'message'. The party should say what it meant and mean what it said. Blair's impatience with the NEC and Shadow Cabinet meant that he relied heavily on his personal aides and some supportive shadow ministers who were committed to the modernising project. They knew his mind and shared his ideas of what needed to be done. Those who were not 'on message' were ruthlessly sidelined.

Labour's policy commitments were presented as Blair's pledges to the electorate. The successful ballots of party members to reform Clause IV of the party consti-tution in April 1995 and approval of the draft manifesto in October 1996 were his initiatives and effectively by-passed the Conference and party activists, always more to the left than mainstream party supporters. It was a plebiscitary style of leadership, in which the leader directly sought approval from party members, without the mediation of union leaders or party institutions. Reforming Clause IV, a classic symbol of 'old' Labour, was also a fundamental statement of Blair's seriousness about changing the party. In 1995, Blair decided to appoint the Chief Whip himself, breaking with the tradition of leaving it to election by Labour MPs. Complaints from PLP or Shadow Cabinet members about the influence of Blair's advisers and speed at which decisions were made by Blair and Brown – with associated lack of consultation – were swept aside. Some compared the style to that of a 'Leninist vanguard' which operated by *fait accompli*. He exploited to the hilt Labour's hunger for election victory and perceptions that he was the party's main electoral asset.

Blair also used 'special events' like press conferences, major speeches, policy launches and seminars to promote new policies, gain media coverage and put his own impress on the party. The idea that there was a 'New Labour' party was advanced relentlessly in major speeches at party conferences, in his 'Mais' lecture on the party's commitment to a 'sound' economic policy in May 1995, in an address to News International executives in June 1995, and in a 'stakeholder' speech in Singapore in January 1996. The approach would be carried over to his premiership.

By the time of the general election in 1997, Labour's image had been transformed. In contrast with 1992, voters now saw it as much more united, trustworthy, economically competent and representative of Britain as a whole than the Conservative Party. Surveys showed that Blair was viewed as a strong leader. His authority in the party and his self-confidence were further enhanced as general election endorsement came from traditionally Conservative newspapers and even from right-wing commentators such as Paul Johnson.

Blair attracted fellow reformers who also wished to modernise the party. Power increasingly rested with the leader's office and associates in whom he invested authority. Significantly, many of these were neither members of the NEC nor, with a few exceptions – notably Gordon Brown – in the Shadow Cabinet. The 'inner core elite', whose influence derived from their proximity and loyalty to the leader, naturally aroused envy in others.[2]

One of his staff spoke privately in December 1997 about Blair having executed a 'coup d'état' over the party in 1994 and about how he would run a centralised government to achieve his objectives: 'There was never any intention of having collective Cabinet government if Tony was to have the policies he wanted. As in opposition, he would have a centralised operation. It was as simple as that.'[3]
[. . .]

Blair's performance in opposition gave clues to the kind of prime ministership he would run. Political strategy had been decided in his office, working closely with his aides and with Gordon Brown. Policy had not been evolved through the Shadow Cabinet or party committees but through his office and his bilateral sessions with Shadow ministers. Party unity was a major and continuing consideration because internal divisions were a gift for an adversarial media. Party discipline and central control of communications were regarded as essential if presentation was to be effective. More than any Prime Minister in our period Blair and his senior aides would enter office with a very clear idea of what they wanted to do in Number Ten.
[. . .]

Many features of the Blair style of operations in government are a carry-over from opposition. These include a belief that political leadership is a stock of capital that can be replenished by personal integrity, good communications, and the achievement of visible objectives (e.g. the 1997 election manifesto pledges) that are effectively within the leader's and government's control; a willingness to change established structures and patterns to enable him to work effectively and achieve his objectives. Radical changes to the Labour Party's constitution to speed decisions and achieve objectives have been followed by reforms at the centre of government to do the same; an acknowledgment of the need for good presentation and rapid rebuttal of criticisms from the media, the opposition or party dissenters; a preference for making decisions in small ad hoc groups of people whose advice he values and on project teams, rather than formal meetings, such as the Cabinet; a practice of relying on known and trusted aides to occupy key positions in Number Ten. There was something akin to a US presidency in the importation of his own staff. It is significant that he starts his working week on Monday mornings with a meeting of his inner group.

Some of the following comments give an indication of the impression that Blair has made on the people who work for him. 'You can't sit around. He wants results,' says a member of the Policy Unit. Another comments, 'This is a very media-oriented operation.' Another Blair adviser remarks, 'He is a Maoist, he is always dissatisfied and wants things done better. At times I wonder if he believes in permanent revolution... Cabinet died years ago. It hardly works anywhere else in the world today. It is now a matter of strong leadership at the centre and creating structures and having people to do it. I suppose we want to replace the departmental barons with a Bonapartist system.'

'I expected him to be more hands-on, more involved in details. He is a big picture man. If it does not fit into his framework he cuts it out,' says an official.

'It is more informal than in a government department or probably than under previous Prime Ministers. In a department the Private Secretary can control the minister's day. Here, it is more pluralistic and different people are providing an input,' says an official. 'It's a Tony operation. There are Tony's people and party people. The former have more regular access,' says a Labour official. 'Tony has a mission. He is impatient to achieve things on Northern Ireland, sorting out health, education and welfare and improving relations with Europe. Early on, he said to me "If I can do those, then I won't have done so badly",' says an adviser.

Talk of creating a stronger centre and promoting greater co-ordination and more strategic oversight are usually code words for combating departmentalism in Whitehall. In opposition, Blair had got his own way on policy and looked to carry on in this vein. Early on in his premiership he told a member of his Private Office that he was aware that the Civil Service provided a Rolls-Royce machine but 'He wanted to do more than to see it. He wanted to get in and drive it,' said the official.[4]

[...]

Blair entered office determined to exercise a grip from Number Ten and has made appointments and created and reformed institutions to suit that purpose. A conventional listing of the Prime Minister's functions includes choosing and dismissing ministers, appointing top civil servants, chairing Cabinet and important Cabinet committees, attending the House of Commons to answer questions, acting as head of government in international meetings of heads of government, and deciding on the date of general elections. These responsibilities are unique to the Prime Minister. But they fail to do justice to Blair's emphasis on setting and overseeing strategy, communicating the ideas of New Labour to the public, and creating a stronger centre.

Blair's longer-term impact on the premiership largely depends on how successful he is. To what extent will initiatives like the SCU and the Performance and Innovation Unit in the Cabinet Office succeed in breaking down departmentalism? Will the introduction of a stronger political element, in the form of a political Chief of Staff in the Private Office, and more aides in the Policy Unit and Press Office, set a precedent? Some features, like the enhanced capacity of the Cabinet Office at the centre and the downgrading of the Prime Minister's role in Parliament and in Cabinet management, appear to be part of a longer-term trend.

By 1999 Blair was showing impatience at the slowness with which departments were making improvements in core public services. Indeed, in a much reported speech in July he complained that it was more rooted than the private sector to the concept 'it has always been done this way'. Civil servants as well as ministers were reminded of their duty to deliver and some of the former reportedly complained of scapegoating. Ministers retaliated with their own complaints of the Prime Minister's office; about decisions and documents being slowed up in an overworked

Number Ten and about Number Ten's negative briefing (John Prescott complained about 'faceless wonders' and 'teeny boppers') over some departments and over the Cabinet reshuffle in July 1999. The last turned out to be minor, although ministers who were targeted for moves have been unsettled over the summer. There was nothing unusual in any of the above. But when added to Blair's style of management, particularly his reliance on his office staff and neglect of the Cabinet, some friendly observers wondered if he was in danger of becoming isolated from his senior colleagues.

A more forceful critique of Blair's 'command premiership' is offered by Professor Peter Hennessy, a long-term observer of Whitehall and Downing Street.[5] He suggests that Blair may have overreached himself, as many of the traditional checks and balances from the Labour Party, Cabinet colleagues and Parliament have all declined. Hennessy's view is echoed by senior civil servants who have worked inside Number Ten and later become Permanent Secretaries. One commented: 'There used to be something [called] Cabinet Government. It was declining when I was there, in the 1980s, but now it seems almost to have died.' Another, who worked under Ted Heath as Prime Minister, gave Blair 'high marks for dealing with long-term strategy, presentation and getting the right mix of politics and administration, which are essential jobs for the Prime Minister'. He added, however, 'Weekly Cabinet is crucial for reminding ministers of the collective ownership of policies and Blair will be foolish to ignore it.'

It is likely that future Prime Ministers will retain a large Policy Unit to monitor departments and promote strategic oversight from the centre. It also provides them with additional opportunities for patronage and opportunities to increase their own political support. It is also likely that a future Prime Minister, particularly when coming direct from opposition, will bring in his own Chief Press Secretary and retain a body like the SCU. A strong communications presence is a necessary response, given the growing importance of the media. Prime Ministers have also long wanted the Cabinet Office to move beyond its remit of acting as an honest broker and ensuring that the Cabinet system works smoothly, and it is unlikely that the steps to encourage policy innovation and better implementation will be reversed. Indeed, if they are judged to have failed, the result is likely to be further demands for a stronger centre.

NOTES

1   Private interview, Blair adviser.
2   Ibid.
3   Peter Mandelson and Roger Liddle, *The Blair Revolution* (Faber and Faber, London, 1996).
4   Private interview, Blair adviser.
5   Peter Hennessy, *The Prime Minister: The Office and its Holders since 1945* (Penguin, Harmondsworth, 2000).

50

Tony Blair

John Rentoul

Despite overwhelmingly favourable press coverage of the new government, Blair, just like Harold Wilson before him, began to complain about the newspapers at an early stage. Wilson frequently devoted considerable amounts of the Cabinet's time to lectures about confidentiality. Only three months after the 1964 election, he circulated a memo to Cabinet ministers warning them against leaking.[1] Blair was more sensitive: he circulated a personal minute to Cabinet ministers on 'Press Handling' just three weeks after the election, on 21 May 1997. 'An interesting idea injected into the media will be taken as a statement of government policy,' he said. 'All new ideas or statements of this sort must be cleared with No. 10,' and he reinforced the point with a hand-written note at the end: 'It is essential we act on this.' Inevitably, the 'gagging order' was leaked within days.[2] [...]

Nor did Blair, however, rely on memos and bans on unchaperoned contact with the Fourth Estate. He ensured tight control over 'the message' by according a central role in the new government's hierarchy to Alastair Campbell. This was another facet of the paradox of simultaneous devolution and centralisation. While the government was pluralistic to the point of promiscuity in seeking allies and supporters from all the power centres of society, it retained rigid control at the centre over presentation.

Campbell's assertion of his control over Whitehall press officers was bound to attract the charge of 'politicisation', and the memo he wrote on 26 September 1997 urging the Government Information Service to 'raise its game' certainly lacked any sensitivity towards the civil service culture of impartiality: 'Four key messages... should be built into all areas of our activity. 1: This is a modernising government...2: The government is delivering on its promises. 3: Its policies are in the mainstream...4: The government is providing a new direction for Britain.'[3]

Campbell could argue that, as he was the Prime Minister's Official Spokesman, and as 'the overall political strategy, direction and style of the government is set by the Prime Minister',[4] he was responsible for presenting everything, party political or not. There is, of course, a fine line between the promotion of government policy, and the promotion of the governing party's policies – a line so fine it hardly exists. Some newspapers became so excited about the Labour Party 'using the civil service to achieve its political objectives' they forgot that was what the civil service was for.

Campbell's political centrality was bound to attract trouble eventually. What was surprising, and a tribute to his brutal charm, was how long it took for him to begin to offend the journalists with whom he dealt every day. He was generally contemptuous of his former colleagues in the parliamentary Lobby – the journalists granted access to the House of Commons, and in particular the Members' Lobby, who were also entitled to attend the twice-daily briefings by the Prime Minister's spokesman. But, as Campbell's biographer Peter Oborne pointed out, this meant he was 'moderately even-handed in his dealings with political journalists'. Peter Mandelson, on the other hand, made the mistake of thinking of journalists as friends and 'when they let him down – in other words did their job – he felt in some sense personally betrayed'. Campbell expected journalists to let him down and, 'when they did so, he therefore felt none of the special rancour that overcame Peter Mandelson'.[5]

The relationship between Campbell, as the new Prime Minister's press secretary, and Lobby journalists started off in high spirits, although with an undertone of menace on both sides. [...]

It was Campbell's favouritism towards the Murdoch press which caused some of the early bad blood. The Downing Street press machine turned out an astonishing quantity of journalism under the Prime Minister's by-line, making Blair the most prolific journalist–Prime Minister in history, with an average of one and a half articles in the national press per week in his first year. Of seventy-six articles, twenty were for the *Sun* and a further four for the *News of the World*.
[...]

When Blair said before the election that he would 'govern by headline', it seemed he was setting out Alastair Campbell's central role in a new kind of government, that would not be the passive object of journalists' attention but would manage the news cycle aggressively in order to maintain its hegemony. It was a double-edged ambition, however, because of the narrow line between trying to dictate the headlines and being dictated to by them.

The single word 'spin' had become, by the middle of 2000, the most devastating weapon against the government, as 'sleaze' became for John Major. A short, headline word which summed up all the complaints about the Blair style, it was, like 'sleaze', too imprecise to shake off. At Westminster, it meant the dark arts of media manipulation, for which New Labour had gained a dangerous reputation in Opposition. For most voters, however, it signified the gap between rhetoric and delivery: the fact that the government was claiming huge amounts of money spent on hospitals and schools and that nothing appeared to have changed. This was the perception which did the real damage: the truth was that New Labour was not – and probably could not be – as good at media management in government as it had been in Opposition. Despite the fearsome reputation of Blair, Campbell and Mandelson, the government was dogged from the start by a string of failures which were largely presentational, from the row over tuition fees, through the early chaos over policy on the euro, to the Ecclestone affair and the lone-parent benefit cut. But none of these had much effect on the government's post-election honeymoon with the voters, and it was not until the government was nearly three years old that the idea of 'spin' started to corrode the opinion-poll ratings. It was only then, when the voters began to expect to see visible and concrete delivery of better public services, that serious disillusionment started to set in and William Hague finally gained some traction on the electoral mountain facing the Conservatives, deriding Blair as 'all spin and no substance'.

[...]

All Prime Ministers want to build a machine around them which will allow them to drive their sleek vision of executive efficiency through the morass of bureaucratic inertia that is modern government. [...]

In Opposition, Peter Mandelson had spent some time thinking about how to translate the 'unitary command structure' of New Labour into government. In his book, *The Blair Revolution*, written with Roger Liddle in 1996, he set out a plan for the Cabinet Office to be strengthened as a Prime Minister's Department. Technically, the Cabinet Office, which backs onto Number Ten and has a connecting door, existed to support the Cabinet as a whole. When he was appointed Minister Without Portfolio, based at the Cabinet Office but answerable to the Prime Minister rather than to his Cabinet minister, David Clark, Mandelson redefined its role as being 'to support the Prime Minister'.[6] Later on, Blair reinforced the Cabinet Office, describing it 'as the corporate headquarters of the civil service'.[7] There was no need to add to accusations of a presidential style of government by renaming it the Prime Minister's Department.

Staff numbers at Number Ten quickly rose by more than half, from 130 before the election to 199 in the mid-term, twenty-five of whom were special advisers.[8] The Policy Unit, another Wilsonian innovation, was expanded under David Miliband – whom Blair had appointed at the age of twenty-nine as his head of policy the day after he became Labour leader. The press office, under the strong political management of Alastair Campbell, was reinforced at the end of 1997 by the setting up of a Strategic Communications Unit. The Political Office, created by Marcia Williams in Wilson's first government in order to fight the 1966 election when Labour scraped in with a majority of five in 1964, was headed by Sally Morgan[.]

[...]

[...] Like a chief executive setting targets for his subsidiaries, Blair introduced a new system of targets which would be agreed between departments and 'the centre'. Instead of conducting business at Cabinet or even Cabinet committees, he did an unusual amount of business in 'bilaterals' – two-sided meetings with his secretaries of state. If he were the chief executive, however, he had to deal with an over-mighty finance department. In an unacknowledged tussle with the Treasury – whose boss thought of himself as chief executive under 'chairman' Blair – the Prime Minister set up a new unit, the Performance and Innovation Unit, to monitor departments and deal with inter-departmental issues. As both those functions had traditionally been the Treasury's, the PIU could be seen as an instrument of asserting Number Ten's control. Or, as Blair put it, 'It will complement the Treasury's role in monitoring departmental programmes.'[9]

[...]

Blair's management style ushered in a new low in the history of Cabinet government in Britain. That style was 'hub and spoke' rather than collegiate, reducing most meetings of the Cabinet to just forty minutes of approving decisions already taken elsewhere, parish notices and short speeches either delivered by the Prime Minister or vetted by him in advance. The usual agenda for Cabinet meetings was 'stunningly unrevealing', according to the doyen of constitutional historians, Peter Hennessy, consisting only of three regular items, Next Week's Business in Parliament, Domestic and Economic Affairs, and Foreign Affairs (for the first two years there was a fourth, 'Europe', which was subsumed in the second and third items from mid-1999), and an attachment known in New Labour language as The Grid – a plan drawn up by the Strategic Communications Unit of events and ministerial announcements for the coming week.[10]

The trend away from the Cabinet as a decision-making forum had been evident for most of the twentieth century, however. Lloyd George and Chamberlain virtually dispensed with Cabinet meetings in their time and Thatcher famously asserted the primacy of an office which had long ceased to be 'first among equals'. Nigel Lawson said of his period as her Chancellor: 'I used to look forward to Cabinet meetings as the most restful and relaxing event of the week.'[11]

It was not surprising, therefore, that Blair's Cabinet rarely engaged in meaningful debate about policy. Nevertheless, the list of critical decisions not even reported to Cabinet is startling, beginning with independence for the Bank of England, the postponement of joining the euro, the cut in lone-parent benefit and the deal on the future of hereditary peers. There was a 'discussion' of welfare reform at Cabinet on 18 December 1997, but only *after* the revolt on lone-parent benefit. And when some issues were debated at Cabinet, such as the Millennium Dome, a decision was railroaded through against the majority view. But even this was not new: Wilson would not let his Cabinet discuss devaluation and Thatcher bounced the Westland decision through when Michael Heseltine might have mustered a majority against her.

Cabinet government was not dead, of course; it was only sleeping. It could clearly reassert itself if the Prime Minister's authority and popularity slipped, as it did over Thatcher in 1990. As a body, the Cabinet's authority derived from its potential power – of two kinds: its power to block the Prime Minister and its power to influence the choice of successor. This second power was greater in a Labour Cabinet than a Conservative one, where the choice of John Major over Michael Heseltine had been decided by Conservative MPs as a whole. Under Labour Party rules, in the case of a sudden vacancy the Cabinet would choose an interim leader and therefore Prime Minister until a full leadership election could be held.

The power of a Prime Minister, on the other hand, is more immediate and more continuously used. Notionally, a Prime Minister has no executive authority in domestic policy, except the power of appointing and sacking the ministers who carry it out. Blair used that power sparingly but without sentiment.
[...]
If Cabinet was not the locus of decision-making, however, this was not because Blair had an alternative centre of power, an informal kitchen cabinet of associates. Although in the political and physical geography of power Alastair Campbell and Jonathan Powell were closest to him, there was no cohesive inner group of trusted courtiers. The model often used of concentric circles around Blair of people arranged in diminishing tiers of influence is not useful, because all of his key relationships were with individuals rather than groups. Ranking them in order of influence is also an imprecise science, because different relationships mattered at different times and in any case served different purposes which cannot easily be compared. But if there were, as Derek Draper suggested plucking a number at random, 'seventeen people who count', they were by mid-2000: Tony Blair, Gordon Brown, Alastair Campbell, Peter Mandelson, Ed Balls (Brown's economic adviser), Anji Hunter, David Miliband, Derry Irvine, Jonathan Powell, Charles Falconer, Cherie Booth, Philip Gould, David Blunkett, Alan Milburn, John Prescott, Richard Wilson and Jeremy Heywood (Blair's principal private secretary).

Some Cabinet ministers were central to Blair's government. The relationship with Gordon Brown, however flawed, was the main one, underpinning the basic strategy of taxing, spending and economic management. David Blunkett was trusted to deliver the government's avowed priority of raising educational standards. Alan Milburn, appointed Health Secretary in the October 1999 reshuffle, quickly gained Blair's respect in delivering a second vital public service.

Others had different kinds of relationship. Peter Mandelson was Blair's envoy in overseeing the concluding stages of the Good Friday Agreement in Northern Ireland, but he retained his role as [...] Blair's personal counsellor and Brown's rival. Derry Irvine's influence declined as the pressures of government crowded in, especially after devolution and House of Lords reform were dealt with.[12]

John Prescott was absorbed in his sprawling department, most of whose policy areas concerned Blair only sporadically, but he was one of the seventeen by virtue of his independent power base in the Labour Party as deputy leader. [...]

Outside the Cabinet, the only minister with a close personal relationship with Blair was Charles Falconer, who had taken over Mandelson's role as his progress-chaser on Cabinet committees – and as impresario for the Millennium Dome. Falconer's progress-chasing role was like a spooling programme on a computer, to work in the background on things the Prime Minister could not focus on immediately. He described his role thus: 'Politicians tend to concentrate on one thing at a time. My concern is with things which are not presently in the foreground.'

Although a lot of the business of government continued to be done in Cabinet committees, the key decisions tended to be 'bilateral', between Blair himself and key ministers. The only other people, therefore, with access to the full picture, the Blair's eye view of government and the world, were Campbell, Powell and the apex of the civil service, John Holmes and then Jeremy Heywood, successive principal private secretaries, with Sir Richard Wilson usually one step back from the fray.

[...]

On the surface, Blair's way of working as Prime Minister was more informal than any of his predecessors. Where John Major held most of his meetings in the Cabinet room, Blair always had his in his study. He also did more business at Chequers than his predecessors. Weekends at the Prime Minister's country home would generally produce rough jottings of his thoughts for the coming week which would be faxed to Anji Hunter and Alastair Campbell. Hunter's husband, Nick Cornwall, would announce the arrival of the fax with an irreverent, 'Here comes your Sunday night stream of consciousness.' The notes would form the backbone of the agenda for the start-of-week meeting in Downing Street.

Blair had scribbled notes to himself for some time. 'I go back and write it down all the time, just for myself. I write notes on how these things must be achieved,' he said just before the 1997 election.[13] Alastair Campbell gave an impromptu idea of the form of the 'Sunday night stream of consciousness'. At the time, in early 2000, it would say something like, he said:

> Spain – where are we on this? Foreign policy – AC speak to me. Northern Ireland – I'm really worried about this, Trimble needs shoring up. Adoption – why does it take six months before a couple gets to know the result of something? Business – three times last week people were complaining to me about too much regulation; do we have a grip on this? London mayor – when should I go and do something?[14]

Blair had always shown a remarkable ability to focus intently on an issue for a short time, absorb the important points and move on. His mental style was well suited to the modern premiership, in which the most precious resource is the Prime Minister's time. 'The reality is different from anything that you might have anticipated,' he told Robert Harris. 'The reality is more intense and more endless, even though in theory you would have anticipated that it would indeed be intense and relentless.'[15] [...]

That intensity, however, partly reflected Blair's own energy and desire for control. If he had wanted to, he could, like Churchill in his second term, have taken naps in the afternoon, or, like Macmillan, have read Jane Austen. The civil service and political machine would have filled the gaps.

One of the members of the Downing Street Policy Unit, Andrew Adonis, was asked if he thought Blair worked harder than Gladstone:

> He does different things. Lots of time on planes, in meetings and doing media interviews – but little time in the House of Commons and virtually no debating. [He] also has a staff, where Mr G had two private secretaries. But that doesn't affect my point – that the weight of the premiership is no heavier than in the past, and that the difference between prime ministers lies in personal temperament and ambition, not the weight of the office *per se*.[16]

Blair was a control-freak, driven Prime Minister, operating a 'command premiership'. But again this was not exceptional. This century Chamberlain, Heath and Thatcher all operated a similar centralised style. Even Major's promise of a more collegiate style was increasingly belied by the reality of a hyperactive and engaged Prime Minister.

'Command premierships have a terrible tendency to end in tears,' Peter Hennessy observed to a Conservative who had resigned from Mrs Thatcher's Cabinet, as they considered the style of a Blair government.

'Yes, but you can get away with it for a very long time,' came the reply.[17]

Notes

1   Memorandum, Cabinet Papers, 19 January 1965.
2   *Daily Mail* and *Daily Telegraph*, 2 June 1997.
3   *New Statesman*, 24 October 1997.
4   Cabinet Office memorandum on Government Information and Communication Service to select committee on Public Administration, 6 August 1998.
5   Peter Oborne, *Alastair Campbell: Labour and the Rise of the Media Class* (Aurum, 1999), p. 139.
6   Speech, 16 September 1997.
7   *Hansard*, 28 July 1998.
8   Charles Falconer, Cabinet Office minister, Lords *Hansard*, 13 December 1999. The Foreign Office in Whitehall at the zenith of the Empire in the mid-nineteenth century had a staff of forty-five.
9   *Hansard*, 28 July 1998.
10   Peter Hennessy, 'The Blair Style', lecture at the University of Exeter, 8 May 2000.
11   Nigel Lawson, *The View from No. 11*, p. 125.

12 Irvine's replacement by Margaret Beckett in July 1998 as chairman of the Cabinet committee on legislation (known as LEG) marked the end of his initial phase of overseeing and prioritising the new government's Bills, but he retained the chair of the more important QFL committee on future legislation and Queen's Speeches.

13 Lesley White, *Sunday Times Magazine*, 20 April 1997.

14 Warren Hoge, *New York Times Magazine*, 14 May 2000.

15 Robert Harris, *Talk* magazine, May 2000.

16 Peter Hennessy, 'The Blair Style', lecture at the University of Exeter, 8 May 2000.

17 Peter Hennessy, 'Patterns of Premiership', The Mishcon Lecture at University College, London, 18 May 2000.

51

Lies, Damn Lies ... and Political Spin

Ivor Gaber

Nothing so graphically illustrates the pre-eminent position of 'spin' within the political process than the fact that on the day of the launch of the Euro [in 1999] the resignation of Charlie Whelan, Gordon Brown's Press Secretary, coming as it did just a fortnight after the resignation of Peter Mandelson, was regarded by most of the British media as the most significant story of the day. There can be much debate as to the appropriateness of that particular editorial decision; what is less contentious is the fact that Whelan (and Mandelson) had been, and still were, at the centre of Labour's communications and campaigning effort. Hence their resignations, and the circumstances surrounding them, did represent events of real political significance. Subsequently Alastair Campbell, the Prime Minister's Press Secretary, appeared anxious to downplay the importance of 'spin' whilst at the same time accepting a modicum of blame for its preponderance as a topic of political discussion. There was, he argued, 'a growing gap between the real agenda and the Media-land [sic] agenda ... and yes we have to be honest enough to think about our own role in how this situation developed. "Spin" never was as important as people imagine, and it's even less important now.' But then he would say that, wouldn't he?

One way of analysing the impact of 'spin' on the political process is to break down its forms into their constituent parts – and to use the marketing concepts of 'above' and 'below-the-line'. 'Above-the-line' publicity activities are those, more or less overt, initiatives that would have caused an 'old fashioned' press officer no great difficulty. The 'below-the-line' activities are those now more associated with the term 'spin doctor' – usually covert and as much about strategy and tactics as about the imparting of information (indeed, it could be argued that they in fact have very little to do with the imparting of information). Although it's important to stress that the below-the-line operations described below, and closely associated with the noble calling of the spin doctor, are not in any sense a New Labour invention. As long as politicians have been politicking, spinners have been spinning.

The most obvious form of above-the-line activity is the stream of daily government announcements. These are made in many different ways – by means of press releases, press conferences or briefings, via interviews and speeches or by a press officer, an adviser or a politician having a discreet word with one or several journalists. But ministers can also make use of all the arcane procedures of the House of Commons – ranging from statements in the House to the issuing of written replies to 'planted' questions. This range of devices means that, on the one hand, political journalists receive a constant stream of stories (on an 'average' day the table in the reporters' gallery at the House of Commons groans under the weight of between 40 and 50 press releases). With such a plethora of material cascading around them journalists find that, on the one hand, it is usually reasonably rewarding to follow up announcements that have been drawn to their attention by press officers but might find it equally easy to miss those announcements that, for one reason or another, nobody has mentioned.

[...] In media terms, politicians spend much of their time simply reacting to what their opponents have been saying. Much of this sort of reaction follows the same procedures as those utilised in reacting to policy announcements and initiatives. The difference tends to be that reacting to speeches and interviews can develop into an electronic political dialogue. For example, a minister gives an interview on BBC Radio 4's *Today* programme; the opposition then picks this up – either directly from *Today*, from the Press Association or from the *Evening Standard*. He or she then puts out a counter-statement, and perhaps gives interviews to the lunchtime radio and TV news bulletins. This in turn provokes a counter-reaction from the government whose response can be heard on Radio 4's *PM* programme or the early evening television news bulletins. The opposition then responds in time for the main news bulletins or the late-night BBC2 programme *Newsnight*. Thus, within one news cycle, an issue can be aired on four occasions, each time both the politician and the media acting in a collusive relationship, within which both have an interest in 'moving the story on'. In fact, the insubstantial nature of the original story and its subsequent trajectory can often be detected by the fact that it is not uncommon for stories that have dominated the airwaves during one day to barely feature in the morning's newspapers the following day.

Ensuring that politicians 'stay on message' is a quintessential part of the activities of spin doctors that characterises so-called 'below-the-line' activities. Maintaining a consistency between the different frontbench spokesmen and women in a party or government is absolutely crucial. At a slightly lower level of the political food chain I recall one incident during the 1997 election when I asked a Labour candidate to comment on a story that had just broken. Before agreeing to do so the candidate called his party's press office to seek both approval and the 'party line'. Then he, and I, had to wait until headquarters had given him the go-ahead and sent the requisite 'message' to his pager for broadcast regurgitation. Such a pattern of events is only possible in an era when mobile communications technology has become commonplace. Equally, of course, it is only the advent of virtually instantaneous electronic journalism that has necessitated such a speed of response.

Labour in government has taken the whole process one stage further with a transcript of what Alastair Campbell, the Prime Minister's Press Secretary, has told the 11am lobby meeting now being transmitted to Labour's media department at Millbank and then faxed to all Labour MPs within 30 minutes of the briefing concluding. Thus armed, backbenchers are now fully 'up to speed' with the Government's policy on the latest breaking stories.

[...]

Driving the news agenda differs from setting the agenda, in that it refers to a sustained campaign of driving the news in a particular direction over a period of time. This can be achieved by feeding selected journalists with a string of related stories. Judicious use of this process enables the journalist to claim each new story as an 'exclusive' whilst at the same time the main thrust of the story remains unchanged. During the summer of 1996, for example, the Labour Party kept their attack against the Conservative Government's privatisation measures on track by ensuring that a constant supply of anti-privatisation stories found their way into the printed and electronic media. One very effective way of intervening in the news agenda setting process is through a relatively new phenomenon, but one that now plays a significant part in the Government's (and to a lesser extent the Opposition's) armoury, that of the 'planted article'. This involves a government or political party supplying a newspaper or magazine with a major article with a senior politician's by-line. This technique is characterised as 'below-the-line' because whilst the activity appears overt it is, usually, not so. For despite the by-line that might appear over the article (the Prime Minister's or the Leader of the Opposition's, for example), almost invariably the article will in fact have been written by a member of the leader's media team. Alastair Campbell, in particular, has been writing regularly for the tabloid press under the name of Tony Blair ever since Blair's election to the leadership of the Labour Party in 1994. This means of dissemination is ideal in terms of media management. It allows the politician to make an argument, on his or her own terms, which is only subsequently open to challenge by journalists and opposing politicians after he or she has established the terms of debate unchallenged.

Spin doctors now speak of constructing a 'firebreak' for a story. This entails creating a media diversion to take journalists off the scent of an embarrassing story that seems, in the journalistic parlance, to have developed 'legs'. A classic of the genre was successfully invoked by Labour in the summer of 1997 when the *News of the World* revealed that the Foreign Secretary, Robin Cook, was engaged in an extra-marital affair with his secretary. As a result Cook, under pressure from Alastair Campbell, announced that he was going to leave his wife. Labour's spin team reacted with speed. Apart from ensuring that Cook dealt with his own personal crisis head on they 'created' two other stories to take journalists' eyes off the difficulties of the Foreign Secretary. First, the *Sunday Times* was leaked the story that MI6 was investigating the former Governor of Hong Kong, Chris Patten, over alleged breaches of the Official Secrets Act, and in a radio interview on the same day Peter Mandelson suggested that the Government was thinking about reprieving the Royal Yacht Britannia, which was due to be scrapped. The results were to be seen on the front pages of the following day's broadsheets with none leading on the Robin Cook story, a result of what one member of the Downing Street press team described as 'a fantastic operation'. [. . .]

A key part of below-the-line activity is building up the reputations of the favoured few. The classic case of this was the exercise undertaken by Peter Mandelson when, as Labour's Director of Communications, he set out to build up the media profiles of two young Labour MPs – Tony Blair and Gordon Brown. This he did by consistently putting their names forward to radio and television producers who were in search of interviewees, drawing journalists' attention to their press releases (and there was never any shortage of these) and by briefing journalists on a regular basis that these two MPs were politicians to watch. [. . .]

The opposite activity, 'undermining a personality', is, in a way, even easier to undertake, particularly if the personality being briefed against is in the spin doctor's own party. [. . .]

Pre-empting is another important arrow in the spin doctor's quiver. An example of this technique occurred towards the end of 1998 when, following the resignation of Welsh Secretary Ron Davies, the *News of the World* informed Nick Brown, who was then Agriculture Secretary, that they were intending to run a story alleging that he was a homosexual. Brown, instead of waiting for the newspaper to appear, issued a statement to all newspapers on Saturday evening, confirming that he was indeed gay. This did not stop the *News of the World* from running their own story but ensured that the story remained a 'one day wonder' and Brown's ministerial career appeared unaffected. [. . .]

A mirror image of pre-empting is 'kite-flying' in which governments or parties use the media to float potentially problematic proposals in order to test public and media reaction. Kite flying can most obviously be witnessed in the weeks leading up to the Chancellor of the Exchequer's budget statement. [. . .]

Yet another ploy much associated with budget-time is raising and lowering expectations. A familiar routine is for the Chancellor to discreetly 'let it be known' that this year the budget is expected to be particularly difficult. 'Informed speculation' appears at regular intervals as to the extent to which taxes are going to have to go up. The worst is expected and then, seemingly miraculously, a little extra is found here, a little less is required there, and the budget is hailed as a triumph. The opposite process comes into play when Chancellors of the Exchequer find themselves in situations of potential conflict with ministerial colleagues. For example, in 1998 during the weeks preceding the budget, the Social Security Secretary, Harriet Harman, or at least her press advisers, were leading journalists to believe that the forthcoming budget would contain significant relief for lone parent families (this would have offset an earlier controversial cut in their benefit). Ms Harman was fighting for her political life and anxious to gain as much political advantage as she could in the pre-budget phase. However, her actions had the effect of raising expectations that the Chancellor, almost inevitably, would find difficult to meet – if there is good news to be broken at budget time then Chancellors tend to want to retain these plaudits for themselves.

'Milking a story' is the technique by which a Government, or for that matter a party, extracts as much positive media coverage out of a given situation as possible. The present Government has developed this almost to an art form. Indeed Betty Boothroyd, the [former] Speaker of the House of Commons, has complained vociferously about the way that announcements, that ought to be made first in the House of Commons, are trailed many days in advance in the newspapers and on the broadcast media. A Political Editor for a national broadsheet described how the process felt from his side of the Parliamentary Gallery:

> Spin doctors are very clever. They work out a strategy for presenting a White Paper and then they say right, we'll give a little bit to the Sundays, another bit to the Mondays, and then another bit to the 'Today' programme on Wednesday when we launch the White Paper, and there's not much the journalist can do about that sort of operation.

Earlier, reference was made to the technique of 'losing' some government announcements in the welter of press releases that daily besiege parliamentary journalists – but there are other ways that stories can be buried. One such is known as 'throwing out the bodies' and was described by a former Whitehall Head of Information who explained that when a 'royal' story broke in the Major years, the Prime

Minister's Press Secretary would immediately phone all government press offices suggesting that now was a good time to put out those awkward announcements they had been storing up, it being a pretty safe bet that the media's attention would be well and truly distracted by the latest chapter in the ongoing saga of the Windsors. [...]

The 'white commonwealth' is the name given to the creation of a favoured group of correspondents who receive special treatment and access above and beyond that available to other political correspondents. The name originated under Harold Wilson and his Press Secretary Joe Haines, who at the time of the Rhodesia crisis relied on a group of trusted journalists to provide favourable coverage and helpful advice. BBC political correspondent Nick Jones described the workings of the 'white commonwealth' under the regime of Bernard Ingham, and how it tended to allow Ingham a relatively easy ride in the lobby briefings: 'Under Ingham's no-nonsense regime those reporters who were employed by newspapers sympathetic to the government had no wish to sour relations by challenging him needlessly. They knew they had every chance of speaking to him by phone after the organised briefing, when they might find it easier to obtain the information they wanted.' Jones makes similar claims about the existence of a 'white commonwealth' under both John Major's and Tony Blair's regimes.

Of course the notion of any privileged 'in group' requires an 'out group' which is less privileged. Reporters 'out of the loop' can find themselves not just excluded from sources of information, but also bullied and intimidated. Bernard Ingham was the first to be charged with such behaviour, but under Labour the tactic has been developed further. Even in opposition, dealing with Labour's media machine posed something of a quandary for the political journalist: accept the line, the spokesperson, the story and all would be well – the journalist would get his or her interviewees, a regular dripfeed of minor 'exclusives' and the sense of being 'on the inside'. However, sign-up for the 'awkward squad' and the result would be interview bids turned down, access to breaking stories denied and no flow of 'exclusives'. It's a dilemma that faces all journalists, in any sort of lobby, all the time, but with New Labour it's particularly acute because the 'game', such as it is, has been and is played with an unprecedented degree of bitterness and brutality, and not just by Alastair Campbell. In the run-up to the 1997 General Election the Political Editor of the *Daily Telegraph*, George Jones, often bore the brunt of attacks from Labour's media managers. He hit back with a front page story 'Why I will Not be Intimidated': 'It is another example of a campaign of intimidation by Mr Mandelson against journalists who write anything with which they do not agree or which is critical of Labour. Mr Mandelson seems to believe that if he can embarrass people in front of their colleagues they will be less likely to write anything that can be seen as anti-Labour.'

Following the problems the Government ran into at the beginning of 1999 with the resignations of Mandelson, Whelan and Robinson much has been made about this being the end of 'government by spin' and the return to a more traditional policy-based political discourse. Indeed, in the weeks following the resignations of Mandelson *et al*, the Prime Minister and his fellow cabinet members launched a series of initiatives designed to turn attention away, as Mr Blair put it, from 'the froth' towards the policy agenda. Yet this in itself was seen as part of a spin operation, with ministers relaunching a series of existing policies ('milking a story' in terms of the above typologies). And there were those, some with significant insight into the workings of the new Labour information machine, who were suggesting that the Government would find it difficult, if not impossible, to wean itself off its addiction to 'spin'. Romola Christopherson, who resigned as Head of Information from the Department of Health at the start of 1999, wrote: 'It is impossible to separate Campbell from Blair from New Labour from government from communication. They are one concept.'

Ms Christopherson's diagnosis of new Labour's addiction is unambiguous; whether or not it is prescient remains to be seen.

52

The Hand of History: New Labour, News Management and Governance

Bob Franklin

On Maundy Thursday 1998, Tony Blair flew to Belfast to resolve what seemed to be an impasse in the Northern Ireland peace process. It was a portentous moment for political developments in the province. The international corps of journalists and broadcasters assembled for a press conference at the airport was more than usually attentive to the Prime Minister's briefing. 'This is not a time for soundbites', Blair announced, 'we've left those at home' and then added, with no discernible note of post-modern irony and much less spontaneity, 'I feel the hand of history upon us. Today I hope that the burden of history can at long last be lifted from our shoulders' (*Guardian*, 11 April 1998). The headlines in the following day's newspapers resonated with the carefully crafted phrase. Politicians' use of such 'soundbites', their need to 'stay on message' and their determination to 'set the news agenda' in their favour, have become crucial components in a modern statecraft which emphasizes the 'packaging' of politicians and policies for media presentation and voters' consumption (Franklin, 1994, 1998).
[…]

Since 1997, the Labour government has imported its election-winning media operation into government: a process described as the 'Millbankization' of government (Gaber, 1998, 10). In his evidence to the Select Committee on Public Administration inquiry into the Government Information and Communication Services, Sir Richard Wilson, the Cabinet Secretary, claimed:

> there is a more systematic determined effort to co-ordinate in a strategic way, presentation of government policies and messages in a positive light across the whole of government, than I can remember since the time I have been in the civil service. (Select Committee on Public Administration 1998, xii)

This process has involved the increasing centralization of communications at Number 10, a more assertive relationship with journalists and broadcasters and the politicizing of the GICS.

'Conducting the Communications Orchestra': The Central Control of Communications

Centralizing communications at Number 10 under the control of the Prime Minister's press secretary has been the key priority in Labour's communications strategy. The intention is to establish the government as the 'primary definer' in media discussions of policy, to ensure the consistency of the government line and to minimize the media profile of any dissenting voices. Central control is certainly strict, but effective. The Mountfield report on government communications suggested that 'all major interviews and media appearances, both print and broadcast, should be agreed with the No 10 Press Office before any commitments are entered into. The policy content of all major speeches, press releases and new policy initiatives should be cleared in good time with the No 10 private office' and finally, 'the timing and form of announcements should be cleared with the No 10 Press Office'. Number 10 also coordinates the work of departmental press offices, via a weekly meeting of information officers which is chaired by Campbell, to 'secure a timely and well ordered flow of departmental communications and to see how best departmental communications can play into the broader Government messages and themes' (Mountfield, 1997, 7): what Ingham delighted in describing as 'conducting the communications orchestra' to ensure that everyone 'was following the same score' (Ingham, 1991, 166).

The establishment of the Strategic Communications Unit (SCU) in January 1998, which includes two special advisers (both ex-*Mirror* journalists), is responsible for 'pulling together and sharing with departments the government's key policy themes and messages' (Select Committee on Public Administration 1998, para 19): i.e. keeping spokespeople 'on message'. The unit liaises with media management organizations in individual departments, such as the Strategy and Communications Directorate in the DfEE, to coordinate government policy messages. The SCU also assists with the drafting of ministerial speeches by including common phrases and soundbites to illustrate the consistency of the government's 'message' and 'no doubt they draft some of those "exclusive" articles the prolific Tony Blair writes' (*Guardian*, 21 May 1998, 20. See also the Select Committee on Public Administration's Second Special report, vi). Since February 1998, the SCU's activities have been supported by 'Agenda', a new computer system which 'helps to co-ordinate government's publicity activities' by listing 'forthcoming newsworthy events, lines to take, key departmental messages and themes and ministerial speeches' (Select Committee, 1998, xiii and Appendix 12).

The government's 'communications day' begins with a 9 am meeting attended by senior communications staffs including Alastair Campbell, Jonathan Powell the Prime Minister's chief of staff, specialist advisers from the Treasury and the Deputy Prime Minister's Office as well as representatives from the Cabinet Office and the Chief Whip's Office [....] The meeting tries to ensure a congruence between strategy and presentation and consigns specific individuals to resolve any particular presentation problems arising that day (Mountfield, 1997, 8). Labour's determination to stay 'on message' requires that nothing is left to chance. The policy 'message' must be carefully scripted, meticulously rehearsed, universally endorsed by party and government, centrally coordinated and favourably presented in the news media (N. Jones, 1999).

[...]

Carrots and Sticks: Labour's Relationships with Journalists

Labour's vigorous and uncompromising news management strategy offers journalists and broadcasters stark choices. If they accept the government line, they will be rewarded with the occasional minor 'exclusive' and be allowed interview access to senior politicians. But journalists who are critical of government will have their bids for interviews denied and will not receive telephone tips about 'breaking stories and exclusives' (Gaber, 1998, 14). In short, the government is playing an old-fashioned game of carrots and sticks (Ingham quoted in Select Committee on Public Administration, 1998, 9–14), although some commentators believe that 'with New Labour ... the game is played with an unprecedented degree of nastiness' (Gaber, 1998, 14).

There is a further reason informing some newspapers' supine coverage of Labour's performance in government; journalists working for the Murdoch press believe their proprietor has agreed a pact with Tony Blair. Murdoch's newspapers' support for Labour since the run up to the 1997 election has been handsomely rewarded by the absence of legislation to outlaw the predatory pricing of *The Times* (despite the opportunity provided by the Competition Bill) and the unwillingness of government to regulate the press's invasion of privacy or Sky's advantageous position in the digital television market. Some journalists argue that Blair is conceding too much policy ground in return for the editorial quiescence of the Murdoch press.

Sticks are more commonplace than carrots. In October 1997, Campbell circulated a memo to all Heads of Information in the GICS arguing that 'media handling' (his preferred term for media relations), must become more assertive. 'Decide your headlines', he insisted, 'sell your story and if you disagree with what is being written argue your case. If you need support from here [Downing Street] let me know' (Timmins, 1997, 1). For journalists writing against the government line, 'the 'handling' has become rough! Journalists are privately bullied, publicly harangued and excluded from off-the-record briefings. Andrew Marr, when editor of the *Independent*, was told 'you are either with us or against us' (McGwire, 1997, 11). Complaints from the Number 10 press office seem to influence even the most distinguished journalistic careers. Rosie Boycott's withdrawal of an offer of the political editor's job at Hollick's *Daily Express* to Paul Routledge was attributed by journalists to Routledge publishing a biography of Gordon Brown which was critical of Tony Blair (*Guardian*, 21 May 1998, 20). Similar rumours surround the departure of *Sun* columnist Matthew Parris after he outed Mandelson on *Newsnight* and the sacking of executive editor Amanda Platell and news editor Ian Walker from the *Sunday Express* following their involvement in the publication of a story about Mandelson's friendship with a Brazilian student (*Financial Times*, 20 January 1999, 10). Given this track record, it is perhaps unsurprising that a biographic article about Campbell observed that 'he performs his onerous tasks with cheerful brutality' (Hattersley, 1998, 3).

Broadcast journalists, especially those working at the BBC, are subject to similar pressures.

[...]

Control Freaks or Designers of a New Democracy?

There is an evident irony in Labour's development of such a robust political communications style and practice: Labour's forceful public advocacy of open government and *freedom* of information (albeit delayed), sits ill with the quieter, more private reality of the considerable *management* of information which is conducted by Number 10. Blair's government is controlling the flow of political communications by and about the government to a degree which is unprecedented in the UK in peacetime. The irresistible question which emerges is whether the Labour approach to news management reflects what leader writers are increasingly describing as a 'control freak mentality' or whether there is a more substantive reason; there seems to be more to this than can be explained by individual psychology which invariably concludes in conspiracy theory.

Three reasons for increased 'control freakery' are suggested. First, these developments may reflect the centralizing instincts of British political parties. Second, the loss of clear policy daylight between the major parties, with few substantive policy issues to define differences, has prompted or exacerbated the focus on presentation. Finally, the hierarchical and centralized control of communications may simply articulate the managerial culture of public institutions.

There is a fourth account which warrants further elaboration. The party seems to be developing a new and emergent conception of democracy which, as yet, is far from fully worked through, but which involves recasting the relationship between government, media and citizens in significant ways. Labour's obsession with the media seems to reflect the opportunities which radio, newspapers, but especially television, offer the executive to communicate directly with citizens. This emphasis on taking the debate directly to the citizens has recently been evidenced in the 'Welfare to Work' Roadshows, the 'Town Hall meetings' and the use of focus groups to test budget proposals: this latter is immensely significant since it reveals the extent to which marketing techniques are involved in policy *making*, not merely policy *presentation* as part of a broader process of policy implementation.

[...]

There are at least two reservations to be entered here. First, this changed vision of democracy involves a changed perception of politicians. Governments no longer seem willing to confront political decisions, preferring to return to citizens to 'test' public opinion on issues, to gain a popular verdict on new policies, and implement them accordingly: the result is populist not popular government. Consequently, the status of politicians is substantially reduced. Instead of making political choices, framing political agendas and presenting them to the electorate, politicians seem more willing than ever to become little more than overpaid messenger boys and girls – ever more frantic distributors of questionnaires and frenzied facilitators of focus groups. For their part, the musings and reflections of these small (sometimes tiny), randomly assembled, unelected and unaccountable groups of individuals increasingly seem to weigh more heavily in the decision-making process than the opinions of elected representatives honed in parliamentary debate.

The new politics require politicians to abrogate their moral and political responsibilities, as politics becomes populist. Political decisions are reduced to market decisions and citizens are transformed into consumers. The public sphere becomes a marketplace. But in this marketplace, politicians are no longer seen to be *market driving* (like Thatcher) but *market driven* (like Blair).

There is a second concern. On this account, politicians make naive or perhaps disingenuous assessments concerning the independence and autonomy of citizens' policy choices. Governments' growing enthusiasm for news management and even the publicly funded advertising of new policy initiatives, makes politicians influential in the shaping of those very choices of citizens which are allegedly driving the policy process. Citizens' policy preferences are not constructed in a vacuum. They draw much of their information as well as orientation from news media that are increasingly subject to news management and spin by the GICS, the COI, the SCU and the Number 10 press office. A crucial constitutional function of parliament has been to act as a bulwark of probity against the overheated enthusiasms and ambitions of all governments and thereby to protect the rights and liberties of citizens. It is less clear who will protect citizens' rights in New Labour's, new model, media democracy.

References

Franklin, B. (1994) *Packaging Politics: Political Communications in Britain: Media Democracy* (London: Arnold).
Franklin, B. (1998) *Tough on Soundbites, Tough on the Causes of Soundbites: New Labour and News Management* (London: Catalyst Trust).
Gaber, I. (1998) 'A World of Dogs and Lampposts', *New Statesman*, 19 June.
Hattersley, R. (1998) 'He has the power, but none of the glory', *Observer*, 18 January.
Ingham, I. (1991) *Kill the Messenger* (London: Harper Collins).
Jones, N. (1999) *Sultans of Spin* (London: Victor Gollancz).
McGwire, S. (1997) 'Dance to the Music of Spin', *New Statesman*, 17 October.
Mountfield, D. (1997) *Report of the Working Group on the Government Information Service* (London: HMSO).
Select Committee on Public Administration (1998) *The Government Information and Communications Service: Report and Proceedings of the Select Committee together with Minutes of Evidence and Appendices*, HC 770 (London: HMSO).
Timmins, N. (1997) 'Blair aide calls on Whitehall to raise its PR game', *Financial Times*, 9 October.

53

Sultans of Spin: The Media and the New Labour Government

Nicholas Jones

[...]
Many of the changes which have taken place within the media have worked to the advantage of those who seek to manipulate the news agenda. The growth of rolling news services on radio and television, and the emergence of seven-day newspapers, have whetted the appetite for a constant diet of fresh stories to feed the relentless demands of the twenty-four-hour news cycle. A fast-moving news agenda, and the speedier turnover of stories, suited the Labour Party well in the run-up to the 1997 general election. As the Conservatives discovered to their cost, every chance was taken by Tony Blair's burgeoning band of spin doctors to exploit the disarray of John Major's administration and the failings of his party. Once in government, Blair and his colleagues reached new heights in their ability to command favourable news coverage and to dominate the newspapers and the airwaves. Through the skilful orchestration of events and the sometimes all too eager support of willing accomplices in the news media, one day's damaging headlines can be obliterated the next. While the party propagandists miss no opportunity to condemn the newspapers for having all but abandoned the straight reporting of political debate, the politicians themselves take every advantage of the growth in personality-led news coverage and, although they frequently seek to deny it, they are prepared to go to almost any lengths to satisfy the constant demand for agenda-setting stories.
[...]
Amid all the frenetic activity which followed the change of government, Blair's closest counsellors seemed to be in danger of misunderstanding what people had voted for. So great had been the general contempt for John Major's administration that the new Prime Minister had in effect been given a blank sheet of paper and told to get on with the job. There was no public appetite for renewed political point-scoring. The electorate appeared to have faith in their own judgement, and moreover to have had quite enough of electioneering and political opportunism. Blair would be given ample time and opportunity to prove himself. As the opinion polls were to demonstrate month after month, voters remained remarkably settled in their thinking. Irrespective of whatever contortions might be taking place within his own party, or the supposedly calamitous events reported by the news media, all the surveys

indicated that the Prime Minister continued to enjoy a virtually uninterrupted political honeymoon. Yet despite these signs of continued voter satisfaction, Blair's strategists remained so consumed by an over-riding obsession to control and dictate the way the new government's affairs were being presented and reported that they gave the impression they feared their election victory might suddenly be snatched away if the headlines went against them for longer than a week.

As the months went by, and events crowded in on the new government, their expertise in massaging the news agenda was to prove no substitute for effective decision-making and substantive action. The new administration had no real need to be fearful of their lack of experience. Senior civil servants had expected and prepared for a change of power. Whatever private doubts cabinet ministers might have had about their own individual capabilities, the virtual annihilation of the Conservatives had demonstrated the power of the incoming administration's collective strength and determination. Nevertheless, the focus seemed to remain firmly on presentation rather than action; and here Labour's self-evident competence while in opposition, and their success in communicating policy announcements to the public, did tend to encourage a sense of superiority. Blair's inner circle remained supremely confident in the infallibility of their news judgement and, when it came to constructing and promulgating a news-driven agenda, it was clear that it would be the civil service which would have to be taking lessons from the Labour Party.

Blair continued to be feted by the news media for far longer than party members could have dared to hope, and there was no doubt that the success of New Labour in catching and holding the imagination and attention of journalists on its ideals and objectives continued after it took up the reins of government, in stark contrast to the Conservatives' failure to construct a coherent message, let alone communicate it. But Labour miscalculated in thinking that the flair they had shown when fighting the election, in ruthlessly pressing forward their news-driven agenda, was necessarily the one and only tactic which they could or should pursue once in power.

Ministers do not need to be constantly tempting the appetite of the news media. If their policies are proving successful and they have established a reputation for effective government, political journalists will soon seek them out. Indeed, there are positive dangers for the government of the day if it tries to perpetuate the kind of hectic feeding frenzy which is not only to be expected but is essential during an election campaign. For a well-run government, a well-planned, well-thought-out ministerial announcement, delivered competently and with style, should look after itself when it comes to setting the agenda and gaining publicity. The far harder task is to devise strategies to minimise damaging speculation or to cope with unexpected events, premature disclosures or embarrassing revelations. The most important lesson to be learned by media managers is to know when, and how, to wind down journalistic expectations. Successful exploitation of the media can take many forms. Blair's spin doctors had built their reputations on being proactive, on courting the attention of journalists, an approach which in some ways was to prove not just unproductive but a distinct liability when press sentiment turned against them. Many senior figures within the government were equally to blame for ill-advised attempts to stimulate high-profile news coverage about themselves rather than about their work as ministers; they too, having been driven for so long by a never-ending courtship of the media, failed – like their advisers – to see the dangers ahead and remained dangerously in awe of the potential power of personal publicity.

[...]

After so long in opposition, [...] habits [acquired in opposition] had become deeply ingrained, and for many in the party, at all levels, treading the byways of media manipulation had become a way of life. In some MPs' offices even junior assistants took delight in tipping off journalists or leaking information. Seeing their handiwork in print – whether as a front-page news story or a mere diary paragraph – was an experience to savour. However small or insignificant their achievements, the ability to engage or even to excite journalists with the information which they could offer provided even these lowly figures with an opportunity to taste real political influence, and the satisfaction was all the greater if their efforts boosted the boss or did down an opponent. And the obsessive fascination with the techniques for influencing the media went right to the very top of New Labour. Tony Blair's two most influential advisers were steeped in the traditions of party infighting and the devious exploitation of political journalism. Alastair Campbell, a committed Labour supporter, was formerly political editor of the *Daily Mirror* and a gifted tabloid journalist; and Peter Mandelson, despite having worked only briefly as a television producer on the ground-breaking political programme *Weekend World*, had built up unrivalled connections in the broadcasting and the entertainment industries.

Most of the major players in Blair's frontbench team were acutely alive to the opportunities to promote the party – and themselves – through the media. As they dug in for the long haul to the general election, they would jump at any opportunity to write articles for national newspapers, and had nothing to fear from high-profile interviews. If offered the chance to take part in a fly-on-the-wall television documentary they would be only too happy to oblige, their sole concern being to ensure that the programme was broadcast at the most beneficial moment for their own personal advancement. While a high proportion of Conservative MPs had, over the years, developed equally strong connections with the world of newspapers, television and radio, far fewer had been practising journalists or broadcasters. Many had closer ties with marketing, advertising and corporate publicity, and as a result the Conservative Party's relationship with media folk was nothing like as close or as fruitful as the links forged by the Labour Party when Neil Kinnock was party leader and expanded and consolidated under Blair. Nevertheless, when it came to the task of achieving successful media management while in government, rather than in opposition, the Conservatives' knowledge and experience of the tactics deployed by big business had at times proved a distinct advantage. Most profitable companies are keen to keep their internal affairs out of the public eye. While they are only too ready to seek favourable publicity for their products and services, they realise that, by and large, their corporate interests are usually best served by maintaining the lowest possible profile; and that requires releasing as little information to the public as possible. Ministers frequently face the same dilemmas as big companies, but do not always understand the benefits of a corporate culture which frowns on the hectic, proactive news management which was second nature to Alastair Campbell and Peter Mandelson.

If news reports keep focusing on an awkward political issue, governments tend to counter the problem by providing facts and figures to justify the stance or decision under scrutiny. But relying on a strategy of rebuttal raises the danger that, as fresh material is released, journalists might discover further damaging revelations hidden away in the small print of the documentation. There are moments in the political cycle when it can become counterproductive to strive too hard to dominate the agenda and a more astute course of action would be to find ways to minimise media interest. Advisers on corporate communications are well aware of the balance which has to be struck and the need to have defensive strategies in place. Promotional work has to be carefully targeted, because a high public profile at the wrong moment, with all the attendant publicity, can become a liability if there is an unexpected commercial mishap and trading conditions take a sudden turn for the worse. Conservative administrations have on occasion proved quite adept at following commercial practice and, by damping down interest at times of actual or potential vulnerability, seeking to avoid damaging political repercussions. A similar ethos has thrived within the civil service: if left to their own devices, government departments would rarely seek publicity for its own sake. Whitehall mandarins are far happier if they can keep out of the public eye, and by nature are far more cautious than ministers when asked to advise on how far the government should go in cooperating with the news media. However, in the after-glow of New Labour's election victory there was no inkling that the party's fabled prowess in news management might one day go awry, and the credo remained unchallenged: the best form of defence is rebuttal, followed by attack.

54

The Electronic Face of Government in the Internet Age [...]

Andrew Chadwick

Political scientists have long sought to explain how political elites maintain them-selves in power. This inevitably raises questions to do with legitimation. Even in liberal democratic states, which may have substantial variations in power structures and societal contexts, there is the problem of democratic control; of the relations between rulers and ruled, the relatively powerful and the relatively powerless. Over the last forty years or so, while the discipline of communication studies blossomed, there have been surprisingly few political scientists who have sought to understand and explain political legitimation with reference to language, symbolism and the manipulation of information. [...] I translate some of these themes and assess their relevance for understanding political legitimation in the age of the Internet through an empirical analysis of executive branch web sites in Britain. [...] It is my argument that the Internet allows for a new 'electronic face' of government which has previ-ously been unavailable. This is controlled by government itself and is subject to the central demands of early twenty-first-century politics, namely presentational profes-sionalism in the form of attention to imagery, symbolism, language use and genre. [...]

[...] I have chosen to analyse what is arguably the most important component of the electronic face of any government: the website of its executive branch. One of the earliest and most successful examples (judged in terms of user numbers) is the US presidential site (http://www.whitehouse.gov). When Internet use began to take off in the USA during the mid-1990s, the White House site rapidly emerged as a first port of call for those seeking information about government. Its perceived ease of use and quasi-portal characteristics proved attractive. By contrast, it was not until relatively recently that the UK Prime Minister's site (http://www.number-10.gov.uk) began to assume the same functionality and popularity. The site was completely redesigned in 2000, and given an intriguing 'brand identity', which I discuss below. It has now emerged as one of the most popular government sites in the UK, and offers a much wider range of content than its US counterpart. It is curious that we often refer our students to executive websites as an information resource, but there has been relatively little critical analysis of their form and content. Much more energy has been spent to date on party websites and election campaigning. But given the symbolic (and very real) power of the executive, even in the most self-consciously liberal democratic political systems such as the USA, an examination of their electronic face reveals some potentially significant aspects of how political legitimation is reinforced through new information and communication technologies.

[...] In the USA, despite the monumentality and continuity conveyed by the White House site, the separation of powers also carries some symbolic weight. It is perhaps fitting, therefore, that the executive branch site is less ambitious. In Britain, where the new Labour government's intensification of the pre-existing tendencies towards spin-doctored, sound bite politics is now such a taken-for-granted part of national life that it is hardly commented on at all, the Strategic Communications Unit controls the executive's web presence, and it shows.
[...]

An examination of the British prime ministerial site, http://www.number-10.gov.uk, reveals similarities and some important differences. [...] The distinction between occupant and role is similarly maintained, with the prime minister's official residence forming the leitmotif. The audience encounters the prime minister sitting within the cabinet section of the site – a nod in the direction of collective leadership.

The established symbolism surrounding 'Number 10' is invoked, with a recurring image of the building's famous front door, complete with a smiling police officer. This obviously symbolizes the authority and stability of the state, but it is combined with a 'friendly' smile – a strategy of mixing genres which may also be found on many corporate websites. The traditional symbols of the British state, the lion and the unicorn, are transformed into a logo which appears at the top of each page, while the inscription 'Welcome to 10 Downing Street' appears in Times New Roman – the font of familiar historical authority.

Yet these indicators of history, authority, power and status sit alongside forms and content of a rather different kind. The redesigned Number 10 homepage is the entrance to a hugely expanded collection of different types of content. The main sections are 'Newsroom', 'Magazine', 'Facts', 'Broadcasts', 'Your Say' and a children's section, '10 out of 10'. The style of the site is eclectic, and has obviously been much influenced by contemporary web design, particularly with its use of small, iconic images, animated buttons, different types of font and an overall colour scheme which is not a reference to established, easily recognizable national colours, such as the red, white and blue of the British flag, but a mixture of black, beige, white and green. In other words, the site, though it makes reference to established 'real world' symbols, appears as a distinct entity in its own right; as a product of some reflection on what the web as a distinctive medium can provide rather than the 'brochureware' approach. In all, Number 10 is a 'slicker' production, but it is also one that is the product of an obsession with presentation and 'modernization' that has emerged as a key component of the 'new' Labour government's strategy. Indeed, the site's 'look and feel' borrows heavily from the hypermedia modernism that is characteristic of 'cutting-edge' web design. Contemporary colour schemes, which differ from section to section, iconic 'lifestyle' representations, and clean lines and well-spaced presentation convey an image of vitality and modernity.

Nevertheless, Number 10 is less overt in its portrayal of executive action and competence than the White House. News bullets feature prominently on the Number 10 homepage, but they cover a more diverse range of activities and policy areas, and, at the sample time of this research, none of the stories portray the prime minister 'acting alone' in the same manner as his US equivalent. Instead, a variety of policy initiatives featuring a range of cabinet ministers are highlighted. The verbal style of the news stories is, at first glance, akin to the pillar of British public service broadcasting – BBC News. But linking deeper into the stories themselves soon reveals that they are little more than government press releases, with their characteristic features: 'The Government has unveiled its vision for a modern, efficient criminal justice system'; '£35 million pilot for pupil learning credits'; 'Courts to get new powers to tackle persistent juvenile offenders'. Thus, executive competence is reinforced, but the collective leadership of the cabinet system is the dominant approach. Competence is demonstrated through coherence and co-ordination; the Number 10 site is therefore an important element in producing an image of government unity.

Clearly the aim of the news bulletins is also to ensure contemporaneity. Indeed, the portal characteristics of Number 10 make it appear to have been designed as a user's browser 'home page'. This may be an excessively optimistic assumption on the part of the prime minister's press office. However, its significance should not be underestimated. The wide variety of audience experiences available on the site make it much more likely that users will click around rather than click through. Governments have always been in the business of self-publishing, but the web makes it much easier to reach a mass audience with news items that would otherwise have to be channelled through the media. The site offers a customized e-mail update service for users who register, and, at the time of this research, provided a quickly updated information section on the farming crisis caused by the outbreak of 'foot and mouth' disease. Government engaging with 'ordinary' individual web surfers as a direct information provider is a new development, and one that is more likely to be achieved with Number 10 than with the White House as it currently stands. Hortatory language styles predominate on Number 10, just as they do on the White House site.

Both of these executive sites do, of course, feature elements that are electronic translations of the average tourist experience. The White House site has its historical essays on the building and its previous incumbents; Number 10 has similar sections. Visitors to the 'real' buildings would be treated to the same thing. However, what is striking, particularly about the British site, is the extent to which 'lifestyle' content, most of which borrows heavily from 'glossy' magazine genres, is intertwined with political forms and content. Thus, the 'Tour Of The Rooms' at Number 10 is reminiscent of an aspirational 'interiors' magazine, and even provides 'panoramic' technology which allows the audience to 'look around' the rooms. Yet the aesthetic description of the rooms is mixed with selected historical observations about their former occupants, safely sanitized down to the level of building materials, but still symbolically powerful. Consider this extraordinary paragraph taken from the description of the Cabinet Room:

> The 23 chairs are the same ones used by Gladstone and Disraeli in the reign of Queen Victoria. Of the set, only the Prime Minister's chair has arms. Some of the silver on the table was presented to the house by President Ronald Reagan. A solid gold sword, presented by the Emir of Kuwait, rests near the window. Those windows are now made of glass three inches thick – a precaution taken following the 1991 mortar attack which shattered the glass.

The '1991 mortar attack' was conducted by the IRA, and came at the depths of the Northern Ireland crisis of the early 1990s. The White House makes similar cultural raids upon established 'lifestyle' and entertainment genres, but it is less pronounced, and mainly revolves around the children's section, 'For Kids'. Nevertheless, the portrayal of the assumption of stable family relationships permeates the site, and constitutes awareness that many adults may be shown the site by their more net-literate children. In both cases, what can be observed here are classic instances of entertainment genres bleeding into political genres. The overall effect is to deflect attention from the reality of executive power and channel the presentation of government into 'safer' areas.

If entertainment genres help to produce a sanitized version of government, then this is only intensified by the presence of the kind of kitsch that can be found all over the Internet. The cult of the family homepage, with its ubiquitous sections on household pets, is very much alive and well in the electronic face of government. Visitors to Number 10 are invited to find out about its famous animal occupants, past and present. As for the White House, the Clintons' celebrity cat, 'Socks', has been replaced by the Bushes rather less charismatic creatures. Taking pleasure in self-publication has long been one of the most popular uses of the Internet, and government is not immune from its characteristic practices. The former British 'e-envoy', Alex Allan, when briefly in charge of Labour's e-government drive, was happy to link from his government pages to his and his partner's 'personal' homepage (http://www.whitegum.com), with its 'Grateful Dead Song and Lyric Finder', Holly the dog, and picture of him windsurfing on the River Thames.

[...] [E]xecutive websites [...] reveal the potential for governments to become self-publicists in ways that have previously been unavailable. Disintermediation in the economy is being mirrored in politics. The symbolic architecture of a government's Internet presence is likely to be just as important in the future as it has been in the past, but the emerging techniques point to a more complex relationship between rulers and ruled, one that will be based upon immediacy of contact, a more direct appeal to lifestyle concerns and entertainment values. It has often been argued that the Internet will empower citizens by providing access to information, and there is no doubt that the sheer volume of government information now available online is immense. But aside from structural issues like the 'digital divide', the underlying dynamics of elite driven politics are not going to change overnight, if at all. 'Hortatory' language, for instance, characteristic of political leaders seeking to establish a link with their audience, is both intensified and curiously modified in the electronic face of government, because the citizen actively seeks information. The relatively (though never completely) passive consumption of political language is replaced by a process in which the citizen becomes an active pursuant. Yet there must be information to pursue, and this is controlled and filtered by government itself. Citizens are brought 'closer' to government through their online 'discoveries', but their interactions with its electronic face are very much on government's own terms.

These sites, especially the British prime minister's, are also typical of the 'infotainment' genres which are fast becoming the stock-in-trade of the more commercial frontiers of the web. That governments are now able to exploit audience recognition of such genres is indicative of the dialectical nature of legitimation identified by Edelman (1995). We are at once in awe of government, and are keen to see the symbolic representation of its power and competence. But we want government to be 'ours' and 'like us'. We want our lifestyle interests reflected and our craving for information and entertainment satisfied by government websites in much the same ways as we would any other site.

The Internet has spawned a new electronic face of government. My analysis of the symbolic forms and content of the UK prime minister's site illustrates a likely future direction for e-government. The rather amateurish, patchy and utilitarian websites of the last three or four years are quickly being replaced by a more professional approach, which ties in with broader government communications strategies. This is undoubtedly a product of the general increase in Internet usage among electorates, but it also represents an increasing awareness of the properties of the web as a medium and how this may contribute to the symbolic dimension of government activity.

The explosive growth of the Internet during the last five years has undoubtedly had an impact on the conduct of politics. But we are only just beginning to appreciate the inevitable balance between continuity and change. Governments will always need support, and the maintenance of support is not always dependent upon rational calculation and the electoral mechanism. Legitimation is a process. It is ongoing, and elite strategies mutate over time. [. . .] [T]he Internet offers political elites many opportunities to intensify and diversify the ways in which they sustain themselves in positions of power. The challenge for social scientists is to interpret and explain how these trends may undermine attempts to use new media to reduce political inequality.

[. . .] [E]ven in cyberspace there will always be a symbolic architecture of power.

REFERENCES

Allan, A. (2001), Homepage. Online. Available: http://www.whitegum.com (5 March 2001).
British Prime Minister (2001) 10 Downing Street website. Online. Available: http://www.number-10.gov.uk (5 March 2001).
British Prime Minister (2001) 10 Downing Street: The Cabinet Room page. Online. Available: http://www.number-10.gov.uk/default.asp?PageId =68 (5 March 2001).
Edelman, M. (1995) *From Art To Politics: How Artistic Creations Shape Political Conceptions*, London: University of Chicago Press.
United States President (2001) The White House website. Online. Available: http://www.whitehouse.gov (27 February 2001).

55

The Commons: Mr Blair's Lapdog?

Philip Cowley

[...] Despite coming to power promising to modernise Parliament, the most frequent complaint from the media, Opposition politicians, and even some Labour back-benchers has been that the independent role for Parliament in scrutinising the government's legislative programme became yet further marginalised under Blair. One Conservative MP even claimed that the 1997 Parliament would go down in history as the 'abused Parliament' (HC Debs, 27 February 2001, c. 726). A common criticism was that Labour's MPs have become excessively loyal and deferential lapdogs, unquestioningly trooping through the division lobbies in support of the government. If these complaints are fair, it suggests that Westminster has lost one of its prime functions in criticising, counterbalancing and checking the excesses of executive power. But are the gripes about the deference and acquiescence of Labour MPs actually valid?

[...]

If the Commons has been 'abused' [...] then this has three separate components.

First, there were Labour's reforms to the House of Lords, where the government was frequently defeated by the votes of hereditary peers. The first stage of the government's reform was the removal of precisely these troublesome hereditary peers, leading to the charge that it was emasculating the second chamber, weakening the one last significant check on its behaviour within Parliament. [...] Second, in the House of Commons, the massed ranks of 418 Labour MPs – 'it's like that scene from Zulu', said one Conservative MP when he first saw them assembled – meant that the government enjoyed the largest majority of any single party since 1935, and Labour's largest ever. This part of the marginalisation thesis was perhaps inevitable – the power of Parliament to influence the executive varies with the size of the government's majority, and because the Blair government enjoyed an enormous majority, Parliament's influence was therefore limited. But the problem was exacer-bated by two factors. There was the contrast between the Blair government and its predecessor. For much of the 1992 Parliament the Conservatives had a majority that was in single figures or non-existent. For five years before May 1997, therefore, the outcome of parliamentary votes was not always known before they took place and things were (almost) exciting. For the four years after 1997, by contrast, they were terribly predictable. And to make matters worse, there were complaints that too many Labour MPs gave unquestioning support to the government. The new methods of whipping implemented just before the 1997 election – including tighter standing orders and the use of electronic message pagers to keep MPs informed of the party line – led to criticism that Labour MPs were too slavishly following the party line. The use of phrases such as 'Daleks', 'clones', and 'spineless' was common. Especially criticised were the new women MPs elected in 1997, who were disproportionately less likely to vote against the party line. Nor did such criticisms come solely from the opposition: one long-serving Labour backbencher claimed that most of his colleagues were a 'model army of programmed zombies' who displayed 'an instinctive bovine loyalty'.

Because of this large, apparently compliant, majority, and the personality of the individuals concerned, a third criticism emerged: that Labour ministers were arrogant and dismissive of Parliament. The changes to PMQs were announced to the House as a fait accompli, even before the Modernisation Committee had been established. Labour ministers were repeatedly accused of releasing information to the media before informing the Commons, provoking several complaints from the Speaker, including a formal complaint to both the Cabinet Secretary and the Leader of the House. The Prime Minister was an infrequent participant in the Commons: Blair led his government in fewer debates and participated in fewer divisions than any recent Prime Minister. Even when the Prime Minister or other Ministers were in the Commons, the complaint was that Labour backbenchers colluded with the government. Three Labour MPs were suspended from the House for leaking Select Committee reports. Others were accused of asking patsy questions to ministers. As one Labour backbencher, Andrew Mackinlay, complained in a now famous question:

> Does the Prime Minister recall that, when we were in opposition, we used to groan at the fawning, obsequious, softball, well-rehearsed and planted questions asked by Conservative Members . . . ? Will [he] distinguish his period in office by discouraging such practices – which diminish Prime Minister's Question Time – during this Parliament? (HC Debs, 3 June 1998, cc. 358–359).

Concern about the marginalisation of the Commons was thus not solely the product of Opposition politicians. Labour's former Chief Whip Derek Foster even complained that the Commons had become the Prime Minister's 'poodle'.

Yet if that is the case for the prosecution, then it does not take Perry Mason to construct the case for the defence. The first problem with most of the criticisms is not that they are necessarily wrong (because many of them are not) but that they pretend to be describing something that is somehow new. Most of the analysis was profoundly, and depressingly, a-historic. Tony Blair did attend parliament infrequently, but the fall in prime ministerial participation in the business of the Commons is nothing new, having been declining since the mid-nineteenth century. There were particularly steep drops in the 1980s and 1990s, under the Conservative premierships of Margaret Thatcher and John Major. Labour backbenchers did frequently ask sycophantic questions to ministers, but it is a trick they perfected after years of watching Conservative MPs do the same. Nor is the Blair government the first to prefer to announce policy outside of the House of Commons. An earlier Speaker, Bernard Weatherill, frequently had to persuade a very reluctant Margaret

Thatcher to come to the Commons to report on policy decisions. She used to complain that it was 'such a nuisance'.

The second problem with many of the criticisms is that they misunderstand or misrepresent what is currently taking place. This is particularly true of complaints about the reform of the House of Lords. Far from removing an independent check on the government, the Lords' reforms (perhaps unwittingly) have created a more assertive and confident body. The change is as much qualitative as quantitative (not so much more defeats, but more significant defeats), but the end result has been an upper chamber that has become increasingly prepared to take on and challenge the Commons. It is also true of the criticisms of the cohesion of Labour MPs. As discussed in more detail below, the real reasons for the high levels of cohesion seen on the Labour benches are far more complicated than any instinctive bovine loyalty. [...]

[...] [T]he PLP elected in May 1997 proved the most cohesive for a generation. There were fewer revolts by government MPs between 1997 and 2001 than in any full-length Parliament since the 1950s. And Blair's was the first government since that of 1966 not to be defeated at least once by its own backbenchers. As we have seen, reaction to this high level of parliamentary cohesion was not entirely positive. Whereas Labour leaders always used to be criticised for not being in charge of their MPs, Blair was criticised for being too much in control. When Labour MPs used to rebel, they were labelled as divided and split; when they rebelled less frequently, they were labelled as spineless and acquiescent.

Most of the criticism was misplaced. For one thing, high levels of cohesion did not mean absolute cohesion. Many Labour MPs were prepared to vote against the government. A third of the PLP – that is, around half of all backbenchers – voted against the government at least once. Moreover, the average (mean) size of rebellions under the Blair government was the third highest of any Parliament since 1945. Labour MPs may not have rebelled very often, but when they did, they rebelled in numbers and across a wide range of issues. [...] Although there were some remarkably sycophantic Labour backbenchers (as there had previously been some remarkably sycophantic Conservative backbenchers), these MPs tended to attract disproportionate media coverage thus masking the three real reasons for the low levels of cohesion.

First, there was a high level of self-discipline by Labour MPs. The legacy of 18 years in opposition created a widespread desire to avoid being seen as divided, almost at any cost. As one MP said: 'If it's a choice between being seen as clones or being seen as disunited . . . then I'd choose the clones any day.' [...]

Many Labour MPs were also keen to stress that they were prepared to rebel against the government but that they rarely felt the need to, because they usually agreed with the government's policies. In part, this was because of a notable rightward shift in the attitudes of the PLP, especially the newer, younger, MPs. [...]

The third reason – and the one most often overlooked – is that, despite its reputation as autocratic, the government was usually willing to negotiate with its backbench critics. Even some of those who rebelled argued that the government listened to their concerns as much as might be expected, particularly after the scale of the lone-parent revolt in December 1997 made the government realise that coercion alone would not suffice in preventing rebellions. Where genuine consultation did not take place, or where the government adopted a macho stance – as with lone-parent benefit or disability benefit – rebellions were noticeable, but where it adopted a more consultative approach, being prepared to sugar the legislative pill, rebellions were muted or non-existent. A good example came in the second session of the Parliament, with the government's plans for dealing with asylum seekers. Some 61 Labour MPs signed an Early Day Motion opposing the proposals, and *The Times* (10 June 1999) claimed that the government faced potential defeat. Yet after concessions granted by Jack Straw, the Home Secretary, just seven Labour MPs voted against the bill.

Seen in this light, the lack of rebellions is rather more positive. Rather than being a Bad Thing – caused by MPs who are too scared to defy their leaders – it is a Good Thing, the result of agreement and consultation as much as of coercion. When the government was not able to placate its critics, there were sizeable rebellions. For sheep – one of the most common phrases used to describe Labour MPs – they could bark loudly when provoked.

[...]

[...] Labour's backbenchers [might well] prove less cohesive in the coming Parliament. As shown above, Labour MPs' cohesion in the 1997 Parliament resulted not from any lack of backbone, but from a general sense of agreement, self-discipline, and an ability to influence government behind-the-scenes. Labour MPs were willing to rebel – and rebel in numbers – when they did not agree and where they could not influence government. The largest revolts were on social security reform and initiatives that involved private finance of public services, and the second term is likely to involve plenty of both. Labour MPs began the new Parliament at a hostile PMQs on 4 July 2001 by making clear their opposition to reforms to incapacity benefit. Moreover, the second Blair government cannot rely on as much deference. There were signs even in the last Parliament of self-discipline beginning to weaken, as the third session saw more revolts than the first two put together. And the early votes of the new Parliament saw more than 100 Labour MPs defy the government over the composition of two departmental select committees. The government will therefore be forced to negotiate; otherwise the second Blair Parliament could see some sizeable backbench revolts. The people in Parliament may largely be the same, but their behaviour may well be very different.

Index